THE

CHRISTIAN

TRADITION

THE
CHRISTIAN
TRADITION

Beyond Its

European Captivity

Joseph Mitsuo Kitagawa

Trinity Press International
Philadelphia

First Published 1992

Trinity Press International
3725 Chestnut Street
Philadelphia, PA 19104

Cover design by Brian Preuss

Library of Congress Cataloging-in-Publication Data

Kitagawa, Joseph Mitsuo, 1915–
   The Christian tradition: beyond its European captivity / Joseph
Mitsuo Kitagawa.
      p.   cm.
   Includes bibliographical references and index.
   ISBN 1-56338-041-2 (pbk.)
   1. Christianity—Asia. 2. Christianity—Western influences.
3. Religious pluralism—Christianity. I. Title.
BR1065.K57 1992
275—dc20   92-20607
                                                 CIP

Printed in the United States of America

For my sisters-in-law
and sisters

Sumiko († 1992)
Fujiko
Michi
Mie

CONTENTS

Preface ix

Part I: The Asian Christian Tradition 1
    1. The Asian Christian Perspective of Christianity 3
    2. The Asian Christian Perspective in Global Revolution 23
    3. The Emergence of Christian Dilemma, with Special
        Reference to Japan 43
    4. Christianity in Japan: Some Reflections 65

Part II: American Experience Through the Eyes of Asian-Americans 89
    5. The Saga of Asian-Americans 91
    6. The Mass Evacuation: Recollections and Reflections 119

Part III: The Christian Tradition: Western and Global 139
    7. Religion(s), Community, Communication, and Faith:
        The Hebrew Paradigm of Christianity 141
    8. The Christian Church and Western Civilization 159
    9. Piety, Morality, and Culture: European and American
        Perspectives 185
   10. Piety, Morality, and Culture in Global Perspective (1) 209
   11. Piety, Morality, and Culture in Global Perspective (2) 233

Appendix: Some Personal Reflections on Autobiographical and
        Biographical Modes of Perception 259

Notes 283

Index 297

Although there may be so-called gods in heaven or on earth—as indeed there are many "gods" and many "lords"—yet for us there is one God . . . and one Lord.

—Apostle Paul, 1 Cor. 8:5–6

From eternity to eternity Buddha [the Absolute] and I [the relative] are separated from each other, yet, at the same time he and I do not fall apart even for a single moment. All day long Buddha and I *live* facing each other, yet he and I have never a chance to *meet* each other.

—Daito Kokushi, 14th century

We have been the recipients of the choicest bounties of heaven. . . . But . . . we have forgotten the gracious hand which preserved us in peace and multiplied and enriched and strengthened us, and we have vainly imagined . . . that all these blessings were produced by some superior wisdom and virtue of our own. Intoxicated with unbroken success we have become too self-sufficient to feel the necessity of redeeming and preserving grace, too proud to pray to the God that made us.

—Abraham Lincoln, 1863

Only if God is revealed in the rising of the sun in the sky can he be revealed in the rising of a son of man from the dead; only if He is revealed in the history of Syrians and Philistines can He be revealed in the history of Israel . . . ; only if nothing is profane can anything be sacred.

—William Temple, 1934

PREFACE

The essays collected in this volume have been written at different times over many years. They are like a series of snapshots taken from three different standpoints that I have been destined to occupy in my life. In these articles I tried to see, to discern, and to depict different subject matters grasped from my own particular situations, even though I knew right along that there are other perspectives from which all these things could be viewed. In writing these articles, my aim was not to defend or justify my own angles of vision or to criticize views of other persons situated in different circumstances. Now that I review my admittedly personal and subjective conspectus, I have to acknowledge once again the import of the age-old truth that there are legitimate differences among various people in perceiving the same events or leitmotifs, seen from divergent perspectives.

I would like to use three imageries to illustrate and portray my tripartite perspectives. I hope that these "pictures painted with words" will somewhat supplement what Toynbee once phrased "the infirmity of human minds and the poverty of human language."[1]

First, it will be helpful, as you read the chapters of Part I, "The Asian Christian Tradition," if you can picture scenes of my personal encounters with Western Christians in the ancient city of Nara, Japan. Born into an Anglican parsonage and raised in the Nara region, I met many foreign tourists who sojourned to see the famous Great Buddha statue and watch the hundreds of deer (considered divine messengers) roaming around the streets of Nara. Among the tourists were a number of Western Christian leaders who were very curious about the Japanese Christian community. According to my experience, those Western Christian visitors either (a) assumed that Asian Christians should hold views almost exactly the same as Western Christians about major aspects of life and the world or (b) thought a priori of Asian Christianity as a B-class tradition within Christendom, inevitably contaminated by pagan beliefs and practices. It did not occur to many of them of either persuasion that their Asian counterparts might have their own Christian experiences and perspectives and that Christianity in Asia was not a pale carbon copy of Western Christian tradition. Thus, most lamentably, I discovered that Asian and Western Christians were separated, of all things, by their different understandings of presumably one and the same Christianity. So from my youth throughout my adult life, I often reflected on the nature of the Asian Christian perspective, as indicated by some of the articles included in this volume.

As you turn to the second section of this volume, entitled "American Experience Through the Eyes of Asian-Americans," picture for a moment the spectacle of an "internment camp—American style" as the epitome of the segregated (self-imposed or otherwise) communities of marginal groups of hyphenated Americans. Coming as I did to the United States several months before the outbreak of the Pacific War, I was arrested early in 1942 as an enemy alien and eventually "paroled" to a camp in Idaho, where American citizens of Japanese ancestry were incarcerated during World War II, together with their immigrant parents who by law had been prohibited from applying for naturalized citizenship and thereby were classified as enemy aliens. There were ten such camps; each one was de facto an internment camp, euphemistically called a "War Relocation Authority" center. I spent three years in the Idaho camp and came to know rather intimately the not-so-readily apparent intricacies of the Japanese-American community.

Our camp was situated in the barren Idaho countryside covered by sagebrush. Out of curiosity, groups of Idaho farmers often drove up to see "their" internment camp—which benefited the neighboring towns economically. Looking at the camp, it would not occur to those Idaho citizens that across the barbed wires were schools where children started and ended their academic years with the Pledge of Allegiance to the Star Spangled Banner. If the armed guards would have admitted them, the visitors would have come upon a huge board on which was listed an honor roll that cited the names of youths from the camp who had lost their lives in the Italian campaign. Ironically, however, these Americans were separated by barbed wires, with one group inside and another outside!

After the war, having been invited by the Episcopal Diocese of Chicago to help the resettlement of displaced persons of Japanese descent, I had the privilege of working with the *Isseis* ("first generation," or immigrant parents) and the *Niseis* ("second generation," or American-born citizen children); and I also came to learn something about other ethnic, racial, and cultural minority groups as well. Thus, although my contacts were by necessity mainly with Asian-American communities (mostly Japanese-American), I often reflected on the larger issues of the tragic realities of various marginal groups in this alleged land of freedom and opportunity. Of most importance, I kept on asking the question: In what sense could Christian members of hyphenated American groups make creative contributions to the larger Christendom and American society?

I rather imagine that readers will have to shift mental gears somewhat sharply in order to follow my third imagery, which portrays the famous remains of Angkor (capital of the Khmer kings in Cambodia from the ninth to the thirteenth century A.D.), a living symbol of the mortality and impermanence of all great human civilizations. Inevitably, we are made to reflect on the durability of modern Western civilization, in which Christianity has been so deeply involved and with which it has been so closely identified. During the heyday of Angkor, Khmer kings ruled a huge territory, which covered from the present French Indochina peninsula in the east to the Bay of Bengal in the west. But the magnificent Angkor, great center of politics, commerce, and religion, with colossal reservoirs, canals, and moats used for water control and irrigation, was abandoned in the midfifteenth century when the Khmers were overcome by invading Thai forces. Angkor remained engulfed by savage jungle vegetation for centuries until the huge city was unearthed in the nineteenth century by French archaeologists. One of the tragic consequences of the Vietnam War was the closing off of Angkor to foreign visitors by the Cambodian government. I was fortunate enough to spend a week there in 1959. While in Angkor, I could not help but be impressed by the similarity between the way Khmer civilization and the Hinduized, chthonic Buddhist tradition, on the one hand, and Western civilization and ecclesiastical Christianity, on the other, supported each other. That type of reflection led me to ask further religious, intellectual, and existential questions, some of which are included in this volume.

I was asked in 1954 by the Canadian Broadcasting Corporation to help cover the Second Assembly of the World Council of Churches held in Evanston, Illinois. Subsequently, after I was allowed to become a naturalized U.S. citizen—a fortunate by-product of the otherwise dubious Walter-McCarran Bill—I attended many ecumenical conferences, such as those held in Davos, Switzerland, and Herrenalb, Germany. The fact that I taught the history of religions for thirty-five years at the University of Chicago and served as dean of its Divinity School for ten years provided me with added incentive to reflect on the nature of encounters between Western and Eastern civilizations, as well as between Christianity and non-Christian religions. I offer these reflections in order to make a modest contribution to the domestic and global problems that now confront this Republic.

Nearly half a century ago, Adolph Keller poignantly observed the predicament of Christianity in the modern world. "In the past," he observed, "Christian faith meant a certainty about life and its future, an assurance which gave a meaning in its continuous changes, an inner security which was a firm foundation from which the moving kaleidoscope of a whole world could be observed and judged."[2] But, as he pointed out, in our century the invisible and intricate network that had supported Christian tradition directly or indirectly—such as the European moral community, Western civilization, democracy, and so forth—is no longer in a position to sustain it. To make the matter more precarious, adherents of Christian faith in the West, in Africa, in Latin America, and in Asia—like mariners—are compelled to rebuild their own "religious ships" while sailing on the high sea. It is my hope that this volume will enhance in a small way mutual understandings among them, for we are all caught in similar quandaries.

1

THE ASIAN CHRISTIAN
TRADITION

1

THE ASIAN CHRISTIAN PERSPECTIVE OF CHRISTIANITY[1]

PROLOGUE

Over the years I have published a number of articles on Christianity in Japan. I am now hoping to place the subject in its broader context, namely, the Asian Christian tradition, a tradition discussed thus far mostly from Western perspectives. Although all of us have learned much from the discussion of the Asian Christian tradition from the perspectives of the former "sending churches" in the West, my views on the subject seek to present another side of the picture, that side seen from the perspectives of the so-called younger churches, that is, Christian communities in the non-Western world.

As a child of a younger church, I have been for years both distressed and amused by the simplistic and erroneous assumption, still held in some quarters of Western Christendom, that Christians in non-Western lands should agree completely and wholeheartedly with Western Christians on all major aspects of Christianity. Of course, in one sense this is not an unreasonable expectation, for all churches share in common many things, for example, sacred scriptures, liturgies, calendars, and so forth. On the other hand, various churches inevitably reflect different types of metaphysical intuition innate to the respective peoples involved. Ironically, so far both ecumenical movements and global confessionalism (of Roman Catholic, Lutheran, Calvinist, Anglican, and other traditions) have not faced this problem squarely. It is worth remembering in this connection that, much as the ancient Hebrew community came into being as the congregation (*qahal*) of various tribal groups, the Christian community from the beginning understood itself as the *ekklesia* (the Greek term for *qahal*) of various peoples (*ethnai*) of dissimilar temperaments, outlooks, and traditions. Unfortunately, from the days of the early Christian community to our own day, there have always been exceedingly vocal persons for whom religion is a sort of cookie cutter, and who expect, say, Christians in South America and Africa or Anglicans in the British Isles and Asia to possess exactly the same kinds of religious orientations as they happen to have. (Evidently, some people are even under the happy illusion that the Almighty and all Christians speak the same language and hold similar views. One of Paul Simon's friends went so far as to tell the senator that "if English were good enough for Jesus Christ, it is good enough for me.") Clearly, we have to be sensitive to the issue of uniformity versus diversity as we proceed to discuss the Asian Christian tradition.

AUTOBIOGRAPHY AND BIOGRAPHY[2]

In our reflections, we also must face two related types of "two-sidedness" —that of (1) our thinking, and of (2) religion itself. The first type of two-sidedness becomes evident in our autobiographical and biographical perspectives. Certainly, one knows himself or herself better than do others, and thus autobiography is an important genre. Indeed, much of what we call faith- or religious-statements is based on an internal language, that is, looking at the religious experience of one's own community from within. Lamentably, many people are exposed primarily to autobiographical religious statements and therefore conclude that all religious statements must be autobiographical. They don't seem to realize that there is also a biographical perspective in religion (articulated in a modest way by such a discipline as the history of religions, or *Religionswissenschaft*), which invariably views all religious traditions from outside, as it were. Furthermore, some people—hold to the misguided hopes of collapsing the autobiographical and biographical perspectives. In reality, there are qualitative, insurmountable, and inviolable differences between these two modes of apprehension of reality, life, and the world.

INNER AND OUTER MEANINGS OF RELIGION[3]

Related to the two-sidedness of our perception is the two-sidedness of what we call "religion"—or the two kinds of meaning of religion itself. As someone said so simply and eloquently, to many of us outsiders, Islam is a religion of Muslims, but to Muslims it is a religion of truth. The same is true of all other religious traditions, including Christianity. The most obvious example of this two-sidedness is Christianity, Islam, and Judaism's "monotheism," or the belief in one supreme deity (their "inner meaning") versus their "monolatry," or the worship of one deity for themselves without excluding competing deities for other traditions (their often reluctantly admitted "outer meaning").

THE RELIGIOUS/CULTURAL/SOCIAL/POLITICAL SYNTHESIS

Equally troublesome for us is the status and identity of religion itself. In this connection, Bernard Lewis stated recently:

> When we in the Western world, nurtured in the Western tradition, use the words "Islam" and "Islamic," we tend to make a natural error and assume that religion means the same for Muslims as it has meant in the Western world . . . that is to say, a section or compartment of life reserved for certain matters, and separate, or at least separable, from other compartments of life designed to hold other matters. . . . In classical Islam there was no distinction between Church and state.[4]

Actually, most of the religious traditions of the world, like Islam, do not share the Western Christian notion of religion as a separate or separable human activity. Rather, as I once stated elsewhere:

> It is a peculiar Western convention to divide human experience into such pigeonholes as religion, philosophy, ethics, aesthetics, culture, society, etc. Obviously, this type of convention is a very provincial usage, even though many Westerners still assume that such a provincial Western mode has universal validity, partly because they are not aware of other, that is, non-Western ways of dividing human experience. Actually people everywhere live and breathe in their own respective "seamless wholes"—what [to Westerners] look like syntheses of religion, culture, and the social and political orders, to use the Western convention of divided categories. Significantly, what we call "religion" [in the Western convention] provides a sense of cosmic legitimation to each synthesis.[5]

As might be expected, in dealing with the case of Western Christianity, people customarily depend on Western Christians' autobiographical notion of religion—following their provincial convention of dividing human experience—as a separable compartment in life.

A propos Christian development in the West, the younger church Christians have no reason to quarrel with Western Christians' autobiographical statements about their "Western Christian" experience, but they rightly resist any suggestion or pressure from Western Christians to adopt the provincial European Christian experience as their own "Christian" experience. To be sure, all younger church Christians are by and large very knowledgeable about the doctrinal, creedal, liturgical, ethical, and institutional development of Christianity in Western history, but many of the controversies and conflicts for which a great deal of blood has been shed in the West do not concern younger church Christians. Take, for example, the heated historical Western-Byzantine controversy as to whether the Holy Spirit proceeds only from the Father, following the Byzantine formula, or whether the Holy Spirit proceeds both from the Father and from the Son, following the Western formula. Although an intellectually interesting theological debate, most younger church Christians do not feel that it is a crucial issue for them, for such a debate was derived basically from the difference between Greek and Latin rhetorics. The younger church Christians believe they have other, more important and urgent things to worry about. For instance, from the perspective of the younger churches, to which the Western convention of compartmentalizing human experience was quite alien, it makes good sense to view Christianity as an integral part of various forms of religious/cultural/social/political syntheses that have developed in Western history. Such a view is not proposed as a better or more adequate version of the Western Christians' autobiographical interpretation of their own experience; but to many younger church Christians, Christianity makes sense only from such perspectives. The following interpretation of Christian development in the West may not conform to Western Christians' autobiographical statements on the subject, but it might adumbrate how the younger churches see the Christian tradition, a tradition that was destined to impinge upon them in the modern period. Regardless, it seems important in these days of ecumenical movements and global confessionalism that Western Christians have some inkling, however slight, of how younger church men and women feel about the historical development of Christianity.

CHRISTIAN DEVELOPMENT IN THE WEST

As far as I can tell, younger church Christians, who invariably have been exposed to other religions, are generally more alert than the average Western Christian to the intricate interrelations that exist between the "religious event" and the "historical event" in the biblical accounts of, for example, the Exodus, Incarnation, Crucifixion, and Resurrection. They are also sensitive to the fact that some biblical scenes portrayed—for example, the Lukan Nativity narrative or Acts' depiction of Pentecost—are more like "pictures painted with words." (Such outlooks may account for the relative insignificance of biblical inerrancy for the younger church Christians.) At any rate, all agree that Christianity was born within the Jewish fold in a corner of the Roman Empire, here emphasizing, of course, what Germans call *Kirchengeschichte* rather than *Dogmengeschichte*. As *Kulturträger* ("culture bearers"), Romans inherited Alexander the Great's dream of unifying all aspects of the *Oikoumene* ("the inhabited quarter of the world"). It must be pointed out that Alexander's vision of the religious/cultural/social/political synthesis rested on the plurality or disunity of religions, the Hellenistic culture and Greek language, the social equality of Greeks, Persians, and other peoples, and a universal political order. Although the Romans modified Alexander's scheme, as, for example, stressing a Roman imperialistic rather than a universal political order, the Roman synthesis continued to accept the principle of religious plurality. Understandably, the early Christian community, which came into being within such a context, affirmed the plurality of religions as its outer meaning side by side with its exclusive loyalty to Christ as Savior as its inner meaning. Such a double orientation was what the apostle Paul affirmed when he wrote: "Although there may be so-called gods in heaven or on earth—as indeed there are many 'gods' and many 'lords'—yet for us there is one God . . . and one Lord, Jesus Christ" (1 Cor. 8:5–6).[6]

CHRISTIAN ORIENTATION—"HORIZONTAL" AND "VERTICAL"

It is worth noting that the Christian tradition, like many other religions, possesses both "horizontal" (historical, from creation to the end of the world) and "vertical" (being the colony of the kingdom of heaven on earth) dimensions. The horizontal aspect of Christianity was inspired indirectly by the eschatology (belief in the end of the world, *eschaton*) of Persian Zoroastrianism "through the medium of the Jewish exiles in

Babylon who seem to have been thoroughly impregnated with Zoroastrian ideas."[7] The vertical dimension of Christianity, which was integrally related to its horizontal dimension, took seriously early Christians' belief in Christ's "second coming." Indeed, the early church was often characterized as the "eucharistizing eschatological community." It was indeed a community of Christ's devotees *in the world* but not *of the world;* in this world, the faithful were "aliens and exiles," to use the expression of 1 Peter (2:11). But when they realized that the anticipated return of Christ (*parousia,* "arrival" or "presence") would not be realized as soon as they had expected, or that it had already been partially actualized at the Pentecost, they were compelled to come to terms with the empirical realities of the historical situation.

APOLOGISTS

The shift of outlook of the early church was also undoubtedly derived from the fact that many intelligent Gentiles—who, unlike the poorly educated Galilean fishermen, were well versed in Greek philosophy—found their way into the early church. In order to make Christian teaching more accessible to the general public, these intelligent Gentiles, often called "apologists," followed the footsteps of the Hellenistic Jews, who had earlier attempted to translate their autobiographical Jewish faith into a biographical mode of Greek language and thought. These Hellenistic Jews, especially Philo of Alexandria, were attracted to the Greek notion of the *logoi spermatikoi,* the "scattered seeds" of truth found in every cultural tradition. Now some of the Christian apologists, like Clement of Alexandria and Origen, appropriated Philo's notion of the *logos* ("word," "reason," "rational faculty") and asserted that the divine *Logos* as teacher (*logos paidagogos*), which had guided all pre- and non-Christian traditions, became the *logos incarnate* in Jesus Christ, thus incorporating in effect the Hellenistic Jews' biographical formula into their own new autobiographical scheme.[8] With this intellectual somersault, the small and powerless Christian community became convinced of the universal validity of its message, at least in its autobiographical affirmation of Christianity's inner meaning.

THE CONSTANTINIAN SYNTHESIS

In A.D. 313, with the Edict of Toleration of Emperor Constantine, Christianity was destined to become the religion of the empire. It should be stressed that Constantine's new religious/cultural/social/

political synthesis was built on the principle of religious unity, effectively reversing Alexander's dependence on religious pluralism, and so expected Christianity to be the sole system to provide cosmic legitimation for his Caesaropapian scheme (i.e., the monarchy as head of both state and church). Inevitably, Christianity, which had been emphasizing less its vertical orientation even before the time of Constantine, became now a full-fledged this-worldly religion. On his part, Constantine felt he had to produce a formula—"Christologically," if possible—equating the cause of his empire with that of heaven. Thus this as yet to be baptized monarch called, and presided at, the Council of Nicaea, held in 325, and strongly urged the bishops—some suspect that he bribed them—to vote for the theological formulation that stated that the Father and the Son of the Trinity were "of the same essence" (*homoousios*). During the Council, Constantine also inaugurated his twentieth year as monarch and invited the attending bishops to the banquet. According to Robert Grant:

> The "men of God" reclined on couches near him, surrounded by security guards with swords at the ready. Eusebius of Caesarea . . . thought that this was what the kingdom of Christ would be. Within a few days the emperor addressed a final meeting on his basic theme, the importance of harmony in church and state.[9]

Many ecclesiastical leaders were very happy with Constantine's synthesis, for it helped the Christian community gain much wealth, prestige, and influence, although some feared that the religious orientation of the church had been soft-pedaled in favor of the expansion of ecclesiastical structures. After Constantine's death, Osius (or Hosius) of Cordoba, adviser to the emperor, told the imperial heir: "God has placed the kingdom in your hands. To us he has entrusted the affairs of the church."[10]

CORPUS CHRISTIANUM: THE MEDIEVAL EUROPEAN SYNTHESIS

With the inauguration in A.D. 590 of the papacy of Gregory I (c. 540–604), Western Europe commenced the era of the *corpus Christianum*, a new religious/cultural/social/political synthesis. Although during this period the ecclesiastical leaders envisioned the establishment of a sort of immanental theocracy under the papacy, reversing Constantine's, which placed the monarchy on top, what actually developed by practical necessity was a dyarchy of political and ecclesiastical heads constantly competing for dominant power. (It is to be noted that the Caesaropapian system, the legacy of Constantine the Great, survived for centuries in the Byzantine Empire; we will carry on our narrative restricted mostly to the developments in Western Europe.) The epoch making event during this period was undoubtedly the rise of Islam, the this-worldly religion par excellence, in Arabia under Muhammad (A.D. 570–632). During the one hundred years following the founder's death, Islam—which evolved its own religious/cultural/social/political synthesis—rapidly expanded not only in Arabia but also into the heartland of the Christian communities in North Africa and Spain. Although the Muslims' hope to penetrate beyond the Pyrenees was barred by Charles Martel in 732, the *corpus Christianum* and the *corpus Islamicum* were destined to coexist side by side for centuries, influencing each other both positively and negatively.

THE IMPACT OF ISLAM

At the expense of oversimplification, let me cite four major areas of Islamic-Christian contact:

1. The *corpus Christianum* learned Greek philosophy and many other humanistic disciplines from Muslim (as well as some Jewish) elites in Spain and Sicily. The fusion of Greek philosophy with Christian thought via the Islamic community greatly helped the Christian cause by enabling theology to become the queen of the sciences and to take a prominent place in the emerging European universities. It is widely recognized that Christian thinkers such as Albertus Magnus (d. c. 1290) and Thomas Aquinas (d. 1274) made liberal use of Aristotle's thought, which they had learned from Muslim scholars. Incidentally, the university (*studium*) was one of the three important medieval European institutions, the other two being the church (*sacerdotium*) and the state (*imperium*).

2. The Islamic community left a strong impact on European Christendom with its scientific spirit. I must hasten to add that philosophy and science were regarded as inseparable in *falsafah* (the Arabic term for the integral approach to knowledge).[11] Central to *falsafah* was the importance of experiment, which also stimulated the scientific spirit then growing in Europe.[12]

3. The complex phenomenon of the Crusades—a series of military campaigns undertaken by European princes from 1096–1291 under the pretext of recovering the Holy Land from Muslim rule, with the active leadership and support of the papacy—defies simple explanation. From the military standpoint, the Crusades hardly threatened the Muslims. That the provincial Europeans at least saw the Middle East could

have been a positive experience, even though the whole enterprise was a colossal misfortune. But the false reports brought back by uninformed Crusaders filled Europe with popular misinformation about Islam that has persisted down to our own time. With the growth of a hostile attitude toward Islam on the part of European Christians, approved and supported by the ecclesiastical leaders, it was but natural for the Islamic community on its part to behave like a stone wall that effectively confined Western Christians primarily to Europe.

4. By far the most conspicuous influence of the this-worldly Islam on Europe was to make the *corpus Christianum*, which already was worldly enough, even more preoccupied with temporal affairs. To highly competitive and paranoic European Christians, Muhammad was the false prophet mentioned in the Johannine apocalypse (Rev. 19:20), and Islam was nothing but an evil religion. It was thus necessary for the *corpus Christianum* to become richer, stronger, and more powerful than the *corpus Islamicum.* Here, European Christians rejected the historical Christian approach to non-Christians. Non-Christians were no longer regarded as traveling companions—on the road to Emmaus, as recorded in the Gospel of Luke—through whom Christ might speak to believers; they were infidels living in the darkness, ready to be conquered, enlightened, and exploited. Once these mundane wisdoms and aspirations were packaged as divine commandments, the *corpus Christianum* found convenient excuses to condone colonialism and patronize crude forms of overseas missionary enterprises.

POSTMEDIEVAL EUROPEAN DEVELOPMENT

The decline of the *corpus Christianum* in the postmedieval period was precipitated by a number of factors, for example, the Renaissance, the Reformation, nationalism, the scientific outlook, and so forth. An interesting footnote might be added in regards to the unexpected role played by the university in this connection. It was during the early sixteenth century that Martin Luther and others became persuaded that what they learned at the *studium* ("university") had its own kind of truth claims, different from but just as valid as the teachings of the *sacerdotium* ("church"). Frightened by this kind of intellectual challenge, Rome asserted its monopoly on the *magisterium* ("teaching authority"), a move that was supported by the leaders of the Counter-Reformation. Consequently, Western Christendom was sharply split between the domains of the papal church and the orbit of Protestantism. Significantly, it was the Roman Catholic nations in the Iberian peninsula, Portugal and Spain, the pious supporters of the Counter-Reformation, that earlier—that is, during the fifteenth century—had initiated both colonialism and the overseas missionary enterprise. Undeniably, implicit in both was a strong and pervasive anti-Islamic impulse.

IBERIAN COLONIALISM

In the Iberian peninsula, the only multiracial and multicultural area in Europe where Muslims, Jews, and Christians lived together for centuries, anti-Islamic sentiment became intensified in the latter part of the fifteenth century with the ascension of the self-styled Catholic monarchs, Ferdinand of Aragon and Isabella of Castille. Spanish Catholicism, no doubt emulating the qualities of rival Islam, was noted for its extreme piety, authoritarian dogmatism, and crude use of power, as exemplified by royal absolutism, the barbarous institution called the Inquisition, and the inhumane treatment of Jews and Muslims. It is not surprising, therefore, that, determined to regain Spain for Catholic Christianity, Ferdinand and Isabella began sporadic military campaigns in 1481 against Muslims in Granada in southern Spain. In this undertaking they became exhausted financially, whereupon Pope Sixtus IV (r. 1471–1484), a great spender himself, came to their rescue by giving them the right of royal patronage "over all benefices reconquered, plus a third of all titles collected."[13] In 1492 Granada finally fell, thus ending Muslim dominion over the Iberian peninsula. This was also the year when Christopher Columbus, with the sponsorship of Ferdinand and Isabella, crossed the Atlantic and discovered North America. In 1493 the notorious Spanish-born pope, Alexander VI (who reputedly secured the papal throne by flagrant bribery), charged Ferdinand and Isabella to send missionaries to the New World for the purpose of the christianization of the Indies.

Meanwhile, Spain's immediate neighbor, Portugal, was not sitting idle. Prince Henry (1394–1460), third son of King João I of Portugal and a well known foe of Islam, nicknamed "Henry the Navigator" because of his interest in maritime affairs, was for years gathering and training mariners for overseas expeditions, not only for the sake of economic gain but also to fight the Muslims on their own soil (presumably Africa). In this situation, confronted by the potential conflicts over colonial spoils between Portugal and Spain, the two loyal supporters of the papacy, each determined to gain as much this-worldly wealth and power as possible, were persuaded by Pope Alexander VI to sign the Treaty of Trodesilhas in 1494, whereby "Portugal and Spain fixed a line

370 leagues west of Cape Verde Islands as the demarcation of their respective zones, [which] . . . thus became the final line of division between the discoveries of the two Iberian states."[14] In keeping with this treaty, Spain now expanded to the New World (and eventually to the Philippines via Mexico), whereas Portugal pursued Africa, India, and East Asia—following the ocean route via the Cape of Good Hope, discovered by Vasco da Gama in 1498.

THE CHRISTIAN OVERSEAS MISSIONARY ENTERPRISE

The colonial expansion of Spain and Portugal gave great impetus to Roman Catholic overseas missionary work. Or rather, using the logic I have been employing in this volume, I might simply say that Roman Catholicism gave cosmic legitimation to the Iberian synthesis of religion (the Catholicism of the Counter-Reformation variety), culture (Iberian), society (hierarchical), and political order (colonialism under monarchical absolutism). To be sure, it was not the first attempt, historically speaking, of the Christian overseas missionary enterprise. We learn that as early as the third century Christianity was known already to have spread to the coasts of the Indian Ocean. One of the most missionary-minded branches of early Christianity was the Nestorian church (the followers of Nestorius, the Syrian born patriarch of Constantinople in the fifth century), which had many congregations in Persia, Central Asia, and China by the seventh century. (The Nestorians were also noted linguists who initiated the translation of Greek science and philosophy, first into Syriac and then into Arabic; many Nestorian scholars were favored by Muslim courts.) The Nestorians were again welcomed in China by the Mongol Yüan rulers during the thirteenth century. It is interesting to remember that Rabban Marcos, born in China, became the Nestorian patriarchate of Seleucia-Baghdad, and that another Chinese-born Nestorian, Rabban Sauma, became the Persian ambassador and was sent to Europe to form an ill-fated alliance with the Crusaders and the Mongols against the Mamlūkes of Egypt.[15] (By the thirteenth century, Nestorians were also well established in the coast of Malabar in South India.) It was during the Mongol Yüan period that Franciscan missionaries were allowed to enter China and a papal delegate was received by the emperor.[16] Unfortunately, both Nestorianism and Roman Catholicism completely disappeared after the Yüan period in China; Syriac Christians (Nestorians), however, remained more or less intact in South India.

THE ROMAN CATHOLIC OVERSEAS MISSION

As mentioned earlier, people in the Iberian peninsula, where Muslim forces received the death blow in 1492, were emotionally anti-Islamic, and their commitment to the cause of the Counter-Reformation made them very anti-Protestant as well. Understandably, both Spain and Portugal agreed to carry on Roman Catholic overseas missionary work under the "patronage" system (*patronato*), an agreement with Rome whereby these governments maintained missionaries and ecclesiastical institutions in their colonies in exchange for extensive power in church matters at home and in Rome. Thus the Portuguese missionaries were sent to Asia, and Spanish missionaries went to the New World. "In fact," says William Sweet, "the early Spanish *conquistadors* considered themselves Christian crusaders and brought over to the New World the ideas which had grown in the long wars which they had fought against the Moors in Spain, using the same battle cries and evoking the same saints in the New World that had served them in the old."[17]

Although Spanish missionary work was decisively important in the Philippines and was a factor not to be ignored in Japan (as those who have read the novel *Shōgun* or those who have seen the television version of it are certainly aware), it was the Portuguese missionary work that directly affected the rest of Asia. After the capture of Goa in South India in 1510, it became a center of Portuguese trade and evangelism in the East; the Bishop of Goa was given a formidable jurisdiction extending from the Cape of Good Hope in the West to China in the East. In 1541, Francis Xavier, known as a conquistador of souls in Asia, appeared on the scene. (Because of his Iberian upbringing, he too was emotionally anti-Islamic and so was happy to leave India, partly under Muslim Mughal rule at his time, for Malacca and eventually for Japan.) In 1575, the Jesuit visitor, Alessandro Valignano, decided to gain more freedom for the missionaries from the civil colonial governments, which were expected to exercise control over missionary work in accordance with the patronage system. It was he who, bypassing conservative and ill-educated Portuguese missionaries, picked an Italian Jesuit, Matteo Ricci (d. 1610), a renowned missionary-scientist, to inaugurate the policy of "accommodation" of some native (non-Catholic) Chinese rites. (This, in effect, was the heart of the so-called Rites Controversy. In the eighteenth century, two popes, Clement XI and Benedict XIV, condemned Ricci's sensible scheme.) In India, another missionary from Rome, Roberto de Nobili, initiated a similar policy of "adaptation" (this time of certain Hindu customs to Catholicism). This policy was bitterly attacked by many missionaries in India and critics in Rome. Later (in 1662), the Vatican established the *Congregatio de Propaganda Fide* to centralize missionary activities under the direct control of the papacy, thus reversing the patronage system.

PROTESTANT OVERSEAS MISSION

The defeat of Spain's invincible armada by the British navy in 1588 symbolized in hindsight the decline of Iberian leadership in colonialism as well as in overseas missionary work. The vacuum was quickly filled, as far as colonial expansion was concerned, by the Dutch, British, and French. As for the missionary enterprise, it is interesting to note that the Protestant churches in Europe had very little to do with it until the eighteenth century. Evidently, most Protestants shared other Europeans' notion of "civilization"—that is, Western civilization—as a de facto pseudoreligion of secularized salvation, which had been gaining ground from the time of the Renaissance. Rejecting the medieval notion that civilization was subservient to the *sacerdotium* ("church"), many postmedieval Europeans came to regard themselves as the inventors and transmitters of true civilization. The phenomenal colonial expansion convinced many Europeans of the superiority of their culture, technology, and socioeconomic and political systems.

Significantly, in the eighteenth century a small group of Protestants called the Pietists rejected the popular European view of the human being as the creator of cultural values. Thus the initial ethos of the Protestant foreign missions, inaugurated by the continental Pietists and English Evangelicals, ran counter to popular European civilization and colonialism. In other words, it was the combined influence of Pietists and Evangelicals, and not the monarchs or church authorities, that promoted the Protestant world mission. In this situation, missionary-minded Protestants had to find a new form of organization for their activity, that is, the private missionary societies. According to Cnattingius: "They were simply associations of individual Christians, both clergy and laymen, who had felt the great call to take up missionary service and banded themselves together to form missionary undertakings overseas."[18] In America, however, many denominations accepted missionary work as a task of the total denomination—starting with the national organization of the Baptists in 1814. Significantly, there was a great double push in America for the establishment of a Christian America and the Christian conquest of the whole world.[19]

COLONIALISM AND PROTESTANTISM

Ironically, despite the initial hostility of the colonial regimes toward the missionary movement, they soon began to persuade themselves that Christianity was the spiritual engine of Western civilization, an engine they wanted to see running among colonial people. On their part, many missionaries came to think that because it was not possible to present a pure gospel anyway, they could at least present a Christian-inspired Western civilization. Thus there developed in the course of time a new modern European synthesis of this-worldly Christianity, Western culture (supported by science and technology), the capitalistic socioeconomic system (with a built-in paternalism), and the colonial political order, a synthesis that was then given "cosmic legitimation" by modern Protestantism. In this way, Protestant missionary work came to mean, in effect, the Westernization of the non-Western world, in keeping with the motto made famous by David Livingston concerning the double aims of "commerce (colonialism) and Christianity." Inevitably, Protestant missionary societies and European colonial regimes in Asia (and, I suspect, in Africa too) betrayed many similarities.

COLONIAL REGIMES AND MISSIONARY SOCIETIES: STRUCTURAL SIMILARITIES

Admittedly, it is very difficult to make general statements about Protestant missionary societies—here we concentrate on Protestant groups because the Roman Catholic missionary enterprise did not regain its vigor until the latter part of the nineteenth century—because there have existed great differences between the European and American, the denominational and interdenominational, and the liberal and conservative societies. Nevertheless, it is safe to state that the early members of all these groups believed in what H. Richard Niebuhr called "Christ against culture."[20] In their singleness to obey the biblical commandment to preach the gospel to the end of the world, they had an oversimplified view that Christianity was bound to be right on every account, while non-Christian religions were simply wrong. We have already mentioned that the colonial authorities, who were at first hostile to the Christian missionary work, began to be more favorably inclined toward it. Oddly enough, many European missionaries, despite their determination to preach the "pure" or "a-cultural" gospel, began to behave as though they were preaching the "Christ of European culture." They began to teach—some no doubt innocently, while others more deliberately—Western cultural values as Christian values. Some missionaries also naively accepted the myth of the superiority of European civilization as well as the myth of the superiority of the white race. And inasmuch as the colonial regimes were eager to spread the gospel of Western civilization, they began to regard missionary programs, especially in education and philanthropy, as their allies. In the course of time, the colonial regimes and Protestant missionary societies even began to exhibit structural similarities.

In colonial administration there was, generally speaking, under the home government, something in the nature of a colonial office, which functioned to supervise the viceroy or governor-general in a given colony. Usually, the latter official ruled the colony, not directly but through a kind of nominal legislative body that embraced a few representatives of the colonial subjects. By far the most complex colonial administrative machine was developed in India under the British rule. According to Sir Reginald Coupland, the main strength of the British raj was the Indian Civil Service, which attracted the flower of English youth. Next in importance to the Indian Civil Service (I.C.S.) was the Indian Police Service (I.P.). There were other technical services, such as education, agriculture, forestry, which were considered less important than the I.C.S. and the I.P., and these permitted a substantial number of native Indians to enter their ranks. Under these so-called All-India Services, there developed many Provincial Services, which were staffed almost entirely by non-British personnel. As early as 1900, the British raj reported that there were over 500,000 Indian and only about 4,000 British personnel. Of course, because of the power structure of the colonial administration, the better-paid and decision-making jobs invariably were held by British personnel.[21] At any rate, such a structure—with the home government, the colonial office, the viceroy's office, and a nominal legislative body within the colony—had its counterpart in many missionary societies. There were, of course, many differences among the missionary societies as well. For the most part in North America, the missionary agencies were the mission boards of the various denominations. In continental Europe, with the exception of the Netherlands, the missionary societies were not integral parts of the churches, despite the close working relationships between the two. Interdenominational missionary societies also developed their own structures.

POSITIVE AND NEGATIVE ASPECTS OF BUREAUCRACY

Broadly speaking, the Protestant churches in the West have accepted the principle of discharging their missionary obligation through missionary societies and mission boards. These latter groups have authorized their missionaries in each of their respective mission fields to organize themselves as a mission, mission council, district committee, or finance committee. In the course of time, administrative responsibility has been transferred to these missions in the field. For example, the appropriation of money is often given in lump sums to the mission, which in turn allocates it to various programs of the native churches, or the mission sends recommendations to the boards or societies in the West regarding the program of the native churches. All missionaries have been painfully aware, however, how difficult—and yet how crucially important—it has been to bring non-Christians to a Christian way of life, a task for which the development of indigenous Christian churches has been fundamental. In retrospect, it is very sad, but understandable, that many Western missionaries, in their wholesale rejection of "paganism," formulated the so-called mission compound in which newly converted natives were kept away from further "contamination" by their "heathen" neighbors. The inevitable result was that these mission compounds became self-perpetuating institutions, identified as the norm of the Christian church. In such a church, it was the missionary who determined what should be done and how it should be done. "The function of the convert was to listen and to obey."[22] Meanwhile, the native Christian churches, small though they were, copied the bureaucratic structure of Western ecclesiastical institutions, and many leaders of these churches began to aspire for top positions in their own ecclesiastical administration. In principle, everybody agreed that the ultimate objective of missionary work was to establish an indigenous church—under native pastors and operating on a self-supporting basis. It was felt that when the time came, the Western missionaries would be able to turn over all pastoral work to native leaders and their superintendence to native pastors. But the when and the how were to be determined by the missionaries themselves. Psychologically, many missionaries accepted the coming of the indigenous church in principle, much as they did the kingdom of God, which was to come for certain but not in their lifetime or in any foreseeable future. For all practical purposes, the native Christian churches were to remain in the status of perpetual tutelage. For example, a missionary was greatly shocked at the very suggestion that the further training of a gifted Filipino might "qualify him to direct the mission some day."[23]

It is not our intention to insinuate that Protestant missionary societies were bound to miss their religious vocations simply because they exhibited uncanny similarities to the ill-fated colonial regimes. All noble ideals need some form of institutional implementations, which often involve bureaucratic dimensions. I realize that the term *bureaucracy* often has some nasty implications, but it is well to remember, as Robert K. Merton reminded us, that "the chief merit of bureaucracy is its technical efficiency, with a premium placed on precision, speed, expert control, continuity, discretion, and optimal returns on input." Generally, those who have served in the church or in the foreign mission field appreciate the vocational security that bureaucracy provides, in terms of tenure, pensions, and regularized procedures for promotion, while they lament the impersonalized atmosphere of the bureaucratic institution. Merton also tells us that the "bureaucracy is administration which almost completely avoids public discussion of its policies." Anyone who is in a bureaucratic organization, be it political, military, or religious, is under constant pressures to "conform to his patterned obligations," with the result that he or she will be preoccupied with the rules and regulations at the expense of the aims of the organization. "Adherence to the rules, originally conceived as a means, becomes transformed into an end-in-itself; there occurs the familiar *displacement of goals* whereby 'an instrumental value becomes a terminal value.'" Merton uses the expression "the bureaucratic virtuoso" to describe an extreme product of such a process of displacement of goals. Another common feature of bureaucracy is the "process of sanctification," whereby certain bureaucratic symbols and status, originally introduced for technical reasons, tend to become rigid and sacred. Inevitably, there develops a discrepancy between a bureaucrat's position within the hierarchy and his position with reference to the public; this results in the formation of in-group solidarity, which resists pressure from the public.[24] Notwithstanding the noble aims of the Christian world mission, it remains true that the church in the West, the mission board or missionary society, the mission in the field, and the native church manifest many of the features of bureaucracy described by sociologists.

MISSIONARY MOVEMENTS AND THE YOUNGER CHURCHES

It is not easy to assess the achievements of modern missionary movements. It is important to state in this connection that although our emphasis has been more on the Protestant endeavors, similar observations can be made in broad strokes concerning the Roman Catholic endeavors as well. Our difficulties are based on the simple fact that the Christian global missionary enterprise, like mother-of-pearl, has many different faces, depending on from which particular standpoint it is

viewed. Undoubtedly, defenders of missionary work would emphasize
its idealism, spiritual mission, and ultraism, virtues rare in the cut-
throat world of international competition. Even though the Christianization of the whole world—the lofty motto of the North American
Student Volunteer Movement around the turn of the century—was
hardly realized, many missionaries themselves were happy that they at
least attempted "Great Things for God," as the first English Baptist
missionary to India, William Carey (d. 1834), advocated. Skeptics are
quick to point out the many shortcomings of missionaries and missionary works, especially their all-too-easy and uncritical compromises
with greedy adventurers and unprincipled colonial officials. Missionaries are also often criticized for turning the clock backward from the real
and chaotic world of today to the anesthetic and illusory certainties of
bygone days. The list of pros and cons could be extended indefinitely.

In attempting to discern and to summarize both the vocal and
the silent reactions of the younger churches to Christian world mission,
I should at least mention the following three reflections:

1. It must be understood that the younger churches have no alternative except to reflect on the modern phase of world history from non-
Western perspectives. They are fully aware that the combined forces of
Western civilization (characterized earlier as a de facto pseudoreligion of
secularized salvation), Christian missionary activities, and European
colonial expansion have brought about political, socioeconomic, cultural,
and even religious changes in much of the non-Western world during the
last two centuries, a period when Protestants were conspicuously active.
Although some members of the younger churches have bought into the
missionaries' official rhetoric that Christian missions, being spiritually
motivated, have nothing to do with exploitive colonialism, many of them
share the feeling of their non-Christian neighbors and are persuaded that
in the past two centuries the non-Western world has come under the yoke
of the modern European religious/cultural/social/political synthesis,
which received its cosmic legitimation from the Western Christian tradition. In this situation, Hendrik Kraemer, the renowned Dutch missionary
to Indonesia, poignantly reflected on himself and his fellow missionaries:
"It seems as if the non-Christian world was spread out before the eyes as a
world to be conquered. It was not only the eye of faith, but also the eye of
the Westerner, who subconsciously lived in the conviction that he could
dispose of the destiny of the world, because the absorption of the Eastern
by the Western world appeared to come inevitably."[25]

2. Many members of the younger churches realize that they live
in an atmosphere inherited from the days of Western missionaries, who

had introduced a very Western form of bureaucracy with a "mission compound mentality."[26] Most of the younger church leaders today accept, reluctantly or otherwise, the necessity of some degree of bureaucracy for ecclesiastical institutions, but they are critical of the type of bureaucracy that the younger churches have been saddled with for two main reasons. First, their bureaucracy was not accountable to the younger churches, which to be sure had many internal problems: it was directed by and accountable to unseen powers in Europe and North America. It was not even involved in the socioeconomic life of various Asian (and, I suspect, African) nations. Second, the younger church leaders inherited their Western missionary-predecessors' incapacity to exercise bureaucratic control. They also became victims of "self-fulfilling prophecy," something that usually accompanies bureaucracy. According to this sociological theory, if people define situations as real, they often become real in their own minds regardless of the objective features of the situation. For example, many Western missionaries held the view during the nineteenth century that all non-Christian religions were doomed to disappear sooner or later. Ironically, this kind of perception infiltrated the younger churches, some of which still today take this notion as their self-fulfilling prophecy, giving them dangerous and unwarranted illusions.

3. By far the greatest problem for the younger churches even today is the history of Christian expansion itself. The fact that Christianity was transmitted to Asia (and Africa, too) as a part of the Western "synthesis," as exemplified by the Roman Catholic enterprise in the sixteenth and seventeenth centuries and by more recent Christian (Protestant, Roman Catholic, and so forth) world missions, is deeply rooted in the memory of peoples in the non-Western world even after the end of Western colonialism. Indeed, many Western missionaries regarded Christians of the non-Western world as semipermanent wards. And even though we call them "fraternal workers" instead of "missionaries," and "younger churches" instead of "missionary churches," the tendency of Christians in the non-Western world to become carbon copies of Western Christians dies hard.[27] Many of them still feel closer to Christians in the West than to their non-Christian neighbors. They still know more about Barth, Tillich, Rahner, or Pannenberg than about indigenous non-Christian thinkers, or non-Christians for that matter. Seminary curricula of the younger churches are slavishly modeled after Western seminary curricula, and many clergy still aspire to pursue "higher" theological training in Europe or North America. Understandably, younger church Christians get incensed when non-Christians point out the "foreignness" of Christian churches in the non-Western world, but they

remain ineffective spectators of, rather than participants in, the social, cultural, and political life of their own homelands.

Part of the dilemma of the Asian Christian tradition (and of the younger churches in general) is due to the fact that the nineteenth century, when the West dominated the whole world, lasted longer than simply year 1899. I agree with the astute observation of Irving Kristol that for the majority of the human race, who live outside of Europe and the Americas, the twentieth century began only in 1945.[28] It is to the twentieth century and the more recent developments of the Asian Christian tradition that we must now turn.

2

THE ASIAN CHRISTIAN PERSPECTIVE IN GLOBAL REVOLUTION

IN RETROSPECT[1]

In the last chapter, I tried to point out that from the time of the Iberian kingdoms' colonial expansion in the sixteenth century to the end of World War II in 1945 many people outside Europe and North America lived in a world order dictated and defined by the Western "world of meaning."[2] There is much truth in Edward W. Said's observation that "the Orient was almost a European invention."[3] I presume that similar stereotyped, oversimplified, and erroneous images of Africa and other non-Western parts of the world have likewise cropped up in many Europeans' minds over the years. Said quotes a statement made by Arthur James, First Earl of Balfour (1848–1930), who simply assumed British superiority and Egyptian inferiority, and argued for British sovereignty in Egypt. Among other self-serving and far-fetched reasons, James insisted: "We are in Egypt not merely for the sake of the Egyptians, though we are there for their sake; we are there also for the sake of Europe at large." Given this kind of orientation, it is not surprising that Earl Evelyn Baring Cromer (1841–1917)—one-time secretary to his cousin, Lord Northbrook—when he was viceroy of India and later British Consul-General in Egypt, to whom both Indians and Egyptians were merely "subject people," was firmly convinced, according to Said, that

23

subject races did not have it in them to know what was good for them. Most of them were Orientals of whose characteristics Cromer was very knowledgeable since he had had experience with them both in India and Egypt. One of the convenient things about Orientals for Cromer was that managing them, although circumstances might differ slightly here and there, was almost everywhere nearly the same. This was, of course, because [so Cromer reasoned] Orientals were almost everywhere nearly the same.[4]

As might be expected, many books and articles have been written on the encounter of Europe and Asia from Europocentric perspectives. Some authors have even insinuated that the modern history of Asia is tantamount to the history of Western expansion. It is not surprising, however, that many Asian intellectuals have voiced their opinions on the same subject from radically different perspectives, resulting, quite predictably, in very different stories; unfortunately, many of their views have not been read in the West.

William S. Haas identifies the two perspectives as such: "*juxtaposition and identity*—this is the structure of the Eastern mind and civilization as contrasted with the *unity in variety* which is the characteristic structural principle of the West."[5] True to this principle, the West aspired for the unity of diverse elements that came into its experience, for example, Hellenism, Near Eastern religious traditions, Roman jurisprudence, and so forth. Understandably, the discovery of the non-Western world during the fifteenth and sixteenth centuries presented yet another great challenge to the West. Mircea Eliade goes so far as to say that the Europeans' discovery of non-Western peoples, especially the strange and fabulous elements in Asiatic societies and cultures, was just as significant a new experience as the maritime discoveries of the Renaissance, the astronomical discoveries that followed the invention of the telescope, and the dramatic confrontations with depth psychology.[6] In each case, the impulse of the Western mind was to try to blend the disparate elements into a synthetic unity. It is understandable, then, that most Europeans viewed Asian peoples, religions, cultures, and political orders as new "ingredients," eventually to be incorporated into the one "universal" civilization destined to come about sooner or later. (This perhaps is the Western meaning of universality and totality, as advocated variously by Christian world mission, Western communism, and the disciplines of intellectual history, social science, and contemporary Western-inspired Asian or Oriental studies.[7])

In sharp contrast to Westerners, who almost automatically think of histories, cultures, and religions of the world in terms of universal principles and unity, Asiatic thinkers, brought up as they are with a tradition of juxtaposition, invariably think of the modern Western civilization—powerful and influential though it was, especially during the nineteenth century—as one of several forms of civilization, side by side with their own. Such a difference in almost intuitive outlooks between Westerners and Easterners will have serious implications for the present and the future of the world. The crucial task before us is not to question which (the East or the West) is right; rather, we must develop the openness, the intelligence, and a sense of respect that will enable both sides to develop mutual understanding while recognizing each other's differences. Of course, this is easier said than done, especially when we are dealing with religious questions, because many religious people are firmly convinced of the rightness of their own particular faiths, views, and convictions.

There have been some individuals who have made valiant efforts to understand the "others" as they are—and not as they should be according to their own views and ideologies—and have advocated the need of mutual understanding and respect as well as genuine dialogue. I already have mentioned the names of William S. Haas and Mircea Eliade. Others who come readily to mind are William Ernest Hocking,[8] F. S. C. Northrop,[9] Paul Tillich,[10] and Arnold Toynbee.[11] Unfortunately, because of their probing minds and daring thoughts, they have often been dismissed flatly by pious Westerners as iconoclastic nonconformists; regardless, their ways of thinking and questioning have already made considerable impact on serious-minded intellectuals in Asia. Ironically, thus far there have been only a few well-read Asian thinkers who have addressed themselves in a levelheaded way to intercultural, interreligious, and intercivilizational problems. I would like to rectify this lamentable situation, for otherwise many Westerners will continue to view the East-West encounter in modern history only through Western glasses. In so stating, I am not saying that Western views are bound to be wrong; I want to state only that Asians have their own perspectives on the subject, and that it is high time for all of us to be exposed to both perspectives.

For our purposes, I would like to avoid dogmatic religious advocates, narrow-minded and avowed nationalists (of which Asian nations have more than their share, almost equal to some Western nations), and self-assured ideologues (such as Asian Communists). Rather, I would like to select a person who is open-minded and neutral on religious, cultural, and political matters and who is familiar with Western as well as Asian views and perspectives. Although there is no such ideal person available, tailor-made for our purpose, I think Western readers, particularly Christians concerned with global affairs, might profit a great deal by reading the views of K. M. Panikkar. He is a modern intellectual, well-versed in classical Asian religions and philosophies, who feels at home with Western thought and culture and who often bends over backward to stress Asia's debt to the Western world. One of his books, entitled *In Two Chinas*, vividly exhibits his ability to be fair to those with whom he does not agree. As the Indian ambassador to China both before and after the rise of Mao Tse-tung, he goes out of his way to point out the merits of Mao's regime.

> It has brought forth great enthusiasm and an irresistible desire to move forward, but the means employed to achieve these very desirable ends are in many cases of a kind which revolts the free mind. Compared to the state the individual has lost all value, and this is the strange thing in China which adds a tinge of sorrow even when one appreciates and admires what the revolution has done for China.[12]

This ability to think rationally even in the midst of a political whirlwind is a rare achievement. Such determined neutrality may irritate partisans; indeed, Panikkar's analysis of the East-West encounter in the modern period would probably disturb as many Asians as it would Westerners. Certainly, for those devout people in the West who have been led to believe that the good and dedicated Western missionaries in defiance of crude colonial governments have saved heathens from darkness and have been loved, respected, and appreciated by Christians and non-Christians alike in Asia, Panikkar's views on Christian missionary work in Asia are strong medicine. My hope is that they will read his small book *Asia and Western Dominance*.[13] As might be expected, Panikkar narrates many stories that the defenders of colonialism or of Christian world mission would prefer to hush up. Despite such boldness, I can assure you that the majority of Asians are far more negative to colonialism, racism, and the Christian missionary enterprise in Asia than even Panikkar would admit.

Briefly stated, Panikkar observes that the modern history of Asia may be divided into the following six periods: (1) the age of the expansion of European nations into India and the Indian Ocean as well as China and Japan (1498–1750); (2) the age of military, political, and commercial conquest of Asia by European nations (1750–1858); (3) the age of European colonial empires in various parts of Asia (1858–1914); (4) the short period of the Russian Revolution, coinciding with World War I, which was destined to change the course of world history; (5) the age of the retreat of European powers from Asia (1918–1939); and finally, (6) the present phase of Asian history, which the author characterizes as the age of the "recovery of Asia" by Asian peoples and nations. What the author finds in this great drama of modern history is "a singular unity" of the Western expansion in its fundamental aspects, such as the "dominance of maritime power over the land masses of Asia; the imposition of a commercial economy over communities whose economic life in the past had been based not on international trade, but mainly on agricultural production and internal trade; and, thirdly, the dominance of the peoples of Europe, who held the mastery of the seas, over the affairs of Asia" (13).

Without resorting to emotional attack, Panikkar nevertheless reveals his negative judgment on the Western approach to Asian peoples and cultures on three major counts, namely, colonial imperialism, racism, and Christian missionary policy. At the root of all three is Western political domination, often accompanied by a streak of racism. Thus it became a common pattern to think in terms of European versus Asian solidarity. Also, seen from an Asian perspective, Panikkar feels that the Christian (Catholic as well as Protestant) missionary endeavor had all the earmarks of being integrally connected to Western political supremacy in Asia. The Portuguese were fanatical in the enforcement of Catholic conformity and persecuted the non-Christians in Goa and their other possessions. The British established a robber state in Bengal and freely plundered and looted under the cover of their "rights." The Dutch in Indonesia went further and reduced a whole population to the status of plantation labor "without accepting in the least degree any obligation for the welfare of the people over whom they had acquired control." Even in China, Siam, and Japan, which were not even under direct European colonial rule, the situation was very bad. For example, the East India Company maneuvered the selling of opium to China against the imperial edict. In a letter addressed to Queen Victoria, the Chinese minister blamed the "unscrupulous traders," stating: "Doubtless, you, the Honourable Chieftainess, have not commanded the growing and sale [of opium]." History has shown how wrong he was! Probably one of the most disastrous turns was the Treaty of Nanking (August 29, 1842), which robbed China of much of its national dignity and sovereign rights. Treaties were also signed with the Americans at Wanghia (July 3, 1844) and with the French at Whampoa (October 24, 1844). The French and Americans demanded and obtained the right that ships of war "cruising for the protection of commerce should be well received in any of the ports of China at which they might arrive," and the British even demanded "compensation *for not plundering the city,* which the soldiers would have done had they occupied it" (92, 99, 101). The frequent dese-cration of Chinese religious edifices sounds harmless in comparison with Lord Elgin's ordering of the burning of the Summer Palace.

Rightly or wrongly, Panikkar feels that the European's racial superiority complex was based on the misguided conviction that the Almighty had elected the European race to subdue and govern the entire world. And because race became the basis of government, the prestige of the white race had to be ensured by an elaborate code, formulae and ceremonies, pomp and grandeur. In many parts of Asia, Europeans did not even conceal their contempt for the native populace. To be sure, Paul Bert, the French Resident General in Annam and Tonking, asserted that "France has but one desire, namely, to give the people prosperity under her moral guidance." A native writer poignantly expressed the sentiment of the people toward the French masters when he wrote: "In your eyes we are savages, dumb brutes incapable of distinguishing between good and evil. You not only refuse to treat us as equals, but even fear to approach us as if we were filthy creatures. . . . There is a sadness of feeling and shame which fills our hearts during the evening's contemplation when we review all the humiliations endured during the day" (166).

Christian missionary work in Asia has been inevitably tinged with imperialism and racism during the past 450 years. The Portuguese and Spaniards were animated by the spirit of the Crusades, and their anti-Muslim attitudes carried over to non-Muslim Asians as well. It is understandable, then, that in 1534, when Goa was made a bishopric, Hindu temples were destroyed and Hindu property was distributed to Roman Catholic religious orders; the Inquisition (surprisingly applied to Hindus) was introduced shortly afterwards. This was the time of the Counter Reformation, when Francis Xavier and others were engaged in active missionary work in India, Southeast Asia, and Japan. The salient feature of Roman Catholic missionary work in Asia was its intimate involvement in the political development of the Western colonial pow-ers, as exemplified by the patronage system whereby the Portuguese government, for example, was commissioned to send missionaries and maintain missionary apparatus in return for certain ecclesiastical privi-leges at home.

With the rise of the non-Catholic European nations as colonial powers in Asia, the situation changed considerably. Protestant monarchs in Europe were not interested in the conversion of Asians. However, in the eighteenth century private missionary societies were established by European Protestants, and their missionaries appeared on the Asian scene. The East India Company did not welcome missionaries, as illustrated by the fact that William Carey's Baptist mission had to settle in the Danish territory of Serampur, outside Calcutta. When Carey started his vigorous evangelism among Hindus in Bengal, Lord Minto prohibited the missionary work and wrote to the Court of Directors: "Pray read the miserable stuff addressed specially to the Gentoos [Hindus] in which . . . the pages are filled with hell fire, and hell fire with still hotter fire, denounced against a whole race of men, for believing in the religion which they were taught by their fathers and mothers" (quoted in 290). In China, Western powers (the Catholic French and the Protestant nations) secured permission in midnineteenth century for missionary work. Significantly, in China as well as in other parts of Asia, the persecution of Christian missionaries offered a classic excuse to Western nations for covering up political aggression. "If the ignorant Chinese Boxers displayed cruelty in their treatment of missionaries . . . the behaviour of the European powers at the time of their triumph was marked by an equally disgraceful exhibition of extreme vindictiveness." No doubt, missionaries were not consciously working for imperialistic ends, but they "were clothed with extra-territoriality and given the right to appeal to their consuls and ministers in the 'religious' interests of Chinese Christians." Although some Christians tried to rationalize this policy on the grounds that "it gave converts a certain assurance of protection," Panikkar is rightly of the opinion that "the missionaries, like other Europeans, felt convinced in the nineteenth century that their political supremacy was permanent, and they never imagined that China would regain a position when the history of the past might be brought up against them and their converts" (149, 292).

The decline of the European colonial powers was accelerated by the rise of America and Soviet Russia. Meanwhile, Asian peoples developed a new sense of nationalism, hitherto unknown in Asia. This new nationalism implied the acceptance of the doctrine of a national personality, of an identification of all people within the territory with the individuality of the state, of a belief in a kind of mystic brotherhood of the people that constituted the nation. Indian nationalism, for example, emphasized the "Indianness" of their people, of their common bond of history, civilization, and culture, mystically united to the land of Hinduism. Side by side with the political and cultural nationalism, Panikkar observes the emergence of "Asianness." This does not imply, however, that the emerging new Asia will be anti-Western. On the contrary, so he argues, the legal systems and principles of government developed in Asia under the impact of the West, for example, will be abiding factors in the civilization of Asia. The author is convinced that the clock cannot be turned back and that the Asian peoples cannot revert to a policy of isolation or pretend ignorance of the existence of other countries. He also feels that the cultural, as much as political, importance of Asia is being felt increasingly by contemporary Westerners. Panikkar's conclusion is optimistic:

> The past of the Great Asian peoples has gradually come to be considered as part of the general heritage of civilized man, and this may in time lead to a breakdown of the narrow Europeanism, which considered everything outside the experience of the West as of secondary importance. These subjects are merely alluded to here to indicate that the influence of the contacts between Asia and Europe is not wholly one-sided and that now, since the political domination of Asia is a thing of the past, the results of the interpenetration of culture may be even more fruitful. (332)

THE ASIAN CHRISTIAN TRADITION IN THE MODERN PERIOD: AN OVERVIEW[14]

There are still many people in Western Christendom who are inclined to divide people in Asia into such oversimplified categories as "Asian Christians," who despite the difference of color of their skin should feel and think exactly as the Western churches do, and "pagan" Asians, who have not been properly enlightened or civilized, presumably, according to "Western" standards and norms.

Most ironically, there are an amazing number of older Asian Christians who in their nostalgia look back to the old days, when they were under the direct control of missionaries, through a rosy haze and refuse to read the signs of our time. Many Christians in Asia have been spectators of and not participants in the revolutionary movements, and even today some of them are not certain how they can relate themselves to their immediate religious, cultural, social, and political environments. In a real sense, Christian communities in Asia are caught in a trap that they helped to build during the past two hundred years, when Christianity made its phenomenal expansion into Asia (and Africa). Among the people in Asia, this situation gave rise to three kinds of attitudes toward Western influence. The first was a positive reaction to things Western by a small group of young people desirous of being emancipated from their cultural and religious traditions. Second, there was a negative reaction among a small group of ultraconservative people who rejected anything new and Western. Third, there was the indifferent attitude of a large majority of the masses. Understandably, Christian missionaries reached the iconoclastic young people, mainly in the urban areas, who welcomed anything novel. In some cases, missionaries were also welcomed by the oppressed peasantry and those who had been looked down upon by the majority; these men and women at the lowest strata of Asiatic society found a new sense of dignity in embracing the Christian faith.

Many European and American missionaries who went to Asia in the last century were Pietists—theologically naive but emotionally dedicated to save all "pagans" from hellfire and eternal damnation. Missionary work to them meant transplanting Western Christianity *in toto* in Asia. They failed to understand that they were addressing themselves to one of the most far-reaching sociocultural revolutions, precipitated, to be sure, by the impact of the West. They hoped and believed that Western "Christian" culture would displace the traditional "pagan" cultures in Asia, so they built churches and schools modeled after those they had known in the West. Western cultural values were taught both consciously and unconsciously as Christian virtues. In all fairness to the missionaries of the last century, it must be pointed out that their attitudes and their approach were welcomed by many of the early Christian converts in Asia. In the nineteenth century, ambitious young Asians in urban areas found Western learning the best means toward their own upward social mobility, and for it they willingly rejected their ancestral ways and beliefs. And the oppressed peasantry who found new meaning and a sense of dignity in Christian faith had nothing to lose, for they had had neither the privilege nor the opportunity to participate in traditional Asian arts and culture anyway.

The combined effects of the Pietism of Western missionaries and the willingness of many of the first generation Asian converts to discard their traditional cultures and religions led to the development of the so-called mission compound. Many non-Christian neighbors accused the Christian churches of being too foreign and alien, but Western missionaries and many of the early Asian converts were convinced that the Eastern cultures were doomed to disintegrate and that they were reading the signs of the time correctly.

But the Eastern cultures did not crumble, and Eastern religions did not die out. Stimulated, to be sure, by the impact of the West, Eastern reformers have made a serious effort to eradicate the evils within the traditional Asian cultures and societies. Starting with the Islamic nations in the Near and Middle East, then in India, Southeast Asia, and the Far East, people found themselves caught in a whirlwind of social, cultural, and political revolutions.

Whether these Asian reformers' criticisms of Christian missionary work were justifiable or not is another question; this certainly is not
the occasion to discuss them. One thing is clear: education, medical and
social work, and the other activities of the Christian missionary endeavor were meant to reflect God's act of redemption of the whole world.
But by equating philanthropy too directly with salvation, some missionaries created "rice Christians"; and by equating education too closely
with the proselytizing effort, they created mediocre schools, preoccupied with chapel attendance and the number of baptisms at the expense
of competent education. There were reasons why many Asians did not
accept the Christian social and educational works as selfless expressions
of Christian love; indeed, they often suspected sinister ulterior motives
behind the Christian philanthropic and educational programs.

Suspicion begets more suspicions, especially when it is con-
firmed by concrete experience. As the Eastern peoples began to recover
from the initial shock of the encounter with the West and began to
regain self-consciousness and self-confidence, they began to be more
critical of the Western nations and Western civilization. For this they
found an easy target in the Asiatic Christians who were so singularly
oriented toward the West. To many Asians, struggling for emancipation
from the political and economic yoke of Western nations, two world
wars hardly inspired them to fight in defense of "Christian civilization,"
even when they had no choice but to fight for their colonial masters. In
the tense atmosphere of modern Asia, it was easy for political, cultural,
religious, and ecclesiastical factors to become hopelessly entangled.
When an Anglican bishop of Ceylon declared that the Christian task in
Ceylon would not be finished until the remaining 90 percent of the
population, who were not Christians, were converted, the spokesman
of Buddhism commented:

> The cry of "conversion" by Bishops in outposts of the Empire is only
> a subdued note of the louder pedal of "win the world for a Christian
> civilization" by imperialists in the heart of the Empire. Winning for
> a "Christian civilization" simply meant winning for the Empire, and
> "winning for the Empire" means enslavement for purposes of ex-
> ploitation. In the figurative language of Churchill and lesser lights
> of the Conservative Party, it was, 'we have not become the King's
> Ministers in order to liquidate the Empire.'[15]

It is not surprising, therefore, that the relationship between Christians
and non-Christians in Asia degenerated noticeably in the twentieth century. Christianity was definitely caught in the struggle of Asian peoples'

revolt against Western exploitation. Even though the missionary enterprise claimed to be a counterweight to the evil of colonialism and economic exploitation, it was seriously embarrassed by the fact that the missionary endeavor and colonialism both originated from the same Western nations. There were even structural similarities between missionary societies and colonial regimes.

Although there have been a few Asian Christian leaders who have urged fellow faithfuls to become involved in the political conflicts against exploitive European powers, the majority of the leaders of Asian churches have been inclined not to take action. For too long, they considered their churches as subdivisions of those in the West, and even now they cannot possibly operate costly institutions, left behind by the missionaries before Western churches lost missionary incentive, without subsidies from the outside. Besides, so many of them, having very little contact with the rest of society, tend to hang on to their own positions, prestige, and meager income within the ecclesiastical communities. They now feel that they have to be more attentive to the nationalistic trends in Asia without, however, antagonizing Christian friends across the ocean. By and large, younger elements within the Asian Christian communities welcomed the change of the nomenclature of their churches from "missionary churches" to "younger churches," which in principle implies that they are no longer subservient to the churches in the West. Then in 1947, the International Missionary Council (IMC), meeting in Whitby, Ontario, Canada, urged older and younger churches to move toward the goal of "Partnership in Obedience." Since then, many leaders of the Asian Christian churches have been made painfully aware that many more realistic steps must be taken before they—together with the older churches in the West—forge ahead toward such a lofty goal.

Undoubtedly, one of the most spectacular events in world history took place after World War II, when more than half of the human race, previously denied the dignity of being their own masters, joined world history as full-fledged human beings. Ironically, many in the former colonial powers have not as yet really faced up to the implications of this turn of events. As for Asia, its map was sharply redrawn with the emergence of many new independent nations: the Philippines (1946), India and Pakistan (1947), Ceylon (Sri Lanka), Burma, South and North Korea (1948), Indonesia and the People's Republic of China (1949), South and North Vietnam (1954), Cambodia (1955), Laos (1956), Federation of Malaya (1957), Malaysia (1963), Bangladesh (1971), and the Socialist Republic of Vietnam (1975). I once stated in this connection:

In a real sense, the basic problem of our time is not the emergence of many new quarrelsome nations in Asia and Africa in the post-1945 era, but rather what both caused and resulted from their political independence, namely, the momentous redefinition of man's conception of dignity, value, and freedom of humankind.[16]

Like it or not, the Asian Christian tradition has to take seriously not only the geographical change in Asia but also this global change in human perception, a change that demands more than a simple rearranging of old furniture in the cozy club of Western philosophies, religions, and cultures. Indeed, it demands the hammering out of new linguistic and conceptual symbols from the present conflicting assertions and affirmations of various peoples and traditions. This implies, among other things, that provincial Western logics and rhetorics, based on a peculiar Western convention of dividing human experience into a series of semi-autonomous pigeonholes—such as religion, aesthetics, ethics, philosophy, and so forth—will no longer be sufficient. For this colossal global task, the Asian Christian tradition is still only vaguely aware of its responsibility to collaborate both with Asian religious and cultural traditions and Christian traditions in the West. For the most part, the leaders of the Asiatic Christian tradition are frightened by the magnitude of such a stupendous task. One serious and legitimate reason for their anxiety is based on the simple fact that the Asian Christian is at the moment not taken seriously by non-Christian Asians and is greatly misunderstood by Western Christians. To make matters worse, for decades Asian Christians have not been encouraged to think for themselves; they have not even produced "juicy heresy," as some unkind critic once mentioned.

A nonreligious Asian friend of mine once commented that Christianity in Asia attracts people who have no "spiritual autobiography" of their own. He went on to say that many Western missionaries arrived in Asia with the amazingly simplistic story that the Christian gospel was something like the "divine scoop" on human destiny and that it was not universally available but had been offered exclusively to the Christian church through a special deal. It was now magnanimously presented even to non-Europeans if they would forsake their traditional spiritual disciplines and accept this "good news" wholeheartedly without doubts and questions, that is, if they would appropriate someone else's spiritual autobiography as their own. This is supposedly the only way for non-Westerners to win "salvation," a salvation already accomplished once and for all (*fait accompli*). Implicit in this approach is the notion of the Christian church as the sole owner of the Eternal Gospel, which is something like a sacred univac; all that is needed is to analyze the situation according to practicality and conventional wisdom so that the church can formulate a new and up-to-date method to push the right button at the right time in order to transmit divine grace to a reluctant and skeptical world.

This may account for the fact that until World War II the goal of the Christian church in Asia was to train as many people as possible, preferably clergy and laity, who were technically intelligent (enough to be able to read and understand theologies, spiritual manuals, and religious education materials imported from the West) but who displayed no real intellectual initiatives of their own. (I am reminded of Deng Xiaoping, who was said to have voiced his opinion to the effect that he did not care what his people believed, religiously or otherwise, so long as they worked hard, paid taxes, and obeyed the Peking regime without raising too many questions.) Of course, in those days "theologies" meant nothing but "Western theologies," whereby all creative intellectual or theological efforts of indigenous Asians were judged (and more often than not condemned) according to theological currents in the West. It is little wonder that the Asian Christian tradition has been accused of being too foreign in religious ethos and belief by non-Christian Asians. In the words of U Khyaw Than, a former secretary of the East Asian Christian Council: "A cultured Buddhist or Hindu, unlike the man from the bush, will . . . wonder why he or she should give up altogether the rich heritage and the long standing refinements for the sake of some other culture and heritage."[17] Only in the Missionary Conference in Madras (1938) was it pointed out that every younger church should develop a "new tongue" that is "in a direct, clear and close relationship with the cultural and religious heritage of its own country."[18] Unfortunately, this great insight was quickly overshadowed by the tumult of World War II.

IN THE POST–WORLD WAR II ERA

After the end of World War II, both older churches in the West and younger churches in the non-Western world found themselves living in a strange world, very different from what they knew before the war—a new world shaped by science, technology, industry, and business that tended to repudiate the sacred pieties, morals, and rituals of all known traditions. Inevitably, the religious topography of the world was transformed by such world-shaking factors as (1) the end of Western colonial imperialism in Asia and Africa, (2) the growth of world communism, which now propelled Asian communist states, for example, China and Vietnam, into the center of world politics, (3) the increasing secularization of Western culture, which coincided with the loss of missionary incentive on the part of the Western churches, and (4) the resurgence of Eastern religions, which now have already converted many ex-Christian and ex-Jewish youths in Europe and America. Ironically, in spite of such a lofty slogan as "Partnership in Obedience," the lack of mutual understanding between older and younger churches seems to be deepening. Let me try to pinpoint this lack of understanding while summarizing the questions (not necessarily criticisms) of the Asian churches regarding the attitudes of older churches in the West.

First, many younger church leaders lament but realize, with sadness, that for the most part, Western churches, although giving lip service, have really lost their missionary incentives. They still fail to understand why many Western churches, once so reluctant even to turn over the insignificant leadership of Asian churches to indigenous clergy and laity, now suddenly are so eager to wash their hands of missionary obligations in Asia on the technical ground that the former missionary churches are now called "younger churches" and that Asia is their orbit. Does the motto "Partnership in Obedience" imply geographical division and partnership (older churches for the West and younger churches in the non-Western world) not too dissimilar to the 1494 treaty between Portugal and Spain, according to which the whole world was divided into these two nations' spheres of interest?

Second, many Asian church leaders seem to feel that the Western churches' loss of missionary incentive and their sudden interest in the dialogue of various religions of the world are more than simple curious coincidences. They rather suspect that the idea of dialogue is brought in as a convenient gimmick to camouflage the bankruptcy of the all too simple historical missionary approach of the Western churches. They often wonder—referring to Max Müller's favorite saying to the effect that before we compare, we must thoroughly know what we compare—about the qualifications and competence of many Western church leaders who are now so passionately engaged in religious dialogue. After all, religious dialogue is not meant to be simultaneous monologue, each person giving publicly his or her autobiographical statements about the natures and kinds of reality, including ultimate reality, without knowing, however vaguely, what others think and believe.

Third, and more basically, many Asian church leaders are puzzled as to whether the Western churches, which after all had spawned the younger churches, really understand the nature of the Asian Christian communities or whether they still think of them primarily as subdivisions and carbon copies of Western churches. Have they really accepted the plain fact that Asian churches at times disagree with Western churches in order to be true to their own divine calling to be integrally related on the one hand to Western churches and to non-Christian religions in Asia on the other, and that their religious, cultural, social, economic, and political outlooks must maintain a delicate balance between their two "faces" (being a part of world Christendom and being heirs to the Asian heritage)? In order to understand more concretely how Asian Christians formulate their thinking, consider the parts of the report of the Indian Ecumenical Study Conference, held at Nagpur in 1952. The report deals with four main themes: (1) the Christian hope, (2) responsible society, (3) mission and unity, and (4) race relations.[19] It might be especially instructive to look at the report's seven observations related to the Indian situation, for I believe that similar observations can easily be made about other Asian situations as well:

1. The report is very critical of both Indian Roman Catholics, who often denounce capitalism and yet resist social change, and the smugly complacent middle-class attitudes of Protestants. In view of the "retardedness" of Indian Christians' social thought, the report strongly recommends a radical scrutiny of Indian social philosophy and a careful analysis of the actual social conditions of India (30).

2. Regarding the "nature of the conflict," the report states clearly that "communism is a symptom and not the disease itself. The real conflict is not communism *versus* capitalism but in the mechanization and psychological conditioning of human being *versus* the responsible society" (53).

3. Under the heading of "the unfinished revolution," the report deals with the agony of India in its transitional period from feudalism to modern society. As such, "India is bound to suggest to Western friends who had their more-or-less violent revolutions a century ago, that they should show some understanding of the social travail through which [India] is bound to pass for some time to come" (53–54).

4. Regarding "the impact of the technological age," the report is particularly concerned with its effect on urbanization and political-economic centralization (54).

5. On "the need of voluntary association," the report stresses that the nature of the responsible society is to be necessarily pluralistic, in the sense that there should be a series of vital, autonomous groups between the individual and the state.

6. The section on "the problem of the secular state" is very noteworthy, and it should be read with care by Christians in the West

even if they disagree with the stance of Indian Christians. The committee strongly upholds the principle of a secular state in a deeply religious society. It further states: "If the secular state is to be a reality in India . . . Christians must learn to initiate activities and schemes for social welfare and social change which may be adopted by men [and women] of good will even if they do not accept the faith which inspires such activities" (55).

7. The report lists a number of possible ventures under the category of "the need for experiment." Among them, it states:

> Trade unions or peasant unions can be of immense spiritual significance, but it is essential to develop an effective working class leadership, and this means that one of the most important forms of activity in which a Christian can take part is working class education so that workers may be increasingly equipped not only to fight for their rights, but to play a significant part in the transformation of the country (55–56).

It might be helpful for us to keep this report of Indian Christians in mind as we look at a series of "new experiments" that have taken place in various parts of Asia: (1) the Church of South India, (2) the "Three-Self Movement" (Protestant) in China, (3) the Chinese Catholic Patriotic Association (CCPA) in mainland China (not in Taiwan), and (4) the Catholic leader's active participation in the bloodless political revolution in the Philippines, headed by Corazon Aquino in 1986.

1. Asian Christians rejoiced in the successful union of Anglicans, Presbyterians, Methodists, Congregationalists, and the Basel (partly Lutheran) mission in South India in 1947. This union is by no means perfect, but it is at least the first successful blending of episcopal and nonepiscopal groups in Christian history—something "divided" Western churches have always prayed for and advocated but have never been able to actualize.

2. The Three-Self Movement ("self-support, self-government, and self-propagation") claims to have jurisdiction over all the Protestant churches in China. As early as 1949, however, the informal group of Chinese Christian leaders who had founded the movement sent a message to mission boards abroad. In it the leaders reflect on how the Christian church in China has been historically related to foreign imperialism and capitalism. But the letter says that "a new chapter in the history of China has begun; a new era has dawned." And "we Christians in China feel the urgent necessity of re-examining our work and our relationship with the older churches abroad." The letter candidly admits

that "heretofore, the Chinese church has been keeping itself aloof from the political torrents" and then goes on to address the challenge of "how the church as an institution and how Christians as citizens in society can perform their Christian functions and discharge their duties to society at the same time."[20] As might be expected, many Western churches tend to dismiss the Three-Self Movement as a political invention of the Peking regime. But the postdenominationalism and the Three-Self principle of the Chinese Protestants are already taken very seriously by other Asian Christians.

3. The complexity of the Roman Catholic situation in Asia in general, and in China (which was never colonized in a technical sense but was mercilessly exploited by encroaching European, Japanese, and American powers) in particular, defies simple explanation. The Roman Catholic mission in Asia has a longer history than its Protestant counterparts. It has had a small number of saintly characters and profoundly learned leaders and a large number (more foreign than Protestant groups) of pastorally competent but otherwise not highly intellectual personnel. (Such people generally taught Chinese Catholics simply to obey the authority of Rome and to accept its ready-made dogmas and teaching, but not to think for themselves.) The fact that Catholic missionary work was unofficially, if not officially, supported by representatives of "Catholic" nations was a mixed blessing, as exemplified by the abuse of diplomatic privileges by missionaries in China taking advantage of Mussolini's concordat with the Vatican. After World War II, the Vatican's official recognition of Taiwan, and not Beijing, complicated the situation still further. According to David Tracy, who visited China in 1981, the Catholic situation there possesses all the ingredients of tragedy:

> The approximately three million Catholics are tragically split. One group—the official Catholic Church of China [otherwise known as the Chinese Catholic Patriotic Association or CCPA]—accepts the Chinese government's Three Self movement and thereby has had no official relationship [since 1957] with Rome. The second [numerically tiny] group—the unofficial, indeed largely underground church—has maintained relationships with Rome.

Tracy goes on to comment that what amazed him was the fact that this official CCPA, which repudiates papal authority, is in fact very doctrinaire and out of date both theologically and liturgically:

> The mass is the Tridentine Latin mass. The structure of authority seems pre-Vatican II, with the notable exception that the clergy is married. . . . Indeed, Vatican II is not accepted [by both groups

of] the Chinese Catholic church so that the now familiar reforms of Catholicism are nowhere present.[21]

It is no doubt understandable that many Western Catholics, who take seriously papal infallibility and the Vatican's "authority," denounce the Chinese Catholic Patriotic Association as illegal, schismatic, and heretical. But Aloysius Jin Luxian, appointed CCPA bishop of Shanghai in 1988, is of the opinion that "for the Catholic church in China to survive, we must attain a political and economic independence. If the Vatican does not fully understand the situation in China, then we must control our fate with our own hands."[22]

4. Not much need be said about the bloodless revolution in the Philippines in 1986, actively supported by the Roman Catholic leaders, as it is still vivid in the memories of many people. Of course, Catholic influence is unusually strong there, as the Philippines is the only Asian nation with a Roman Catholic majority. It must be pointed out, however, that the Catholic leaders' participation in the revolution symbolizes the Catholic and Protestant Asian Christians' profound concern for social justice and a stable political order. There was a time when many Asian Christian leaders were saddened when the visiting U.S. Vice President praised Marcos publicly as the defender of democracy. Ultimately, it was their strong sense of social justice—above political expediency— that helped topple a powerful and greedy Marcos even in favor of an untried and inexperienced Corazon Aquino.

Finally, I might add that although many Asian Christians still slavishly imitate, import, and appropriate current Western theologies (some of them are also interested in Latin American liberation theology, whereas others are in feminist, African-American, and other new types of theological formulations) as if Western theologies were the only authentic Christian views, there are some signs that indigenous thinkers, both Roman Catholic and Protestant, are now trying to hammer out their own understanding of religious truths discovered in an Asian context. They are caught, to be sure, between the traditional and the modern, between Christian and non-Christian, and between the East and the West.[23] After decades of simple imitation and being told by Western missionaries "what" (but rarely "how") to think, many of them are now learning the importance of thinking for themselves out of their own Asian experience. As a Filipino theologian Jose M. de Mesa states: "If there is one thing that gradually dawned on the consciousness of Christians with regard to theological re-rooting of the Gospel from one cultural and historical milieu into another, it is the necessity of re-thinking rather than just translating this Gospel with a new frame of reference."[24] And they hope, in the words of Kōsuke Koyama, that "the study of theologies of Asia by Westerners and the study of theologies of the West by Asians [to which I might add the *genuine* 'dialogue' of religions crossing cultural and religious lines] may lead to Christianity's emancipation from its Babylonian captivity."[25] Such is the prayerful hope of the Asian Christian tradition.

3

THE EMERGENCE OF CHRISTIAN DILEMMA, WITH SPECIAL REFERENCE TO JAPAN

JAPAN'S RELIGIOUS HERITAGE: JAPAN IN ASIA

In my article "Some Reflections on Theology in Japan" (1961), I dwelt heavily on the theological trends of the Japanese Christian community partly because at that time there were few Western books on the subject.[1] Since that time, this lamentable situation has been rectified somewhat by the publication of several helpful Western books. (I am not certain, however, how widely they have been read by Western Christians.)[2] Be that as it may, my present primary concern is to relate the Japanese religious and cultural tradition in general, and its Christian development in particular, to the broader Asian context, especially to that of the Asian Christian tradition—and not so much to repeat what I have already said about technical theological trends in the Japanese Christian community. In this attempt, I am aware that many people are not familiar with Asian geography. Harold Isaacs tells us that in 1942 more than 40 percent of the American population could not locate China or India on a map. In 1945, after America's direct military involvement in Asia for over three years, only 43 and 45 percent of the American population could locate China and India, respectively—a very slight improvement.[3] I trust that the situation on this score has by now changed for the better. At the very least, I hope people are aware

43

that Japan is a small island archipelago off the Asiatic continent and that its total area is smaller than that of California. Its land is very mountainous and volcanic, and arable portions of the archipelago, mainly along the coastal lines, are very limited. No one is absolutely certain how far back we can trace human habitation on the Japanese islands. Most archaeologists tell us that Japan's prehistoric culture can probably be traced back some four to five thousand years, and it is safe to assume that by roughly 300–250 B.C., inhabitants in the archipelago had attained a degree of self-consciousness as one (proto-Japanese) people.[4] For the most part, however, Japanese historians are of the opinion that the early period of Japanese history as such commenced around A.D. 250 or 300. It should be remembered that Japan at that time barely had emerged from the state of prehistory, whereas continental Asia, particularly China and India, had already experienced centuries of sophisticated cultures, civilizations, and social and political structures. They already had the benefit of the lofty teachings of such sages as Confucius and Buddha, and they had witnessed the glories of King Aśoka's Buddhist empire in India (third century B.C.) and the stupendous and urbane Han empire in China (202 B.C.–A.D. 220). Ironically but understandably, the early Japanese took it for granted that the world meaningful to them was the world they knew and experienced on the Japanese archipelago. They were, of course, vaguely aware of the existence of other lands, other peoples, and other civilizations, all of which were exaggerated in contradictory ways in the Japanese imagination, sometimes as objects of adoration and sometimes as objects of contempt. This kind of contradictory existential background may account for the hyperbolic streaks of ethnocentrism and the deep-seated inferiority complex that have always characterized the spiritual autobiography of the Japanese throughout history.

WA-KAN—THE JAPANESE-CHINESE STYLE OF LINGUISTIC-THOUGHT FORMS

It is important to realize that the early Japanese, like every other people in the world, had their own unique ways of dividing human experience. Their way was certainly different from the Western convention of discerning human experience in terms of a series of semiautonomous, separable pigeonholes—religion, ethics, aesthetics, philosophy, psychology, and so forth. Significantly, the Japanese convention in this regard was very different from the Chinese and Indian-Buddhist ways of carving the texture of human experience as well. It is not surprising, then, that the massive penetration of Chinese civilization and Buddhism into

Japan during the fifth and sixth centuries forced the Japanese to adjudicate their differences. For example, in early Japan:

> Good meant beauty, excellence, good fortune, and nobility—goodness was identical generally with the activation of life-giving power. Bad was the opposite. A good person was a noble person, not a morally good person; and a good thing was a fortunate thing, not something morally good. The Chinese term *shan-hsin* ("virtuous heart") was translated into Japanese as *uruwashiki kokoro* ("fine heart"), and denoted an affectionate heart.[5]

In order to face this cultural crisis, the Japanese, who didn't have a written language, concocted at least two convenient but cumbersome systems of writing by borrowing the Chinese script. One system used Chinese characters but read them in Japanese; the complexity of this system—used in the compilation of one of the oldest mytho-historical writings, the *Kojiki* ("Records of Ancient Matters")—is such that "the modern reader of the *Kojiki* . . . has a sort of bilingual puzzle which he must decipher as he goes along."[6] The second method used Chinese characters only for their sound value, disregarding their lexical meaning in order to express Japanese sounds.[7] In both systems, adopting the Chinese script while ignoring its highly developed pictographs, ideographs, and phonetic compounds proved to be more cumbersome and misleading than the Japanese had originally thought. In this respect, the early Japanese did not understand—and curiously enough, modern Japanese still do not comprehend—Gadamer's wise exhortation that language "is not only an object in our hands, it is the reservoir of tradition and the medium in and through which we exist and perceive the world."[8] It is an astounding thing that there were enough Japanese intellectuals during the seventh and eighth centuries who, without having been to China, had enough command of the Chinese language to compile their own historical memories or even to express their poetic sentiment. For example, the ill-fated prince Ōtsu (662–687), shortly before his execution, wrote the following two poems—one in Japanese, included in the *Manyō-shū*, and the other in Chinese, included in the *Kaifūsō*, the collection of Chinese verses composed by Japanese poets:

> (In Japanese) Today, taking my last sight of the mallards
> crying on the pond of Iware,
> Must I vanish into the clouds!
> (In Chinese) The golden crow lights on the western huts;
> Evening drums beat out the shortness of life.
> There are no inns on the road to grave—
> Whose is the house I go tonight?

In commenting on these two poems, Donald Keene remarks that whereas the first is purely Japanese in feeling, the second "not only uses Chinese language and allusions but attempts to give philosophical overtones lacking in the simple Japanese verse."[9] In reading these two poems, I am, however, impressed more by the fact that the Chinese language, probably not fully understood, and the poetic allusions, reflecting the Chinese convention of perceiving the texture of life, were already appropriated by the early Japanese in order to express their—inevitably no longer so simplistic—apprehension of life and the world. The two poems mentioned above dramatically indicate the new Japanese linguistic-thought forms usually referred to as the *wa-kan* ("Japanese-Chinese") style, forms that dominated the Japanese mental universe until Japan's encounter with Western civilization in the midnineteenth century. Significantly, it was through this hybrid and cumbersome medium that the Japanese (a) tried to understand Chinese philosophical systems—for example, Confucianism, Taoism, the Yin-Yang school, and Buddhism—on the one hand, and (b) tried to reconstruct their own historical memories, as exemplified in the compilation of two mythological histories, the aforementioned *Kojiki* and the *Chronicle of Japan* (*Nihon-gi* or *Nihon-shoki*), on the other. It is not surprising that some people—the Japanese, the Chinese, and more recently, Westerners—interpret the Japanese-Chinese (*wa-kan*) system either from a China-centric or Japan-centric perspective. As late as 1961, Paul Tillich reflected on the relationship between Japan, where he had paid a visit, and China, which he characterized as "the ultimate source of Japan's culture and religion." Thus he jumped to the hasty and misleading conclusion that "China is the mother, she remained the mother in the Chinese-Japanese war and she has not ceased to be the mother in spite of her being conquered by communism."[10] Clearly, Tillich thought of the *wa-kan* system primarily as a Chinese-inspired linguistic-thought form.

THE RITSURYŌ—JAPAN'S FIRST SYNTHESIS

At any rate, through the hybrid, or rather, Japanized Chinese, *wa-kan* system, the early Japanese imported various Buddhist schools from China: the six officially recognized schools were introduced in the eighth century, the Tendai and Shingon schools in the ninth, Pure Land Buddhism in the eleventh, and the Zen traditions in the twelfth and thirteenth centuries.[11] Of more importance, the *wa-kan* system provided the necessary intellectual foundation for Japan's first major religious/cultural/social/political synthesis, called the Ritsuryō ("imperial rescript") system, which remained intact until the sixteenth century. Elsewhere I have characterized the Ritsuryō synthesis as a form of "immanental theocracy" with the emperor functioning simultaneously as (a) the living deity, (b) the reigning monarch, and (c) the chief priest. It is important to recognize that the Ritsuryō synthesis was built on three basic principles: (1) the mutual dependence of ō-bō ("emperor's law") and *Buppō* ("Buddha's law" or "teaching"); it should be understood that ō-bō implied in effect a homology of the indigenous Japanese notion of the tribal-chieftain and the Taoist-inspired semimagical monarch seen within the context of a political order defined by the Confucian affirmation of *T'ien* ("Heaven"); (2) an institutional syncretism between the native Japanese Shinto religious tradition and Buddhism, which had originated in India and had been introduced from China—known as *Shin-Butsu Shūgō*; and (3) the eclectic belief that Japanese deities were manifestations of the Buddhas and Bodhisattvas in India—*honji-suijaku*. The inclusion of these principles indicated that the two "universalistic principles"— namely, the *Dharma* (hō in Japanese) of Buddhism, and the *Tao* (*michi* in Japanese) of the Chinese philosophical tradition—had to be subordinated to the "particularistic" experience of the Japanese, epitomized by the throne.[12]

In comparison with its rather impressive and grandiose beginning, the career of the Ritsuryō synthesis was found lacking. It displayed many contradictions and inconsistencies, partly because some of the Chinese models considered to be paradigmatic did not fit into Japanese social realities. Inevitably, the Ritsuryō model was destined to undergo changes under the pressures of the Fujiwara oligarchy (which monopolized the imperial regency from the midtenth to mideleventh centuries), the *insei* (de facto rule by nominally retired monarchs), and the feudal regime (rule by strongmen).

Through it all, however, Buddhism penetrated deeply into Japanese culture and society, due partly to the fact that in comparison with its experience in China, where it had to contend with the powerful traditions of Confucianism and Taoism, Shinto in Japan presented very little spiritual or intellectual challenge. Another important reason for its prosperity was the strong favor and support it received from the imperial court and the government, which depended on Buddhism to solidify the fabric of the nation. By far the most impressive period of the Buddhist tradition in Japan was the thirteenth century, also referred to as the Kamakura era, when a series of truly outstanding native Japanese leaders, such as Yōsai (or Eisai) of the Rinzai Zen school, Hōnen of the Pure Land School, Shinran of the True Pure Land school, Dōgen of the

Sōtō Zen school, and Nichiren of the Nichiren school upheld high religious standards, even though their outlooks betrayed the strong particularistic spiritual ethos of the Japanese people rather than the universalistic orientation of historical Buddhism.[13]

EROSION OF THE RITSURYŌ SYNTHESIS AND THE INTRODUCTION OF CATHOLICISM

The civil and political life of Japan broke down in the midfifteenth century. It took three strongmen—Oda Nobunaga (1534–1582), Toyotomi Hideyoshi (1536–1598), and Tokugawa Iyeyasu (1542–1616)—to unify the nation and eventually establish a new order, rejecting the historic Ritsuryō religious/cultural/social/political synthesis. The first two, Nobunaga and Hideyoshi, had nominal allegiance to the throne, but rejected the crucially important principle of the Ritsuryō synthesis, namely, the mutual dependence of the sovereign's and Buddha's laws. They mercilessly attacked powerful Buddhist institutions. It so happened that Nobunaga's time coincided with the coming of Portuguese Roman Catholic missionaries, who had followed the chance arrival of shipwrecked Portuguese merchants in southern Japan. Understandably, Roman Catholicism was welcomed by Nobunaga, who had no use for Buddhism. Catholic activities took on new vigor with the coming in 1549 of the famous Jesuit, Francis Xavier (1506–1552), one of the leaders of the Counter-Reformation in Europe. Brought up in Navarre, where Roman Catholicism had been in a centuries-long struggle with Islam, Xavier was emotionally anti-Islamic. In 1541 Xavier went to India as papal legate and representative of the king of Portugal, but he was not comfortable there because of the existence of the Muslim Mughal dynasty. As might be expected, he voiced his strong opinion to the effect that the conversion of Asia to Catholicism should start from Japan to China, and not from India. True to his medieval European outlook, Xavier always attempted to approach those in power, expecting their followers to comply with their leaders' religious allegiance. Japan was no exception.

Fascinating though it is, we cannot go into a detailed discussion of the missionary policy of Roman Catholicism in Japan during the sixteenth and seventeenth centuries.[14] We should point out, however, that the Jesuit-inspired Catholic groups in Japan followed the general pattern of the tightly knit medieval Japanese Buddhist groups, for example, the True Pure Land sect and the Nichiren sect. Also, they freely employed Japanese Buddhist terms—for example, Hotoke ("Buddha," used as another translation of the term God), Jōdo ("Pure Land," used for heaven), *Buppō* ("Buddha's Law," used for Christianity or religion in general), and *Sō* ("Buddhist monk," used to describe Catholic clerics)— to explain Catholicism as though it were a sect of Buddhism.[15] Following the death of Nobunaga, Hideyoshi became de facto the ruler of Japan. He astutely pursued foreign trade with European nations without supporting Catholicism. It was his megalomaniacal ambition to subdue China. He dispatched his crack forces, including those of several *daimyō's* who had been converted to Catholicism, on two occasions (1592 and 1597) to Korea as preliminary steps. Oddly enough, the honor of saying Roman Catholic mass for the first time in Korea goes to the clerics who accompanied Japanese Catholic troops in Hideyoshi's expeditionary forces. Incidentally, Hideyoshi's death in 1598 ended this misguided nightmare.

THE SECOND SYNTHESIS (THE TOKUGAWA) AND ITS ANTI-CATHOLIC POLICY

With the death of Hideyoshi, Tokugawa Iyeyasu rose to power, and in 1603 he inaugurated his feudal regime (*shōgunate* or *bakufu*), destined to rule Japan until 1867. His regime was another form of "immanental theocracy." Although it was very different from the earlier Ritsuryō synthesis, it was also a similarly comprehensive synthesis. In sharp contrast to the Ritsuryō synthesis, which depended heavily on the Shinto-Confucian-Taoist notion of the emperor, the Tokugawa synthesis depended on the legitimation of the Neo-Confucian notions of natural law and the natural norms implicit in a human society grounded in the Will of Heaven.[16]

Significantly, the Tokugawa synthesis—which rejected the Ritsuryō principle of the mutual dependence of the sovereign's law and the Buddha's law for its claim that the Tokugawa *shōgun* (generalissimo) had the prerogative to rule the nation—upheld, however, the two other Ritsuryō principles, that is, institutional Shinto-Buddhist syncretism and the belief that Japanese deities were manifestations of Buddhas and Bodhisattvas in India. In fact, the Tokugawa regime skillfully maneuvered to support and utilize Buddhist institutions to serve as the arm of the regime in exterminating the dreaded Catholicism and to serve as the regime's agent in maintaining thought control. In order to implement the regime's anti-Catholic policy, the Tokugawas ordered every Japanese household to register in neighborhood Buddhist temples, thus creating the hitherto unknown nationwide Buddhist parochial system. It should be noted that the cause of Roman Catholicism was greatly damaged when Spanish clerics from the Philippines, colonized by the Spaniards who had crossed the Pacific Ocean from Mexico, muscled into Japan, then under Portuguese jurisdiction. The fierce rivalry between Portuguese Jesuits and Spanish Franciscans as well as between Portuguese and Spanish traders—well dramatized in the television miniseries "Shōgun"—caused untold harm to the well-being of Japanese converts to Catholicism, who were already being persecuted so brutally by the feudal regime. In the end, a severe blow came to Catholics when in 1637 thousands of Catholic men and women joined other disgruntled elements on the southern island of Kyūshū and rebelled against the government. When the uprising was finally quelled, they were either tortured or shipped out of the country. Thus ended the official history of Roman Catholicism in Japan. Thereupon, the Tokugawa regime took the far more drastic measure of "national seclusion" (sakoku), cutting off all trade and other relations with most foreign nations (excepting non-Catholic Holland). This national seclusion lasted two and a half centuries until the arrival of Commodore Matthew Perry in 1853. Opinions vary sharply as to whether it would have been better for Japan not to be "nationally secluded," even at the risk of being drawn into the colonial orbit of one of the greedy European powers. Although we are not in a position to settle this interesting question, we cannot help but notice that the national seclusion for two centuries and a half certainly enabled the Tokugawa synthesis to take root. Even given this opportunity, inevitable transformations were to come with changing social realities in Japan.

Briefly stated, the very success of the Tokugawa regime to maintain a permanent martial law, the original aim of the regime, eventually undermined the very hierarchical social-political order and cumbersome apparatus created by the regime to implement martial law. For example, three hundred odd social classes, rigidly defined in a descending order— the shōgun and his circles, the emperor and the courtiers, feudal lords (daimyō) who were masters of nearly three hundred fiefs, the well-known castelike classes of soldiers (shi), farmers (nō), artisans (kō), and merchants (shō), down to the pariah group—inevitably loosened in the course of time so that merchants, for example, who had held a relatively low social status, became in fact far more powerful and influential than other supposedly higher class people. Also, over the years, prescribed nomenclatures and symbols did not always keep pace with changing realities. For example, Neo-Confucianism—the official system that gave cosmic legitimation to the Tokugawa synthesis—was earlier monopolized by Zen priests, but eventually the anti-Buddhist sentiment of ex-Zen

Neo-Confucianists drove them close to the causes of Shinto and the National Learning (*koku-gaku*). To complicate the picture further, there was a group of Japanese Roman Catholics who maintained their faith under the disguise of Buddhism, commonly referred to as the "hidden Christians" (*kakure Kirishitan*),[17] and a group who followed Dutch Learning (*Rangaku-sha*) through an almost microscopic contact with the Dutch trading center in Nagasaki and who managed to import books on medicine, astronomy, and various sciences, translating them for their own edification. From the late eighteenth to the first half of the nineteenth century, the gradual loosening of the Tokugawa regime's control over the nation resulted in the crisscrossing of various social, political, ideological, and religious currents. In several localities, a series of messianic cults emerged from the soil of folk religious traditions. Externally, ships of foreign powers began to appear off the Japanese shores. In this situation, various voices, for example, anti-Tokugawa, royalist, antiforeign, and pro-Western (or rather, antinational seclusion), were beginning to be heard in crescendo. One thing became abundantly clear to everyone—Japan was hopelessly isolated from the rest of Asia and the world community.

MODERN JAPAN: THE THIRD SYNTHESIS (THE MEIJI)

The combined effect of internal and external pressures resulted in the dissolution of the Tokugawa feudal regime. Thus began a new Japan under the presumably direct rule of the boy emperor, Meiji. His advisers attempted to create a third great synthesis by combining the earlier Ritsuryō and Tokugawa syntheses and by adding Western technology and learning, which they were eager to appropriate. Accordingly, the Meiji regime elevated the throne in the manner of the Ritsuryō synthesis, but it rejected the Ritsuryō principle of the mutual dependence of the sovereign's and the Buddha's laws. In fact, the Meiji regime by fiat separated the native Shinto religion from its amalgamation with Buddhism, whereby the new State Shinto—presumably the nonreligious national and patriotic cult to be practiced by every Japanese regardless of his or her religious affiliation—alone would give cosmic legitimation to the Meiji synthesis. Thus, although the Meiji regime rejected the first and second of the Ritsuryō principles, it kept—as did the Tokugawa synthesis—the third principle, namely, the belief in the Japanese deities as manifestations of the Buddhas and Bodhisattvas in India *(honji-suijaku)*.

The architects of this new Japan were determined to rectify the lamentable state of Japan's isolation from the world community. Some of them went so far as to accept uncritically the European claim made frequently during the nineteenth century, that modern Western civilization was the most enlightened system of the world and possessed universally valid norms to be adopted globally. In this situation, leaders of the new Japan wanted to expand the aforementioned *wa-kan* linguistic-thought system to embrace the Western symbols, logics, and syntaxes, whereby the *wa-kan* system now came to be transformed into a newer *wa* (here including Japanese and Chinese) *yō* (Western) system. Through this new eclectic Japanese-Chinese-Western linguistic-thought system, not only did many new words, concepts, idioms, and symbols penetrate Japan from the alleged "superior and universal" Western civilization, but also, as Ichikawa astutely observed, "even the structure of the Japanese language" itself was greatly modified.[18] This does not imply that the Japanese language became a new tongue, but that it now depended heavily on the Western convention of dividing human experience into a series of separable pigeonholes, a radical break with the traditional Japanese way of discerning human experience. (Sadly, most Western missionaries as well as many Japanese Christians have been insensitive to this linguistic predicament of the modern Japanese.)

The Meiji regime, which inherited its anti-Christian policy from the Tokugawa feudal regime, was surprised to discover the existence of the *kakure-Kirishitan* ("hidden Christians" who had preserved their faith under the disguise of Buddhism for two centuries) and brutally punished them. The government, then eager to improve the unequal treaty provisions with Western powers, was yet more surprised by the strong protest made by the representatives of Western powers over the Meiji government's harsh treatment of the hidden Christians as well as its stance against religious liberty. The government also could not ignore the cries for religious freedom voiced by liberal Buddhists and other Japanese intellectuals, and so the regime in 1873 lifted its anti-Christian ban, which soon resulted in the evangelistic activities of various Christian groups, such as, Russian Orthodox, Roman Catholic, and Protestant. (Because the Protestant denominations were most conspicuous, we will primarily follow their activities in the following pages.)

It should be remembered that even before the lifting of the anti-Christian edict, Christian missionaries had been allowed to live in Japan under the terms of the treaty of 1858—signed by the Tokugawa feudal regime—which allowed for the free religious activities of foreigners in the treaty ports. For example, as early as 1859, L. Liggins and Channing Moore Williams of the Episcopal church, J. C. Hepburn, M.D., and his wife of the Presbyterian church, and S. R. Brown, D. B.

Simmons, M.D., and G. F. Verbeck of the Dutch Reformed church in America arrived in Japan. In 1890 Jonathan Goble of the American Baptist Free Mission Society joined the group. By 1872 already seven missionary organizations were engaged, sub rosa to be sure, in some kind of missionary activity. Understandably, the official lifting of the ban against Christianity in 1873 was a great boon for missionaries. Their educational activity was especially noteworthy. For example, in 1874, C. M. Williams established Rikkyō (St. Paul's) College, and the American Methodist Church established another school, which later became Aoyama Gakuin. In 1875, Joseph Hardy Neesima (Niijima), who had unlawfully left Japan and graduated from Amherst College (1870) and Andover Theological Seminary (1874), established Dōshisha College in Kyoto. The fact that the establishment of these Christian institutions preceded the founding of the first official government institution, Tokyo Imperial University, in 1877 indicates the seriousness with which educational work was taken by Christian missionaries.[19] In addition to youths' being exposed to Christianity through these church-related colleges, there were other young people who came in contact with Christianity through foreign teachers on the faculties of government institutions. (From the latter group came many prominent Christian leaders, e.g., Nitobe Inazō, Uchimura Kanzō, etc.)

It should also be pointed out that, of the Christian institutions mentioned above, Dōshisha was not a school established by Western missionary societies. It was founded as a Japanese university by Niijima. Of course, Niijima was an ordained minister, and several Western missionaries cooperated with him. But Dōshisha's administration and management have always been in the hands of Japanese leaders. This may also be the right occasion to put on record that there was a sizable group of young Japanese intelligentsia with Neo-Confucian orientation, as exemplified by Uchimura Kanzō (1861–1930) and others like him, who embraced Christianity "on their own," as it were, on two main grounds (even though some Western missionaries tried to claim credit for their conversion). First, the Neo-Confucian principle that there is only one *li* (*ri* in Japanese, "principle" or "truth") in the universe prepared the minds of these Japanese youths to be receptive to any new alien religious philosophy. Second, although they hardly knew the main tenets of Christianity, they persuaded themselves that the *logos* ("word," "speech," "reason," "rational principle") mentioned by the Greeks, Hellenistic Jews, and Christians (John 1:1) was no other than the *li* taught by Neo-Confucian masters in China. Especially attractive to these young Japanese-Confucianists was the notion of the scattered seeds of the *logos* (the *logoi spermatikoi*), which dwelt in all non-Christian and pre-Christian traditions.

In retrospect, it becomes evident that these ex-Confucian-Christians wanted to make sure that the Meiji era became a truly revolutionary period for Japan so that, by homologizing Neo-Confucian metaphysical intuitions and the Christian teaching of love, it could move forward to what Johann Gottlieb Fichte (1762–1814) once called *Die Bestimmung des Menschen.* Understandably, they did not see eye-to-eye with the Western missionaries' approach to higher education because of the tension, as pointed out by Uchimura Kanzō, that existed between Japanese (here including ex-Confucian-Christians and nonreligious but pro-Christian Japanese) "who were desirous of making the institutions primarily academic, and the missionaries, who were conducive neither to effective education nor Christianization."[20] Ironically, this particular tension has remained deep-rooted in the Christian community in Japan until our own time.

WESTERNISM AND CHRISTIANITY

As mentioned earlier, the architects of modern Japan were extremely pragmatic and essentially conservative statesmen determined to create, at any cost, an up-to-date modern nation-state as rich and strong as any European power without, however, losing its traditional magico-religious polity. Thus, in a way reminiscent of the contradictory attitudes of the sixth- and seventh-century ancestors, who on the one hand were intoxicated with an unduly-idealized Chinese civilization known mostly only through books and on the other hand regarded themselves as a superior "divine" race, the Meiji leaders were determined to emulate unseen Western powers as possessors of universal norms while they themselves displayed impressive streaks of self-righteous ethnocentrism. At least initially, the government went all out to promote Westernism (*ōka-shugi*). In 1887 Foreign Minister Inouye Kaoru went so far as to say: "Let us change our empire into a European-style empire. Let us change our people into a European-style people. Let us create a new European-style empire on the Eastern sea."[21]

Some of the government leaders candidly admitted that the ulterior motive behind such a determined Westernism was the calculated notion that only by modernizing Japanese language, culture, and society along Western lines could Japan rectify the humiliating clauses of various unequal treaties with European powers, such as the one on "extraterritoriality." As might be expected, the Meiji regime, due to its paranoia over such a treaty revision, grudgingly lifted the ban against Christianity in 1873, as Western powers were taking a dim view of the anti-Christian policy of the Japanese nation. Of course, this act allowed the proselytizing activities of various Christian groups to surface. The short-lived popularity of the Westernism also gave ample opportunities to the Japanese intelligentsia, especially those leaders of the so-called Japanese enlightenment, to demonstrate their frivolous lack of integrity and consistency. We are told:

> It was just as if the people had become drunk. In a short period they would have to come to their senses, but right then they were intoxicated with foolishness. . . . Fukuzawa Yukichi proposed that Japanese improve themselves as a race by marrying with white men [and women]. . . . Kanda Naibu and others . . . established a society to encourage the Romanization of Japanese. Toyama Shōichi's intellectual switch was particularly interesting. He had written a book entitled *The Contradictions of Christianity* for which the arch conservative Inouye Tetsujirō wrote the preface. Within a year, he recommended the adoption of Christianity because of its concern for social reform.[22]

This Westernism undoubtedly gave encouragement to Western Christian missionaries (and Japanese Christians who swallowed the Westerners' perspective), for during the early Meiji era the Japanese desire to learn Western culture made their evangelistic activities easier. Even though Westernism as such did not last long, while it did last "those who worshipped [it] rushed to Christianity."[23] Understandably, in that kind of atmosphere the prestige of being Westernized was such that foreign missionaries' opinions became dominant, not only in the Russian Orthodox and Roman Catholic groups (in which leadership remained primarily foreign in ethos if not in numerical strength until World War II) but in Protestant groups as well. It should be noted in this connection that as early as 1873 there was a small but effective native leadership in Protestantism. Three main characteristics of the native Protestant leadership in the early Meiji era were (1) its antidenominationalism, (2) its proud independence (including its urge to create self-supporting churches), and (3) the multiplicity of its activities, for example, ecclesiastical as well as political, cultural, literary, pacifist, and socialist movements.

Ironically, although the popularity of Westernism propelled the influence of Western missionaries, such popularity brought with it an unfortunate emphasis on denominationalism, which to be sure had richer financial resources.[24] Winburn Thomas tells us that at that time Protestant missionaries in Japan were primarily American and secondarily British.[25] They were preoccupied with evangelistic expansion, including educational and philanthropic activities, but tended to be indifferent to social, cultural, or political developments in Japan. It is not surprising, therefore, that some of the native Protestant leaders and Western missionaries (as well as their faithful Japanese followers who were brainwashed by the missionaries) perceived the same events very differently. For example, in 1881 the noted pastor Uyemura Masahisa sharply criticized the shallowness of Westernism as advocated by the Meiji government, which used it only as a gimmick for the sake of improving the inequalities of its treaties with Western powers. "To remedy this, they [the government officials] decided to make us the equal of the other nations even in this respect [meaning the practice of Christianity]. But religion is religion. . . . One cannot lightly change or exchange it as he can food, drink, or clothing. Therefore, many thinking Christians felt that this attempt to adopt Christianity was a positive harm rather than a benefit."[26] But, if Westernism was a positive harm for the cause of Christianity in Uyemura's eyes, Western missionaries and their faithful followers were persuaded that "Christianity was being borne along with [the] popularity of western civilization. It [Christianity] was even discussed as a potential religion of the state. . . . Some missionaries predicted that the land might be Christianized within a decade or fifteen years."[27] From the early Meiji period until World War II, the Christian tradition in Japan was split between those who aspired to pursue their own understanding of Christianity under indigenous leadership, exemplified by Uchimura Kanzō's "Non-Church" movement,[28] and those who followed denominational lines, following Western churches under the leadership of Western missionaries and/or native leaders endorsed by the missionaries. Both groups produced persons of great intelligence and learning, even with regard to Western theological minutiae. But in the main, the Japanese Christian communities had no integral connections with Japanese religious/cultural traditions or with fellow Christian communities in other parts of Asia, although they did have some influence among the Westernized middle-class intelligentsia in urban areas. No wonder Raymond Hammer wonders whether or not the Christian church is no more than a "'caller' at the 'genkan' (doorway)," for it still has not entered deeply into Japanese society.[29]

NOTES ON THE JAPANESE SCENE FROM 1889-1945

Ironically, even while many Western missionaries and new native converts were still dreaming about the Westernization/Christianization of Japan, the Meiji regime abruptly gave up Westernism, and very quickly a number of nationalistic and anti-Christian movements and societies came into being around the year 1890. Although the Meiji Constitution, adopted in 1889, gave lip service to a very restricted kind of religious freedom, no one was fooled concerning the intentions of the regime, now determined to superimpose on the whole nation the emperor cult, nationalistic patriotic virtues, and a nonreligious Shinto to be practiced by every Japanese regardless of his or her religious belief. The government's intention became more apparent in the Imperial Rescript of Education, based on the homology of Shinto and Confucian morality, promulgated in 1890. Understandably, some Christians, tired of being accused of disloyalty to the nation, were inclined to make compromises with this rising nationalism. The whole Christian community shamefully capitulated completely to the government's claim of "righteous war" at the time of the Sino-Japanese War, 1894–95.

The events in the 1890s indicated clearly that in a relatively short time Japan had "inhaled" the logic of imperialism from the European "more advanced nations" (*senshinkoku*). After the Sino-Japanese War, Formosa (Taiwan) and the Pescadores Islands were ceded to Japan. Three European imperialist powers—Russia, Germany, and France—dissuaded Japan, however, from acquiring Liaotung Peninsula. Japan was later angered when all three of these Western powers demanded and received from China huge concessions as a reward for their "Triple Intervention."

Anti-Christian groups in Japan made the most of the discrepancy between the official stance of the supposedly Christian European nations and their actual practice. There was much talk about eventual revenge against Russia, Germany, and France with the popular motto *gashin-shōtan*, or "perseverance under difficulties." When the anti-Western Boxer Rebellion took place in China in 1900, Japan sent expeditionary forces to aid the Western powers. Impressed by the bravery and discipline of the Japanese forces, Britain signed a treaty of alliance with Japan two years later. Meanwhile, Russia continued to push southward into Manchuria, greatly threatening the well-being of Korea and its self-styled guardian, Japan. In this situation, Japan—with British help—engaged in the Russo-Japanese War (1904–1905), which was indeed a national gamble. After Russia's defeat, Theodore Roosevelt of the United States arranged a peace treaty, which greatly fattened the military and financial cliques in Japan at the expense of northern China (Manchuria) and Korea. Significantly, Uchimura Kanzō and other Christian pacifists, together with nonreligious liberal pacifists, took a public stand against the Russo-Japanese War, but they were powerless in the face of the strong militaristic and expansionist ethos of Japan. In 1910 Japan, now an imperialist power, annexed Korea forcefully with the support and approval of Britain and America and in 1911 finally managed to eliminate the unequal clauses from its treaties with various Western powers. As far as the Meiji regime was concerned, it had achieved its original goal of making Japan a modern nation-state with a traditional polity, and a rich nation with a strong defense (*fukoku-kyōhei*). By importing Westernism and its scientific technology without its spiritual engine, that is, Christianity, and by buying into the international capitalistic network, Japan had become a militaristic, colonial power similar to the European imperialistic powers in Asia.

Early in the twentieth century, Japan watched with great interest the potential conflict between "Pan-Germanism," headed by the newly united (1871) German empire with the help of Austria and Italy, and "Pan-Slavism," advocated by Russia with the support of France and Britain. When World War I finally erupted, Japan fought on the side of its ally, Britain. Moreover, taking advantage of the chaotic global scene, Japan made in 1915 its most aggressive and reprehensible "twenty-one demands" on China. Intoxicated by the victory of World War I, Japan exhibited a great appetite for expansion. The throne, occupied by the sick Emperor Taishō, was nominally venerated, but no longer, however, as a political authority but as a tool of the oligarchy. Buddhism and Christianity, as well as the Sect Shinto denominations (separated from nonreligious State Shinto between 1882 and 1908) had to cowtow to State Shinto. Much to the consternation of the government, however, during the era of the so-called Taishō Democracy following World War I, the demands of universal suffrage became vocal. Industrial workers began to organize unions, political parties were established, labor strikes were frequent occurrences, and a small but articulate Marxist group began to attract students. All these movements were suspected as Bolshevik propaganda. The emperor cult, State Shinto, the Japanese spirit (*Yamato damashii*), and nationalistic ethics (*shūshin*) were trumpeted as ideological weapons against all "foreign" and "dangerous" systems, including Christianity.

In 1931, the Japanese army, reluctantly controlled by political parties during the Taishō democracy, began its blatant aggression, usually referred to as the Manchurian Incident, partly under the pretext of solving an economic depression that threatened the financial foundation of Japan. During the 1930s, all liberal thinking and expression in religion, philosophy, art, or culture was condemned as dangerous. The rights of freedom of the press, thought, and assembly, as well as the freedom of conscience and belief, were violated. Some elder statesmen and moderate parliamentarians who resisted these militarist expansionist policies were assassinated. In 1936 Japan joined Germany (with which it had always had a Freudian relationship; that is, one of love and hate) in an anticommunist pact, and the government began to press all religious bodies to cooperate with the national aim to extend the imperial rule over East Asia. In 1939, the Religious Bodies Law was enforced, by which the government could control all aspects of religious organizations, and Buddhist and Christian groups were strongly "encouraged" to form united bodies. Further, a Religious League composed of Christian, Buddhist, and Sect Shinto denominations was organized in 1941 to provide a spiritual bulwark for the nation during World War II.

REFLECTIONS ON JAPANESE THEOLOGY
BEFORE AND AFTER WORLD WAR II

William Temple once remarked that God, being the creator of heaven and earth, may not be exclusively concerned with the church; this is an important reminder as we reflect on so-called Japanese theology. By and large, Christians in the West, Roman Catholic or Protestant, have been brought up with the fifteenth-century dogma *extra ecclesiam nulla salus* ("outside the church there is no salvation"), and so they tend to look for propositional doctrinal statements of the ecclesiastical community in dealing with Japanese theology. Admittedly, no one quarrels with such an autobiographical affirmation of the exclusivistic faith of one's own religious community. In Japan, however, as hinted earlier, some of the Christians of the early Meiji period were ex-Samurais brought up in a Neo-Confucian tradition that emphasized the one universal *li* ("truth" or "principle") and were attracted by the notion of the *logos* dwelling in every human tradition rather than in the ecclesiastical institution called the church per se. Those ex-Samurais, who had lost their old *raison d'être* with the toppling of the Tokugawa feudal regime, considered the Meiji Restoration a radically revolutionary turning point for Japan, whereby it could now move forward toward *Die Bestimmung des Menschen*. Kozaki Hiromichi (Kōdō), an influential pastor, has spoken of a time when he and others like him, in order to pursue

primarily political ends, entered the Kumamoto School of Western
Learning. (The school was founded in 1871 by the lord of Kumamoto
fief, sensing the eventual doom of the Tokugawa feudal regime and
wanting able youths of his fief to learn something about alien Western
civilization to prepare themselves for a new Japan.) Kozaki asserted that
"all had politics as their aim when they entered school. Asked his professional objective, there was not one who would not reply 'statesman.'"[30]
He and some of his friends, however, came to know Christianity
through Captain L. J. Janes, who was not a missionary but had been
hired as the instructor of the school. Then

> they realized that their old [Neo-Confucian] ethical system was
> nothing but an unsatisfying community mechanism for preserving
> the feudal stratified society. The new [Christian] God whom they
> faced made demands on their consciences. . . . A covenant with
> God demanded that each man offer up his entire being. . . . They
> turned from unquestioning obedience toward their lord [of the fief]
> and parents to help other persons by pledging their loyalty, in this
> case, their souls, to God.[31]

This was probably the reason why so many early Japanese Christians
entered education, government service, creative writing, and even politics as their "Christian" duties, some of them, of course, becoming pastors, as well.

Thus, instead of looking very narrowly at the doctrinal theology of the Christian community in Japan, I hope more people can look
at the broader social-cultural-political activities in which Japanese
Christians took initiative, using, for example, H. Richard Niebuhr's
helpful concepts contained in his famous little book *Christ and Culture.*[32] Parenthetically, I might add that early Japanese Christians had
nothing against the church as such. In fact, they took it for granted that
there ought to be fellowships of persons representing different backgrounds, opinions, and temperaments, all dedicated to Christian service. However, they were not impressed by denominational divisions;
moreover, the church was not the highest item in their priorities. Some
of these characteristics of the early Meiji Christians have been partially
transmitted to Uchimura's *Mu-Kyōkai* ("Non-Church") movement, although this group has been decisively colored by Uchimura's unique
form of biblicism. Incidentally, Uchimura has come to be known in the
West primarily for his Non-Church Christian activities, but, like many
other early Meiji Christian leaders, Uchimura

> did not confine himself to spiritual matters. He also wrote on social
> problems and joined the socialists like Kōtoku Shūsui [who was

eventually executed by the authoritarian government] and other Christians like Abe Isoo at the time of the Ashio Copper Mine Incident and the Russo-Japanese War. . . . Uchimura continued to criticize injustices, but he never became a socialist. The Unitarians, [on the other hand] because of their modern interpretation of the Bible and desire to apply Christian [social] ethics, gradually moved from theology to direct concern with social evil. People like Abe Isoo, Katayama Sen [who became an ardent Christian socialist while studying at Grinnel College and was later involved in the Japan Communist Party; he died in the Kremlin where he is now buried] and Kinoshita Naoye followed this path from Unitarianism to socialism.[33]

Admittedly, many of these ex-Samurai and ex-Confucian Japanese Christians were not meek and conforming orthodox Christians of the ecclesiastical type. But they took very seriously their Christian vocations to improve the social, cultural, and political conditions of Japan, as exemplified by the activities of Kataoka Kenkichi, Nakajima Nobuyuki, Saitō Mibuo, and Shimada Saburō—all later to become members of the Diet.

As the Meiji regime lifted the ban against Christianity and actively promoted Westernism in the 1870s, if only for the sake of political expediency (especially for the benefit of treaty revisions with Western powers), many (predominantly American) missionaries arrived on the scene. With their coming, the Japanese Christian community inevitably began to be dominated by their activistic energy, financial power, and their norms of what the church ought be: a simplistic biblicism and highly individualistic puritanical mores, for example, prohibition, no smoking, no card playing; denominational orthodoxies; the popular nineteenth-century vision of establishing a "Christian America," repackaged for Japanese consumption, and the tendency to equate America's manifest destiny with the kingdom of God on earth; strict Sunday observance; and finally, an emphasis on revivalism.[34] To be sure, those missionaries also pioneered many worthy causes, notably women's education and an antiprostitution campaign. Curiously, though, they exhibited a strong antiintellectualism in spite of their fondness for educational ministry. These characteristics of the missionaries, especially those of the Protestant traditions, were not confined to early Meiji Japan. Much later, William Ernest Hocking criticized the same traits of Protestant missionaries in India:

> Our Protestant institutions are set for prompt delivery of partly prepared men. It is as though the graduate level of adept preparation were out of tune with our sense of haste and scantiness of

means. . . . The real lack, among Protestants, is a lack of perception; a certain triviality and crudity in the sense of the work to be done; a *supposition that we already know enough, and that more thinking is a luxury that can be dispensed with.* [35]

Fortunately, there were a tiny minority of learned missionaries in the case of Japan who went beyond the usual language study and pursued serious inquiries into Japanese as well as Western religious/cultural traditions—for example, Hans Haas of Germany, Arthur Lloyd of Britain, August Karl Reischauer, George W. Knox, and (later) Daniel C. Holtom of the United States—but they were so very few in number. Many others were, in Hocking's term, "partly prepared" career-oriented missionaries. Convinced that they already knew the eternal truth and persuaded that they were the official representatives of normative (Western) Christianity, they acted more often than not as inflexible guardians of what they understood as the religious/moral standards of tiny but divided missionary churches in Japan. For example, many of them required strict Sabbath observance as a condition for baptism, whereupon a poor person who had to work on Sundays sent a letter of petition to a missionary who was in charge: "I beg you by your mercy to allow me into your organization even though I cannot go to church on Sundays. Please show me this compassion." [36] As might be expected, many of the Japanese Protestant churches under the control of Western missionaries were greatly threatened by the coming of the new liberal and critical European theologies and the Unitarian/Universalism from America. Understandably, many of them reacted extremely negatively against the World's Parliament of Religions, held in Chicago in 1893, which incidentally served as the first occasion for Buddhism, Hinduism, and other Asian religions to be introduced to the West. In 1896, thanks to the astute wisdom of Shaku Sōyen, a leading Buddhist delegate to the Parliament, the first Conference of Religionists, commonly referred to as the "Buddhist-Christian Conference" (*Butsu-ya Ryōkyō Kondan-kai*) was held in Viscount Matsudaira's villa. [37] By that time, it had become apparent that such issues as those of the World's Parliament of Religions, the Buddhist-Christian Conference, new liberal European theology, and Unitarianism were splitting the tiny Japanese Christian groups sharply between the conservative, "orthodox" (traditional) denominational groups and the more liberal and progressive factions ready to raise difficult intellectual issues, willing to relate Christianity to vital socioeconomic and political problems, and open to engage in dialogues with other religionists about matters of mutual concerns. As might be expected, most Western missionaries who thought it was their mission to convert Buddhists and Shintoists were emotionally against the World's Parliament of Religions, for it was inviting delegates from Buddhism and Shinto as religious equals to the Parliament sessions.[38] (It is interesting to recall that the Archbishop of Canterbury and many Christian groups in the West also objected to the Parliament for treating all religions alike. Curiously, the Sultan of Turkey objected to the Parliament, using almost identical language.) Many missionaries were just as negative to the Buddhist-Christian Conference as well, but happily, some of the more levelheaded Japanese Christians, such as the influential pastor Yokoi Tokio and a widely recognized philosopher Ōnishi Hajime, were convinced that it was their Christian duty to cooperate with Buddhist leaders in order to face jointly with them the many crucial problems confronting Japan. Unfortunately, the opinions of those able Christians who did not share the missionaries' orthodoxy became increasingly less influential within the church groups; it was these same groups who went along with the rising nationalism before and after the Sino-Japanese War. The growing nationalistic ethos within the Japanese Christian communities during the 1890s was illustrated by the revoking of Tamura Naoomi's ministerial status on the ground that he was too critical of Japanese social customs that degraded women. Ironically, while most church papers did not raise any objections, it was the secular press, *Kokumin-no-Tomo* ("Friends of the People"), which bitterly criticized the Christian community's dismissal of Tamura. It reminded the Christian communities: "The Christian Church should not truckle to an extreme and narrow patriotism; rather it should show its own magnanimity."[39] It was most unfortunate that a number of able and daring Christians, both clergy and laity, who were highly respected political, social, and cultural leaders and were desperately needed as pillars of the infant churches, felt caught between the missionaries' myopic orthodoxy and the irrational nationalism of the church groups and began to drop out in despair from the narrow-minded Christian communities in Japan.

Because this kind of analysis is not readily available in most Western books, I have indulged in a fairly detailed analysis of the Christian development in Japan in the late nineteenth century in order to trace the contradictory traits of the Japanese Christian community in the first half of the twentieth century. They are (a) its singular orientation to Western Christendom with utter disregard for Christian communities in other parts of Asia (or Africa or Latin America, for that matter) and (b) its willy-nilly acceptance of an exaggerated nationalism, an acceptance not too dissimilar to the sixth- and seventh-century Japanese who regarded themselves as the divinely elected paragon of humanity while exhibiting a deeply rooted inferiority complex (especially vis-à-vis Chinese civilization). The Japanese Christian community in the first half of the twentieth century reflected and also accommodated the national ethos of modern Japan, (characterized astutely as "Asian Westernism" by Vera Micheles Dean), which considered itself above all other Asian nations and acted accordingly until 1945.[40] These critical comments about the Japanese Christian community were made, significantly, not by outsiders who did not share the agony of the Japanese churches in the difficult situation under hostile authoritarian regimes, but by many insiders who had lived through those critical years that seriously tested the very survival of Christianity in Japan, the years immediately after World War II. As might be expected, younger church leaders were inclined to be particularly impatient with older leaders, who during the 1930s and the war years felt they had no viable recourse except to succumb to the government policies and to compromise with the nationalistic mood of the nation. Accordingly, various church assemblies in the immediate postwar period took seriously the public act of collective "repentence" for their past mistakes. Ironically, many of those who "repented" often overlooked a small group of war-time heroes and martyrs who dared to buck against the tyrannies of the government for the sake of their Christian conviction, partly because most of those unsung heroes represented anti-intellectual charismatic wings of Christendom. More ironically, many leaders of the mainline church groups, younger as well as older—brainwashed as they were with an unbiblical notion based on the fifteenth-century dogma "no salvation outside the church"—conceived of divine activities in Japan primarily in terms of the concrete programs of the churches. It may be pertinent for us, however, to appropriate a broader perspective and to reflect on the nineteenth and twentieth centuries' Christian activities "both outside and inside churches."

4

CHRISTIANITY IN JAPAN:
SOME REFLECTIONS

PROLOGUE

In the three previous chapters, I have attempted to portray (a) some features of the Asian Christian tradition, and (b) its relationship, or lack of it, with the Japanese Christian community, which ideally should have been its integral part right along. Readers no doubt also recognized the fact that although the Asian Christian tradition has been thus far discussed primarily from the perspective of the "former sending churches" in the West, I have tried—as stated in my Chapter 1—to bring to bear the perspectives of Asian Christians on the subject—perspectives derived from their experiences, which are, of course, very different from the experiences of their counterparts in the West.

The lack of meaningful rapport between the Asian Christian tradition and the Japanese Christian community until after World War II is extremely lamentable, although it is understandable because of various geographical, historical, psychological, and cultural factors. In a sense, Japan, being an archipelago surrounded by ocean, has always been isolated from other Asian nations and peoples as well as from the rest of the world. Moreover, Japan's isolation was officially institutionalized by the policy of national seclusion imposed by the Tokugawa feudal regime from 1639 until the arrival of Commodore Matthew

Perry in 1853. The modern Japanese imperial regime, which followed the Tokugawa shōgunate, pursued a policy of exchange with the West to compensate for the previous exclusion experience. Some viewed the new policy as "promiscuous Westernism," although the hidden motivations of the government were (a) to use some features of Western civilization precisely in order to keep the West at arm's length, (b) to become sufficiently Westernized and "civilized"—ostensibly for foreigners' consumption—for the purpose of revising and improving unequal clauses in treaties with Western powers, while at the same time consolidating the national community internally by depending on the mystique of the emperor cult, on the newly-concocted, allegedly nonreligious State Shinto, and on the traditional ethics of loyalty and filial piety, and (c) to emulate rich and powerful Western nations, whereby Japan would become a new Eastern colonial power, dominating other peoples and nations in Asia. Such an offensive attitude on the part of the Japanese government leaders toward Asia was not conducive to the development of fraternal interrelations between peoples and groups in the Asiatic continent and Japan.

On the part of the Asian nations, many of which had been colonized by Western nations, there were good reasons for them to be preoccupied with their unilateral relations with their respective colonial powers; for example, Indonesia with the Netherlands, countries on the French Indo-China peninsula with France, India and Burma with Britain, and the Philippines with the United States, at the expense of their horizontal relations with other groups and peoples in Asia, including those in Japan. To be sure, delegates from churches in various Asian nations were always invited before World War II to attend the ecumenical and/or global confessional meetings, such as those of the International Missionary Council or of the World Lutheran or Pan-Anglican groups, but it was rare for indigenous church groups in Asia, crossing denominational and national lines, to meet before the war for the purposes of mutual edification and fellowship. Thus, although Christian churches have existed historically in Asia for a long time, the self-conscious phenomenon called the Asian Christian tradition is a fairly recent, in fact postwar, development.

As I reflect on the contemporary Japanese as well as the Asian Christian traditions, I am struck by the fact that there is an overwhelming, uncritical, and naive equation on their part between Christianity and the institutionalized churches, which is no doubt the mixed legacy inherited from Western Christendom and its world missionary movement. With this problem in mind, I indulged in spelling out the common Asian Christians' understanding of the paradoxical biblical view of

Christianity and of the church, based on the apostle Paul's double orientation (see 1 Cor. 8:5–6); that is, monotheism as inner meaning and monolatry as outer meaning. I also touched on the common mode of human apprehension that we all share, namely, the autobiographical and biographical perceptions. Ironically, it is always tempting, where one religious tradition (Islamic, Hindu, Buddhist, etc.) dominates others for any length of time, for the adherents of the dominant religion to assume that their autobiographical understanding of the inner meaning of their tradition has unquestionably objective universal validity. And Christians in the West from the time of Constantine and Theodosius fell into this trap, especially in reference to their understanding of the intricate relationship between divine reality—one who transcends the *ekklesia*; one who uses, judges, and transforms the church, but who is never identical with it—and the organized Christian ecclesiastical establishment. Admittedly, European Christians in principle affirmed the visible and pneumatically inspired, but history testifies that Western Christendom became essentially more preoccupied with the visible, earthly side of the church.

We are told that *Credo . . . communionem sanctorum* of the Apostles' Creed was added later to *credo . . . unam sanctam catholicam ecclesiam.* According to Gerardus van der Leeuw:

> Its original meaning was: "I believe that there subsists a participation in the sacred elements (of the sacrament)," while in the Middle Ages the expression acquired the [new] significance—community of all, both living and departed. The Reformation, however, opposed the community of saints to the visible hierarchy of the Roman church, and [affirmed that] the essence of this community rests on election by God and the constancy of Christ.[1]

Nevertheless, European Christians, both Catholic and Protestant, took it for granted that their own provincial autobiographical understanding of the inner meaning of the church—as formulated in the nonbiblical dogma *extra ecclesiam nulla salus* ("no salvation outside the church"), as declared by the Council of Florence in 1438–45—was based on eternal truth. Once the earthly church council invaded the divine territory of salvation—deciding for God as to who should be saved—many religious activities, including global missionary programs, increasingly came to be seen as matters of human deed and assertiveness, however pious they might be, while the Almighty became more like the inactive *deus otiosus* to many Westerners, even though people constantly invoked the deity theoretically as the Ultimate Reality and the Lord of History.

Some years ago, I was deeply moved by the General Introduction to the Christian Presence Series by Max A. C. Warren. In his own words:

> Our first task in approaching another people, another culture, another religion, is to take off our shoes, for the place we are approaching is holy. Else we may find ourselves treading on men's [and women's] dreams. More seriously still, *we may forget that God was here before our arrival.*[2]

My impression is that the tone of profound humility exemplified by the above statement by Warren was not always exhibited by many missionaries who have gone to Asia during the past four centuries. To be sure, missionaries—just because they happen to be engaged in pious calling— were not exempted automatically from such human aspirations as ego, jealousy, desire for prestige or success—that is, the usual manifestations of the classical notion of original sin. Be that as it may, many Western missionaries and missionary societies gave distinct impressions to people in Asia that their own activities, their success or failure, directly determined the effectiveness of the divine enterprise as such. Moreover, as Warren states: It has also to be admitted quite frankly that during these centuries the missionaries of the Christian Church have commonly assumed that Western civilization and Christianity were two aspects of the same gift which they were commissioned to offer to the rest of [humankind]."[3]

As I examine the recent history of the Japanese Christian community, it pains me to notice a deep tension that existed between some of the articulate indigenous Japanese Christian leaders, who took their Christian duty seriously enough to go into politics, education, labor relations, and so forth (outside the ecclesiastical orbit), and most Western missionaries and their slavish followers, who were preoccupied by the promotion of churchy programs of sectarian institutions as the sole Christian enterprise. In so stating, it is not my intention to judge either the past Western missionaries or indigenous Christian leaders. Rather, I cite the Japanese case as an example of similar tensions that must have existed in other parts of the Asian Christian communities. And it is my sincere hope that future leaders of the Asian Christian tradition, including, to be sure, those of the Japanese Christian community, will resist the all-too-common temptation to equate the ecclesiastical institution with the One who judges and transforms it. Keeping this in mind, let me now briefly discuss both the nonecclesiastical (especially philosophical reflection and sociopolitical action) and ecclesiastical (particularly systematic theological works in the narrow sense) dimensions of the Japanese Christian tradition.

JAPANESE PHILOSOPHY

Philosophy (*philo-sophia*, "the love of wisdom") is clearly a Western term. And it may be, as William Haas argues, that in Asia the term *philo-ousia* ("love of reality or essence") may be closer to what the Asian thinkers traditionally sought after.[4] At any rate, philosophy—here using the Western term—covers diverse related intellectual pursuits such as, metaphysics, logic, and ethics. Philosophy in this broad sense has had a long history in Japan.[5] Certainly, during the premodern period, it was the Neo-Confucian philosophy that provided cosmic legitimation to the Tokugawa synthesis of religious/cultural/social/political/legal/moral orders. And very shortly after the time when the Tokugawa feudal regime was compelled by American gunboat diplomacy to open Japan's door to the West in the 1850s, Japan was eager to find a new "philosophy" to give cosmic legitimation to the new synthesis destined to come into being. Thus in 1863 (a few years before the surrender of the feudal prerogative to the Meiji emperor), the Tokugawa regime sent two men— Nishi Amane and Tsuda Masamichi—to Holland, a country that had maintained limited intercourse with Japan from the seventeenth century. These two men studied philosophy and the social sciences in Holland until 1865. It was Nishi who coined the term *Kitetsugaku* ("the science of questioning wisdom") in order to differentiate his form of thought, informed by Western philosophy, from Confucian and Buddhist systems of thought. That is to say, the term "philosophy" (*Kitetsugaku* or simply *tetsugaku*) had a rich nuance as the foundation of the new order in Japan, and it was so conceived by the architects of modern Japan.

In retrospect, it becomes apparent that modern Japan has produced a number of first-rate philosophers. Especially well known are those who belong to the so-called Kyoto school founded by Nishida Kitarō (1870–1945). Concerning this school, one of its contemporary spokesmen has written:

> Adopting Western methods, utilizing Western categories, and at the same time criticizing both, they endeavour to find a new way to express their original philosophical insights and often, in view of the results so far achieved, their own life and world views, nurtured in the tradition of oriental thought.[6]

It should be noted that one of the philosophers who taught at Kyoto was Hatano Seiichi, who attempted to contribute the metaphysical profundities transmitted through Western Christian tradition to the new Japanese philosophy. For him, philosophy of religion was the theoretical retrospection of religious life-experience. Hatano differentiated the task of philosophy of religion from that of theology, which to him implied a practical concern to clarify and develop the truth of a particular religion for the life of a religious community. Inevitably, however, the cognitive study of any religion demands a philosophical view. Nevertheless, Hatano rejected the theologian's temptation to use philosophy primarily as a means. Basically, he did not accept the view that there is only one true philosophy of religion, to be affirmed universally by all seekers of truth. He argued cogently that there is no such thing as *the* true philosophical standpoint for the religio-philosophical approach to the structure and essence of religion in general. Thus, a philosopher of religion must determine the kind of philosophical viewpoint he or she will accept for his or her religio-philosophical endeavor.

For his own philosophy of religion, Hatano accepted the key concept of *agape* as his starting point and developed the thesis that the structure of time is correlated with the different types of love: *epithumia*, or desire, with the temporal structure of natural life, *eros* for that of cultural life, and *agape* for that of religious life. It must be made very clear that his use of *agape* does not make his philosophy of religion subservient to Christian theology, as some church people think; rather, it enriches his philosophy of religion with the Christian insights that he had experienced. Although his philosophical study has been ignored by many church people in Japan, his works remind Japanese intellectuals at large, prone to dismiss Christianity merely as a provincial magico-religion of the West, that they must take seriously the truth claims handed down in the Christian tradition in their inquiry into religious truth.[7]

CHRISTIAN SOCIAL ACTION

One of the unfortunate consequences of the emphasis on individual religion and morality, a feature of Protestant Christianity in Japan during the first half of the twentieth century, has been the general tendency toward the privatization of religion and an accompanying sense of disdain for Christian social or political action. Even so, there have been a small group of active, articulate, restless, and able Christians who have considered themselves a creative religious minority, both in the nation and in the churches. They have been effective in various activities and movements for the improvement of the social, economic, cultural, and political life of Japan; for example, in education, philanthropy, labor, peace and socialist movements, cooperatives (both agricultural and industrial), purification campaigns, voting rights education, and numerous other causes. Certainly, millions of people who suffered during the Great Earthquake of 1923 will never forget the impressive selfless activities of the Salvation Army.[8] And even the most bigoted anti-Christians would recognize the great contributions Kagawa Toyohiko (1888–1960), evangelist, writer, and social activist, made almost single-handedly for the Co-Operative Movement, Labor and Farmers Unions, and so forth, even though, according to some critics, Kagawa's socialism was not too different from a bourgeois democracy of the American type.[9] In this respect, it is interesting that Katayama Tetsu, a renowned Christian layman and former Prime Minister of Japan, reminisced in 1967 how other types of socialists, especially Abe Isoo, once a pastor and the founder of the *Shakai-Minshu-tō* (Socialist Democratic Party), endured the persecutions and restrictions imposed by the authoritarian government in order to campaign for nonbourgeois but also anti-Marxist Christian socialism.[10]

JAPANESE THEOLOGY

Not much can be added to ᵗhe descriptions of the theological development, in the technical sense, within the Christian community in Japan in the prewar period of such perceptive works as Carl Michalson's *Japanese Contributions to Christian Theology*[11] or Germany's *Protestant Theologies in Modern Japan: A History of Dominant Theological Currents from 1920–1960.*[12] Michalson's book is a helpful overview, whereas Germany's book is a more detailed study of what he calls "theological currents," especially the "rise of dialectical theology," which is exceedingly helpful. I am delighted that Germany presented the main points of Takakura Tokutarō's "biblical evangelicalism" as an indication of the faith of the reformers that "once again moved out of theological and denominational isolation to influence the church at large."[13] Equally important for our purpose is Michalson's description of the systematic theological enterprise of Kumano Yoshitaka, characterized by him as the most Westernized of all the leading Japanese theologians even though he never traveled abroad. (In a sense, his case is similar to the philosophical work of Nishida Kitarō, who was well versed in Western philosophy although he never studied abroad.) Kumano's *Dogmatics (Kyōgigaku)* is based on the doctrines of predestination, creation, anthropology, the church, and ethics. Kumano's doctrine of predestination is deeply grounded in his eschatological faith, more fully developed in his *Shumatsu-ron to Rekishi-tetsugaku* ("Eschatology and Philosophy of History").[14] He manages to interrelate creation, incarnation, and eschatology. Kumano interprets eschatology as a dialectic movement between existence toward death (anthropology) and existence under God (revelation).[15] Kumano also was one of the early interpreters of dialectical theology in Japan; it was he who initially introduced Brunner's *Philosophie und Offenbarung.*[16] Although Kumano managed to incorporate many Western theological insights into his *Dogmatics*, he lacked the theology of culture and the notion of the particularity of the church, which is at least one aspect of the doctrine of the incarnation. This may account for the fact that in spite of his autobiographical affirmation of the theme "outside the church there is no salvation," the Japanese Christian community, on which he had exerted such a great influence, remained an introverted, complacent, and ineffective community, uprooted from the chaotic reality of Japan in the 1930s, which became even more chaotic during World War II.

POSTWAR JAPAN

Regarding the religious situation in Japan after the end of World War II, I can present here only a brief account of my reflections on the topic. Obviously, Japan's surrender to the Allied Powers at the end of World War II was the most traumatic event in the historical memory of the Japanese people. What is less obvious is the fact that the year 1945 also signified the end of the Meiji synthesis, which had propelled Japan into modernity in 1868. And, as stated earlier, the Meiji synthesis in itself was a synthesis of two earlier syntheses, namely, those of the Ritsuryō (seventh–sixteenth centuries) and the Tokugawa (1603–1867). Each of these three religious/cultural/social/political syntheses depended on the cosmic legitimation provided by a particular religious or semireligious system: for example, the Ritsuryō depended on a Shinto-Confucian-Buddhist homology, the Tokugawa on Neo-Confucianism, and the Meiji on the newly-concocted nonreligious State Shinto. It becomes abundantly clear, then, that the year 1945 signified not only the defeat of Japan (the first of its history) but also—equally significant in many ways—the end of its cosmic legitimation.

   At any rate, it was a new experience for the Japanese people to be ruled by foreign (predominantly American) occupation forces, symbolized by the person of General Douglas MacArthur, who issued directives ordering the captive Japanese government to enact a series of measures as guiding principles for a new Japan. By far the most significant new feature was the religious policy of the SCAP (the Supreme Commander for the Allied Powers), as illustrated by the following clauses of the new postwar "Constitution" (promulgated on November 3, 1946—to take effect as of May 3, 1947):

> Article 20: Freedom of religion is guaranteed to all. No person shall be compelled to take part in any religious act, celebration, rite, or practice. No religious organization shall receive any privileges from the State, nor exercise any political authority. The State and its organs shall refrain from religious education and other religious activity.

> Article 89: No public money or other property shall be expended for the use, benefit, or maintenance of any religious institution or association, or for any charitable, educational or benevolent enterprise not under the control of public authority.[17]

The SCAP also persuaded the emperor to promulgate on January 1, 1946, the Imperial Rescript, "renouncing claims to divinity." In all fairness, it should be pointed out that the emperor's renouncing of his *kami* nature meant more to Washington, which interpreted "divinity" in Jewish or Christian theistic terms, than to most Japanese people, who understood *kami* nature in a much more pantheistic way. Nevertheless, the fact that the emperor had made a special reference to this matter was something new. He said (in translation):

> The ties between Us and Our people have always stood upon mutual trust and affection. They do not depend upon mere legends and myths. They are not predicated upon the false conception that the Emperor is divine and the Japanese people are superior to other races and are fated to rule the world.[18]

The postwar policies under the inspiration of the SCAP signified Japan's "second opening" to the family of nations. The first opening in the midnineteenth century, compelled to be sure by Commodore Matthew Perry's gunboat diplomacy, opened up Japan's ports to foreign trade. It was soon followed by the policy of the Meiji regime, which aimed at making Japan a rich and strong, modern nation-state with Western knowledge and technology, without however losing its traditional magico-religious foundation.[19] It meant that in spite of the external "opening" of Japan, the architects of modern Japan were determined to preserve, and even solidify, the de facto national seclusion policy as far as the political, ethical, and magico-religious framework of Japan was concerned. In fact, the external Westernization and internal "immanental theocracy" were the most contradictory features of the Meiji synthesis, which lasted until 1945. It was this internal, spiritual national seclusion of Japan that the SCAP was determined to break down.

Undoubtedly, the American occupation policies exerted directly or indirectly tremendous influence on the postwar recovery and development of Japan: secularization, modernization, industrialization, a new educational orientation, the instant transformation of a gigantic "national" Shinto to "Shrine" Shinto, the splitting up of old Buddhist schools into numerous independent sects, a phenomenal mushrooming of hundreds of new religions, and so forth. The immediate postwar situation was also marked by some curiosity about Christianity, reputed to be the spiritual engine of the victorious Allied nations, on the part of the general populace in Japan. And there was no question that the constitutional guarantee of religious liberty benefited Christianity. On the other hand, MacArthur's ill-advised promotion of Christianity and the SCAP's all-too easy equation of the American type of democracy with Christianity proved to be a disservice to Christianity as well as to the cause of separation of religion and state, the stated principle of the American-inspired postwar constitution. Popular interest in Christianity waned quickly, due partly to the naïve assumption of the Occupation leaders that Christianity was an effective anticommunist ideology. Moreover, the swarming of so many new missionaries from Europe and North America, especially of the extremely Evangelical persuasions, who had little understanding of Japanese culture, religion, language, and history, compounded the problems of Christianity in Japan.

Understandably, the ever-changing American policies toward Japan muddled many dimensions of the American-Japanese relationship as well as internal Japanese development. The most far-reaching effect was caused by the sweeping change of the American policy from its initial goal of the democratization of Japan to the establishment of Japan as an anticommunist citadel in the Pacific. Then came the Korean War, in which MacArthur served as the supreme head of SCAP in Japan and simultaneously as a commanding officer of Allied forces in Korea. As might be expected, Japan then became an important manufacturer and supplier of arms to the Allied (predominantly American) forces. The situation became more entangled during the long and misguided Vietnam War. As someone has candidly pointed out, although Americans wanted to remake Japan legally as a stronger military ally for the

United States in East Asia, Japan coyly declined the honor by quoting the postwar constitution, written by American democratic crusaders, right back to Americans. A cartoonist portrayed the situation graphically by drawing two pictures: in one, Americans were telling Japanese not to make bombs but to start making automobiles; in the second, Americans were asking Japanese to stop making automobiles and to begin producing arms.

Japan, which regarded itself as a faithful and reliable ally of the United States, was greatly mystified by Nixon's overture to Peking without any prior consultation with Tokyo. All these shifts of American policy greatly determined the maneuverability of Japan, which since the end of World War II had been walking on a tightrope, caught between its own economic and political survival and the preserving and strengthening of goodwill toward itself on the part of North American, European, African, and Asian nations. It is encouraging to see Japan's hitherto unprecedented efforts to improve its relations with Korea, China (both Peking and Taiwan), Southeast Asian nations, Africa, and even Latin America in the postwar years.

The complexity of the Christian situation in postwar Japan is such that we might consider at least three different but often overlapping phases of this tangled affair, seen from three different perspectives: (1) Japanese Christianity seen from the West, (2) Japanese Christianity in its institutional aspect, including its doctrinal development, and (3) Japanese Christianity in its noninstitutional aspects.

JAPANESE CHRISTIANITY THROUGH WESTERN EYES

Japanese Christianity means different things to different people in the West. To some Western Christians, the Japanese Christian situation in the postwar period meant a challenge and/or golden opportunity to engage in vigorous evangelistic, educational, and philanthropic ministries. Many of them recognized that churches and other institutions were now directed by native leaders, and they were willing to work cheerfully and faithfully under Japanese colleagues. Also there were many new groups, such as Evangelicals, who had begun their activities only recently. On the other hand, there were individuals, Catholic and Protestant, from Europe and North America who were reluctant to serve in various capacities if native Japanese personnel were available. They would, however, gladly work in Japan if their special talents, training, or calling—those unavailable among native personnel—could be utilized. Already, many foreign personnel have made great contributions in such areas as education, philanthropy (e.g., KEEP, a combination of educational, medical, and agricultural projects in the Yamanashi highlands), and radio ministry (as successfully initiated by Lutheran groups). Special mention should be made in this connection of the NCC (National Council of Churches) Center for the study of Japanese Religions (Protestant) in Kyoto and the Nanzan Institute for Religion and Culture (Catholic) in Nagoya, which has already sponsored several dialogue sessions between Christian (including Roman Catholic and Protestant) and Buddhist or Shinto groups and has published a series of important studies on the Kyoto school philosophers.[20] Thanks also to Nanzan Institute, there is now for the first time a network of Protestant and Catholic organizations for interreligious encounter in Eastern Asia (e.g., Hong Kong, Indonesia, Japan, Korea, Malaysia, Philippines, Taiwan, and Thailand).[21] These are but a few examples of the many projects for which foreign personnel are exercising their special talents or training, normally not available to people in Japan.

JAPANESE CHRISTIANITY:
THE INSTITUTION AND ITS DOCTRINE

Concerning the institutional aspects of the Japanese Christian community, I have already touched upon the reasons why the Christian (especially Protestant) churches under the leadership of missionaries became tight little communities, confined largely to the middle-class urban intelligentsia before the war. To be sure, the national climate was extremely unfriendly to Christianity, and the authoritarian militarist government was determined to superimpose the emperor cult and the national Shinto on every Japanese subject. Tragically, both Catholic and Protestant leaders buckled under this persistent pressure. In 1936 the papal delegate was instructed by Rome that obeisance at the Shinto shrine was not considered a religious act and as such could be practiced by Japanese Catholics. Meanwhile, Protestant leaders too accepted the government's interpretation that State Shinto was nonreligious in character. Some prominent Protestants even concocted the Christian *norito* (liturgical prayers in the manner of the Shinto tradition). Understandably, after the war some Christians made public repentance for their wartime compromises with militarism, and others—again publicly—accused the wartime church leaders of their shameful submission to the government's pressures. Curiously, shortly before and during the war, an amazing number of Protestant ministers became devotees of Karl Barth, and more specifically, of his eschatology, which, as they understood it, made life in the wartime Japanese state more bearable by stressing that "the real end of Christianity is not on this earth but in the Kingdom of God which does not arrive by man's power but by God's."[22] One realizes, of course, that the Japanese Christian community was small and weak and that it was suspect in the eyes of the government, and thus "psychologically and emotionally, resistance to the state had become for [Japanese Christians] an impossibility."[23] Still it is curious how Japanese Barthians, convinced that they were faithfully following Barth, ignored so completely Barth's public statements on the issues of church and state or the unmistakable thrusts of the Barmen Declaration, even if they could not follow the examples of resistance set by the German and Swiss theologians.

As one looks back at Christian development in Japan since the end of World War II, one cannot help but notice the growing emphases on the notions of church, theology, and mission. Curiously, the combination of these three have had the unexpected effect of boxing in Japanese Christians into sect-type communities (in Troeltsch's sense) with such traits as an exclusivistic in-group consciousness; a subculture dominated by institutional bureaucratization, which appears on the surface as the implementation of a democratic spirit but more often than not is really more of a dissipation of peoples' energy by multiplying committees and meetings; a church-centered outlook, as if the ecclesiastification of the cultural, social, and political orders of Japan were possible today; and a clerical paradigm of the Christian community. Parenthetically, I might add that by clerical paradigm I do not mean to imply that only clerics are active in church affairs, but that their mores and ethos dominate the churches. (I recall one Japanese Christian visitor who, after having attended some church conventions in North America, remarked that he was struck by the fact that church conventions in North America operate with the lawyers' ethos, so that even clergy behave like lawyers, whereas in the Japanese churches, lawyers and businessmen are inclined to behave like ordained ministers.)

This may be an appropriate occasion to interpret the nature of the religious/cultural/social/political synthesis—to which what we call religion provides cosmic legitimation—in terms of three layers: (1) the level of religion in the narrow sense of the term, with its theoretical, practical (liturgical and philanthropic), and ecclesiastical expressions (to use Joachim Wach's favorite phrases[24]); (2) religion as expressed in various aspects of culture; and (3) the religiously oriented or religiously inspired sociopolitical order.[25] Ironically, such a singular preoccupation with church, theology, and mission, as in the case of

Japanese Christianity in postwar Japan, might give some psychological satisfaction to the people involved to the extent that it is able to fit every aspect of life into a coherent pattern inspired by the theology of the mission of the church. However, this is a dangerous illusion based purely on a self-authenticating logic, and not on social, cultural, and political realities.

As far as one can ascertain, this singular preoccupation with the empirical church in postwar Japanese Protestant Christianity may be explained in terms of the convergence of many factors. Chief among them are (a) the residue of the prewar authoritarian government's pressure in establishing a united ecclesiastical structure (because both the government and Christians thought of Christianity only in terms of church structures); (b) the wartime development of sect-type small groups that justified themselves by interpreting theologies of Karl Barth in their own unique ways; and (c) a misunderstanding of Emil Brunner (who taught for two years in postwar Japan), as though he were a second Barth, whereby Japanese Christians thought of Brunner's notion of justice, for example, only in a narrow ecclesiastical context. Once this kind of rigid "church" tradition was established, Japanese Christians interpreted newly imported thoughts only through their ecclesiastical glasses; for example, those of Rudolf Bultmann; Reinhold Niebuhr, who addressed himself to broader social and political issues, transcending ecclesiastical boundaries, and Paul Tillich, who consciously stood on the boundaries between religion and culture. Although their theological vocabularies were greatly enriched by the new heavy emphasis on ethics, thanks to the contribution of John C. Bennett (who visited Japan in 1949), many Japanese Christians tried to fit the contributions of various European and American thinkers primarily into a new mode of Christian ethics. Japanese Christian churches felt encouraged by the ecumenical movement, then in vogue, with its modified Barthian glorification of the church. And finally, there was the abominable ignorance of Japanese Christians concerning the ecclesiastical as well as nonecclesiastical developments of Christian groups in other parts of Asia.

Even when you understand the gentle tyranny of the above mentioned factors, it is still a mystery how so many Japanese Christians failed to understand the thrust of Emil Brunner, who, after all, spent over two years in Tokyo. It was his clearly stated aim to interpret Christianity to the intellectuals in Japan, that is, interpreting Christian approaches to the questions about life and culture in contradistinction to the outlooks of Karl Barth. In his own words:

> In distinction from Karl Barth whose main work is *Die Kirchliche Dogmatik* [Church Dogmatic] . . . my theological thinking was, from the very start, dominated by the endeavor to preach . . . to those outside the Christian Church. . . . This difference between the one who has his eyes fixed on the believers and the [one] who thinks of the non-believers was at the basis of our disputes which began as early as 1917. . . . Maybe the interpretation of the Gospel from the point of view of *philosophy of society and culture* is the special service into which I was called.[26]

I am sure this writer is not the only one who regrets that the Japanese Christian community did not take more advantage of Brunner's contribution when he was so readily available at such a critical time.

Happily, today an increasing number of younger Japanese Christians are breaking out of such narrow theological and ecclesiastical frameworks and actively cooperating with other Asian theologians in their cooperative inquiry. Over ten years ago, a Japanese lay woman theologian, Kiyoko Takeda Chō, stated:

> We are seeking to be freed from our own misunderstanding which has led us to treat Western Christian traditions or Western theologies as universally normative. . . . Often westernized Christian forms have been accepted as being the Christian form. This is due to the Western imperialistic cultural domination and also to the laziness or lack of dignity and effort on the side of receivers in the Third World. We have to be freed from this misunderstanding.[27]

And there are some signs that the Japanese theologians are addressing themselves to, and also from within, their religious, cultural, social, and political contexts. Already, as early as 1960, Carl Michalson spotted Kitamori Kazoh, a young Lutheran and now a member of the United Church (Kyōdan) as the most self-consciously Japanese theologian. In *Theology of the Pain of God*,[28] Kitamori's concern for involvement in the Japanese spiritual experience of suffering enables him to refer to Buddhism as "our tradition," and to him, "suffering is the common term that links God, the Christian faith, and Japanese experience."[29] He believes that pain is the essence of God, insisting, however, that his theology should not be confused with Patripassionism.

Because Kitamori's book is now available in English, we do not have to say too much about its contents at this time. It is worth mentioning, however, that he, being self-conscious both of his Japanese and Christian roots, concerns himself with the relevance of communism in postwar Japan and with the significance of the traditional poetic form *haiku*. He is also sensitive to the relationship that exists between the pain of God and

the Buddhist attitude toward suffering. Undoubtedly, Kitamori was
deeply influenced by his Buddhist Neo-Hegelian teacher Tanabe Hajime,
the advocate of a philosophy of metanoetics, whose work is now available
in English, thanks to the Nanzan Institute mentioned earlier. Tanabe
insists that a metanoia in the "death and resurrection" experience of conversion alone enables one to transcend noetics or metaphysics as speculative philosophy in the realm of subject-object relationship. Thus, rejecting
the Hegelian speculative synthesis "as well as" and Kierkegaardian dichotomy "either/or," Tanabe advocates "neither/nor,"

> a thoroughgoing negativity of our immediate (the repentance of
> one's radical sin) by the mercy of the Absolute, who also negates
> himself for the sake of Love and Mercy. Our repentance of sin means
> the forgiveness and negation of it by the grace of the Absolute. For
> the very reason that God or Buddha is the Absolute Nothingness, He
> is the power and mercy of absolute self-surrender.[30]

Tanabe's influence on Kitamori is evident when the latter holds that,
according to the law, there is a fundamental either/or between God
and man. "But Jesus Christ is the righteous apart from the law. In him
the *either/or* is overcome by a *both/and.*"[31] And, "Christ's acceptance
of *neither/nor* transcends the *either/or*, reconciling *both/and.*"[32] Although I cannot pursue this fascinating subject any longer, I hope it is
sufficiently clear that it is exciting indeed to see a dialogue of this sort
in Japan between Buddhist philosophers, who usually know a great
deal of Western philosophy and Christianity, and some—lamentably
few—articulate Christian theologians, who are at home with Buddhist
and other Asian religious and philosophical traditions.

NONINSTITUTIONAL ASPECTS OF JAPANESE CHRISTIANITY

By noninstitutional aspects, I refer both to the second level of religion,
mentioned above, namely, the facets of culture—values, ideologies, arts,
and imagination—and to the third level, that is, sociopolitical structures and organizations.

    As to Christian activities on the sociopolitical level, we have
seen already how Japanese Christians of the early Meiji era, especially
those ex-Samurais and ex-Confucians, played amazingly active roles as
members of the Diet or government—for example, the ministries of
education, foreign relations, the cultivation of Hokkaidō island, and the
administration of Formosa. They were not particularly "churchy"
Christians; or rather, to them their churchly duties were to reform the

polity of Japan, to enlighten the citizens with the meaning of participation in parliamentary democracy, to improve the status of women, to pioneer a Tolstoyan utopian movement, and to guide labor, peace, and socialist movements. Although these activities were neither understood nor supported by the Western missionaries and Japanese leaders of the institutional denominational churches, who were more concerned with the expansion of institutional churches, the sociopolitical activities of prominent Japanese Christians nevertheless proved to be very effective, especially during the "Taishō democracy." Significantly, during the immediate post–World War II period there were some visible carryovers of the prewar Christian activities in the sociopolitical domain, even though a conservative force began to dominate the Japanese political scene with strong support from the SCAP and Washington. Even then:

> As the Socialist Party reorganized, continuing social Christians such as Tetsu Katayama, Motojirō Sugiyama, Isō Abe, Toyohiko Kagawa, and Bunji Suzuki were among the party leaders and advisors. In 1947, for the first time in Japan's history, the Socialist Party formed the cabinet, with Katayama as premier. As of February, 1948, there were twenty-seven Christian members of the Diet and five Christian cabinet members.[33]

Ironically, after those well-seasoned and tough-minded prewar liberal Christians retired or died (e.g., Abe, Katayama, Kagawa, and Sugiyama), this brand of prominent Christian social activists was no longer available. Instead, the leadership is now in the hands of institutional churches, for example, the *Shakai Mondai Semmon Iinkai* ("Social Problems Committee") of the United Church, founded in 1952. The committee consists of competent and liberal-minded laypeople (mostly scholars) and ministers; some members have been engaged in a series of excellent research projects on social, economic, and political problems, often in close cooperation with various committees of the World Council of Churches in Geneva. But they seem to work only within the framework of the institutional churches. I cannot think of many well-known active, individual Christians operating outside of church boundaries at the present, although there were many before the war and during the immediate postwar period. To cite a few concrete examples: Japanese society will have to deal with the question of Japan's minority groups, such as, the pariahs (*Eta*), the Korean-Japanese, and the Ainus. I fully realize that there are numerous committees and research projects within institutional Christian churches dealing with these problems and that they all say that solutions for these problems must be found eventually. But the question is, How soon is eventually? When the issue of "boat people" was much talked about, we all expected that the churches in Japan would at least discuss the question of refugees, but not a ripple has been heard so far.[34]

It is my personal observation that the scenery has changed a great deal in postwar Japan in regards to what Ishiwara Ken once aptly called the intermediate zone (a sort of halfway house) between institutional and noninstitutional Christian activities, and between the sociopolitical level of religion (category 3) and the sphere of culture (category 2), mentioned above. In depicting the case of the philosopher of religion, Hatano Seiichi, mentioned earlier, as an illustration of the intermediate zone, Ishiwara, emphasizes the relevance of theology more directly than I am inclined to do. According to him:

> Theology in Japan now has the experience, the secure foundation, and the maturity to permit a growing use of the intermediate zone. There is a great deal of guidance, worthwhile material, and intelligence available in Japanese culture for the enrichment of the church and theological thought. Already a widening conversation between Japanese theology and resources of Japanese culture can be observed.[35]

I, on the other hand, tend to stress the importance of Christian public individuals who are motivated by their Christian religion to undertake various nonecclesiastical activities, such as, the broad adult education aiming at solid human characters advocated by such individuals as Nitobe Inazō[36] and Uchimura Kanzō.

In a sense, Uchimura's Non-Church group itself might be regarded as a somewhat churchy movement in the intermediate zone. (Actually, I recall that some leaders of the Non-Church group persistently and courageously criticized the expansionist policies of the authoritarian government throughout World War II.) Of course, many of these individuals, including those already mentioned (e.g., Abe Isoo, Katayama Tetsu, Kagawa Toyohiko, and Sugiyama Motojirō), as well as those who have not been mentioned, such as Nambara Shigeru and Yanaibara Tadao, both of Tokyo University, were well known as Christians, but with the possible exception of Kagawa Toyohiko, most "Christian public individuals" won the respect of Japanese society primarily for their respective public (nonecclesiastical) activities. I personally lament the growing de-emphasis of the relevance of these Christian public individuals, even though I have nothing against the participation of ecclesiastical groups in the works of the intermediate zone, that is, if the church groups really do exert more energy than they seem to be doing today. Take for example such obvious issues as the peace and antinuclear movements. We recognize that a number of church groups, both Catholic and Protestant, are cooperating with these movements now, but their leadership is clearly in the hands of new religious groups (*Shinkō Shūkyō*), especially the Nichiren-related lay Buddhist movements like the *Risshō-Koseikai* and the *Sōka Gakkai.*[37]

As far as I can ascertain, unlike Europe and America, where churches and culture and/or the sociopolitical order have maintained close relationships with each other (so that a Reinhold Niebuhr can preach to a church on Sunday and turn around and address himself to democratic action or the secularization of culture with the assurance that people inside churches and those in society at large have a similar understanding of the meanings of such fundamental notions as justice, order, and charity), in Japan or in any other part of the non-Western world, where cultural traditions and the sociopolitical order have been built on non-Christian and non-Western metaphysical assumptions, the importance of the intermediate zone and of Christian public individuals cannot be underestimated. This is a matter that deserves much more reflection.

Finally, we cannot possibly overlook the relevance of Christians' activities in the domain of culture. It has often been said in Asia that people in India are very sensitive to philosophical matters, whereas Chinese are more ethical and Japanese more aesthetic, and there is a grain of truth in that kind of oversimplified observation. At any rate, considering the fact that Japan has a long tradition of aesthetics-oriented culture, it is amazing how Christianity—both the Roman Catholics in the sixteenth and seventeenth centuries and the Protestants groups in the nineteenth and twentieth centuries—have never exhibited a real understanding and appreciation for the aesthetic or cultural forms of Japan. Unfortunately, native Christians in Japan inherited the missionaries' "unmusicality" in this matter. (As far as I can see, this lamentable situation is not confined to Japan. This is a grossly neglected problem for the entire Asian Christian tradition. Only in recent years, as Takenaka's article on Christian art indicates, has the consciousness of Asian Christians regarding aesthetic-cultural matters been raised.[38]) Parenthetically, I might add that I am not unaware of attempts—some of which are rather successful—at adopting indigenous aesthetic and cultural symbols, idioms, and styles to express Christian meanings; for example, Christmas cards that emphasize Japanese features in the infant Jesus or that put a kimono on Mary, or church buildings that accommodate Shinto or Buddhist characteristics. I am not altogether against such efforts, but these attempts belong to what Sierksma calls "ritual art" or what I think of as ways of using indigenous cultural forms primarily to express Christian religious and theological meanings. Ritual art, according to Sierksma, implies that "its sole or primary meaning is that of religious act, e.g., ritual dance, gesture, music, or that of religious expression, e.g., images visual symbols, painting and architecture." That is all to the good, but that is not my real concern. Rather, it is my hope that Japanese Christians would do what Sierksma calls "religious art" (not a satisfactory expression, I'm afraid). In this category of art, "the meaning of art as ritual act or expression remains, but it also *provokes and allows the artist scope for his own artistic creativity.*"[39] I have used Sierksma's categories to make a point—that the time will soon come when Japanese Christians will participate fully in producing genuine works of art as intricate expressions of their own native Japanese cultural tradition *and* Christianity. No longer will the Japanese Christian have to bear the common accusation of being a "banana," with its yellow skin and white insides.

It might be helpful if I chose a concrete example, namely, the creative writing of Endō Shūsaku, who happens to be a Catholic layman. I have chosen him for my example because he is, first and foremost, a good writer. Besides, many of his novels already have been translated into English, and several perceptive studies of his work are readily available, so that I do not have to translate pertinent passages from his Japanese writings. Also, for our purpose I recommend Jean Higgins' article "East-West Encounter in Endō Shūsaku," for her article reinforces my thesis nicely.[40] In all Endō's writing, two themes interest me deeply: (1) his autobiographical account of his own religious pilgrimage, and (2) his historical novel, especially his work concerning the Roman Catholic missionary work of the seventeenth century, as illustrated by his famous novel *Silence.*[41]

His religious pilgrimage began at the tender age of eleven when his mother embraced Catholicism. As a filial son, he was baptized, but throughout his student days and during his study in France, he felt caught between two diametrically opposed worldviews, the Japanese and the Christian. He felt that at baptism he had been given a ready-made suit that did not really fit him. He envied some of his friends who as adults chose to be converted to Catholicism—freely, as in a love marriage—in contrast to his own case, a sort of arranged marriage. After years of anguish and pain, externalizing his own problems in creative writing, Endō gradually came to the understanding, as Jean

Higgins observes rightly, that "at the heart of the cultural problem of the gulf between Japan and the West lay the religious problem of incompatibility of images of supreme (superior) being and the ramifications of such images for an understanding of the self and cosmos."[42]

Let me now take up the main theme of his novel *Chimmoku* (Silence). The scene is seventeenth century Japan at a time when the Tokugawa feudal regime is proclaiming its ban against Catholicism, which had earlier been presented ably by Francis Xavier and other European missionaries. Many missionaries and thousands of Japanese Catholics, called *Kirishitan*, have been brutally tortured and persecuted. Some of the priests, mostly foreign but some native, have been shipped out of the country—mainly to Macao and to Manila. In 1633, Christovao Ferreira, then the Vice-Provincial of the Society of Jesus in Japan and the administrator of the Japanese Diocese, is arrested; he apostatizes the following month.[43] Renamed Sawano Chūan, he is hired by the feudal government and spends his time criticizing Catholicism as a misguided Western religion; in some cases, he is successful in persuading Japanese *Kirishitans* to renounce their Catholicism. In Endō's novel, Ferreira apostatizes because he can no longer maintain his image of a triumphant, majestic masculine deity of European Christianity as advocated by the Counter-Reformation (brought to Japan by Francis Xavier and his companions). God's absolute "silence" in the midst of the tortured Japanese *Kirishitans'* cries for miraculous rescue is simply too much for him.

In this emotionally charged scene appears Endō's hero, Rodrigues, a young Portuguese Jesuit, and his fellow priests, former students of Ferreira, who after many trials and difficulties arrive in Japan to shepherd the Japanese *Kirishitans*, deprived of clerical guidance, and to find out for themselves what has actually happened to their former teacher. Higgins astutely observes:

> The image of Christ constantly before [Rodrigues'] mind's eye is that of the risen Christ, serene in conquest; a Christ of glory, whose example calls for heroism in his followers, for fidelity unto death, even in martyrdom, if such must be. Rodrigues' God is a judgmental God. Had he not said: "Whoever denies me before men, him will I also deny before my Father who is in heaven." (Matt. 10: 33) He is clearly a God of the strong; a God who would surely banish the betrayer, the apostate, from his sight.[44]

As might be expected, Rodrigues makes every effort to uphold the teachings of the church, hiding from feudal officials in the mountains or in fishing villages while he shepherds and comforts the discouraged faithful. The feudal government soon demands that people walk on the *fumie* (copper tablets of the crucifix) to test whether they are the followers of Christ. Those who hesitate or fail to step on the *fumie* are brutally tortured.

Rodrigues—betrayed by Kichijirō, whom he had tried to help—is arrested. He knows, of course, that Peter had betrayed Jesus three times and was forgiven, and he begins to wonder if even Jesus' love was big enough to forgive Judas, who had betrayed him for a few coins. He sadly comes to learn of the feudal government's plot of severely torturing many *Kirishitan* men, women, and children unless he (Rodrigues) publicly apostates by walking on the *fumie*. His mental agony is further increased by Ferreira's statement to the effect that he too had had a similar experience. Ferreira tells Rodrigues that he (Ferreira) offered ardent prayers to God to rescue those poor victims, but God did nothing for them, whereby Ferreira could no longer preserve his faith in God. In one of the most poignant scenes, Ferreira tells Rodrigues that were Christ himself there, he (Christ) would apostatize out of love for the suffering *Kirishitan*. He gently urges Rodrigues to perform that most painful act of love, stepping on the *fumie*.[45]

Was Ferreira right about God's silence? This is a difficult question. At least Rodrigues is persuaded that even if Christ had kept silent, his (Rodrigues') own life up to that moment had spoken for and about Christ, including Jesus' love toward Peter and Judas. Now, however, he realizes that his long journey from Europe and his exposure to the *mundus imaginalis* of Japan has transformed the image of Jesus from one of the triumphant, majestic king to that of the tired, worn, bony faced man of the *fumie*. He even hears a faint voice speaking to him: "Trample! Trample! It was to be trampled on by [you] that I was born into this world. *It was to share [your] pain that I carried my cross.*"[46] The climax is narrated very simply, reminding us of the gospel account of Peter's betrayal: *Kōshite shisai ga fumie ni ashi o kaketa-toki, asa ga kiga. Niwatori ga tōku de naita.* "When the priest (Rodrigues) stepped on the *fumie*, morning came, and the cock crew in the distance!"[47]

In Endō's novel, Ferreira warns Rodrigues about the price he will have to pay for his so-called apostasy. "The clerics of the church would surely condemn you. You would be driven out by them just as they had judged me and driven me out [of the church]. But what you are about to do is something much larger than the church or mission."[48] The act of liberating Jesus from petty orthodoxy, making it possible for Jesus to carry his cross and share the pains and torments of the people, is somewhat reminiscent of Zen Buddhists' way of killing man-made

Buddhas, Bodhisattvas, and scriptures if they stand in the way of *satori* ("illumination").The Christian religion that Ferreira discovers in the midst of the agony and suffering of the Japanese is a far cry from that of the proud, well-established church of Europe, which vies for power and prestige with earthly kingdoms, and which is exported outside Europe in the name of Christian world mission.

As Higgins poignantly points out:

> When Rodrigues, at Christ's invitation, apostatizes in order to spare Japanese Christians further torture, he renounces all that was previously meaningful to him: his mission, his priesthood, his membership in the Church, his membership in his own religious order, his good name, his Western self-image, his Western conception of God.[49]

Ironically, Endō's *Silence* has been read widely for its implicit theology. Many of my Catholic friends, both clerical and lay, in Japan and in the West, are extremely touchy about what they consider Endō's "heretical" theological views. My hope is, however, that more people will read Endō's *Silence* for what it is, a work of creative writing. That he has his own way of interpreting the meaning of love—both as a Japanese and as a Christian—is very apparent. It is clear, however, that Endō here is writing a novel, not a B-class book of theology or apologetics. On the other hand, in writing this novel, especially in creating such characters as those of Ferreira and Rodrigues, Endō discovers for himself (and others) a new way of being true to the Japanese and Christian traditions. In so doing, Endō presents a good example of how Japanese Christians can contribute to the domain of aesthetic culture without appropriating indigenous cultural forms, symbols, and idioms merely for the sake of Christian propaganda.

I should make it clear that my outlook for the Christian situation of Japan is neither very optimistic nor hopelessly pessimistic. Like it or not, Christianity in modern Japan has developed primarily as an urban, middle class intellectual's religion. As early as 1959, Charles Iglehart characterized it in this way: As "cosmopolitan, international, enlightened, ethical and rational, it commends itself to the movable class in the cities. [And yet] neither the people of the villages nor the workers in the cities have been deeply reached, much less won."[50] Iglehart admitted then, in theory at least, that Christian thinking must widen its base "from that of the traditional formulations of the West to include insights offered by Japan's own great truth-seekers and spiritual geniuses of the past."[51] I am inclined to add two other recommendations: (1) a singular ecclesiastical approach without contributing anything to the domains of culture and the sociopolitical order of Japan will be a fatal mistake, and (2) the Christian tradition in Japan must recognize itself as an integral part of the Asian Christian tradition. Only with the cooperation of Christian and non-Christian religious and cultural traditions—those in Asia, but eventually with those of Africa, Latin America, and Europe—can it make relevant contributions ultimately to *Die Bestimmung des Menschen.*

II

AMERICAN
EXPERIENCE
THROUGH
THE EYES OF
ASIAN-AMERICANS

5

THE SAGA OF
ASIAN-AMERICANS

MYTHS ABOUT ASIANS

All Americans trace their ancestry to other parts of the world, except, of course, for the Native-Americans. Historically, most European immigrants have largely managed to merge into the American scene, because they did not encounter a serious and enduring race problem. In the case of non-European immigrants, however, the situation seems to be quite different. Their rate of absorption has been rather slow and has been hindered by curious fictitious myths developed from figments of the imagination. Considering the fact that the total number of persons of Asiatic descent, for example, is negligible, it is simply astonishing that the myths about Asians have been so widespread and so carelessly accepted by many people even today. Although many persons admit that they have never had firsthand contact with persons of Asiatic ancestry, they are convinced that Asians constitute problems because "Mrs. Jones told us that Mr. Smith said Mrs. Henry informed him, saying Mr. Adams had mentioned that he heard Mrs. Johnson relate . . ." Professional race-baiters, yellow news journals, and cheap movies provide these gullible folks with abundant tales and incidents concocted out of sheer imagination. These myths about Asians—like so-called scientific theories about other ethnic and racial groups—are kept alive in the minds of the people by ignorance.

The question as to how any fictitious myth develops is an interesting and complex problem. Some time ago, novelist Franz Werfel described the process of myth making in The Song of Bernadette. According to his novel, a young girl of Lourdes claimed one day that she saw "a lady in white with a blue girdle and a golden rose upon each foot." Immediately, villagers assumed that the lady in question was no other than the Blessed Virgin, despite the cautious attitude of the officials of the church on the subject. The author seems to speak through one Monsieur Hyacinthe de Lafite. "I feel that all you men miss the essential point. The true problem is offered not so much by the little visionary as by the great crowd that follows her."[1] Similar observations may be made concerning the myths about Asians in America. No doubt, Asians, like other immigrant groups in this country, have had their share of problems among themselves as well as with others. However, we might say, paraphrasing Franz Werfel, that the true problem is provided not so much by the tiny group of Asiatic immigrants as by the rest of the people who accept the myths about Asians.

Once myths about Asians are created, the general public expects Asians to play the roles that fit into the mythical image. Asians are said to be submissive, shrewd, secretive, enigmatic, industrious, and clannish. Although Asian immigrants encounter less discrimination than some other immigrant groups in American society, they are nevertheless subjected to persistent and stereotyped labels and categorical judgments. In short, many people expect Asians not to be individual persons, but rather to be predictable categories, such as farmers, gardeners, laundry operators, shopkeepers, owners of Chop Suey and Sukiyaki restaurants, and so forth. Indeed, like all myths about racial groups, myths about Asians have little or no reference to specific cases or persons.

Furthermore, mythmakers and myth believers constantly confuse in their minds (a) Asians who are actually from Asia and are temporarily visiting this country, such as diplomats, representatives of business firms, exchange professors and students, and short-term travelers; (b) Asiatic immigrants from China, Korea, Japan, the Philippines, and Southeast Asian countries, who are permanently settled in this country (many of whom are now naturalized citizens), and (c) American children born of Asian parentage. Also, a number of ex-GIs had married Asian war brides, while some other people adopted Asian children, thus making the problem all the more complex.

In the last 150 years, many prominent individuals from Asia, such as Hideki Yukawa, nuclear physicist who taught at Columbia

University, have found a second home in America. However important they were, these persons did not represent the "Asian problem" in America. To understand clearly the problems facing Asians in this country, the primary concern must be with the Asiatic immigrants and their descendants.

At the risk of oversimplification, I will discuss this matter in the following three stages: (1) the problems of the Asiatic immigrants, spanning a time interval roughly from the middle of the last century to the early 1920s; (2) the problems of Asian-Americans, that is, American citizens of Asiatic ancestry, and their relationship to their immigrant parents and the American society at large, which covers a period from the 1920s to World War II; and (3) the complicated problems of Asiatic immigrants and Americans of Asian descent in the period following the end of World War II.

Historically, the Asiatic immigrants first settled in Hawaii and on the West Coast. Consequently, their problems were considered as a local issue on the one hand, and as complicated by legal and international considerations on the other. All in all, the problems of Asiatic immigrants and Asian-Americans are not only political, legal, and economic, but they also involve social and cultural dimensions.

After World War II, the coming of many refugees, especially Koreans following the Korean War and those from Vietnam, Cambodia, and Laos following the Vietnam War, added many new wrinkles to the already bewildering problems of Asian-American communities. It must also be pointed out that an increasing number of Americans are becoming Asia-conscious. Whereas before the war, the public expected only eccentrics, scholars, and missionaries to love Asia, today it has become fashionable and respectable for average citizens to be versed on things Asian, and although this new trend is in many ways desirable from the standpoint of international and intercultural understanding, it has added some confusion in the minds of many Americans who have enough difficulty in differentiating the "Asians among us" from the "Asians across the ocean." In fact, the current vogue about Asia often expects Americans of Asian ancestry to be ready to appear in Asian dress and interpret Asian cultures. The Asian-Americans' knowledge about Asia is far from reliable in many cases, and some of them have a definite emotional bias against the cultures of their immigrant parents. Thus it should be borne in mind that the current (postwar) myths about Asia and Asians are equally as dangerous as the traditional myths about Asians among us.

ASIATIC IMMIGRANTS

The Land of Aloha

The kingdom of Hawaii, before its annexation to the United States in 1900, was known as a haven for shipwrecked Asiatic fishermen. Situated at the crossroads of the Pacific, Hawaii attracted Chinese, Koreans, South Sea Islanders, Filipinos, Japanese, as well as some Europeans. We are told that in 1879 the population of Hawaii was only 57,985. That year, the United States won the right to import sugar through a reciprocal treaty, and American sugar interests began actively to recruit Asiatic labor, particularly Japanese. The census of 1900, after the annexation of Hawaii to the United States, reported the population of the Hawaiian islands as approximately 154,000, including 37,000 Hawaiians and part-Hawaiians, 28,000 Caucasians, 5,000 Chinese, and 61,000 Japanese.

The overwhelming majority of Asiatic immigrants worked as plantation laborers, although in time many became shopkeepers in the cities, too. Life on the plantation was anything but easy, yet these new immigrants accepted menial tasks and hard labor with patience, fortitude, and determination. During the latter part of the nineteenth century, the planters were extremely satisfied with the hardworking and cheap Asiatic laborers, but gradually the immigrants' determination to rise economically began to threaten the planters' vested interests. The workers' industriousness had been praised as long as it did not aspire to more than a laborer's reward. But once the workers had begun to better themselves, their traits, which had been praised as virtues, became threats to the dominant group. Because Hawaii had allowed more freedom to Asiatic immigrants than did the continental United States, private sentiment of the *Haole* ("wealthy whites") toward Asians became increasingly negative; and it was the views of the *Haole* that carried weight in the political domain. Hawaiian statehood was resisted for many years by the combined efforts of entrenched business interests in the islands and crafty politicians in the continental United States. Thus, for many years—for much too long—neither laws nor education made it possible for the Asiatics in Hawaii to enter a voting booth.

The West Coast

Asiatic immigrants began to arrive at the West Coast after the Civil War. From that time on, the U.S. immigration policy, which once had been relatively free from discrimination on account of race or color, became increasingly biased against nonwhite immigrants. The first

Asiatic immigrants to come to America were Chinese. Records show that there were fewer than one hundred Chinese in the United States before the middle of the nineteenth century. Following the gold rush in California in 1849, however, railroad builders and gold prospectors actively recruited and welcomed Chinese immigrants as a source of cheap labor. But as soon as business waned, the welcome turned into racial animosity. The Burlingame Treaty of 1868, which gave Chinese subjects in the United States the rights of citizens of the most-favored nation, was soon abrogated by congressional action. Between 1860 and 1890, California politicians used the Chinese immigrants as a political issue, both within the state and in Congress. A bill was passed by Congress in 1870 to exclude Chinese laborers, but it was vetoed by the president. In 1882, Congress passed an act to suspend Chinese immigration for ten years, and this policy was extended for another ten years by an act passed in 1892. In 1902, this exclusionary policy became permanent.

Pattern of Discrimination

In retrospect, we can understand why West Coast pressure groups were so successful in their campaign against the Chinese immigrants. Because China's prestige was at its lowest ebb in the international sphere, America's discrimination against Chinese immigrants did not result in international repercussions. In the domestic scene, politicians from the West Coast and the southern states were allied in Congress in promoting anti-Chinese and anti-Black measures during the period following 1876. But more basically, the success of the California politicians was due to the general unfamiliarity of the public with the plight of the Chinese immigrants. The public regarded the Chinese problem as a localized West Coast issue, and the average citizen naïvely accepted the propaganda of California politicians as the truth. Mr. Justice Field, persuaded by California pressure groups, pronounced—as though he was an authority on the Chinese problem—that Chinese "remained strangers in the land, residing apart by themselves, and adhering to the customs and usages of their own country. It seemed impossible for them to assimilate with our people or to make any change in their habits or modes of living."[2] It was on such an extralegal basis that the Chinese were denied the right to citizenship through naturalization. Moreover, the Chinese person "was held ineligible to testify in any case in a court of law for or against a white person; he was subject to special heavy taxes; he could not vote; he was excluded from schools" (10). The Chinese were made the scapegoat for business slumps as well as the cause of crime waves. Behind every problem, so the California politicians argued, was the menace of the Chinese, and the American government and public accepted these fabricated myths about the Chinese. And once the vicious and effective pattern of discrimination against one Asiatic group was successfully established, protected by a legal facade and abetted by the press, the West Coast pressure groups applied the same techniques against Japanese, Korean, Filipino, and other Asiatic immigrants as well.

Legal Myths

It is well known that the 1790 naturalization act stipulated that any free white alien was eligible to become a citizen of this Republic, and that the statute was enlarged to include Blacks in 1870. In 1922, the Supreme Court declared that Japanese were ineligible for naturalization because they belonged to the "Mongolian" race. Mr. Justice Sutherland, speaking for a unanimous Court, interpreted the 1790 naturalization act to mean that only members of the white race were eligible for citizenship (in spite of the fact that "Blacks" were included later into the de facto "white" category). In this connection, Milton R. Konvitz points out that there are three ways of interpreting the term "white": (1) white signifies a color quality; (2) it refers to people of the original race stock called "Caucasian" or "Aryan"; or (3) it embraces only the European peoples. Clearly, the 1922 Supreme Court decision settled on the theory of race regardless of color. In that same year, however, dealing with a case involving a high-caste Hindu, the Supreme Court declared that a Hindu, even though he belongs to the Caucasian "race," is not eligible for citizenship. The same Mr. Justice Sutherland, again speaking for a unanimous Court, unashamedly reversed the reasoning of the previous case and came to the strange conclusion that a person may be Caucasian and not white on the ground that "the words of the statute are to be interpreted with the understanding of the common man from whose vocabulary they were taken" (89). One admires the amazing flexibility and legal ingenuity of those justices!

Even more irrational was the basis on which the Filipinos were excluded from naturalization. As American nationals, the Filipinos were not aliens; however, in the eyes of the law, they were not citizens. The 1870 naturalization act, which could transform an outsider into a citizen, was applicable only to aliens, so the legal mythmakers concluded that the Filipinos were ineligible (93). Thus, before World War II,

Asiatic immigrants were held to be ineligible for naturalization either because of race, color, or because they were not aliens.

Chinatowns and Little Tokyos

Despite the legal, social, economic, political, and cultural barriers that confronted them, the Asiatic immigrants managed to survive somehow both in the Hawaiian islands and on the West Coast from the latter part of the nineteenth century to the 1920s. At first, the majority of immigrants were laboring-class males, many of whom were "birds of passage," eager to make quick money and then return to their homes in Asia. Unfamiliar with their new environment, American mores, and the English language, the pioneers of Asiatic immigration experienced unspeakable hardships. As was true with all other immigrants, the Asiatics were destined to start their life at the bottom of the scale. Many of them were under contract to recruiters who demanded unreasonable commissions from their meager rewards, which were earned in the main from farm labor, dishwashing, and railroad gang work. Although they had heard fabulous tales about "easy money" in America before leaving Asia, the immigrants soon discovered that it would take years before they could save enough money even for their return passage. As their first hopes of "getting rich quick" gave way to the reality of the situation, the Asiatic immigrants began to settle down enough to make everyday living in America possible. Women began arriving as picture brides, with high hopes of finding their husbands or fiancés successful and comfortable. They too soon sobered up from their daydreams. Although beset by such trying conditions, or more likely because of them, family life became the source of their strength. And, with the increase of family groups, the immigrants soon felt the need to create some kind of community life for themselves.

In this effort, the Asiatic immigrants received no assistance from the consular officials of their countries of origin, for these officials looked down on the immigrants because the latter had deserted their homelands. Thus, virtually abandoned by their native governments and ignored by American officials, the immigrants had to develop their own community life, as exemplified by Chinatowns or Little Tokyos. At least in their own communities, the immigrants were not refused service in restaurants and barbershops, or accommodations in hotels or boardinghouses. Their wives could depend on the services of midwives and could borrow a cup of sugar from a neighbor, for instance, without embarrassing language difficulties.

The problems of the immigrant-parents became harder and more complex when the children began to grow up. It is to be noted that their children, born in this country, were American citizens. How were these offspring to be raised and educated? This was a great concern for the immigrants. For a long time, most of the parents had no way of knowing what the future held for them or for their children. One thing was certain: The children were to attend American schools. However, because many parents wanted their children to grow up with at least some appreciation of the cultures of the old countries, they used a part of their scant income to establish language schools (e.g., Chinese or Japanese) that operated after regular school hours. Little did those parents realize that their American-born children would grow up with an emotional bias against the "old country" cultures!

Religious Activities

If the Asiatic immigrants' problems of adjustment to their life in America were ignored by the governments on both sides, they were equally neglected by the religious groups—Buddhist, Shinto, Taoist, and Christian—during the initial period. Many immigrants maintained some type of religious devotion at home, mostly of their ancestral families, but organized religious activities among immigrant groups were few and far between. With the establishment of community life, however, various religious groups started their temples, shrines, and churches, served often by itinerant clergy. Because most immigrants did not come from the higher strata of Asian societies, their education, let alone religious training, was very limited, but many of them were eager to learn. Gradually, religious institutions within the Asiatic communities began to play an important role as religious, as well as social, recreational, and cultural centers of community life. Many religious institutions operated nursery and language schools, and offered classes in English, sewing, cooking, and so forth.

The Christian activities among the Asiatic immigrants had several dimensions: first, interpreting America and American Christian churches to the immigrants; second, interpreting the Asiatic immigrants to Americans, more particularly to the churches; third, providing the immigrants with social, cultural, recreational, and welfare activities; and fourth, meeting the spiritual needs of the immigrants. In my opinion, most churches failed miserably in the first and second objectives, and used the third primarily as "bait" for the fourth. Christian churches in America, for the most part, shared the indifference of the general public; in fact, some ardent church members on the West Coast were also noted for their anti-Asiatic campaigns. There were, of course, some individuals, notably Sidney Gulick, who were vocal about problems of Asiatic immigrants. Their chief interests were not with the immigrants' welfare, however, but more with international political issues pertaining to China, Japan, Korea, and the Philippines. By and large, Christian leaders— Asiatic and American—who worked directly among the immigrants stressed personal salvation, revivalistic campaigns, the temperance movement, and rigid moralism. They had little appreciation or understanding of the frustrations and difficulties being experienced by the immigrants as they sought to adjust themselves to life in America. Ironically, the program of some Christian groups among the Asiatic immigrants was regarded de facto as an extension of "foreign" missionary work.

There were three different, but related, problems about the Christian work among Asiatic immigrants: (1) lack of adequate financial resources, (2) lack of personnel, and (3) total absence of overall programs as well as imagination and understanding of the nature of the issues of immigration in America. The perennial lack of financial resources resulted in (a) the poorly organized services of poorly trained volunteers, (b) more emphasis on such self-supporting programs as language school, flower arrangement, and so forth, at the expense of spiritual ministry, or (c) dependence on donations from well-to-do (but bigoted) white Americans who dictated churches' policies.

The lack of personnel often led churches to turn to missionaries to Asia on furloughs or retired ex-missionaries, people who rarely understood the unique problems of Asiatic immigrants in the hostile West Coast (or Hawaii for that matter). Often theological students or young clergy from Asia were asked to spend a few years on their way to or from American seminaries to minister to churches among Asian communities. Of course, they had no appreciation of the situation pertaining to immigrants and their children. Obviously, such makeshift approaches further complicated the already bewildering church work among the Asiatic immigrant communities.

ASIAN-AMERICANS

Marginal Groups

All of us as social beings live in multiple groups. Any person may be a member of one or more groups, depending on the complexity of the social situation in which that individual lives. In our society there are many groups, each having more or less cohesive relationships among its members. The individual becomes a social being as a result of that person's integration into the family, the school, company, shop, and other social and occupational groups. The individual incorporates into his or her personality the experience within these groups and the expectations of behavior that he or she shares with its members. In the course of time, the individual organizes within himself or herself various kinds of shared expectations of behavior, and that individual begins to understand his or her role and status in society. It is to be noted in this connection that the racial group plays an important role in determining for those who are its members their status in American society. The individual who does not belong to the dominant white group, regardless of his or her achievements in other areas of life, becomes what is known as the "marginal person."

Like it or not, Americans of Asian ancestry were destined to be born and raised in the racially segregated community of their immigrant parents. In most places on the West Coast, economic and social pressures as well as restrictive covenants forced the Asiatic immigrants to remain "marginal groups." This, in turn, was used as evidence of "unassimilable-ness." Their immigrant parents, labeled as ineligible for naturalization by American law, had of necessity resorted to the racially segregated pattern of community life. Their communities provided for them something of a haven in the midst of the surrounding prejudice and discrimination of the larger American society. However, with their children, the situation was much more complicated and tragic.

Asian-Americans, born here and educated in American schools, are culturally Occidental even though they are racially Asiatic. The tragedy of Asian-Americans, like other marginal individuals, is that they are responsive to the values of the dominant group, which nevertheless rejects them on the ground of racial background. Like children of other immigrants, many children of Asian immigrants react against the culture of their parents and share the values and goals of the dominant group in American society, even though they are not accepted by the invisible establishment of their own society. In this connection, most people accept the three phases of the life cycle of the marginal individual in the United States. The first phase is one in which the individual is not aware of his or her minority-group status. The second phase is one in which the individual becomes aware of his or her marginality. The third phase encompasses the longer period of the more permanent adjustments, or lack of them. All Asian-Americans are bound to experience these three stages to a greater or lesser extent.

In their childhood, Asian-Americans are exposed to an admixture of Eastern and Western cultures. Soon they grow up as full-fledged American kids, because of the influence of public schools and their relationships with children of other races outside their homes. In the main, hostility in the social sphere does not become noticeable until adolescence. By that time, ironically, they realize self-consciously that they are inwardly very American, mentally, psychologically, and psychically, but they also realize—externally—that they are expected to keep away from the normal social life of the wider American society. After several bitter experiences of being refused by barbers, restaurants, or hotels, the fear of being humiliated in public tends to draw them together in the racially segregated community of their parents, the very community they detest.

Psychological Ghetto

We earlier noted that the Asian communities on the West Coast came into existence because of a number of factors—cultural, political, legal, social, and economic. Now we must consider the significance of these communities as "psychological ghettos" as well.

At the outset, it must be recognized that the segregated community had many positive meanings for first-generation Asiatic immigrants. Barred from naturalization, denied participation in the broader social and communal life, they felt they had to establish a community of their own. In a sense, they had every reason to be proud of their success in establishing security for themselves and for their wives and children in a new world whose welcome was less than ardent. And these Asiatic immigrants, like all other immigrants, managed to live with two (American and Asian) sets of perception and behavior. For the most part, in their dealings with non-Asian and/or other Asian groups, they depended on American business codes and practices. In their own home and community life, however, they resorted to their respective traditional values and customs, such as the conception of society as one large family, the patriarchical and male-dominated family organization, and family customs at birth, marriage, and death. They tried to solve the problem of their children's education by sending them to public schools and providing them with vernacular-language schools after regular school hours. All in all, these segregated communities were products of the ability and imagination of the immigrants in their efforts to solve their social dilemma in America, and they gave unstintingly to establish their own communal life.

The emotional insecurity of their American-born children, as in the cases of many other hyphenated Americans, was chiefly caused by the citizen children's realization that they were self-consciously Americans, even though they were not warmly accepted by American society. At the same time, they were not understood by their parents, and they were not basically at home in the racially segregated communities. At public schools, they were indoctrinated about the rights and privileges of American citizenship, although many of their non-Asiatic classmates did not accept them fully as Americans. In their own homes, they did not understand or appreciate fully the language and ways of their immigrant parents. Whereas the immigrant parents took the traditional Asian concept of filial piety for granted, the children's response was based on the American principle of individual initiative.

The relationship between the immigrant parents and their citizen children became increasingly more complex as the latter finished their high school education. Many Asian-American youths aspired to professional careers, yet they were aware that American business practices meant that as Asian-Americans they tended to be the last ones hired and the first ones fired. Ironically, in the meantime they were expected to become the legal owners of their family farms or businesses, because their "alien parents" were unable to hold legal titles because of discriminatory restrictions. And yet, the citizen children, despite the fact that they were the "legal employers" of their parents, were expected to acknowledge parental authority. More ironically, many Asian-Americans reached their adulthood or early adulthood at the time of the Great Depression. Accordingly, even those who had professional training either had to accept menial, nonprofessional positions such as gardener, cannery-hand, and houseboy, or they had to work on their family farms and/or in family businesses. Because Asian-Americans proved too thoroughly American to become "reverse immigrants" to Asia, they were compelled to find a realistic compromise in their home situations in Hawaii and on the West Coast. Thus it was common to see during the 1930s a graduate engineer working as an auto mechanic, or a plant pathologist working in a nursery. Many others went back grudgingly to the trades of their parents as a last resort.

Sense of Belonging

The first generation of Asiatic immigrants encountered discrimination primarily because they were (a) a foreign-language speaking group, (b) a non-Western cultural group, and (c) a racial group with an identifiable physical identity that was different from white or black Americans. Thus, for them, segregated racial communities offered a semblance of security essential for the well-being of any human being.

Once the pattern of prejudice and discrimination against the Asiatic immigrants developed on the West Coast, based on the three primary reasons mentioned above, the same pattern of bias was carried over to their children, that is, Asian-Americans who were English-speaking people and ardent upholders of American culture. Tragically, Asian-Americans endured discrimination solely on account of their racial physical identity. Also, American society, which accused Asian-Americans of being clannish, had mortal fear of mixed marriages. In fact, miscegenation laws have affected Asian-Americans in many states until very recently. For instance, California at one time barred marriages of white women and Mongolians; Oregon also prohibited white-Mongolian marriages; Utah and Wyoming had laws prohibiting marriages of white persons (both male and female) with Malaysians and Mongolians. Actually, the miscegenation matter was not too crucial a problem because many Asian Americans married among themselves (at least until recently). Far more serious was the discrimination in housing, employment, and social life. In addition, Asian-Americans were made to feel as though they were perpetual tourists—being looked at and remarked upon—in their own country.

Where and how should they find the sense of belonging? This indeed was a crucial question in the minds of Asian-Americans in the late 1920s and 1930s. There were a minority among Asian-Americans who advocated an immediate integration into American society by leaving the segregated communities on the West Coast. But, in order to do this, they needed adequate professional training, freedom from family obligations, and proper contacts—a combination not easily available to many. There were some who looked for job opportunities in business firms that require knowledge of two languages. Unfortunately, most Asian-Americans had only a smattering of the language of their parents, and in any case, such opportunities were very limited. For the majority of Asian-Americans, there was no easy way out. Gradually, and only gradually, did many of them begin to realize the painful fact that their American citizenship did not automatically guarantee equality of opportunity, and that they had to "earn" the rights and privileges of citizenship. Thus, slowly they began to assume a more active role in the Democratic or Republican parties, in citizenship league movements, and in labor unions. Paradoxically, those who were born in the continental United States were more ardently American in their cultural orientation but less at ease in their manners than their Hawaiian-born cousins—due probably to the greater prejudice directed against them. In the main, however, both in the Hawaiian islands and on the West Coast, Asian-Americans went as far as prejudice in society would permit them in assuming the place that American ideals assured them was theirs.

A few words might be added about the efforts of religious groups—mostly Buddhist, Catholic, and Protestant—that tried to help the soul-searching and maturing process of Asian-Americans in the 1920s and 1930s. Indeed, these groups did help interpret the immigrant parents to their citizen children, and vice versa. But these religious groups were originally set up to meet the needs of the Asiatic immigrants and could not easily be transformed to become adequate centers of activities primarily for Americans of Asiatic ancestry. The clergy, elders, and non-Asiatic volunteers made various attempts to keep young Asian-Americans in respective religious groups, and although these religious groups provided opportunities for boys and girls to meet, many young people dropped out of sight after marriage. Christian groups also attempted to create occasional fellowships with non-Asiatic church groups, but usually a polite air of sociability dominated such occasions. In fact, enduring friendships crossing racial lines, even within the same Christian denominational groups, were very rare. Curiously, there were not many attempts to create fellowship occasions within an individual Asian-American community. More successful were gatherings of Buddhist or Christian groups within the same racial context but in different localities. In general, these religious activities cemented, rather than loosened or transcended, racial solidarity of segregated Asian-American communities.

THE ASIAN-AMERICAN SITUATION SINCE WORLD WAR II

The situation of Asian-Americans has become infinitely more complex during the fifty years 1940–1990, and we can only briefly touch on two main phases: (1) World War II and (2) the Korean and Vietnam Wars. These wars and their aftermaths affected the destinies of Asian-Americans a great deal.

During World War II

Understandably, World War II, and more particularly the warfare in the Pacific zone, spotlighted the problem of Americans of Asiatic descent and of their parents, who had remained aliens because they were ineligible for naturalization according to American law. It is not surprising, therefore, that the undercurrents of pro- and anti-Asiatic sentiment, which were stalemated in the 1930s, particularly on the West Coast, came to the fore with the outbreak of war. On the positive side, we can cite the repeal of the Chinese exclusion laws; on the negative side, we can cite the tragedy of the mass evacuation of all persons of Japanese descent, including a large number of American citizens, without any due process of law, from their homes on the West Coast to incarceration in ten camps (de facto internment camps).

During the war, the problem of Chinese aliens, who had been declared ineligible for naturalization by American law, presented an embarrassment to the United States, which considered China an important ally during World War II. In short, Congress—recognizing the importance of goodwill between China and the United States—repealed the Chinese exclusion laws in 1943. Although the 1943 repeal act had some discriminatory features, it was nevertheless a step in the right direction, characterized by President Roosevelt as an act to correct a historical mistake. The repealing of the Chinese exclusion laws, the enactment of legislation authorizing a Chinese immigration quota of 105—which after all was not such an astronomical number—and the granting of U.S. citizenship to permanent Chinese resident aliens through naturalization encountered very stubborn resistance and active protests in Congress. Milton Konvitz characterizes the temper of many members of Congress through the statement of Congressman Elmer of Missouri, who said:

> "You enact this law and you have taken off the stakes and riders of the immigration fence. It will be easy to push down the rest of it. Raise it higher, strengthen it more, close the gaps. Make it like the Missouri lawful fence: horse-high, bull-strong, and pig-tight."

What the congressman objected to was the implication that the United States had been wrong for about sixty years in enforcing the exclusion act. "'We were not wrong. The Chinese people . . . had previously been called Chinese devils. When did the Chinese devils become saints?'" (29). On the other hand, Earl G. Harrison, the Commissioner of Immigration and Naturalization, urged the repeal of all racial barriers to immigration on two grounds: (1) such repeal would admit not more than one thousand immigrants from all Asian countries, and (2) the only nation in the whole world outside the United States that enforces racial discrimination relating to naturalization was Nazi Germany, and in his opinion, "this is not very desirable company" (81).

As to the Japanese aliens and Japanese-Americans, I intend to make references to them in other sections of this book. It is important, however, to include some observations here. For the most part, the Japanese immigrants were confused and frightened in the weeks following Pearl Harbor. Former friends turned on them with suspicion. Business practically stopped at their stores, and many lost jobs overnight. Various West Coast groups, such as the California Joint Immigration Committee, the Native Sons of the Golden West, and the Hearst press, which had for years agitated against the Japanese on the West Coast, were quick to take advantage of war hysteria and to translate it into political action to evacuate the Japanese. Although German, Italian, and Japanese aliens against whom there were grounds for suspicion had been rounded up by the Department of Justice soon after the outbreak of war, such measures did not satisfy the hate-Japanese groups. Not only did they cry for the evacuation of alien Japanese, they also agitated for the removal of all American citizens of Japanese descent. According to the strange logic of the then Attorney General of California, Earl Warren (later Chief Justice of the Supreme Court), the absence of sabotage in the early months of the war was a positive indication that Japanese-Americans had plans for a program of concerted sabotage. (This was his famous thesis of concerted sabotage.[3]) The climax came early in 1942, when the Commanding General of the Western Defense Command, John L. DeWitt, ordered all persons of Japanese ancestry— 110,000 of them, mostly American citizens—to be removed from their homes on the West Coast on grounds of military necessity: "The Japanese race is an enemy race. While many second and third generation Japanese, born on United States soil, possessed of United States citizenship, have become Americanized, the racial strains are undiluted."[4]

The mass evacuation of all persons of Japanese ancestry on the West Coast was a tragic, and yet logical, result of race prejudice and fictitious legal myths—and was not based on "military necessity," as was claimed by General DeWitt. In sharp contrast, General Emmons of Hawaii, who was in the center of the war zone, cautioned against war hysteria in reference to persons of Japanese ancestry in Hawaii, by declaring:

> Hawaii has always been an American outpost of friendliness and good will and now has calmly accepted its responsibility as an American outpost of war. . . . [I]f the courage of the people of these islands is to be maintained and the morale of the entire population sustained, we cannot afford to unnecessarily and indiscriminately keep a number of loyal workers from useful employment.[5]

Evidently, the legal myths that were the stock in trade of politicians and pressure groups did not persuade some jurists. Said Mr. Justice Murphy, defying the claims of the White House, congressional leaders, and the military:

> Distinctions based on color and ancestry are utterly inconsistent with our traditions and ideals. They are at variance with the principles for which we are waging war. . . . To say that any group cannot be assimilated is to admit that the American experiment failed, that our way of life has failed when confronted with the normal attachment of certain groups to the lands of their forefathers.[6]

As Morton Grodzins points out, "The evacuation was a major event in the history of American democracy, without precedent in the past and with disturbing implications for the future."[7] The evacuation was particularly disturbing to Japanese-Americans, for if such a measure could be taken against them under any pretext, it could happen to any group of citizens as well. Thus Japanese-Americans took their duty as citizens with utter seriousness, not only because they were consciously fighting the enemy at the front, but also because they had to fight against the creation of two classes of citizens at home—those of the dominant majority and those of marginal groups. The 100th and 442nd Infantry battalions, which were composed of Japanese-Americans—many of whom had volunteered from the camps into which they had been thrust—are examples of this fact. (There were a sizable number of Japanese-Americans serving in various branches of the armed forces in the Pacific Theater, as well.) Thanks to the patriotism of Japanese-Americans and other Asian-Americans, gradually the prejudice against persons of Asiatic ancestry began to be counterbalanced by a sense of fair play. For example, through the efforts of religious groups and citizens groups in cooperation with the War Relocation Authority of the Department of Interior, persons of Japanese ancestry were able to leave the camps and resettle in various parts of American society even before V-J Day in 1945.

In the Period Following World War II

The makeup of Asian-American groups since World War II, especially during and after the Korean and Vietnam Wars, has undergone tremendous changes, partly because many new immigrants, refugees, and asylum seekers have been added to the ranks of prewar Asiatic immigrants and Asian-Americans. Clearly, the ever-changing drama of the international scene—from the independence of the Philippines and the rise of Mao Tse-tung in Mainland China to the Russian withdrawal from Afghanistan and the Tiananmen tragedy—has had direct bearing on the posture of Asian-Americans in the United States.

In 1946, with the independence of the Philippines from American political control, the new Philippine republic was given an annual immigration quota of 100, and a similar quota was also given to India. Meanwhile, the United States, which was chiefly responsible for the occupation of defeated Japan, radically changed its occupation policy from creating a "Switzerland in Asia" to that of establishing an "antiCommunist citadel in the Pacific." In 1948, the Communists' victory in China, which drove Chiang Kai-shek's party to Taiwan, changed China from a close ally to an antidemocratic menace. With the outbreak of the Korean War in 1950, the United States had to depend on Japan both as a military base and a supplier of arms. I might add that the Korean War saw the beginning of economic recovery in Japan, and it also marked the beginning of a sizable number of Korean immigrants, war brides, and refugees. In 1952, under the terms of the Immigration and Naturalization Act (Walter-McCarran Bill), Japan was given an annual quota of 185. Although these figures are numerically very small and insignificant, they are important symbols in counterbalancing the discriminatory measures of the pre–World War II period, which effectively had prohibited the immigration and naturalization of Asiatics for decades. Then, the Refugee Relief Act of 1953 allocated 3,000 visas for East Asian refugees, 2,000 to Chinese, 4,000 to orphans under ten years of age, and 5,000 more to those who came under the category of "Adjustment of Status." Incidentally, of a grand total of 326,867 immigrants from all over the world during the fiscal year 1957, there were only 23,102 from all Asian countries, and a large number of Asiatic immigrants were nonquota immigrants, such as wives and husbands of U.S. citizens.

The prolonged Vietnam War (1955–1975), which had expanded into Cambodia and Laos as well, is conservatively estimated to have cost about $200 billion for the United States alone, resulting in "high inflation, recession, unemployment, and slow growth in many sectors of the U.S. economy."[8] The troubles in Southeast Asia also produced a large number of refugees, displaced persons, and asylum seekers, who are different from traditional Asiatic immigrants. The United States does not feel it can refuse Southeast Asians, who had fought on the American side, from applying to settle in America. The fact that the United States has now suddenly become the country of "first asylum" has also many far-reaching implications. Meanwhile, the influx of Korean and South-east Asian settlers has inevitably created tensions, conflicts, and misunderstanding between Asiatics and non-Asiatics in American society as well as among different ethnic and racial groups within Pan–Asian-American communities.

It is also not surprising that Asian-Americans' well-being has been positively and negatively affected by the political and economic changes in Asian nations and their relationship with the United States. Take, for example, the amazing economic prosperity of Japan, Korea, Taiwan, Singapore, and Thailand during the 1980s, which has resulted in the temporary residence in the United States of many business representatives from these Asian nations—with schools for their children, food markets and restaurants for their families, and so forth. The relationship between these temporary Asians' new communities and traditional Asian-Americans' communities is precarious, to say the least, even though the non-Asiatic populace may find it hard to distinguish members of these two Asiatic peoples' communities. Such an understandable confusion sometimes has tragic consequences, as demonstrated by the killing of a Chinese-American who was mistaken for a Japanese from Japan by two unemployed auto workers in Detroit. They blamed automakers in Japan for the loss of their jobs. Equally devastating are the series of incidents, real or assumed, involving different Asian ethnic groups, old or new, like the power struggles between Korean, Vietnamese, and Chinese groups in New York, which greatly damage the rapport between Asiatic and African-American populations.

Observations on the Current Scene

This may be an appropriate place for us to take a brief look at the current situations of Asian-American communities in the narrow sense, that is, communities of American-born citizens (children of Asiatic immigrants). The diversity of their situation is such that we have to resort to the well-known wise saying that the only valid generalization is that there are no generalizations. However, we could probably and safely differentiate three major settings: (1) the situation in the Hawaiian islands, where Asian-Americans are culturally comfortable even if they are a numerical minority; (2) the situation on the West Coast, where Asian-American communities are loosening up from within but still carry emotional strains inherited from the past, both in terms of inner-community modes of behavior and the relationships between their communities and the non-Asiatic populace (which now includes an expanding Hispanic dimension in addition to whites and African-Americans); and (3) the situation outside of Hawaii and the West Coast, where many—except hardy individuals—tend to suffer from insecurity, restlessness, and the sense of impermanence despite considerable achievements in their chosen fields. Beyond these differences in the three kinds of settings, there are infinite variations, each with its unique ethos. Here I rely on my firsthand contacts with the Japanese-American community in Seattle, Washington, and the more fluid situation for Japanese-Americans and other Asian-Americans in Chicago. I offer the following observations:

1. Although my knowledge of the Hawaiian situation is very limited, I cannot help but feel that the relative isolation of Hawaii from the continental United States is quickly becoming a thing of the past. The fact that Hawaii is now represented in Washington by Asian-American members of Congress is but a symbol of active participation of Asian-Americans in the closer integration of the islands into the whole United States, politically, economically, socially, and culturally.

2. The frustrating experience of Asian-American communities on the West Coast amply testifies to how slow and painful the social integration of any minority group into American society is. Goodwill on both sides and repeated resolutions by civic and religious groups, indispensable though they are, do not automatically solve difficult social, political, economic, and psychological problems involved in making integration a reality. Also, the integration of marginal groups requires the persistent cooperation of well-integrated personalities on both sides. This is not an argument in favor of gradualism, which usually degenerates into apologies for the status quo and pious do-nothingness. I am stressing the need for honest and realistic—and yet sympathetic— diagnosis rather than simply advocating only lofty principles. Of course, this is easier said than done. Especially on the West Coast, which had a stubborn pattern of discrimination against all marginal groups, semi-segregated Asian-American communities admittedly provide a measure of mental and psychological security, even though they may discourage and annihilate individual initiative. The perennial danger of the West Coast is its tendency to treat members of ethnic minority groups primarily in terms of their ethnic background. In this situation, many Asian-Americans, in their eagerness to be integrated into American society, often fall into the pitfall of considering the American heritage as simply an extension of Western (European) tradition in contradistinction to the Asian cultural traditions of their parents' original homelands. And they often overcompensate for their frustration of being discriminated

against by identifying themselves, of all things, with a particular view of American culture as a transported form of a European paradigm.

3. Many Asian-Americans scattered in various parts of America, outside Hawaii and the West Coast, also are tempted to identify themselves with the European paradigm of American culture, partly in order to differentiate themselves from various kinds of Asians from Asia now residing in the United States. In doing so, they do not realize that this is precisely what the now-fading invisible establishment of the dominant American culture understood, interpreted, and advocated American culture to be. It was on this ground that the dominant class regarded as second-class citizens the members of marginal groups, who cannot easily be assimilated into the white European-inspired elite culture. And strangely enough, Asian-Americans, as well as members of other ethnic minority groups, have been hypnotized for too long by such self-serving, one-sided rhetoric. In reality, America had never been and is not now a part of Western Europe. If anything, America came into being by rebelling against a hierarchical, royalty-and-aristocracy-ridden European pattern. The American ideal of government is not government from above, but government by the people and for the people. American education rejected the two-tier system, based on birth, lineage, and wealth; it revolutionized education by forging ahead with a one-tier system for all children. And, as Daniel J. Boorstin reminds us:

> It is time we cease thinking of ourselves as an outpost of Western European civilization. . . . [W]e must not doom ourselves to remain an epilogue to European history, making ourselves only a newer Old World. This cannot be avoided unless we learn to treat non-European cultures as equals. Only if we can relate ourselves to, and acquire the new habit of comparing ourselves with, the cultures of Asia and Africa . . . [o]nly then [can] we remain part of a New World.[9]

Such an *orientatio*, which is undoubtedly based on a more adequate perception of the nature of American culture, however, places a double-edged burden on members of Asian-American and other hyphenated American groups. On the one hand, they have become cocreators of this fluid, never-to-be-completed American culture, rather than being creatures of a ready-made cultural form, dominated by the invisible establishment of an elite group that discriminates against members of marginal groups as second-class citizens. On the other hand, in dealing with foreign, especially Asian, cultures, Asian-Americans should be crystal clear about their own identities, because they are not ambassadors of

Asian nations and traditions to the United States; they are indeed full-fledged Americans who happen to have some familiarity with and interests in Asian traditions because of their particular backgrounds. In so doing, Asian-Americans, like all other Americans, especially those of marginal groups, should avoid the fateful pitfall of considering themselves primarily in terms of their ethnic and racial backgrounds. To be sure, the stubborn pattern of this racial discrimination will continue to haunt them. But ultimately, this type of psychological reorientation that enables them to become an integral part of the ever-growing American culture should alone serve as a corrective to the Asian-Americans' ambiguous self-image.

It is far from my intention to urge Asian-Americans and members of other minority groups to play it safe and advance themselves in society, following the rules of behavior established by someone else. Some people think that such an approach is the only way to avoid unnecessary prejudice, but in reality, such an attitude is based on a concept of inverted prejudice; that is, it implies that members of minority groups are hypnotized by their own prejudice constituted by their versions of the prejudice that is thrust on them, instead of intelligently coping with the reality of the situation.

Ironically, all Americans, including members of the minority groups, have to live under the strong pressure of uniformity and utilitarianism. "The most striking paradox of American life," according to Robert Maynard Hutchins, "is that this system, which must rest on individual differences, produces the most intense pressure toward uniformity. The fact that any [person] can become President, instead of making every [person] an individual, tends to make [that person] a replica of everybody else."[10] The pressure toward uniformity is particularly strong on members of minority groups, for in the name of acceptance and integration, they are pressured by well-meaning people to wear the right clothes, say the right things, hold the right opinions, and think the right thoughts—the rightness, however, that is determined by the amorphous society. The second pressure toward utilitarianism comes from the fact that modern life rests on specialized knowledge, ability, skill, and competence, which require various kinds of vocational training. This factor has great bearing on the rather impressive achievement of Asian-Americans in all levels of education because of their utilitarian attitude toward education for the sake of upward social mobility. All in all, Asian-Americans have been pressured to look, act, and think in acceptable manners, afflicted though they often are in their solitude by the ambivalence and schizophrenic tendencies in their own existence as Americans of particular ethnic and racial backgrounds.

My reflection on Asian-Americans is based on the notion that they are as much an integral part of American society and culture as any American can be in the midst of the confusing world of our time. They must realize that their feeling of being cut off from the mainstream of American life is the result of impossible demands they often make on themselves. Racially and ethnically, they are not any better or worse than all other Americans, and they, like others, suffer from inner inconsistencies between their aspirations and practical necessities. But they should be mature enough to sustain contradictory elements without torturing themselves by searching for an unbiased society that does not exist. One thing is clear, though. They must become tough adults, self-conscious about their own rights as citizens and human beings as well as cognizant of their responsibilities and duties to be cocreators/partners in charting the course of society and culture—instead of being victims, beneficiaries, or spectators of courses of society and culture that are to be determined by other peoples in their own country. In so stating, I hope I am not romantically idealizing the structure of American society or overestimating the potentiality and influence of Asian-Americans.

Finally, it must be admitted that the shape of American society and culture has been changing over the years, and it is probably possible to depict such significant general trends as the slow erosion of the once powerful but invisible establishment of the dominant elite group (class) or the gradual rise of the once degraded minority and marginal groups. However, no one can predict solutions of deeply rooted problems such as racial discrimination, which haunts Asian and other minority groups directly everyday. It may be that our formula of dichotomy—quick solution versus rigid dogma of gradualism—does not do justice to an involved issue such as racism. Without resorting to gradualism or admitting defeat, we may have to realize that for betterment, as Edward Shils has said, some issues require the passage "of time which resolves problems through supplanting them by new problems, and through the . . . generation of new traditions which only the passage of time can nurture."[11]

The problems of Asian-Americans will find their more enduring solutions to the extent that problems of any ethnic and racial minority group in America are ever solved—only by the strengthening and cementing of the democratic system, which nurtures individuality and creativity. Fresh insights, wisdom, and faith will come to Asian-Americans in the midst of their participating in this basic endeavor. Then the inconsistent elements within them will be seen in a larger perspective. Ultimately, I share Shils's sentiment that the more adequate synthesis of various social, cultural, and psychological threads and factors will emerge

> not from deliberate efforts at synthesis but from ardent exertions to solve real scientific problems, to discover something true and important through scholarship, to write poems and novels about what one sees with one's own eyes, feels with one's own feelings, imagines with one's own imagination and to apply one's own knowledge and skills to the handling of tasks for which one is responsible with a responsibility which one accepts.[12]

SOME REMARKS ON THE EASTERN CULTURAL HERITAGE OF ASIAN-AMERICANS

Any discussion of the situation of Asian-Americans requires some references to the impact of the so-called Eastern cultural heritage on them. This, however, is an extremely elusive issue for three reasons: (1) The uniqueness of each group of Asiatic origin defies easy generalizations. (2) The situation of those groups that had settled in America before World War II is grossly different from that of, say, newcomers from Korea or groups from Southeast Asia. (3) Each group—prewar as well as postwar—is marked by a series of internal differences based on individuals and subgroups. (Although my contact has been primarily with prewar groups from East Asia, I hope that my observations have some relevance to other groups as well.) Invariably, all groups of Asiatic origin were influenced to some degree by Eastern cultures, but it is very tricky to determine what sorts (levels) of Asian religious and cultural traits were transmitted to Asian-Americans, by whom, and to what extent.

As far as can be ascertained, most of the first-generation immigrants, especially from East Asia (but I presume others as well), did not come from the higher strata of society, and their outlooks had not been shaped by elite cultural/religious traditions in Asia. It is my impression that many people in the lower strata of East Asian societies, mostly in rural areas, lived in a mental, spiritual, and psychical world that cannot easily be identified in terms of the traditional elite cultures (e.g., Buddhist, Confucian, or Taoist), but one characterized by a more amorphous blending of various cultural and religious features. Although it is virtually impossible to depict theoretical strands of such Pan–East-Asian folksy syncretism, we might succinctly sketch some of the underlying assumptions, as follows:

1. Spirit has no higher place than matter; spirit and matter, which are both aspects of nature, coexist on the same plane, and both are subject to the cosmic urge (termed the original or cosmic principle in elite traditions).

2. Ethical values are basically relative. Good and bad are both necessary, and they both deserve our respect or devotion. Also, the law of retribution, which is believed to be rooted in one's past, allows new possibilities for one's future.

3. In primordial time (or at the root of the structure of the cosmos—not unlike the logos doctrine of the preface to the Johannine Gospel), before spirit and matter, or good and evil, were separated, there was an original harmony (or state of undifferentiation, as advocated by some Zen Buddhists in the past). From this original state of harmony emerged opposites—light and darkness, good and evil, and so forth. All differentiated beings—such as human beings and deities, angels and demons, animals and plants—are not permanent entities.

4. If we could only retrieve the state of original harmony by attaining, for example, the unity of human beings and nature, there would be no need for a special agent such as a savior to bridge the gap or to overcome the fact of separateness. Religion is essentially a technique of training for realization (and actualization) of this truth. Sages and semidivine beings (e.g., Taoist deities and Mahayana Buddhist divine bodhisattvas), however, can expedite this kind of religious (soteriological) process.

5. Cults and symbols are essential for religion, for religion— with their help—defines levels of reality. Religion is also a necessary "glue" for life itself, which is a seamless homology of culture, social, economic, and political orders, and aesthetics, and so forth (which are seen as separate dimensions of life in elite traditions of Asia or as a series of separate independent entities, as has been deeply ingrained in the Western mode of thinking).

6. After death comes another life, which is followed by another death. (To use Western terms, we might say that death and resurrection are interchangeable in a never-ending process.) Such a chain of interaction is affirmed in terms of the unbroken family lineage on the empirical plane (although deliverance from such a never-ending repetition of the life-and-death process is sought in elite Buddhist traditions).

Let me reiterate that the above is my characterization, in a more discursive way, of the seemingly this-worldly (and nonsoteriological, except in reference to funerary rites and ancestral cults) religious/cultural orientation of Pan–East-Asian folk tradition. It is to be noted that this kind of pragmatic religious/cultural heritage—which also stressed courage, honesty, hard work, endurance, frugality, filial piety, and so forth (all of which were idealized as common Eastern cultural virtues)— served as the guiding principle for the first-generation immigrants from Asia. Their sense of pride as human beings, in spite of all the discriminations and difficulties they had to endure, was expressed in the somewhat romanticized poem entitled "My Hand" by Yonejiro Noguchi (1875– 1947), who at one time (before he joined Rabindranath Tagore at Santiniketan) was a resident of California. It reads:

> Please look at my hands.
> Don't you think that the clumsy thick bones
> of my hands look like the joints of a winter bamboo?
> Their rough hard skin tells that my ancestors
> used to grab muck for many generations.
> Their reddish short nails remind you of the face
> of a poor clodhopper.
> My ancestors, according to my genealogy,
> had been looking into the face of the earth
> for four hundred years,
> tending lovingly the seeds they sowed.
> I thank my ancestors who found an honest living
> in the plough and the sickle.
> The love they gave to the earth for such a long time
> was not in vain,
> for I can bring so much love to nature.
> The love my ancestors gave
> has been repaid in me.
> Please look at my hands,
> the proof that I am a descendant
> of the family who prayed silently
> to the earth for so long.
> I am thankful for the answer to those prayers
> that was fulfilled in me.
> Please look at my hands.
> The history of an honest, simple life
> that my ancestors defended so zealously
> is written in my fingers.[13]

We have already mentioned that what most first-generation Asiatic immigrants brought with them were not elite religious/cultural traditions of Asia but this-worldly oriented Pan–East-Asian folk traditions—plus some respective Chinese, Korean, or Japanese cultural trappings. To be sure, more elite religious/cultural traditions were introduced to Asiatic immigrant groups later on after the arrival of missionaries from Asian religious establishments. But the pragmatic this-worldly orientation persisted as a main characteristic of the first-generation Asiatic immigrants' mental outlook. Two other factors might be added in this connection. First, for the most part, American-born children of those Asiatic immigrants, like the second generation of many other immigrant groups, did not appreciate the East-Asian cultural values that their parents had tried to uphold and to transmit to their children. Second, more often than not, it took the third generation of Asian-Americans to show more positive appreciation of the legacy of their grandparents. Although such is a familiar pattern repeated in various immigrant groups, there was an added dimension in the case of the third-generation Asian-Americans; for their positive response to Asian cultures coincided with, and was encouraged by, the sudden receptivity on the part of many Americans and other Westerners toward Eastern religions and cultures. It is not surprising, therefore, that many young Asian-Americans, who are eager to look for cultural roots as the basis of their new sense of self-identity, are attracted not by the folksy syncretism brought by most East-Asian immigrants, but rather by the more elite traditions of Asian religions and cultures that are fashionable today in the West. Of course, familiarity with the more elitist contemporary Asian religions and cultures might inspire young Asian-Americans in their attempt to define or redefine their own cultural identities, but they have to know that even the most intimate acquaintanceship with sophisticated Asian cultures will not help them to understand their own particular Eastern cultural heritage, which had been transmitted by their immigrant forebears.

6

THE MASS EVACUATION: RECOLLECTIONS AND REFLECTIONS

INTERNMENT CAMP—AMERICAN STYLE[1]

For many years, it has not been easy for me to talk or write publicly about my experience of being incarcerated during World War II, even though I often have had sleepless nights thinking about it. Because it was such an emotionally taxing and demanding experience, I have felt that one either must give much time and energy to do even a semblance of justice to talking or writing about it or must try not to think about it but do other things to occupy one's mind. Besides, I have had a feeling, rightly or wrongly, that not many people can believe that such an appalling thing could happen in America in the presumably civilized and enlightened twentieth century.

Shortly after I was released from the camp, I read Claire Huchet Bishop's book *France Alive*, in which she mentions how a lasting bond united those men and women who had come back from concentration camps.

> When they met in their local units they [identified themselves] as having been "there." "There" they had endured the same physical torments and experienced the reality of human communion. "There" they were all human beings, suffering persecution. . . . "There" they rediscovered and lived the communion of the "faithful." They were kept alive by it, physically and mentally.[2]

119

It may well be that we can talk about the depth of our feelings only with those who have shared the same experience or at least have had a similar experience. About ten years ago, while visiting California I had an opportunity to visit an elderly Japanese gentleman whom I had not seen for the nearly forty years since we had shared the same barracks in the detention camp in Santa Fe, New Mexico. He was a successful farmer in Salinas before the war, raising lettuce on a huge, choice piece of land. At the outbreak of the war he lost practically everything. When I first met him, he was still a youthful forty years old. Now, after forty more years, his face bore the creases of years of hardship, disappointment, and suffering. Words did not come easily in our emotional reunion. Quietly, he showed me a notebook in which he kept the names of everyone we knew in the camp, and I noticed that most of the names were marked with red ink, "deceased in such and such year." He told me what had happened to many of them after the war. Some were too old to start a new life, while others made a meager comeback in spite of seemingly unsurmountable difficulties. When I was leaving, my old friend handed me the notebook containing the names of our mutual friends and admonished me to overcome my reluctance to talk about our internment experience, so that others would remember those innocent farmers, shopkeepers, and fishermen who had been the victims of race prejudice and war hysteria.

Much has been written about the mass evacuation of persons of Japanese ancestry from their homes on the West Coast and Alaska in 1942. Some narrative accounts as well as historical background will be given in other sections of this volume. Here I want to stress mainly the far-reaching significance of this extraordinary event. In the words of Morton Grodzins:

> No charges were ever filed against these persons, and no guilt was ever attributed to them. The test was ancestry, applied with the greatest rigidity. Evacuations swept into guarded camps orphans, foster-children in white homes, Japanese married to Caucasians, the offspring of such marriages, persons who were unaware of their Japanese ancestry, and American citizens "with as little as one-sixteenth Japanese blood." Evacuation was not carried out by lawless vigilantes or by excited local officials. The program was instituted and executed by military forces of the United States with a full mandate of power from both the executive and the legislative branches of the national government.[3]

Indeed, it was the first instance in American history when ethnicity alone defined a group of Americans who were to be incarcerated behind barbed wire.

It must be mentioned that there were four kinds of camps. One was the Assembly Center, such as the one at Santa Anita (a temporary center—a converted racetrack), to which all persons of Japanese descent were sent initially from their homes on the West Coast and Alaska. From the Assembly Centers, people were sent to the ten War Relocation Centers, which were more permanent camps scattered in remote parts of the United States. A third kind of camp was called an Enemy Alien Detention Camp, such as the one in Santa Fe or in Missoula, Montana, where many leaders among the Japanese communities were detained until their cases were cleared by the FBI and the district attorneys and they were released to join their families in the War Relocation Centers. Those alien Japanese who could not prove to be harmless were sent to the fourth kind of camp, the Army Internment Camp in Lordsburg, New Mexico. In my case, I had spent a few months each at the Enemy Alien Detention Camp in Santa Fe and the Army Internment Camp in Lordsburg before I was sent to the Minidoka War Relocation Center Camp at Hunt, Idaho, where I remained until October 1945—altogether three and one-half years. During that period of time, I was initiated into the world of the *Isseis* (the first-generation immigrants from Japan), and the related but different world of the *Niseis* (the second generation, the American-born children of the *Isseis*). In fact, my exposure to those camps was the real introduction to American society for me. Thus I initially came to learn about the American experience through the eyes of persons of Japanese (later, other Asiatic) ancestry.

As a newcomer to this country, I did not understand all the political, economic, social, and legal factors that were involved in the mass evacuation. Even then I was struck by two features that were obvious to anybody. First, Japanese immigrants were considered enemy aliens because of the legal restrictions imposed by the American government. Had they been given opportunities to become naturalized citizens, the West Coast situation would have been very different. Second, I could not believe how a group of U.S. citizens could be removed from their homes and incarcerated without any due process of law, even in a time of emergency. I was also disappointed when respected columnists like Walter Lippmann advocated the evacuation. After all these years, the important issues to me now are not how badly persons of Japanese descent were treated, and there were many tragic instances, or how much they had lost economically, and here again their loss was considerable. Rather, the two main issues are the legal and human implications. The mass evacuation affected only one ethnic minority group during the war. But the fact that the principle of evacuation was introduced into the constitutional system by the U.S. government has left an important legal precedent. More important were the human factors, such as emotional frustration, the loss of confidence in the government, and the breakdown of morale on the part of the 110,000 or 120,000 persons who were incarcerated.

In retrospect, the most amazing fact was that the tragic event of mass evacuation was not widely known by the bulk of the population. Many of those who learned about it were inclined to believe that the government knew what was best, while others dismissed it as a West Coast problem. However, there were some people who tried to do something about it. Let me cite only one example. A group of Quakers with the cooperation of some other Christian and Jewish groups had established the Japanese-American Student Relocation Council with headquarters in Philadelphia. Those of us who were inside the camp depended heavily on this organization to encourage colleges and universities to accept and offer financial aid to qualified Japanese-American boys and girls. Even from our camp alone, we managed to send several hundred young men and women to various colleges, universities, and vocational schools. It was not easy to raise money for Japanese-Americans during the war, and not everyone we sent did well. But a surprising number of Japanese-American youths found new rays of hope when some unknown American friends cared enough to do something for their unfortunate fellow citizens.

Today, even after so many years, my memory of those days is still overwhelming. Over the years, I have seen many of those who had been "there" with me. Some are well-established lawyers, businessmen, and artists. Many older friends who have survived the ordeal are now retired. They too remember the camp experience with mixed feelings. I am still overwhelmed by that visit with my elderly friend whom I had met after forty years. In spite of his years of hardship, success, and disappointment, he maintains a remarkable sense of serenity. After I left him in his humble home in Salinas, I thought of a saying attributed to a great philosopher-teacher: "If you seek wisdom, listen to those who have suffered." I too hope to have gained some measure of wisdom from my own experience!

THE LEGACY OF THE ISSEIS, THE FIRST-GENERATION JAPANESE IMMIGRANTS[4]

Unfortunately, an increasing number of the *Isseis* are getting very old, and before long they will disappear from our midst. Thus it may be appropriate for me now to present my personal account of how I came to know the world of the *Isseis* through our shared life in the internment camps. In the fateful year of 1941, my peaceful study at Berkeley, California, was rudely interrupted by Pearl Harbor, and I found myself eating canned beans in the Alameda County Jail. From there I was shipped successively to the Enemy Alien Detention Camp in Santa Fe and to the Army Internment Camp in Lordsburg, New Mexico, with my fellow internees, all of whom were *Isseis*.

During my internment camp days, I often read and reread the story of Daniel in the Old Testament. According to the story, Daniel's enemies persuaded the king to sign a document that was designed to cast Daniel into the den of lions. When he learned one day that the document had been signed, we are told that Daniel went to his chamber, where he had windows open toward Jerusalem, and got down upon his knees three times and prayed. This story had special significance to all of us then, because in those days we all prayed with our windows open toward home. Like Daniel, who was vexed by the uncertainty of his life, my fellow internees were haunted by the ambiguities that enveloped their existence.

Every day, as the bright New Mexico sun faded behind a skyline decorated only with sagebrush, we all gathered together and shared our frustrations and problems. It was through these daily contacts that I came to know the *Isseis* intimately. I was fascinated to listen to the endless tales of these new friends, these simple, hardworking people who had crossed the Pacific earlier with adventuring hearts. By the time I knew them, however, their faces, once youthful and proud, bore the creases of years of hardship. Many of them were from California, Oregon, and Washington, but some were from Hawaii and Alaska. All of them had worked tirelessly throughout their adult life on their farms or in their shops, enduring humiliation and discrimination, with a firm determination to provide a better future for their offspring. I could readily understand what a traumatic and baffling experience it was for them suddenly to be uprooted from their homes because of war on the grounds that they were not citizens of this country, when by law they could not seek citizenship. And as we walked together along the barbed wire in the daytime, or as we tried to cover ourselves against the cold at night in the drafty wooden barracks, I could sense that my *Issei* friends were deeply troubled, not so much by the experience of physical discomfort or even the loss of their homes and property, but more by the sense of uncertainty they felt concerning their own future as well as the future of their wives and children from whom they were separated. It was on such an occasion that I suddenly realized the emotional impact of the Hebrew psalm: "By the waters of Babylon we sat down and wept, when we remembered thee, O Sion!" The Hebrews too must have prayed with their windows open toward home.

Even now I cherish my memories of those fellow internees, who allowed me to glimpse into the world of the early Japanese immigrants through our life together. Many of them originally came from the areas of Japan that had been greatly affected by the transition from the feudal regime to the imperial rule that took place in 1868. The year 1868 marked not only the political upheaval but also social, economic, and cultural changes as well. Gone were the social and political institutions of the feudal age, and with them many of the traditional values and mores of the culture. In this circumstance, some of the ambitious youths came to America. Little did those young Japanese youths realize that they were coming to Hawaii and the West Coast, where agricultural and business interests, which had initially welcomed them as cheap contract labor, would soon turn against them. Moreover, persistent pressures from the West Coast eventually led to the U.S. Supreme Court decision in 1922, which ruled that Japanese were ineligible for American citizenship, and to the passage of the 1924 Quota Act, which legally terminated Japanese immigration altogether.

Understandably, the life of the Japanese immigrants on the West Coast was not an enviable one. I still get nightmares when I recall the horror stories told by my *Issei* friends about the long hours they had to work each day for meager pay, part of which was pocketed by their bosses. But then they were still young and eager to make quick money and return to Japan, as indeed some lucky ones did. However, for many, their first hopes of getting rich quick soon gave way to the reality of the situation, and they settled down on the West Coast by bringing wives from the old country. Being unfamiliar with their new environment, American mores, and the English language, the *Issei* pioneers underwent extreme hardship. The only source of comfort to them was their family life, which was made possible by the loving care of long-suffering *Issei* women, the unsung heroines of the tortured drama of Japanese immigration to America. In the course of time, with the increase of family groups there developed a need for some kind of community life. Although we may argue today in hindsight whether or not such a ghettolike community pattern was desirable over the long run, it was the only option available for the early settlers.

My exposure to fellow internees taught me the simple yet important lesson that *Isseis* were not categories but persons—individuals with an amazing variety of habits, temperaments, and backgrounds. If there are common *Issei* traits, as I think there are, they were derived from the common experience of living under trying conditions in a new land and from the common concern the *Isseis* had for their descendants. The more I listened to their life stories, the more I came to admire the strength of their character as well as the courage, fortitude, and sense of dedication of *Issei* women. No doubt, the *Isseis* had their share of limitations and blind spots. After all, their upbringing in Japan did not prepare them to cope with many of the problems they had to face in their new environment. Chief among them was the question of how to raise their children, who were Americans by birth. In spite of their serious effort, the *Isseis* were not prepared to appreciate the depth of their children's emotional insecurity caused by the *Niseis'* own realization that they were not accepted completely either by the community of their own parents or by the American society at large. To make the matter more complex, many *Niseis* reached early adulthood during the 1930s and 1940s under the shadow of the Great Depression and the mass evacuation. And it was only when their *Nisei* children, who by virtue of their birth and education were citizens of this country, also were uprooted from their homes and sent to war relocation centers without due process of law, that many *Issei* parents came to realize the dilemma and the depth of agony of their children.

I remember a man with whom I was taking a walk on day. I did not know him very well, but he confided in me his sense of bewilderment. Evidently, he had been fairly successful in his business, but he could not stand to see his children go through humiliating experiences. So, against his wife's counsel, he took his whole family to Japan, thinking that there his children would not be regarded as second-class citizens. But when they arrived at his native town, he knew immediately that Japan would not be the place for his "American" children. So he and his family moved back again to the West Coast and rebuilt their business. He sent his sons and daughters to college and hoped that with a college education and professional training they could hold their own in society in spite of racial prejudice. "But now," he said sadly, "everything we had worked for is gone. I am here in this internment camp, while my

wife and children are sharing one dusty room in a relocation center."
Then he continued, "I still think we were right in coming back to this
country, because as my wife says, this is where our children belong, and
we should be where they are. True, we have lost everything, but there
are good times and bad times, and my wife and I can live somehow. But
what hurts me is the fact that my children's loyalty to their own country is questioned!" Not knowing what to say, I simply nodded my head,
and we kept on walking silently. At the end of the walk we parted. My
walking companion did not say a word, but he had tears in his eyes. I
knew then that he was going to pray that night with his windows open
toward the relocation camp that was the temporary abode of his wife
and children. Later, after I was sent to the Minidoka War Relocation
Center Camp in Idaho, I learned that one of his sons had volunteered
from his relocation camp for the army and was killed in action on the
Italian front when his battalion (made up of Japanese-American volunteers) was assigned to rescue the lost battalion from Texas. I prayed for
the repose of his son's soul and felt unusually close to my Buddhist
friend in another camp, who no doubt was in deep agony for losing his
beloved son.

It is not strange, therefore, that even today I remember many of
my fellow internees at Santa Fe and Lordsburg. I still correspond with a
few, but lamentably, many of them are gone. Most *Isseis* never attained
fame nor acquired much wealth. They have, however, left a precious
legacy in their valiant spirit, which enabled them to endure and overcome almost insurmountable difficulties, disappointments, and set-
backs throughout their life.

Once a famous rabbi touched the hearts of a Jewish audience
when he said, "You are perhaps the children of dealers in old clothes, but
remember you are the descendants of prophets." In a similar vein, I
often remind the *Niseis* and *Sanseis* (the third generation) that they are
the descendants of those heroic *Issei* men and women, and I fervently
hope that they will live up to the legacy of the *Isseis*.

"THIS CANNOT HAPPEN AGAIN!"[5]

Outsiders visiting relocation centers have usually been impressed first
by the stark physical setup. One arrives at the gate to Minidoka after
traveling several miles through uninhabited, rolling sagebrush country.
From the distance loom the two water towers, the tall hospital chimney,
and then row on row of one-story tar-papered barracks. These extend
approximately three miles along the canal that provides irrigation for

the farm and residence blocks. A cluster of white buildings overlooking the canal are the administrative apartment barracks. Until the last few weeks, "the gate" has been a real barrier as well as a symbol. In the shadow of a guard tower, which during the early days was manned by a soldier with a machine gun, stands the little stone gatehouse with its sign *"STOP:* U.S. Army Guard," a guardrail across the road (like the gates at rail crossings), and a turnstile for pedestrians. It was necessary for evacuees and visitors to conform to an elaborate pass procedure carried out jointly by the Military Police and the War Relocation Authority (WRA) gate staff. Some of the residents never went beyond that gate from the time of their arrival in August or September of 1942 until their departure in the summer or fall of 1945! For most people, it was too difficult or inconvenient to arrange for a pass more than a few times throughout the whole period.

Just inside the gate is the memorial park and the honor roll dedicated to the community's servicemen. This small plot of grass, trees, and flowers is an oasis in the landscape and a symbol of loyalty to their country under the most adverse conditions. Although persons of Japanese ancestry were at first barred from military service (some were even discharged at the time of Pearl Harbor because of their ancestry; others were refused when they volunteered December 8, 1941) and only the army has opened its doors to them so far, names are listed. (When volunteers were recruited in February 1943, Hunt, Idaho, sent a larger proportion of its population than any other community in the United States.)

Beyond the park lies the administration area, a maze of offices manned by evacuees and frequently changing appointed personnel who have had less and less understanding of the significance of the project and the life within the community. "Necessary" red tape, lack of vision, and actual maladministration have resulted in frustration, tension between administration and residents, and general low morale of all concerned.

As one descends the hill (the residents have nicknamed it "Capitol Hill") from the administration area in either direction, he or she crosses an open space—in keeping with the gulf between the governing and those governed—and enters the row of residence blocks. Each of these consists of twelve barracks, a recreation hall, a mess hall, and a utility building that houses toilet and bath facilities, laundry room, and boiler room. Within each barracks are from six to eight one-room "apartments." The WRA furnished only one electric light suspended from the center of the ceiling, a potbellied stove set on a box of earth for fire protection, and a 30-inch army cot with two army blankets for each member of the family. The charm and elaborateness of individual apartments depends upon the means and the resourceful-ness of the individual inhabitants. Except in special cases, groups of five or fewer have only one room, twenty feet square or smaller.

Recovering from the shock of the physical environment, new-comers marvel at the residents' ability to maintain an approximation of normal life behind barbed wire. Children have been occupied in nursery schools and in elementary and secondary schools accredited by the state of Idaho. Adults have been able to learn English and vocational subjects under the adult education program. The community activities section has sponsored outdoor basketball and baseball, community sings, dances, entertainments, and exhibits. A cooperative, Community Enter-prises, has maintained two movie houses at either end of the project, showing two pictures each week. There has been a weekly newspaper published by evacuees under the joint sponsorship of the Community Enterprises and the Reports Division of the WRA. Weekly services, Sunday schools, and other religious activities have been sponsored by the Federated Christian Church (Protestant), Roman Catholic Church, and the Buddhists. Barring employment cuts, most of the employable adults and many children have at one time or another worked in project offices or in other activities necessary to the maintenance of a commu-nity of ten thousand. Community Enterprises maintained general stores, beauty shops, barber shops, shoe repair shops, watch repair, and so forth. Professional workers were paid $19 per month; the standard wage was $16 for others. There was leisure for hobbies, clubs, and social gatherings. But this life was not satisfactory.

Beyond the obvious problems resulting from such abnormal life—lack of personal privacy; weakening of family unity because of new arrangements for eating, recreation, and so forth; tensions arising from conflicting values; frustration at the curtailment of civil liberties; and America's failure to fulfill her creed of democratic equality—there were more complex situations that even the most understanding out-sider would find difficult to analyze, much less untangle. These might be attributed to a peculiar "Japanese psychology," but are more accu-rately described as stemming from the unique background with which the evacuees faced their unprecedented status.

Analyzing and evaluating the evacuation of persons of Japanese ancestry from the West Coast, with all its ramifications, will require the perspective of time. It has been a temptation to assign responsibility for errors and grow vindictive against the results of human frailty. But the need and inescapable task for the church at Minidoka was to develop spiritual resources for facing this especially trying period and to help in the solution of crucial personal problems that were not being met by the WRA for a variety of reasons. Beyond that, however, there was an urgent need to interpret the circumstances and thinking of the residents to the local staff, and, vice versa, the legislative limitations and administrative considerations to the residents. Also, we tried to bridge the growing distance between project life and thinking, and the stream of outside life. We were guided by the belief that, in addition to ministering to individuals, it was crucial to try to influence society and to try to lift it up to the Christian standard so that the minority groups would be treated in a Christian manner and not have to suffer unnecessary discrimination and prejudice. The whole issue of the evacuation and the relocation centers has often been clouded by confusing it with international affairs; it is, and must be recognized as, a matter of our American domestic policy.

Perhaps a few typical situations will serve to illustrate the complex difficulties we faced.

The Sato Family

Many families like the Satos were concerned about their children, who had to grow up under abnormal circumstances, in unusual danger of becoming delinquents or at least growing less fitted for the pattern of outside society. In this family, the high-school-age son would leave the cramped apartment at breakfast time and often remain gone until bedtime. Mr. and Mrs. Sato worried about his companions and his activities, but they had little control over the situation. When George ate his meals in the block mess hall, he would join his friends rather than be seen in public, eating with his Japanese-speaking parents and childish younger brothers and sisters. Besides, sitting at long picnic tables with benches attached, closely associated with two hundred or more people of various degrees of polite table manners, is not a satisfactory family meal arrangement. Aside from chores like bringing in kindling, coal, and drinking water, there was little to keep George at home. He hesitated to bring his friends "home" to the crowded quarters. The other boys felt the same way, so they would wander around the camp in groups. There wasn't much to do. Recreation halls were closed except to organized groups; there were no gymnasium facilities except rough outdoor basketball courts and baseball diamonds. Athletic equipment was scarce. Musical instruments had been left behind in an effort to reduce baggage. There were a few clubs, but they left much to be desired. There simply wasn't much to do, so the boys would "make the rounds," buying snacks at the co-op canteens, lounging around the offices where their acquaintances worked, and swapping stories in the laundry room. George had lost interest in school—the buildings were merely remodeled barracks, the equipment was limited, student morale was low. As the years passed, juvenile delinquency in the form of gambling, drinking, and property damage became more prevalent. The Satos were very eager to return to a better environment for their children's sake.

Why, then, would a conscientious family chose to remain in a relocation center? Perhaps in their case the economic factors are strongest. In the hysterical period between Pearl Harbor and evacuation, Mr. Sato had disposed of his farm and equipment for a fraction of their worth. His small principal had diminished after three years during which it was necessary to withdraw funds to supplement the pattern of life provided by the WRA. Alien land laws made it difficult to return to the coast as a farmer. Without elaborate legal proceedings, Mr. Sato could not even run his Purple Hearted soldier son's orchard for him while he was overseas. At that, there would be difficulties in marketing the goods in the face of boycotting by the teamsters' union and packing houses. Two hazards stood in the way of taking up a small business in a West Coast city: first, the difficulty enemy aliens faced in obtaining municipal licenses; second, the scarcity of adequate housing. The WRA has not been of appreciable help in either of these problems. Mr. Sato was hesitant to attempt farming in some other part of the United States because he was not acquainted with the climate or the methods required outside of the coastal region. It was too great a gamble at his age of sixty-one to risk his whole investment. Mr. Sato is no longer as young and vigorous or as adventurous as when he came to America in 1902.

Apart from financial considerations, there were very real fears for the security of the family. It was hard to believe that, if the people of Japanese ancestry were evacuated for their own safety (this is one of the justifications offered by the army), it would be desirable for them to return with the war in the Pacific still in progress. If the evacuation had been the result of pressure groups among those who knew the Japanese-Americans, what security could be expected among the absolute strangers to the east? Even the constitutional rights of the second generation, American citizens, had not protected *them* from the confinement behind barbed wire. At least, in the centers one could be reasonably sure of minimum housing, food, education, and medical care. What of the persistent rumors in camp about Japanese who had been refused hospital care because of their race? What would be the chances for them when the veterans returned to the labor market to swell the numbers of workers released from defense jobs? Mr. Sato's dilemma, whether to suffer continued life in camp or to risk venturing "outside," is not unusual; it is typical of that facing most family heads in the camp.

Amy Suzuki

Let us turn to Amy Suzuki's problem, which is representative of many. She was the oldest of several children; her father was sixty, not an unusual age for the father of a recent high school graduate. Amy had just completed her high school course, after three years in the project high school. She wanted to go to college to become a laboratory technician. She was a brilliant student. Mr. and Mrs. Suzuki believed that higher education was a waste of time for a girl; it would unfit her for marriage. Furthermore, they positively refused to approve her initial proposal to become a nurse. Such a profession was not "nice." Having obtained the reluctant consent of her parents, Amy began to have misgivings: Could her parents manage to get along in this new community without her to bridge the gulf of language difficulty? Would she be able to meet all of her expenses, since the family could contribute nothing? Would her project education be sufficient for the demands of college? How would she be accepted on the campus and in the college town? Could she "catch on" to the etiquette that had been neglected in camp? Going away to college was a major experience in any girl's life; how much more it meant to a girl who had lived in a relocation center!

Mr. Kimura

Mr. Kimura was a widower. His children were grown up and had relocated with their families, leaving him in camp to enjoy the companionship of other elderly Japanese who were now able to live less strenuously than they had since coming to the United States. Mr. Kimura asked little of life; he accepted the necessity of evacuation philosophically and did not complain unduly about the project inconveniences. When his children went out, early in the history of the center, he would not accompany them because he did not wish to be a burden while they established themselves, and he would have been without social contacts because he spoke little English. By the time the close of the center had been announced, Mr. Kimura had lost all interest in "the outside." The old men who daily met in the shade of the boiler room to swap rumors and philosophize were quite convinced that the WRA would not carry out the closing orders, because so many other policies had been reversed in the past. While the war lasted, the WRA would not dare to oust them.

Hadn't the boys who volunteered for the army been promised that their parents would be provided for? It was better to wait and see what the government would do for them; they had nothing to lose.

Readjusting to Outside Life

In one way or another, most of these situations have been met by patient effort on the part of the individuals concerned, by intercession with the administration, and with invaluable help from persons outside the centers. Now we are faced with a new set of problems—the difficulties met in readjusting to outside life.

The plight of those returning to the West Coast is extreme, but it is affecting the lives of thousands and is duplicated to a lesser degree in other cities throughout the country. To begin with, many have been forced by circumstances to return without assurance of permanent housing. As a result, hundreds have spent weeks and months in makeshift hostels or crowded into the homes of friends. Employment for most people is limited to menial tasks, regardless of the worker's qualifications. These factors are, after all, basic to security. The situation now is not good.

The attitude of society toward these returning neighbors is discouraging. The consensus of most Japanese-Americans is that they are tolerated but not accepted. This is especially serious in the case of the school-age youngsters. Scattered as they are throughout the Caucasian communities, they miss the close daily contacts with their friends, which formed the basis for the more-or-less satisfactory pattern of social life in camp. Making friends in a new location is difficult and slow in any case. It is very discouraging when the *Niseis* bring to the problem their sensitiveness to discrimination and their feelings of differentness bred by past experience. Well-meaning organizations, like church fellowship groups, may offer one invitation, but they do not follow up their hospitality and the *Niseis* are reluctant to "break in."

Even school is not the source of satisfaction it once was. It will be some time before the *Niseis* can resume their traditional academic leadership after the lax atmosphere of the project schools, which could not help reflecting the disintegration of the rest of the community. The social resistance carries over into school athletics in some cases. Also, the returning evacuees have not had the facilities for athletics that their classmates have had (except, perhaps, baseball—which won't help them until spring), and it is thus more difficult to overcome Caucasian indifference by athletic prowess.

We can only guess at the outlook for very young children who cannot remember pre-evacuation life. Meeting new situations on the basis of camp life alone may lead to bewildering results, especially if the other children and the adults concerned are not prepared to be very patient and understanding.

Now that the whole thing is over, all of us—Americans, whose country stands for the Christian way—must either forget this sad experience of the mass evacuation of one of our minorities or learn something from it. Unfortunately, some people still are totally unaware of what has happened to our Japanese-Americans. The bulk of the population has never known them; and if they think about the matter at all, they are inclined to accept unthinkingly that "the government probably knew best," without remembering that *they* are responsible for "the government."

The scars remain. Personal resources have been wiped out. Parents' relationships with their children have been jeopardized. People have lost confidence in themselves and in American society. Youngsters have acquired manners and outlooks quite foreign to "outside" standards.

Surely, this cannot happen again!

RACISM VERSUS LEGAL EQUALITY

In concluding Part II of this volume, it is not my intention to assert that the Asian-Americans' perspective is the most important or well-balanced approach to the American experience. Far from it. The American experience, like mother-of-pearl, has diverse shades of meaning seen from various perspectives, each of which has its particular sensitivity, amplified by different groups' collective discernment of their existential situations. And it is hoped that all groups will try to know, understand, and appreciate others' perspectives—as well as be aware of their own—for the mutual benefit of the common life of the Republic. My late brother used to talk about three types of racial minority groups in America: (1) the indigenous minority (the Native-Americans), (2) the imported minority (African-Americans), and (3) the alien minority (persons of Asiatic ancestry, e.g., Chinese, Korean, Filipino, Japanese, and Southeast Asians).[6] I presume that the so-called Latinos also belong to the third category, because they too are neither indigenous to America (even though some of them belong to regions south of the border), nor were they forcibly imported to this country.

I have no firsthand knowledge of the Latinos, but I have some familiarity with Asian-Americans, and I can appreciate the designation of "the alien minority" for Asiatic immigrants who were originally encouraged to come here as neither colonists nor immigrants. "They were alien laborers employed for a definite period of time. The logical extremity of this outlook on the part of the Americans was the Oriental Exclusion Act of 1924."[7] And although many of these alien laborers from Asia inevitably became immigrants rather than remaining as contract laborers, they—and even their American-born children—were treated as "aliens, unassimilable to American life," by agricultural and business interests on the West Coast, who used various legal and nonlegal means, such as humiliation, restrictions, and prohibitions to keep Asiatics permanently as aliens. The most extreme example of treating Asian-Americans as though they were aliens was the mass evacuation of all persons of Japanese ancestry that has just been discussed.

I can understand why some people on the West Coast are now trying to soft-pedal the effect of the infamous mass evacuation, which was not one of the brightest pages of recent American history. The latest effort along this line, according to the *New York Times,* is a resolution proposed in California "to revise what schoolchildren are taught about the internment of Japanese-Americans during the World War II." The *Times* continues:

> The legislator, Assemblyman Gil Ferguson . . . seeks to have children taught that Japanese-Americans were not interned in "concentration camps," but were held in relocation centers justified by military necessity. . . .
> The resolution is intended to counter a measure passed last year urging that children here be taught that there was no military basis for the internment, and that it resulted primarily from "race prejudice."

And the article adds:

> The Federal Commission on Wartime Relocation and Internment of Civilians, which was created in 1980 . . . concluded that the internment was not justified by military necessity. It listed the "historical causes" shaping the decision to relocate Japanese-Americans to be "race prejudice, war hysteria and a failure of political leadership."[8]

Undoubtedly, the aforementioned 1980 federal commission was painfully aware of how difficult and time consuming it is to reverse the myth of military necessity regarding the mass evacuation, which after all had been executed by the United States Army and was mandated both by the executive and legislative branches of the federal government.

Luckily, there was a seed of sanity among some people, more particularly in the Supreme Court. Konvitz informs us:

> Mr. Justice Murphy, in the opinion for the majority of the court, said that while it was the duty of the court to carry out the will of Congress, the judgment of the court must be guided . . . "by the spirit of freedom and tolerance in which our nation was founded, and by a desire to secure the blessings of liberty in thought and action to all those upon whom the right of American citizenship has been conferred by statute, as well as the native born." This guiding principle in construction of the law of Congress is not itself contrary to the will of Congress, for "we certainly should presume that Congress was motivated by these lofty principles."[9]

Although Murphy assumed that General DeWitt must have "acted in good faith" when he ordered mass evacuation, the justice was equally certain that the Bill of Rights is not suspended by "the mere existence of a state of war," which implies that—according to Konvitz's account of Murphy's opinion—"there are constitutional boundaries which military authorities and Congress, engaged in the effective prosecution may not transgress."[10]

Understandably, therefore, serious efforts to undo the damage of the legal basis of mass evacuation were initially focused primarily on lawsuits presented to the Supreme Court, for example: (1) the Hirabayashi case (*Hirabayashi v. United States*)—as to whether the curfew restriction was adopted by General DeWitt in 1942 "in the exercise of an unconstitutional delegation by Congress of its legislative power and whether it unconstitutionally discriminated between citizens of Japanese ancestry and those of other ancestries, in violation of the Fifth Amendment"; and (2) the Korematsu case (*Korematsu v. United States*)—"The evacuation order was without adequate military justification and itself was a deprivation of Korematsu's constitutional rights." The true issue was "whether or not a citizen of the United States may, because he is of Japanese ancestry, be confined in barbed-wire stockades euphemistically termed Assembly Centers or Relocation Centers—actually concentration camps."[11] But the cumbersome process, to say nothing of the huge cost, required for the undoing of the alleged legitimacy of the evacuation was amply testified to by the dismal failure of the Korematsu case in the Supreme Court in 1944. Twenty years later, in November of 1963, Fred Korematsu appealed the decision, and the ruling was overturned. In October of 1987, Gordon Hirabayashi finally won his case as well, after forty-five years of court battle.

Of course, during those years—1944 to 1983/1987—a number of other factors came into the picture. The patriotism of Japanese-American GIs in the aforementioned 100th Battalion and the 442nd Regiment, for example, undoubtedly had some effect in tempering the extreme form of war hysteria. No less significant was the fact that a large number of Japanese-Americans had won respect from others in various trades or professions in terms of their endurance, perseverance, and determination to excel. Also, the tremendous number of books and articles, scholarly researches and nontechnical narrative accounts, autobiographies, poems, novels, and picture books about the inhumane and degrading facts of the mass evacuation and camps, written with the help of the Freedom of Information Act that enabled the authors to dig up many hitherto concealed official and unofficial measures of discrimination, had salutary effects in informing and enlightening the general populace. As I once stated in my review of R. Drinnon's *Keeper of Concentration Camps: Dillon S. Myer and American Racism* (Berkeley, 1987), and D. Casensway with M. Rosemann, *Beyond Words: Images of America's Concentration Camps* (Ithaca, 1987):

> Particularly in the wake of the Iran-contra affair, these books are timely reminders that there have been various previous attempts on the part of the United States government to bypass the Constitution. They remind us that majority opinion is far from a guarantee of basic human rights. Given this tragic history, the Constitution needs to be respected as a "majority of one."[12]

By far the most persistent and effective endeavor to reverse the wartime injustice was undertaken by a large number of ordinary citizens of diverse racial, cultural, and religious backgrounds who gave time, money, and labor for compensatory redress (called the "redress movement") for the internment of Japanese-Americans. Year after year, these dedicated men and women endured numerous hardships, disappointments, and delays. At long last, in August of 1988, President Ronald Reagan signed the so-called redress bill—H.R. 442, the Civil Liberties Act, declaring that the internment of Japanese-Americans during World War II was a mistake. Although the act provides a restitution payment to each surviving Japanese-American (roughly 60,000 of the 120,000 who were originally relocated), the amount of money was hardly designed to make up for those huge financial losses or all those lost years. The president made it clear that "what is most important in this bill has less to do with property than with honor. For here we admit a wrong. Here we reaffirm our commitment as a nation to equal justice under the law."[13]

With the Civil Liberties Act enacted on August 10, 1988, the hopes of Japanese-Americans were greatly restored. Moreover, by acknowledging the fundamental injustice of the evacuation, relocation, and internment of U.S. citizens of Japanese ancestry and of their parents, America redeemed equality and freedom, which were robbed not only from persons of Japanese ancestry, but also from all Americans. However, in spite of this positive outcome, the ugly heads of racial bigotry seem to pop up elsewhere without any encouragement. Many concerned citizens have been deeply disturbed by the reported increase in death threats and harassment pointed toward Arab-Americans since the Iraqi invasion of Kuwait in the summer of 1990. The mass media seem to have an abundant supply of incidents, each of which involves untold suffering, shattered hopes, and huge losses of property and maimed lives. Certainly, a great many of us have been immensely inspired by Martin Luther King, Jr.'s dream of a color-blind America. Even though King's dream may not be actualized soon, we should at least make every effort to achieve the minimum standard of the American way of life, namely, the equality of all citizens before the law, which alone leads us to liberty in thought and action envisaged by the architects of our Republic.

III

THE CHRISTIAN
TRADITION:
WESTERN
AND GLOBAL

7

RELIGION(S), COMMUNITY, COMMUNICATION, AND FAITH: THE HEBREW PARADIGM OF CHRISTIANITY

PROLOGUE

Part I of this book was meant to depict an Asian Christian's perspective of Christianity as I personally experienced it in my childhood and youth in Japan, while Part II attempted to unfold some of the inner fabrics of Asian Americans' mental universe—shared presumably to a great extent by America's other marginal and/or minority groups—in which I have been privileged to participate since 1941. Now in this section I intend to deal with Western Christian tradition, with special reference to the American scene, as a member of the Christian community here, as a naturalized citizen of this Republic, and as a student of religion(s). Inevitably, my perceptions on the subject are colored by my thirty-five years' experience of teaching the history of religions at the University of Chicago, including ten years of serving concurrently as dean of its Divinity School.

In adumbrating my reflections on this subject, I have a modest hope of sharing with readers a slant that holds in balance both (a) an external and phenomenological approach to Christianity as one of the significant religions—indeed as one genuine experience of religious reality underlying various religious experiences, and as such constitutes one part, albeit an important one, of the whole of humanity's religious experience, and (b) an autobiographical understanding of the inner meaning of Christian tradition as a tradition of faith to be affirmed from within.[1] I am firmly convinced that just as we are entitled to be illumined in human affairs both by the two legitimate, even though different, perceptions (biographical and autobiographical), we can ill afford to neglect either the external or the internal approach to religious phenomena and not-so-readily-apparent religious reality. Ironically, there are some people who want to collapse the external and internal approaches in favor of either humanistic, social scientific, or philosophical (external) study of religion(s) or narrowly theological (internal), say, Christian or Jewish, study. I am persuaded, however, that both the autobiographical and biographical genres as well as external and internal modes of religious comprehensions are qualitatively different and basically uncollapsible in the end, and both are legitimate and necessary.

Admittedly, many of those who approach religions from outside are suspicious of autobiographical understanding and/or affirmation of the inner meaning of religions from within, because the latter orientation is bound to unfold the uniqueness of individual religious traditions, thus greatly complicating the task of generalizing about religions, which is essential for any external attempt to delineate the common features of various religions. Many of them would rather depend solely on such general categories as myths, symbols, rituals, doctrines, devotions, and types of leadership, or—especially when confronted by an individual religious phenomenon—resort to primarily objectified descriptions, using aforementioned general categories in their eyeball approach. Thus, in many cases, the external (biographical) approach to religions elucidates histories, systems of doctrines, contents of scriptures, and even devotional practices of, for example, Hinduism, Buddhism, Christianity, or Islam, without explicating how the faithful of those traditions interpret their daily experiences in the light of their religious faiths or attain the sense of certitude of salvation by following their inherited spiritual paths. To be sure, the external study of religions is undoubtedly one of the legitimate approaches, especially because in recent decades it has developed many sophisticated theories and methods that are greatly enriched by the cooperation with and contributions of up-to-date humanistic, historical, and artistic scholarship and of the social sciences, such as psychology, sociology, cultural anthropology, neo-Marxist insights, and/or poststructuralist criticisms. Appreciative though I am of critical, humanistic, and social scientific (nontheological) study of religions, I have two main reservations about their approaches. First, many practitioners of external study, partly because of their overconfidence in their methods and partly because of their emotional antireligious attitudes, seem to be persuaded that their orientation is undoubtedly the most and only authentic mode of study of religion(s), and they find no room or justification for what I call the autobiographical perception of the internal meaning of religions. Second, in their enthusiasm for their perspective, many of the practitioners rightly appropriate insights and methods derived from a variety of other disciplines but often neglect what Mircea Eliade once called the dimension of the "sacred," which cannot be neglected altogether in dealing with religious reality.[2]

On the other hand, my reservation with the one-sided exaggerated claim of the nontheological (humanistic and social scientific) study as the only legitimate mode of study of religions is mild in comparison with my frustration with pseudotheological studies, which seem to advocate that the autobiographical discernment of the inner meaning of religions is the only authentic religious approach, thereby rejecting all claims of legitimacy of the approach to religious phenomena and reality from outside. Such a stance often takes place among adherents of one religion, when the said tradition becomes an official or dominant religion in one place for any length of time. It is somewhat analogous to the mental habit of residents in an area where one language has been spoken for generations. It is a temptation for them to succumb to the mental complex that theirs is the best, if not the only true, language, and that all other languages are pale shadows of the genuine (their) linguistic expression. To be sure, Christians in the West are not the only group of religious adherents to fall into this kind of common error; in fact, various other groups, such as Muslims, Hindus, and Buddhists in their respective Islamic, Hindu, and Buddhist regions, have often developed similar mental traits over the years. But because we are now dealing with the Western Christian tradition, I will discuss presently how Western Christians have been historically led to such misguided delusions about their faith, and how simplistic "theologians" among them have come to assert the claim that their autobiographical understanding of the inner meaning of Christianity is the only true path, while all others are false and not worthy of respect.

RELIGION(S): SOME PRELIMINARY REFLECTIONS

Before we go into a more pointed discussion of Western Christianity, a few general remarks about some common features of religions might be in order. In this connection, I have often quoted the statement by a sensitive Islamicist, Bernard Lewis, ostensibly to demonstrate that, in dealing with global religious scenes, many of the things that have been taken for granted in the West are not universally valid or accept-able.[3] By appealing to Bernard Lewis's statement, I am not trying to contravene the value of the Western convention of dividing human experience into a series of semiautonomous domains, for example, aesthetics, ethics, art, culture, religion. However, the fact that this kind of perception has worked fairly well in the West in the past does not imply that such a provincial convention now has universal valid-ity, as some Westerners—either because of blind confidence in their inherited ways of thinking or ignorance of other options—seem to assert. On this point, it should be stated that our ignorance of other (in this case, non-Western) ways of perceiving the nature of human expe-rience is understandable and, humanly speaking, forgivable, but, as is often said, our ignorance of how ignorant we are about other peoples' ways is no longer forgivable.

It is worth noting that many peoples in various places through-out the ages have accepted the orders of "heaven, human, and nature" (different dimensions of space) as well as the notions of the "past, present, and future" (dimensions of time). But there are an amazing vari-ety of perceptions of these dimensions of space and time, handed down in different traditions. Some of them envisage a coherent overall cosmos, consisting of celestial, earthly, and netherworldly strata, all governed by some sort of comprehensive order, moral or otherwise. Others reject any notion of cosmic order and find only chances, accidents, and brute law of survival in the entire universe. Notwithstanding the almost infinite vari-ety of views proposed by different traditions on dimensions of space and time, many religious traditions, developed in history, are securely an-chored in (a) the "empirical order" (social, cultural, economic, political, etc.), even though it is usually seen in its relationship to heavenly or netherworldly realms; (b) the "present time sequence," organically con-nected to be sure to the past and the future; and (c) the "destiny of human beings" both individually and collectively. It is to be noted in this con-nection that, contrary to the wishful thinking of current academic stu-dents of religions, the tasks of religion have been primarily soteriological (how can we be saved or enlightened?) and only secondarily cognitive (regarding such subject matters as the nature of human life, different levels of reality, including Ultimate Reality, and relationships between, say, the order of heaven and the order of nature). My mentor, Joachim Wach, speculated that human beings throughout the ages had the reli-gious impulse to believe and worship and also the intellectual impulse to try to understand. I might add that there have been various degrees and kinds of combinations of soteriological and cognitive sensitivities even within the same religious traditions.

Religion, according to one definition, is belief in a divine or superhuman power or powers to be obeyed and worshiped as the creator(s) and ruler(s) of the universe. Not all divine powers are, however, believed to be creators or rulers of the universe, as testified by Hinduism, and there is a religion, Buddhism, that does not believe in any deity or creator of the universe. Buddhists affirm that it was Buddha who had gained insight into the meaning of existence and the holy path of deliverance from the transitoriness of the finite world, enslaved as it is in the time-and-space complex. Various Chinese sages have taken seriously the "Will of Heaven" (not just Heaven), the transcendental source of the "Heavenly Mandate," which, in accordance with the eternal cosmic principle (tao), is on the one hand intrinsically involved in the regular rotation of celestial and terrestrial movements, and on the other hand underlies the normative structure of human, social, and political orders. These illustrations might be sufficient to elucidate my point that there are a wide variety of religious orientations in the experience of humankind. Even then, the all-too-Europocentric definition of religion cited above may profitably be kept in mind as we reassess Western Christian tradition, which was greatly influenced by, among other things, predominantly theistic Near Eastern religions (Zoroastrianism, Judaism, and Islam) to say nothing about Christianity itself, as well as mystery cults and other Mediterranean and European local traditions.

This may be an appropriate occasion to add a brief note on the notions of "sacred" (often equated with religion) and "secular" (opposite of sacred), which are mentioned in most discussions of religion. In discussing sundry matters, I remember asking my learned senior colleague, Mircea Eliade, for his considered opinion as to when secularism emerged. According to him, secularism as such arose when specialists of the sacred—seers, diviners, tricksters, shamans, priests, prophets—came into existence. I often recall this comment of Eliade's as I think of the development of religions, which exhibit the principle of *coincidentia oppositorum* between the sacred and the secular, held together in a mutually supportive and/or critical correlation. Ironically today, especially in the Western world, there is a great deal of misapprehension and loose thinking on the proper relationship between "sacred and secular (or profane)" dimensions, which greatly distort our understanding of religions in general and Christianity in particular. Thus it might be worth considering this matter a little further.

Today it is fairly common to equate religion with the sacred, and society and culture at large with the secular (profane) dimensions. Thus, both many clerics and social scientists tend to treat Judaism or Christianity (sacred) and society (secular) in oppositional terms (based on different motivations). But history amply testifies that Christianity, for instance (but other religious traditions and their societies/civilizations follow more or less similar patterns), has "two faces": (1) the Christianity that is embodied in the church, or the ecclesiastical structure, and (2) Christianity as this-worldly religion, one of the dominant features within the framework of Western civilization (embracing social, cultural, artistic, economic, political orders), which incidentally received its cosmic legitimation from Christianity both as (a) "church" and (b) "religion," or civilizing agency. In dealing with this intriguing historical phenomenon (a sort of double exposure), we are often misled either to equate the two faces or to completely separate the two (based mostly on wishful thinking, sentimentality, or loose thinking). It is worth remembering, too, that sacred and secular dimensions are involved in Christianity both as a church and a this-worldly religion.

1. Christianity, like many other religions, is rooted in the experience of invisible religious reality, based on faith, involving a quality of mind and of will and spirit. Such sacrality, however, in order to be shared by others, has to be expressed in myths, symbols, rituals, doctrines, and ethics, and is embodied in the ecclesiastical structure (called the church, in the case of Christianity), based on sacramental and incarnational principles. In this process of the embodiment of the sacral experience by "earthen vessels" (the profane or secular dimensions of the ecclesiastical structure), the church often ends up distorting sacred experience and faith by resorting to yesterday's experiences as the soteriological formulas for today and by superimposing such dead formulas (dogmas and canon laws) on the faithful in the name of ecclesiastical authority. In other words, the church that came into being as the servant of Christianity, being the embodiment of Christian experience, now claims to own Christianity outright with its own all-too-human and secularistic understanding of what the sacred experience, or even religious reality, ought to be. Also invariably, as it has happened to many other religious communities, the autobiographical perceptions of the later faithful brought about perspectives that were different from those of their forebears. For example, just as Buddha, who was originally venerated as the pathfinder of the soteriological path, came to be the object of worship himself by later Buddhists (as indicated by the sacred formula "I take refuge in the

Buddha; I take refuge in the Buddhist teaching—*Dharma,* law; and I take refuge in the Buddhist community—*Samgha"),* Jesus of Nazareth, who preached the gospel of the kingdom of God, became himself the center of the gospel.

2. In Europe, Christianity as a this-worldly religion was compelled to be "domesticated" so as to become an important cornerstone of the bulwarks of Western civilization. Whereas earlier followers of Jesus were urged to hold in balance, and not mix up, the things that are *God's* and the things that are *Caesar's,* after the fourth century, when Christianity became the official this-worldly religion of the Empire, loyalty to the *Caesar* began to be mixed up with loyalty to *God.* To be sure, Caesar's kingdom and Western civilization were legitimated by the sacred aura of Christianity, but according to the emerging autobiographical perception of Western civilization (which gradually blended Hellenistic thought, Christian tradition, and Roman jurisprudence), religion had to be subservient to the growing civilization. Thus, in a sense, this-worldly Christian religion was regarded most ironically as a shield—reminiscent of a fig leaf in the Genesis myth, which was used by Adam to hide him from the divine presence—against the sacred dimension of Christianity itself.

The most confusing fact is that the development of the church and the development of Western civilization were not so neatly differentiable. Their paths intersected at many points negatively and positively. The competition and conflict between the church (*sacerdotium*) and the state (*imperium*) in European history are legendary, and the university (*studium*), the third prestigious institution, was often caught between *sacerdotium* and *imperium.* On the other hand, the church and Western civilization have mutually penetrated and influenced each other, so that it is virtually impossible to discuss the history of either the church or Western civilization independently. To put it another way, it is far from an easy task to trace the development of Christianity, which had been based on the experience of religious reality, embodied on the one hand in the church (ecclesiastical tradition), and on the other hand objectified as a this-worldly religion, blended into Western civilization. In this respect, we should remind ourselves that such a dual character of Christianity is by no means its unique feature. Certainly, many other religious traditions also follow a similar pattern because in any human history, "community," "communication," and "faith" are closely interrelated but could not be boxed into one and the same framework. Rather, the unique character of Christianity was derived from its adherence to the Hebrew paradigm, which will be discussed later in this chapter. But first I will briefly touch upon the general issues of community, communication, and faith, common to many religious traditions.

COMMUNITY, COMMUNICATION, AND FAITH

Today we are keenly conscious of the crucial importance of the problem of communication, stimulated no doubt by the ever-growing cultural and idea industries (e.g., radio, television, movies, newspapers, and magazines) that not only influence fashions and idioms but also mold the minds and spirits of the masses. We should keep in mind, however, that communication has always been a fundamental and perennial factor in human history.[4] This problem has concerned religious people, too, because they realize that in the domain of religion they can ill afford to ignore the relationship between the techniques of communication and its contents.

The term *technique* is not used here only to refer to the gimmicks of communication, which are exploited, for example, by semicommercialized hucksters of the gospel. On this point, more consideration than superficial gimmicks should be given to a careful semantic analysis, and use of, symbols that are essential to meaningful discourse. Clearly, certain meanings cannot be created in peoples' minds only by artificial manipulation of symbols. At the same time, there is not much point in employing certain symbols that do not evoke in other minds something pointing to what the communicator is trying to communicate. Hence the importance of the "contents" of communication, too. In this respect, religious communication is peculiarly complex and ambiguous because the contents, or the "what," of religious communication has to deal with invisible and amorphous faith. Significantly, all religions acknowledge that their faith is ultimately based on a claim and not on a proof. It implies, then, in the area of religion, that even the most rational thinkers reach a point where they have to invoke a "religious Fifth Amendment" when rational communication fails. Thus, as Louis de la Vallée Poussin rightly observes, Buddhism, for example—by far the most philosophical of the various religions—"ends in an act of faith."[5]

No religious faith has ever existed in a vacuum; it has been conditioned by particular historical and cultural traditions, even though it in turn conditioned the history and civilization in which it existed. One of the intricate issues involved in this mutual relationship is that of a "magical circle of words," which—as astutely observed by Wilhelm von Humboldt—implies that any person or persons brought up in a particular civilization cannot be altogether emancipated from various kinds of ambiguous but real associations of emotional reactions to symbols and words.[6] (It is a matter of great significance that universalistically oriented religions such as Buddhism and Christianity dared to claim that their faith can be divorced from civilization-bound symbols. Yet ironically, Christianity depends on the Hebrew paradigm, which in principle affirms the inseparability of symbols and faith, as will be discussed below.)

In many religious traditions, it is taken for granted that the nature of faith is such that the deepest dimension of faith can only be pointed to; it cannot be delineated. How, then, can a listener develop a mode of becoming aware of inner values and meanings that are not spelled out by the communicator? Different people have given different answers, such as intuition, imagination, the existence of fore or prior knowledge, fantasy, and congenial understanding. There is no denying that poets and novelists can describe the joy of love even when they themselves are in a state of misery, and that a sincere Sufi Muslim or a Hindu Bhakti believer can feel congenial with the writings of Jewish or Christian mystics. When Marian Anderson sang "Lead Kindly Light" in front of the statue of Mahatma Gandhi during her goodwill tour of India in 1957, the Hindu listeners undoubtedly sensed something of the inner meaning of the great hymn. The meaning communicated, however, was probably a unique blending of the diverse backgrounds exemplified by the British Roman Catholic, John Newman, author of the hymn; the black American singer, Marian Anderson, who happens to be a Protestant; and a group of Hindu listeners. Furthermore, this particular hymn was a favorite of Mahatma Gandhi, and as such the Hindu listeners were prepared to "participate" in the act of dedication of this hymn to the memory of Gandhi. It is quite another thing to ask, however, whether or not Newman's theology, Christology, and ecclesiology were communicated to the Hindu audience. Here lies the knotty issue in the "magical circle of words," involved in the values, meanings, histories, and so forth, of civilizations and secular or religious communities. Inevitably, therefore, we are confronted by the intriguing relationship between community and communication.

Nowadays we use the term *community* rather loosely, often interchangeably with *society*. But I would like to retain the meaning of community as it was depicted in Ferdinand Tönnies's classic *Gemeinschaft und Gesellschaft* (1887) as "groupings based on organic sympathy (*Wesenswille*)," in which "the accident of kinship or proximity is responsible for an association which no one has particularly sought to arrange," whereas society consists of groupings based on personal preference (*Kürwille*), "in which mutual selection has led to an association deliberately designed by its participants."[7] On community, Louis Wirth says that it is "a territorial base, distribution in space of men, institutions, and activities, close living together on the basis of kinship and organic interdependence, and a common life based upon the mutual correspondence of interests tend to characterize a community."[8] It should be noted in this connection that some of the religious fellowships—especially in the case of founded religions such as Christianity or Buddhism—emerge as societies; but in the course of time, adherents of those societies begin to interpret the inner meaning of their fellowships autobiographically as communities, because to their orientation there is an element of "something not manufactured, but given." Thus, as van der Leeuw points out, insiders feel they "do not become members of it, but 'belong to it.'"[9]

In discussing the relationship between community and communication, we might profitably differentiate two aspects of communication: (1) "communication between," which according to Hendrik Kraemer refers to the realm of "all possible manifestations of human intersubjectivity" and (2) "communication of," which refers to the "forms and subject matters of communication," such as information, teaching, discourse, discussion, and debate.[10] Many scholars speculate, as did Robert Redfield, that in the so-called primitive communities, communication was a relatively simple matter because their members were "held together essentially by common understanding as to the ultimate nature and purpose of life. . . . [T]he people were homogeneous in that they shared the same tradition and had the same view of the good life."[11] The homogeneity of community life also characterized some of the ancient communities, such as the ancient Greek *polis*, which, according to some scholars, had simultaneously the characteristics of both the religious community and the city-state. With the gradual disintegration of the dual character of the *polis*, however, "communication between" began to erode and the need for "communication of" arose.

We are told by Josephus that when Roman conquerors entered Jerusalem and went to the Holy of Holies in the Temple of Solomon, they found it empty. Although the absence of manmade symbols indicates, as Josephus interprets autobiographically from the perspective of the inner meaning of Judaism of that time, "the purest type of religion, the secrets of which we may *not reveal to aliens*," it could also mean that the Jewish community at that time still maintained a sufficient degree of "communication between" without having to depend on external symbols.[12] Later on, however, the homogeneity of the Hebrew community eroded under the impact of Hellenism, alien rule, and the spread of Aramaic as the language of the people, rather than traditional Hebrew. And by the first century B.C.E., many Jews no longer shared the same values even within the Hebrew community, which now witnessed the mushrooming of many societies within it—the Sadducees, the Pharisees, the Herodians, the Zealots, and the Essenes. And in this soil and climate Christianity was born!

THE HEBREW PARADIGM OF CHRISTIANITY

The unique character of Christianity is said to be rooted in its "Hebrewness." Whether or not Jesus of Nazareth belonged to one of the old societies or founded a new one, both insiders and outsiders of Christian religion seem to agree that Jesus was conscious of standing in the tradition of the Hebrew community of faith. Evidently, he felt called to restore not the political independence of the Davidic kingdom but the religiously inspired foundation of the Hebrew community. This was acknowledged in a Gospel account that he was "sent to the lost sheep of the house of Israel" (Matt. 15:24). Even that controversial figure, Paul, who was undoubtedly a full-fledged Hellenistic Jew and a Roman citizen, was proud of his Jewish heritage and affirmed the theme: "If you are Christ's, then you are Abraham's offspring." (Gal. 3:29). Accordingly, we should briefly reassess the main essentials of the Hebrew paradigm. It is significant that the Hebrew Bible stresses the point that the ancient Hebrew community was not only a tribal community (actually a congregation of many tribes) but also a covenanted community. According to the biblical tradition, Abraham had two sons, Isaac and Ishmael. Isaac was not only Abraham's son, but also the son of promise. He in turn had also two sons, Esau and Jacob, and it was the younger twin brother, Jacob, who received the birthright and the paternal blessing. These narratives emphasize the point that "an order of *salvation* separates off from that of *nature,* a divine *possibility* from the—likewise divine—*givenness*," to use van der Leeuw's expression.[13] Opinions vary, however, as to whether the human community and covenanted community were homologized or whether one side (tribal or covenanted thrust) embraced the other.

At any rate, the motif of the covenant runs through the Hebrew Bible. We are told that when the Israelites were suffering and enslaved in Egypt, God told Moses, the hero of the biblical tradition— even though Moses did not even know God's name—to tell his fellow Israelites the divine plan to rescue them, whereupon "the people believed and . . . they bowed their heads and worshiped" (Exodus, chapters 3 and 4). It should be noted that God's own reference to himself as "I am/shall be what I am/shall be" is based on the Hebrew notion of *hayathology* (the dynamic notion of *action,* in sharp contrast to the static Greek *ontology*—metaphysics—of *being,* which later Christians accepted after the encroachment of Greek metaphysical tradition invaded Christianity through scholastics in the medieval period). To Pharaoh, however, what was evident to Israelites had no meaning for him, as he told Moses and Aaron: "Who is the Lord, that I should heed his voice and let Israel go? I do not know the Lord." (Exod. 5:2), clearly indicating self-authenticating circularity and nontransferable particularity of the notion of the covenant. It is also worth adding that, according to the ancient Hebrew notion, "God is LORD of the community yet in some sense *a member of the community also.* He participates actively in its life, maintains his relationship to it, and assumes the responsibility of one who is in covenant with his people," to quote James Muilenburg's astute statement.[14]

Once the Israelites were delivered from bondage in Egypt, they were expected to renew their covenant with God, no longer as slaves of the Egyptian king but as free children of the divine king's promise. But in the course of time, the ethos of the covenanted community underwent changes when the Hebrew community developed into a bureaucratic kingdom; the kingship of God now was to face a competing authority of the earthly king. Then, it was seer-judge Samuel who maneuvered to elevate David to the throne, ousting the tragic figure of King Saul. David, in turn, appointed his son Solomon "to be ruler over Israel and over Judah" (1 Kings 1:35). Solomon dared to expel Abi'athar from being priest to the Lord. He also brought pagan cults into the Hebrew community, even though he was credited to dedicate the Temple of the Lord. To be sure, the covenanted community preserved its external forms but became subservient to monarchy, which governed the human community. No wonder, when the prophet Amos dared to proclaim the universal judgment of God even on his own Israelites, a spokesman—an ecclesiastical elite of the bureaucratic kingdom (political community)—greeted the prophet in the name of the king: "O seer, go, flee away to the land of Judah, and eat bread there, and prophesy there; but never again prophesy at Bethel, for it is the *king's sanctuary,* and it is a *temple of the kingdom"* (Amos 7:12–13; my italics). It is to be noted that a political community and/or a civilization have often developed their own "temple of the kingdom."

Space does not allow us here to go into detailed discussion of the intriguing role of the prophet. Suffice it to say that although Hebrew prophets functioned exclusively within the Hebrew language and symbols (despite the fact that they often transformed customary meanings), they were credited with the power of transcending their time and space. According to Joachim Wach: "The prophet illuminates and interprets the past, but he also anticipates the future. The *kairos* (moment) is interpreted by the prophet in this dual light."[15] In other words, the prophets were patriots (not nationalists), but their primary loyalty was to the Lord of history, and not to the Jewish kingdom. Some of the prophets also talked about a *new covenant* between God and Israel. "This is the covenant which I will make with the house of Israel," so prophesied Jeremiah: "I will put my law within them, and I will write it upon their hearts" (Jer. 31:33).[16] Thus, the automatic equation of the Hebrew community and the covenanted community was to be elevated one notch above to a new spiritual covenanted relationship, and the order of salvation (divine possibility) was to be differentiated from the order of nature (the divine givenness). In short, a new kind of community was promised; and men and women must now seek membership in this new spiritual community with a new attitude, for "the sacrifice acceptable to God is a broken spirit; / a broken and contrite heart . . ." (Psalm 51:17).

The Babylonian exile in the sixth century B.C.E. was another turning point in the spiral history of the Hebrew community. There in Babylon, Israelites imbibed many features of Persian Zoroastrian religious tradition, such as, angelology and demonology, and above all, the notion of the end of the world (*eschaton*).[17] Understandably, the influence of the Persian concept of the end of the world refined many Hebrew ideas, such as the day of the Lord that comes at the end of history, and the sophisticated theory of the "history of salvation" (*Heilsgeschichte*), which is different from empirical history but has been intertwined with it. The Babylonian captivity also made Israelites ask penetrating questions about the rationale about their suffering and theodicy (a vindication of divine justice in allowing evil to exist). The prophet Ezekiel asserted, on the one hand, that the Israelites' suffering was caused by divine wrath because of the Israelites' failure to live up to the covenant, and on the other hand the suffering was part of a divine plan to "cleanse" the Jews' hearts so as to make them worthy instruments of the divine enterprise (Ezekiel, chapter 36). The realization that the new covenanted community was to be commissioned to become the messenger and instrument for God's universal salvation reached its peak in the prophecy of Deutero-Isaiah:

"'You are my witness,' says the LORD / 'and my servant whom I have chosen, / that you may know and believe me / and understand that I am He'" (Isa. 43:10).[18] Deutero-Isaiah was also persuaded that the God of the Hebrew community was indeed a universal deity, governing the whole universe, punishing the sins of Babylon, and anointing Cyrus as king of Persia, and so forth. The Babylonian captivity of the Jews away from their homeland also compelled them to devise a series of activities to sustain their inherited tradition in new situations. This was done by regular worship and teaching (both of which centered around the synagogue because of inaccessibility to the Temple in Jerusalem), which became regular features of Rabbinic Judaism in subsequent periods. The Jewish captives who were released by the Persian king Cyrus (600?–529 B.C.E.) to return to Palestine came under the control of priestly elites. Both the Torah (religious law and teaching) and the prophetic oral tradition were codified.[19] Meanwhile, cultural and political maps of the Near East were redrawn several times. Following the conquest of Alexander the Great of Palestine in the fourth century B.C.E., Jews were destined to be ruled by the Hellenistic-Ptolemies of Egypt, the Syrian Seleucid dynasty, and eventually by Rome. Culturally, the Jews felt the strong impact of Hellenism. Many Jews began to settle in diaspora communities in various parts of the Mediterranean world, and the Hebrew Bible itself was translated into the Greek Septuagint. Understandably, extreme traditionalists among the Jews must have resented the encroachment of Hellenism into the Jewish fold, but many, especially Hellenized Jews, rejoiced that they now became acceptable to the larger world. And as I once said:

> The Hellenistic Jews wanted to convey their autobiographical affirmation of the inner religious meaning of Judaism biographically to non-Jews through the Greek language and Hellenistic thought patterns. . . . [T]hey wanted non-Jews to understand some aspects of the contours of their monotheistic faith, or mono-Yahwism. Conversely, the non-Jews [in the religiously pluralistic Mediterranean world] who could not enter into the "inner meaning" of the Jewish religion at least biographically understood the "outer meaning" of Judaism in terms of a "monolatristic particularism," a special accent on a particular deity within the context of "monolatry" (acceptance of many deities, each one worshipped as the supreme deity by different groups).[20]

The spiral development of the Hebrew community—both the tribal and (old and new) covenanted communities—clearly illustrates the important fact that any community maintains a relative equilibrium of values and history. Of course, ideas and values do change, but changes of values are not completely divorced from history, and both cultural and religious symbols reflect the way in which values and history are held together. As values change, the old symbols are either discarded or used (or re-used, in Paul Ricoeur's term) to represent a new meaning.[21] In this context, we should remember that the history of a community (especially *Heilsgeschichte*) is not an impartial account of chronological events. History has a dimension of values that are shared by the community, because history is interpreted by the shared values (even though the values in turn are constantly modified by the historical experiences) of the community. In this sense, the community is the bearer of the tricky and ever-changing relationship of values and history, as testified by the ancient Hebrew experience. To be more specific, the Hebrew Bible tells us that the covenanted relationship presupposes faith, which is a new dimension unknown to the order of nature, even though the covenanted relationship was not against nature, which was taken for granted to be a state of divine givenness, exemplified in the Hebrew Bible by the nature covenant of Noah's story (to be contrasted with the faith covenant of Abraham and Moses, etc.). And in a way, the story of the tower of Babel is the continuation of the nature motif of Noah's account, both indicating that there is a basic divine order in God's creation. The biblical theme is that every tribe and nation of the world has the benefit of the nature covenant that God made with humankind.

I am sure it was not a sheer accident that biblical writers placed the story of the tower of Babel just prior to the account of Abraham. We can easily see two obvious reasons: (1) While the sons of Noah decided on their own to build a "city of the sons of men," Abraham—as later the New Testament speculated—"looked forward to the city which has foundations, whose builder and maker is God" (Heb. 11:10). (2) The covenant God made with Abraham is related to the nature covenant he had made with Noah and all living creatures, but the former is not automatic as is the latter; it requires faith, which has elements of uncertainty, absurdness, and risk in human eyes (because God does not explain everything to men and women of faith as he did to Noah). In faith, Abraham and Jacob were assured of the promised land, even though their faith was tested. And Moses, that indefatigable hero of the Exodus experience (it is unclear whether it was a historical or religious event), was not allowed to step into the promised land; in faith he had a glimpse, however faintly, of the reality of the promised land. Indeed, the motif—God's promise, the Israelites' faith, the covenant, and the promised land—was repeated many times in the biblical accounts, even though each event in this spiral development moves upward, acquiring new meaning. Let us briefly reexamine Deutero-Isaiah's account of the "suffering servant" with this in mind.

As the biblical account portrays it, the Babylonian captivity follows the similar pattern of the Hebrew captivity in Egypt. God's promise is given: "Fear not, for I am with you. . . . I will uphold you with my victorious right hand" (Isa. 41:8–10). With the success of Cyrus the Persian, the Jewish captives were encouraged with the hope of returning to the homeland: "Who says of Cyrus, 'He is my shepherd, and he shall fulfil all my purpose'" (Isa. 44:28). But God, the Lord of history, judges the sins of Babylon as much as the faithlessness of the Israelites. Even then, the Jews' suffering is not basically due to God's punishment on them, which they certainly deserved. Rather, it was meant to be a discipline and preparation for a divine purpose: "Behold, . . . I have tried you in the furnace of affliction. For my own sake, for my own sake, I do it" (Isa. 48:10–11). And God urged the Israelites to be faithful to the covenant: "Keep justice, and do righteousness, for soon my salvation will come, and my deliverance be revealed" (Isa. 56:1). The scenario of the drama of the Babylonian captivity is obvious: God chose Israel to be God's messenger: "I will give you as a light to the nations, that my salvation may reach to the end of the earth" (Isa. 49:6). And, following the motif, the reward of the promised land was assured—in terms of the future glory of Zion, which it must be noted, is not an earthly kingdom, but a new world order: "For behold, I create a new heaven and a new earth . . ." (Isaiah, chapters 65 and 66).

As the biblical account tells us, in the context of this grand eschatological hope of universal salvation, moral and social *restitio in integrum* in this world had only a preparatory meaning, at least in the eyes of Deutero-Isaiah. He saw clearly a hidden meaning of the motif of the suffering servant in the experience of the Jewish captivity in Babylon: "He was wounded for our transgressions, he was bruised for our iniquities" (Isa. 53:5). The significance of the Hebrew community—its achievements and sufferings—was no longer understood in terms of the reward of the earthly promised land envisaged by Abraham, Jacob, and so forth. The Hebrew tribal community as a whole was called to be the spiritually inspired covenanted community, which implied, as far as Deutero-Isaiah could see, that the community had to be a corporate servant of the Lord, who had chosen the Hebrew community as an instrument to relate the order of nature to the new order of Salvation. Such a spiral view of the history of salvation, based on a particular value-history motif, could not be understood intellectually; it could only be experienced and most likely grasped only faintly in faith. Ironically, as it happened in various other traditions, spiritual experience and faith became neglected in favor of external cognitive certainties, supported by ecclesiastical, religious, and legal trappings. By the first century B.C.E., "Hebrewness" lost its covenantal values and connotations, and sadly, it came to be regarded primarily as a historical accident.

In this situation, as mentioned before, a series of sectarian groups, both political and religious, emerged, each advocating its own brand of Hebrew tradition. Most audacious among them was a small new group of followers of the son of a Galilean carpenter. This group of followers, convinced of its calling to restore the ethos of the Hebrew covenanted community and following the spiral upward movement of the history of salvation, was to be elevated to become a new community of faith both for the Jews and for the Gentiles.

8

THE CHRISTIAN CHURCH
AND WESTERN CIVILIZATION

THE BIRTH OF CHRISTIANITY

In many parts of the ancient world, what we refer to as "religion" was inseparable from the tribal, ethnic, social, cultural, and political life of the people, so it is well nigh impossible to talk about the beginning of religion per se as a separate entity. Also, even in reference to the so-called founded religions, objective, historical data, which we moderns seek, about their births are hard to come by. As far as we can ascertain, based on random sampling of comparative materials, there seem to be two main plausible types of founding myths that trace the inceptions of the founded religions.

One type of founding myth seems to stress the centrality of the religious community as a more decisive factor in the emergence of a new religious tradition, even though by so doing it was not meant to denigrate the importance of the founders, their lives and teachings, and so forth. Such an orientation was ably articulated by Edward J. Thomas in his depiction of the birth of Buddhism. According to his analysis, Buddhism began "not with a body of doctrine, but with the formation of a society bound by certain rules," so that "to begin by analyzing the doctrine without first examining the community and the circumstances in which it originated would be likely to lead to quite arbitrary results."[1]

Significantly, biographies of the founder, which developed in abundance shortly after the founding of the Buddhist community, originally came into existence primarily as career models for novices. And it should be noted that the Buddhist community (*samgha*, which soon came to be dominated by monastics to the extent that the term *samgha* often came to be used as a synonym of the monastic orders, especially in the southern or Theravada tradition) remained one of the three objects of all Buddhists' affirmation, together with the Buddha and the doctrine.

The second type of founding myth stresses the supreme importance of the founder for founded religions. Chief among many examples of this category is that of Muhammad as the seal of prophets.[2] Of course, the Islamic tradition stresses *Qur'an* as the saving word of Allah and the prominence of Islamic community (*Umma*) as the paradigm for the united human community. But the *Qur'an* was transmitted by Muhammad, and the *Umma* was commenced by the Muslim community (*umma muslima*) under the leadership of the prophet in Medina.

Significantly, the founding myths of Christianity—as far as the authors of the New Testament attempt to portray—are based on the subtle mutuality of the first and the second types, that is, the centrality of the religious community and the importance of the founder. Or rather, the myth of the inception of the Christian community is authenticated by the myth of the founder, and vice versa, even though the myth of the community most likely had preceded the myths of the founder chronologically speaking—contrary to the expectation of many of the faithful. In other words, here accepting the expressions of the Book of Acts, the Christian community came into being by miraculous divine intervention on the day of Pentecost, after which the infant Christian community presumably collected appropriate lores about Jesus of Nazareth, as exemplified by the Gospels. The compilers of the New Testament, however, placed by design the lores about Jesus of Nazareth prior to the Book of Acts, which contains the narrative of the Pentecost, following the *mundus imaginalis* of the early Christian community, which had a sort of escalator mentality, directly relating the life and teaching of Jesus—epitomized by the account of the commission of the twelve disciples—to the autobiographical interpretation of the Pentecost event, in which the universalistic pneumatic gift (Holy Spirit) of grace was believed to be provided to the provincial (Jewish) Christian human fellowship, represented by the twelve disciples. In short, from the perspective of the early Christian community, the life and teaching of Jesus, culminating in the commission of the twelve disciples, was to be looked back on through the spectacle of the Pentecost event, while in turn the emergence of a new community of faith at Pentecost was claimed to be a continuous development of the spiral soteriological movement of the Hebrew history of salvation with Jesus as its center. Let us reassess the highlights of the dovetailing scenario presented by the compilers of the New Testament—first, the lore of the founder, followed by the narrative about the miraculous founding of the Christian community.

In reviewing the lores about Jesus, with minor variations in the Synoptic Gospels, we find two common underlying themes. The first follows what Martin Dibelius once called a "law of biographical analogy"— with certain fixed features also found in biographies of other saints and religious founders (e.g., Buddha, the Jina, Muhammad, Zoroaster, Lao-tse, etc.), including the realization or announcement during their childhood or youth about religious calling and the notion of supramundane powers that protect them in the time of distress. The second theme insists on the unmistakable Jewish identity that characterized Jesus' life and teaching. I might add that it was this unabashed particularity (Jewishness) which, according to the compilers of the New Testament, remained at the center of the motif of universality of the new Christian community that came into existence at the Pentecost. Accordingly, the Gospel accounts portrayed Jesus as a typical Jewish boy: he was presented in the Temple for purification; his parents and friends were all Jews; he worshiped regularly in the synagogues; and his religious outlook was decisively influenced by the traditional motif of the aforementioned Hebrew heritage, that is, God's promise, the Israelites' faith, the covenanted relationship between them, and the promised land (which is significantly claimed as the kingdom of God by Jesus, however). Notwithstanding insignificant variations among them, all the Gospel accounts seem to agree that Jesus' mission was to restore not the political independence of the Davidic kingdom but the more spiritual Hebrew covenanted community. Thus, although he was very conscious of being "sent only to the lost sheep of the house of Israel" (Matt. 15:24), he understood the meaning of the covenanted community in the more universalistic eschatological sense, and not in the provincial biological (ethnic) sense. To Jesus of the New Testament, the history of the Hebrew community from the time of Abraham was taken for granted as a spiral development of the hidden drama of salvation, and evidently Jesus took with utmost seriousness the role that he and the remnant of the household of Israel were destined to play in the history of salvation (which to be sure was accepted self-consciously in full-scale universalistic terms by the new Christian community in the Pentecost narrative).

Such an angle of vision on the part of the New Testament compilers may account for their attempt to cast the life of Jesus in the inherited frameworks of the biographies of their Jewish forebears, such as Abraham and Jacob. Accordingly, the account of Jesus' baptism was highlighted by the Holy Spirit's descent upon Jesus in bodily form, with the divine announcement of his unique relationship to God. This was followed by the narrative about the temptation of Jesus in the wilderness, which tested his faith. Then he was certain about his covenanted relationship with God, who now commissioned him to announce his mission in public by reading in the synagogue in Nazareth the portion of Isaiah's prophecy that included the proclamation that "today this scripture has been fulfilled in your hearing" (Luke 4:21). How then did he understand the end of his life? Opinions no doubt vary widely on this subject. As a plausible conjecture—and it is nothing more than conjecture—we might turn to the well-known parable of the prodigal son. According to this story, the prodigal son—after he wasted his inheritance—struggled in his mind as to whether to go home or not. Clearly, his struggle was not solely against hunger. He must have felt in the image of his father a combination of judgment and love. It was this unique character of fatherhood from which he had alienated himself. In the end, he made up his mind to return to his father's house. Significantly, his father saw him from far off, was moved with compassion, and accepted his prodigal son warmly (Luke, chapter 15). In a real sense, it was "death" that enabled the prodigal son to be "resurrected" as the Son of God. The narrator of this parable was well acquainted with the paradigm of Jacob's legend, according to which Jacob beyond the river was dead, but crossing the river, "Israel"—the new and resurrected person—found the fulfillment of life or the "promised land" in the experience of reconciliation with his alienated brother.

It is this picture of Jesus as the new Israel that is portrayed by the author of Mark's Gospel, too. Jesus in this Gospel is not a triumphant king, as in the Fourth Gospel. The author of Mark, however, skillfully weaves together two themes regarding Jesus. First, from the viewpoint of his disciples, Jesus was the agent through whom God revealed his mighty work, as testified by Jesus' talk to a paralytic: "Your sins are forgiven," because "the Son of man has authority on earth to forgive sins" (Mark 2:5 and 10). His disciples were also given a glimpse of God's plan in the vision of the Transfiguration. Second, from Jesus' own standpoint, he played the role of the suffering servant; he was tormented about the prospect of his tragic end, and even asked God to remove that tragic role. And, although he dared to go forward when the time came, he cried out to God on the cross: "Why hast thou forsaken me?" (Mark 15:34). Significantly, these two themes—Jesus as the suffering servant and new Israel, and Jesus through whom God's salvation of humankind was revealed—find harmony at the cross in the words of the centurion: "Truly this man was the Son of God" (Mark 15:39). In fact, these two portrayals of Jesus were inseparably interwoven throughout Mark's narrative. Thus, following the traditional Hebrew motif, God's promise was given to Jesus, Jesus' faith was tested, God and Jesus entered into a covenanted (Father-and-Son) relationship, and after the suffering on the cross he was resurrected. Seen from the standpoint of the disciples, again following the traditional motif, God's promise was given to them through Jesus, their faith was tested, they were given the new covenant through Jesus, and after losing the earthly Jesus they received the gift of the Spirit at Pentecost. In all fairness, it should be made clear that the New Testament compilers' interpretation of Jesus' understanding of the *raison d'être* of the Hebrew covenanted community was not the only correct, or the most logical and/or acceptable, option of the Jewish religious heritage. On this issue, I often think of the contention of R. T. Herford, as cited by Judah Goldin, that the Pharisees and Jesus (and by implication Paul) had much in common, but that their obvious disagreement was based on

> two fundamentally different conceptions of religion, viz., that in which the supreme authority was Torah and that in which the supreme authority was the intuition of God in the individual soul and conscience. The Pharisees stood for one; Jesus stood for the other.[3]

Moreover, it was not only Jesus' understanding of the inherited Jewish spiritual heritage but also "his tremendous personality that gripped those first disciples," as cogently pointed out by Morton Scott Enslin.[4] To be sure, many of his first disciples were not known for learning or professional training. In fact, many of them were humble partners (koinonoi) in the fishing trade; the precursor of Christianity as the new community of faith and koinonia was heralded as Jesus "initiated them [the disciples] into a higher partnership, for which they left all to follow him."[5] The elevation of their partnership to a higher dimension was culminated, according to the Gospel accounts, in the commissioning of the twelve disciples, which incidentally symbolized the twelve tribes that had constituted the Israelite community or congregation (qahal; after the Pentecost, the Christian community came to be referred to as ekklesia, which was a Greek term for qahal).

As to the narrative of the divine intervention that fostered the formation of the Christian church at the Pentecost, some scholars suspect—as mentioned earlier—that it had actually preceded, at least chronologically, the collection of the lores about Jesus, but that the Book of Acts reversed the order based on its own reasonings. Thus we are told by the Book of Acts that the disciples of Jesus were discouraged and dispirited after his crucifixion. But in the midst of the depth of such a disappointment and distress, the remaining few of Jesus' followers in Jerusalem experienced an unusually uplifting ecstatic joy and assurance about their calling to the higher partnership, initiated by Jesus. Clearly, such expressions as the flame, wind, and speaking in tongues indicate that they had an extraordinary spiritual experience, which to them was a decisive event reminiscent of the Exodus, but that they could not express this experience in a more adequate rational language (Acts, chapter 2).

Understandably, however, their responses to such a traumatic experience were conditioned to a great extent by the main features of their world of inherited meanings. For instance, they were steeped in the Jewish understanding of God, who is a transcendental creator deity and the Lord of history and yet "in some sense a member of the [Hebrew] community also. He participates actively in its life, maintains his relationship to it, and assumes the responsibility of one who is in covenant with his people."[6] Also, as pious Jews, they had high hopes of the coming of a Messiah. And thus their experience of encountering Jesus of Nazareth, who was utterly dedicated to the cause of the kingdom of God as a historical reality, must have led them to see in him the mysterious coming of the divine into a human person and the Jewish covenanted community, a hypostatization, the embodiment (incarnation) and epiphany (*phanesis*, "the notion of God's becoming visible"). In short, the messenger of the gospel of the kingdom of God himself became for all intents and purposes the central object of the gospel. This is exactly what the Fourth Gospel had in mind when it put the following statement into the mouth of Jesus:

> "You search the scriptures, because you think that in them you have eternal life; and it is they that bear witness to me. . . . If you believed Moses, you would believe me, for he wrote of me." (John 5:39–46)

The meaning is clear: Anyone who worshiped God in spirit and truth was assured of the kingdom of God, for Jesus was the agent through whom a "new covenant" was given (John 13:34).

The new covenanted community, in principle at least, held that biological and ethnic factors were not decisive for salvation, because God's divine enterprise has cosmic significance. Thus, for example, on the day of Pentecost, Peter—quoting the prophet Joel—declared: "And in the last days it shall be, God declares, that I will pour out my spirit upon all flesh . . . and I shall show wonders in the heaven above and signs on the earth beneath. . . . And it shall be that whoever calls on the name of the Lord shall be saved" (Acts 2:17–21). Indeed, according to those who experienced it, the Pentecost was the reversal of the course of the tower of Babel: "Whatever their birthplace with its own language and tradition, men hear the messengers of the Gospel speaking in their own tongue the wonderful work of God."[7] Notwithstanding their theoretical affirmation of broader orientation of the new covenanted community, those followers of Jesus, nurtured in traditional Jewish upbringing, were hung up about such practical issues as circumcision for Gentiles who wanted to come into their fellowship, as dramatically illustrated by the story of Peter and Cornelius. Peter was told by God in a dream: "What God has cleansed, you must not call common" (Acts 10:15). Thus, so the Book of Acts tells us, he dared to call on the house of Cornelius, saying: "You yourselves know how unlawful it is [according to the Jewish legal tradition] for a Jew to associate with or to visit any one of another nation; but God has shown me that I should not call any man common or unclean. So when I was sent for, I came without objection" (Acts 10:28–29). And after Peter's preaching, the Holy Spirit descended on all who heard him, and Peter "commanded them to be baptized in the name of Jesus Christ" (Acts 10:48). This incident enabled the infant Christian community to avoid an unhappy division between the circumcised and uncircumcised faithful in the new *koinonia*. In the meantime, the Christian group developed simple rites and religious practices; the new concepts summarized their faith, and the new symbolism and new attitudes gave expression to their solidarity. Also, the infant Christian group was knit together with joyful anticipation of the coming of the end (*eschaton*) of the world, when their Messiah would return as redeemer and judge. Accordingly:

> They devoted themselves to the apostles' teaching and fellowship, to the breaking of bread and the prayers. . . . And all who believed were together and had all things in common. . . . And day by day, attending the temple together and breaking bread in their homes, they partook of food with glad and generous hearts, praising God and having favor with all the people. (Acts 2:42–47)

Indeed, the infant fellowship (of largely Jewish-Christians) had all the earmarks of what someone called an "eschatological eucharistizing community." Significantly, the author of First Peter wrote: "Beloved, I beseech you as aliens and exiles," (2:11), paraphrasing Psalm 39. There is a difference in outlook, however. Although the ancient psalmist thought of himself as a sojourner because he could not find his end, the early Christians considered themselves as sojourners precisely because they knew their own end (*eschaton*) in terms of the return of their Messiah (*Parousia;* "presence or second coming").

The mental horizon of the early Christian group was greatly expanded with the unexpected emergence of Paul, the self-styled apostle to the Gentiles, as an articulate spokesman of the Christian message. We know little about his life before his conversion, and biblical accounts about his youth, and even about his dramatic conversion experience, have some contradictory elements. And, although there were enough suggestions that Paul and other leaders disagreed on some important issues, his own letters eventually came to be accepted as prominent parts of the Christian Bible. In retrospect, there is no question that he left a decisive influence on the subsequent development of Christianity, due greatly to his profound concerns that reflected his own tripartite self-identities, namely: (1) the centrality of *piety* as an essential quality of his new religion, no doubt stemming from his devout Jewish background, for he was "circumcised on the eighth day . . . of the tribe of Benjamin . . . as to the law a Pharisee" (Phil. 3:5); (2) the importance of *learning* in general, but especially about Greek thought, a transcultural and not a provincial thought pattern, which was a hallmark of a Hellenistic Jew, in sharp contrast to the intellectual poverty of uneducated Galilean fishermen; and (3) the relevance of *citizenship*, with its rights, responsibilities, and obligations, which he took for granted as a Roman citizen. (It is interesting to observe that subsequently European civilization came to consider itself built on three foundational institutions, echoing dimensions of Paul's three concerns: *sacerdotium*, or church; *studium*, or university; and *imperium*, or state.) Evidently, Paul had an unshakable conviction, inherited from Jewish tradition, that he was above all a human, made in the image of God (*imago dei*). He learned from Greek tradition as a Hellenistic Jew that he and every other human being have intrinsic value as individuals, each possessing uniqueness (but according to his new faith, all united in sin, which is derived from an innate rebelliousness against the Creator that is shared, unfortunately, by all descendants of the first human being, Adam). Paul also had no qualms, for example, in appealing to the officials and kings, as a citizen of the Roman Empire, and his extensive evangelical activities presupposed the existence of the peaceful and orderly geopolitical framework provided by *Pax Romana*.

Paul's writings indicate that he shared with Jewish-Christians in Jerusalem the belief in the impending arrival of the end of the world and the return of Jesus as Christ and Redeemer—which added intensity and immediacy to Paul's message. (It should be noted that earlier Jewish captives in Babylon transmitted this Zoroastrian-inspired notion of the end of world history, *eschaton*, to post-Babylonian Jews.) And, when the early Christian community realized that the end of the world was not so imminent, or perhaps had been already partially actualized in the descent of the Holy Spirit at the Pentecost, it had to make adjustment to the historical reality of the second century. In that difficult situation, Paul's tripartite formula of piety, learning, and citizenship provided sufficiently helpful resources for the Christian community to cope with various perplexing issues.

Unlike other, especially Jewish-Christian, leaders, Paul had a more sophisticated understanding of the nature of religion based on the principle of *coincidentia oppositorum*. Accordingly, although he proclaimed the ultimacy of the God of Jesus Christ (monotheism) as his autobiographical affirmation of the inner meaning of the Christian religion, he readily acknowledged the existence of plurality of religions in the Mediterranean world, of which Christianity was one—based on the outer meaning of Christianity (monolatry). As he stated:

> Although there may be so-called gods in heaven or on earth—as indeed there are many "gods" and many "lords"—*yet for us there is one God, the Father,* from whom are all things and for whom we exist, *and one Lord, Jesus Christ,* through whom are all things and through whom we exist. (1 Cor. 8:5–6; emphasis mine)

(Incidentally, such a double-edged orientation of religion was almost totally rejected by European Christians after Christianity became the dominant religion of the Roman Empire, much to the impoverishment of their understanding of their faith.) As might be expected, Paul's dual orientation to religion was not shared by other early Christian leaders either. For example, Irenaeus of Lyons proclaimed during the second century that only Christianity was a genuine religion, and Christians have nothing to learn from other religions about truth.[8] Lamentably, Irenaeus and most Western Christians in subsequent periods, down to our own day, also failed to comprehend Paul's subtle contention that one particular religion (Christianity more successfully, according to his experience and conviction) can and should unfold adequately the contour of the hidden, invisible religious reality that underlay all religious traditions. Meanwhile, this new eschatological community inevitably developed its own group consciousness and structure. Through its faith in Jesus as the Risen Lord, through the identification of Jesus with the Messiah and Logos, and through Baptism and the Lord's Supper as the means of communication with the Risen Christ, who was believed to be sitting at the right hand of the Father, the new covenanted community began to have a visible structure of its own. Although it was influenced by the examples of the synagogue and the mystery cults, "the fundamental point is the growth of an independent religious community possessing the essential ideas of the Gospel and equipped with its powers, which then develops its own dialectic over against the synagogue and mystery cults."[9] In that connection, we agree with Thornton that a combination of the following four factors provided a unifying bond for the early Christian community: (1) the teaching of the apostles, (2) the fellowship or sharing of a common life (*koinonia*), (3) the breaking of the bread, and (4) prayers.[10] Although the new *koinonia* of Christians, who had a profound religious experience at the Pentecost, had no intention of severing the relationship with the old Hebrew community, gradually the Christian community developed its own inner cohesion and outward thrust, resulting in the separation of Christianity from Judaism.

After separating itself from Judaism, Christianity was destined to preserve an ambiguous orientation of being simultaneously a heavenly and an earthly—an eschatological and transcendental as well as a pragmatic and this-worldly—community, "in" this world but not "of" this world. Accordingly, at least until the time of the emperor Constantine the Great (r., 306–337), Christians were expected to offer two kinds of *leitougia:* (1) liturgy, in which they communed with God through the Risen Christ, who imparted grace to the faithful in the earthly existence, and (2) public service, such as paying tax and serving for the welfare of the society and the empire. Indeed, as van der Leeuw poignantly observed: "Until its elevation to *ecclesia triumphans* or its dissolution in *communio sanctorum,* [the Christian community was understood to be] the *salt of the earth,* the actual ground of the world's continued existence."[11] Due to its twin nature of the *leitougia,* both insiders and outsiders often failed to comprehend the subtle relationship between the two aspects of Christianity—as spiritual-ecclesiastical community (church) and this-worldly religion of Western civilization. (As I will discuss presently, the overlapping relationship between the church and the religion of the empire became more complex in the Middle Ages because the church developed along the paradigm of the earthly kingdom and behaved as one of the states from time to time, as reflected in the nature of the papacy as de facto a monarchical episcopate.) To be sure, Christianity taught the equality of all human beings, but it was not easy to explain that "it is an equality which exists purely in the presence of God, and in Him, based solely on the religious relation to God as the centre of the whole."[12] This negative equality, to use Ernst Troeltsch's expression, was not based on a common claim of nature. Thus, with all its religious affirmation about the equality of the grace of God, the early Christian community was "very cautious towards any attempt to carry over this equality into the sphere of secular relationships and institutions, which [are different from] the real religious basis of this equality."[13] (In this respect, throughout history the ethos of Jewish and traditional Roman Catholic ethics are far less complicated.)

Some scholars suspect that the death of the last of Jesus' disciples must have been a traumatic experience for the early church. As long as the disciples (apostles) lived, they were unquestionably the guiding spirits of the Christian groups in various places: for example, James in Jerusalem, Philip in Samaria and Ethiopia, Andrew in Scythis, John in Asia, Peter for dispersed Jews (Paul for the Gentile groups). Under them developed various kinds of ministries, such as presbyters and deacons. When the last apostle died, the early church entrusted the bishops to maintain the unity of the church with the help of graded ministries and by preserving the apostolic teachings.[14] By the midsecond century, there existed writings that had come to be considered the nucleus of sacred scripture by common consent, although it was not until two centuries later that the present New Testament became canonical. At any rate, with its own forms of worship, its own orders of ministry, and sacred scriptures, the Christian community had all the marks of an independent ecclesiastical institution by the end of the third century.

The first three centuries in the common era, which witnessed the growing institutionalization of Christianity, were also the time of the phenomenal expansion of the Roman Empire, which successfully blended the universalistic Hellenistic thought, inherited from the Greeks, and their legal tradition, military power, and administrative skill. Invariably, Christianity too felt the impact of Greco-Roman civilization. Thus, already in the second century, intellectual Christians—Justin, for example—attempted to explain the Genesis account of the creation of the world in terms of Platonic cosmology. Others adopted the Stoics' reason (logos) and advocated that every civilization had a scattered seed of logos, which ultimately became fulfilled in Jesus Christ as the logos incarnate.

Some of the philosophically oriented Christian apologists tried to synthe-
size Greek wisdom and Jewish-Christian ethics so as to guide Christians
as faithful citizens of the growing empire. Although most Christians
managed to live peacefully in two (God's and Caesar's) realms, some
purists among Christians refused to pay homage to the caesar, the visible
symbol of loyalty to the earthly empire.[15] The so-called martyrs, whose
names dotted early Christian history, are those who thus took their citizenship in heaven more seriously and emulated Christ's death in their
own situations, with the hope of acquiring eternal life beyond death.
(Martyrdom came to be regarded as the highest paradigm of Christian
faith in the early church.) There were still others, who—like the author of
the Johannine apocalypse—did not choose martyrdom but were highly
critical of the absolutistic tendency of the earthly kingdom and of the
arrogance of human civilization. Little did early Christians realize, however, that this-worldly benefits, such as power, prestige, and wealth, that
came with the official recognition of Christianity in the fourth century
were dubious and mixed blessings to their faith.

THE CONSTANTINIAN TWIST

With Constantine's edict of Milan in 313, Christianity became a legitimate and favored religion in the Roman Empire. (It was made the state
religion by Emperor Theodosius late in the fourth century.) In this new
situation, the biblical exhortation of holding "things that are God's"
separate from "Caesar's" gave way to a new formula that loyalty to God
was to be tested by loyalty to the caesar and vice versa. Curiously,
Constantine—even before he was baptized—called and presided over
the so-called ecumenical council of Nicaea held in 325, and boasted the
title *pontifex maximus* (which later was taken over by the pope). The
pattern thus developed under Constantine (and Theodosius) is called
Caesaropapism, according to which the earthly ruler also had jurisdiction over religion, the pattern that lasted for centuries in Eastern
Rome. Meanwhile, with the establishment of Constantinople as the
capital, the neglected and declining Western wing of the empire rallied
around the bishop of Rome (self-styled as "eternal city"), who assumed
more of a monarchical role in addition to his patriarchal functions.
Both the Byzantine (Eastern Roman) pattern of secularization of the
religious community (in which church became in effect a department
of state) and the Western Roman pattern of ecclesiastification of nonreligious dimensions of life (justified by the notion of "two swords")

sought legitimation in terms of self-authenticating circular logic, amplified by pious opinions turned into doctrines or dogmas.

It is to be noted that all religious traditions have produced an abundance of pious opinions and practices, not necessarily as essentials of salvation or enlightenment based on a central core of sacred teachings or historical facts, but derived from adherents' autobiographical, "pious" understanding of sacred scriptures or traditions. In the case of Christianity, how to interpret certain scriptural passages became a serious issue. For instance, the Gospel account of the conversation between Jesus and Peter could be interpreted minimally as Jesus' affirmation that the church should be built on faith in Jesus as Christ (as eloquently uttered by Peter) or maximally—here the pious opinion tends to sway the judgment of the faithful insiders—as Jesus' appointment of Peter as his vicar on earth. (We don't even know whether the author of the Gospel recorded verbatim Jesus' speech or whether he put the consensus of the early Christian community, either minimally or maximally, into the mouth of Jesus.) It is not possible in this context to document how effectively both ecclesiastical and political leaders used such pious opinions to enrich their status, prestige, and power; for example, the legendary accounts of Peter as the first martyred bishop of Rome, of Constantine's donation, of Constantine's and his mother's dreams, and a series of popular devotions and inferences about Jesus' mother Mary, including her alleged ascension and her being co-redeemer. With these pious opinions, practices, and devotions turned into de facto new church doctrines, and with the absorption of popular "cults of saints," which developed side by side with martyrdom, the early Western Christianity acquired proficient resources to reach unsophisticated and superstitious masses.

We should keep in mind that the Mediterranean world underwent far-reaching social changes and transformations from the third to the fifth century. The traditional structure of Roman civic society—a federation of city-states, each with its civic religion, governed by a coherent system of jurisprudence—eroded, and the Senate as well as the provincial city-states were helpless, leaving only the imperial power and the army retaining enough power. In this situation, a series of military monarchs attempted to transform Rome into a centralized state, which incidentally required unity of, or one common, religion rather than the traditional plurality of locally based religions. And Christopher Dawson is probably right in giving credit to Constantine for recognizing Christianity as potentially "the one living creative force in the social and spiritual life of the age."[16] Meanwhile, the Roman Empire was also exposed to the threat of "barbarians." The Vandals crossed the Danube in 406, and the Visigoths took Rome in 410.

The fall of Rome in 410 motivated Augustine of Hippo to formulate his philosophy of history, based on the well-known notions of the *Civitas Dei* and the *Civitas Mundi.* To him, the *Civitas Dei* was both earthly and heavenly; and as such the Christian church was integrally related to the two-dimensional kingdom of God, even though the two cannot be identified. Of prime importance in his thought was the supreme value he placed on the church as the representative of the City of God on earth. Augustine thus left a legacy of the image of a Christian state, and many people regard him as the "originator of the medieval theocratic ideal." Indeed, he initiated the Western European ideal of "the church as a dynamic social power."[17] Thus the Christian community—with its newly acquired status and prestige in the empire, assured by Augustine of its direct pipeline to the divine source in heaven—reflects, in the words of Peter Brown, "the attitude of a group confident of its powers to absorb the world without losing its identity. . . . It is a group . . . ready to fulfill what it considered *its historic mission, to dominate, to absorb, to lead a whole empire.*"[18] There is no question that the Christian church in Western Rome benefited a great deal from the Germanization of the Roman Empire by cuddling up to the Frankish Territorial churches (*Landeskirche*) as the basis for the church of the empire (*Reichskirche*) and as the potential framework of the universal catholic church. On the other hand, German (Carolingian) rulers deftly used the church, especially its growing monastic system (according to which monks led the life of "daily dying" for their Lord), as the civilizing agent for consolidating the state. It was the famous Charlemagne (768–814) who rescued Pope Leo III from enemies by pledging the imperial power to protect the papacy in return for the benediction of the papal church. We are told that Charlemagne likened the pope to Aaron, the high priest, and himself to Moses, who led the chosen people.[19]

Meanwhile, Christianity and Europe (here including both the Eastern and Western wings of Rome) were destined to encounter the growing power of Islam both as religion and empire, which started in the seventh century in Arabia. Within one century after the death of Muhammad in 632, the Islamic community embraced not only crucial parts of the Byzantine territories but also northern Africa, the traditional stronghold of Latin Christianity, as well as the Iberian peninsula. By that time, Christianity, now that it was made the state religion of the Roman Empire, began to assume that its autobiographical approach to the inner meaning of Christianity is the most objective and universal perspective—following its own self-authenticating circular logic—in relation to all religions of the world. Accordingly, Christianity reproved (and began to persecute) Jews for not accepting Jesus of Nazareth as the Messiah. It also, especially after the time of Augustine, became doctrinaire and denounced those who did not conform to its main tenents as heretics. And, as might be expected, most European Christians, convinced as they were that the salvation of humankind had already been accomplished by Jesus Christ, rejected Muhammad's claim to be the seal of prophets. Indeed, many Christians thought of him as a false prophet like those mentioned in the Johannine apocalypse. Thus began the lamentable relationships between the *corpus Islamicum* and *Christendom* that have lasted not only through the medieval period of the misguided and bloody Crusades but to our own time.

As to the main features of European development, it should be noted that there developed the Holy Roman Empire, 962–1558 (begun with the coronation of Otto I as Holy Roman Emperor and virtually terminated by the abdication of Charles V from that office), established on the soil prepared by Carolingian monarchs. This meant, however, the transition from the German tribal-oriented Carolingian civilization to the Latin imperialism oriented to and supported by a new phenomenon called feudalism, Gregorian civilization. Then, as Troeltsch poignantly pointed out, "the papal universal church became a civilizing, spiritual, and uniform principle. . . . The combination of Italian jurisprudence and French theology, philosophy, and poetry, created the spirit of the ecclesiastical universal civilization."[20] The papal church was based on a number of factors, including ecclesiastical universalism, the canon law, the sacramental doctrine, and the religious orders. Significantly, the idea of the Holy Roman Empire was inseparable from a particular way of organizing life as the *corpus Christianum* (Christianity-inspired general community), of which the spiritually and ecclesiastically disciplined inner core was known as the *corpus Christi*. Again, there were three pivotal institutions in medieval Europe: (1) *sacerdotium* (the church, symbolizing both explicit religious structure and less stringent devotional practices of the people), (2) *imperium* (state, symbolizing domains of social, economic, political, etc., life and systems), and (3) *studium* (university, and the sphere of ideas, education, culture, arts, and civilization). All three were believed to be divinely inspired, because all good things of life— piety in religion, morality in civic life, and learning and virtue—were considered as gifts, to be bestowed from above. It is interesting to note, however, that the outlook regarding the hierarchical order of the three institutions varies according to the perspectives of *sacerdotium*, *imperium*, and *studium*.

1. The perspective of *sacerdotium* was represented by the leadership of the papal church, whose ideal was the consolidation of the total society, especially, of course, *imperium* and *studium*. The church, which had originally been understood as the spiritual community *in* this world but *not of* this world, developed into a gigantic Christendom of the Middle Ages. It implied that the synthesis of all dimensions of life in medieval Europe received cosmic legitimation from the Christian church. The underlying ideology of the *Corpus Christianum* was not the spiritual independence of the church. "The full freedom and independence of the church was only reached when the temporal powers [i.e., *imperium*, etc.] were subordinated to [*sacerdotium*] . . . and directed by her in all matters pertaining to salvation."[21] And, as everything is ultimately related to salvation, soteriology became equated with ecclesiology. To be sure, the tension between the earthly *ecclesia* and the *ecclesia triumphans* was more accentuated in a way by the insertion of purgatory between them. On the other hand, the church as the body of Christ came to be understood almost in a physical sense in that the priest directly had Christ's power and authority to impart grace on earth. Accordingly, the church, with its power to impart grace on people and control their consciences, became very influential in the life of the *imperium*, no longer "in the service of a theocratic royalism, but in the service of an hierarchical theocracy of an ecclesiastically controlled civilization."[22] By far the most appalling evidence was the so-called Crusades, 1096–1290, in which the pope—who claimed to be the faithful servant of the Prince of Peace—demanded the "Christian" princes of Europe to capture Jerusalem militarily from Muslim control. We can understand historically how Christianity as a this-worldly religion of European civilization boasted the papacy to be above emperors and kings, exemplified by the reign of Innocent III (pope, 1198–1216), who was undoubtedly the most powerful ruler in Europe in his time. But one wonders on what legitimate Christian or religious ground Pope Boniface—who issued in 1302 the bull *Unam Sanctum* ("One Holy"), advocating that submission to the earthly pope in Rome was essential for salvation—made such an extravagant assertion. By that time, the Western church took Augustine's notion of the church as the representative on earth of the kingdom of God too seriously and literally in that it assumed that the church leaders' decisions, especially the so-called dogmas, reflected the divine will. Thus the Council of Florence (1438–45) went so far as to invade God's domain of salvation by deciding for

God as to who should or could be saved in the dogma *extra ecclesiam nulla salus* ("no salvation outside the church").[23] (Oddly enough, this notion was carried over into the churches of the Reformation.)

2. From the perspectives of the state and the emperors, particularly powerful forces, however, *imperium* was seen as the most prominent of the triad, whereby *sacerdotium* and *studium* were subservient to the political authority. Indeed, such rulers as Henry III (d., 1056), Henry IV (d., 1106), Frederick I (d., 1056), and Henry VI (d., 1197) managed to dominate papal power. Even the aforementioned Pope Boniface reluctantly acknowledged defeat to Philip IV (r., 1285–1314) of France over the issue of taxation of the clergy. (It is often said that Boniface marked the beginning of the erosion of papal power.)

3. The perspective of *studium* was more ambiguous, unstable, and changeable, partly because originally some medieval universities in Europe, such as Paris and Oxford, allied themselves with *sacerdotium* in treating theology as the queen of science. This kind of intimate relationship and mutuality between *studium* and *sacerdotium* began to crack after the fourteenth century by the advocates of the Renaissance and humanism in Italy—initially not the mainstays in *studium*—who affirmed the values of Greek paganism, much to the annoyance of *sacerdotium*. During the fifteenth century, some of the Reformers, who studied in the university, defied the authority of *sacerdotium* on the ground that the truth-claims of *studium*, different though they were from the church's teachings, had as much validity as those of *sacerdotium*. Subsequently, influenced by scientific revolution and the Enlightenment, various branches of learning taught in *studium* became independent from divine aura and theology (and by implication became liberated from the influence of metaphysics and *sacerdotium*).

COLONIALISM, THE CHRISTIAN WORLD MISSION, AND SECULAR SALVATION

In any part of the world throughout history, peoples' hopes and ideals have often been restrained, modified, or transmuted by historical realities, and medieval Western Christianity and medieval Europe were no exceptions. Part of their dilemmas and existential contradictions might be traced to the audacious vision of Constantine, who tried, as someone once stated, to incorporate the heavenly domain into his earthly empire by equating loyalty to God with (which implies for all intents and purposes making it subordinate to) loyalty to Caesar, thus nurturing Christianity to become a full-fledged this-worldly religion while continuing doctrinal and liturgical affirmation of faith in a transcendental deity. It is a matter of some significance, too, that the *sacerdotium* in Western Europe developed ecclesiastical structure along the imperial Roman paradigm, following Emperor Diocletian's design of different prefectures, each subdivided into dioceses ruled by vicars. It also deftly transformed the notion of martyrdom, the early church's ideal of sacrifice for faith, into the monastic practice of the daily martyrdom, and assimilated the saints' and Virgin cults, and so forth, in order to make Christianity more palatable to former barbarians and the masses while boasting the supramundane nature of the church by utilizing pious legends, traditions, and opinions such as Petrine doctrine and Constantine's donation. For its part, the *imperium* took full advantage of Christianity in return for making it the state religion by claiming sacred aura over the authoritarian political structure (the *Civitas Christiana*), which was now unabashedly proclaimed to be the "Holy Roman Empire."[24] The "holy" Roman emperors heavily depended on ecclesiastical leaders in consolidating the political fabric of the empire and relied on monastic orders as civilizing agents in the hinterlands and outlying districts. Understandably, the rise of Islam threatened both the church and the empire, whereby the *sacerdotium* and the *imperium* jointly fought the *corpus Islamicum* in a series of military campaigns called euphemistically the "Crusades." The *studium* (and the *sacerdotium*, even though it was often reluctant to acknowledge it), however, benefited much from the *corpus Islamicum*, which was instrumental in introducing Greek thought, especially Aristotelean metaphysics, which provided the theoretical framework for medieval Christian scholastic theological systems. The popularization of Greek tradition and classical learning also provided positive impact on the Renaissance.

The overlapping interrelationships among the three pivotal institutions, which greatly strengthened the blending of the political, religious, and cultural features of medieval Europe, were destined to be altered due to changing historical realities that confronted all three institutions respectively.

1. The *sacerdotium*, claiming as it did to act on behalf of the heavenly deity, earlier separated itself from the Byzantine half of Christendom in the ninth century by mutual excommunication. Unhappily, it had to confront a new trying experience of the removal of the papacy to Avignon in the fourteenth century. Although the papacy was brought back to Rome after a period known as the Babylonian Captivity, it was inevitably followed by the "Great Schism," which separated followers of the French popes from followers of the Italian popes. Even though the

schism was finally brought to an end after repeated attempts by the councils in the fifteenth century to resolve the tension between the two groups, the papacy was not restored to its former power. The church leaders also tried to stamp out such heresies as those of Wycliff and Huss. But the seams of the colossal Western *sacerdotium* finally came apart in the sixteenth century with a series of Protestant (Lutheran, Calvinist, Anglican, etc.) Reformations, which in turn precipitated the Council of Trent and the Counter-Reformation. At any rate, the religious map of Western Europe was no longer painted with one color, that is, that of the papal church. (It is worth mentioning that Luther rejected not only the theological systems but also the canon law of the papal church.)

2. As to the *imperium*, from the beginning of the Holy Roman Empire in 962, absolute temporal authority of the emperor had to contend with universal spiritual (which often intruded into the temporal sphere) authority of the pope. To be sure, many emperors managed somehow to manipulate the ecclesiastical authority, but some popes, notably Gregory VII, had enough actual power to excommunicate Henry IV, releasing Henry's subjects from their oaths to him, in the late eleventh century. Toward the latter part of the Holy Roman Empire, however, the balance of power shifted in favor of the emperor, so that Charles V (the last papally crowned emperor), for example, thought nothing of taking Pope Clement VIII prisoner, in spite of the fact that Charles was a passionate adherent of the papal church. By that time, the foundation of the *imperium* itself was mercilessly shaken by the decline of feudalism, the growth of the vernacular, coupled with intense nationalism, the development of towns, trade, and industry, the phenomenal rise of the middle class, and the persistent threat of the *corpus Islamicum*.[25] (It might be noted that although Charles, as much as the papacy, was anti-Protestant and condemned Luther and Lutherans at the Diet of Augsburg in 1530, he was in no position to pursue this matter because he needed the support of Protestant princes in Germany in his war against the Muslim Turks' invasion of Vienna. In the end, Lutherans were officially recognized in Germany due to Charles's pragmatic compromise.)

Following the disintegration of the Holy Roman Empire, the accession of Ferdinand I as nominal emperor in 1558 ushered in the period of territorial monarchies, which lasted until the abdication of "Emperor" Francis II in 1806 and the official termination of that empire by the decree of Napoleon, who incidentally initiated the modern era of autonomous nation-states. The division and territorialization of Europe had many implications. First, assumption of the importance of the empire as a coherent unit gave way to the growing recognition of a territorial or national group as a more realistic political unit. Second, while the *imperium* continued to recognize the spiritual relevance of the *sacerdotium*, it now controlled the destiny of territorial or national churches, even in presumably traditional Roman Catholic nations such as Spain and Portugal. Third, territorial monarchies and nations, in comparison with the papally inspired Holy Roman Empire, gave greater freedom to the *studium* (university), learning in general, and arts as culture, as evidenced by the growing vitality of the Renaissance, scientific revolution, leading up to the Enlightenment. Parenthetically, Christianity, which had prospered as a this-worldly religion from the time of Constantine throughout the period of the Holy Roman Empire, made smooth transition to the new order of territorial monarchies and later on to that of autonomous nations. For example, within the political and ecclesiastical territorial structures, churches became important units of social and political life. Within the papal church traditions, monastic orders had always been accepted as the sphere set aside from daily life. Besides, there were a small number of very pious clerical and lay mystics who took the supramundane goals of *unio mystica* seriously. Most of the faithful, however, were more concerned with the here-and-now, with simple piety consisting of a round of church and home cults and practical guidance provided by confessionals. Understandably, churches of papal tradition stressed moral theology and instructions for people in both upper and lower strata of society. Significantly, the ever-growing body of canon law that blended legal and theological features helped iron out the intricate relationship between the *imperium* and the *sacerdotium*. In the Protestant communities, too, there were overlapping but somewhat different concerns, that is, piety (feeling and religious experience) versus morality (emphasis on conscience). The majority of clergy and laity willingly accepted the givenness of church situations within the sociopolitical reality dictated by territorial monarchies, and they sought instruction and teaching about individual civic and Christian life from influential "moralists."[26] In the course of time, there developed a small group of "pietists" (more among Protestants, but some among Catholics), who reacted against the secularized state of territorial or national churches and considered themselves as constituting spiritual inner circles (*ecclesiola in ecclesia*), taking biblical heritage very seriously. (It was these pietists who initiated and promoted Christian world mission.)

 3. The gradual decline of the *sacerdotium*—and the concomitantly decreasing influence of the church on the *studium*—starting with the fourteenth century, continuing to the period of territorial monarchies and to the modern era of autonomous nations, fostered the

impressive development of the Renaissance, scientific revolution, the Enlightenment, and so forth, all of which in turn transformed Western civilization into a pseudoreligion of secularized salvation. We can hardly exaggerate the magnitude of the effect these new developments had on the consciousness of Europeans. For example, in the words of William Clebsch:

> Two investigations based on observation challenged the traditional views of the human body and the stars. A Belgian anatomist, Andreas Vesalius, published *On the Structure of the Human Body,* and a Polish astronomer, Nicolaus Copernicus, published *On the Revolutions of the Heavenly Bodies* (both in 1543). . . . Then four men produced studies whose implications Alfred North Whitehead called "the greatest single intellectual success which mankind has achieved." He referred to Galileo's research into the acceleration and deceleration of moving bodies, to Descartes's mathematical models of scientific concepts, to Huygens's powerful telescopes and wave theory of light, and to Newton's unified theories of the forces at work in the universe.[27]

Side by side with such thoroughgoing intellectual somersaults, the discovery of non-European peoples, their languages, religions, and cultures, coupled with the rediscovery of Greek and classical learning and the exposure to the Islamic concept of *falsafah* (the Arabic notion of the integration of science, philosophy, and other spheres of knowledge), made the new European intellectual elites breathe in an unprecedented new mood. Although they were products of medieval Christian tradition, and many of them never rejected the traditional authority of the church, revelation, and doctrines, the center of their world gradually shifted from heaven to the earth. To be sure, many of those creative thinkers continued to affirm the transcendental deity, but their sense of the mystery of the universe was radically altered by the sudden rearrangement of space and the dislocation of the earth from the main stage of the bewildering vastness of the universe. The fact that the laws of the world, of nature, hitherto considered the exclusively mysterious prerogative of the deity, could be at least partially comprehended by mathematical calculation greatly enhanced their sense of the autonomy of human beings.

Elsewhere I have asserted that notwithstanding the Western convention (which even today often misleads people) of dividing human experience into a series of semi-independent compartments (e.g., religion, aesthetics, ethics, politics, etc.), human life throughout history in every continent has been a sort of seamless synthesis of what we still regard as semi-independent compartments. In this situation, what we normally designate as "religion" has functioned in, among other things, two different ways: (1) it becomes an integral part of the (religious-cultural-social-political, etc.) synthesis, as dramatically testified by European history itself, and (2) it has a special role (which no other component of the synthesis is expected to fulfill)—that of providing the sense of cosmic legitimation to the whole synthesis itself.[28] I hope that readers will readily see that this-world-centered Christianity gave such a sense of cosmic legitimation both to the Constantinian synthesis and to a slightly different synthesis called the Holy Roman Empire. Significantly, after the decline of the Holy Roman Empire, the traditional Christianity (which had provided cosmic legitimation to earlier syntheses in Europe) came to play second fiddle to the pseudoreligion of secularized salvation—namely, Western civilization itself (of which Christianity continues to be an integral ingredient, however)—which provided cosmic legitimation to the new European form of religious-cultural-social-political synthesis evolved during the period of territorial monarchies and the more recent era of autonomous nations. Conversely, many Europeans from the midfifteenth or sixteenth century onward began to feel that they were the creators of new cultural values and the chosen bearers of true civilization—much as the ancient Hebrews felt chosen to be the bearers of true religion—which they now "magnanimously" share with non-European peoples, even though the latter were expected to be enslaved and exploited by the bearers of true civilization. This exploitation was justified because European civilization, given cosmic legitimation by the pseudoreligion of secularized salvation, was destined to be, in many Europeans' eyes, the triumphant universal civilization. This view was the underlying feature of not only the Industrial Revolution and the French Revolution later on, but of the European colonialism commenced by two Iberian nations, Portugal and Spain, as early as the sixteenth century. Such a pseudoreligion of secularized salvation was no doubt the underpinning notion of Kipling's view of the white man's burden, characterized by William Haas as "a strange compound of genuine idealistic responsibility, blindness and hypocrisy, with a strong dose of will-to-power as the basic component."[29]

Inasmuch as the problem of colonialism was already discussed in Part I, Chapter 1, of this volume, we should not reiterate it in this context. It is worth recalling, however, that the so-called Roman Catholic overseas missionary expansion program was delegated initially to two Catholic nations, Portugal and Spain, through the patronage system. As such, the civil governments initiated and financed the church's programs, personnel, and institutions in their colonies, in exchange for extensive power over church matters at home and in Rome. (Later on, with the increasing initiatives of religious orders, coupled with the inauguration of the *Congregatio de Propaganda Fide* in Rome, the patronage system declined.) More important, perhaps, were the nostalgic attempts by monarchs of three Catholic *nations* to restore a semblance of the past glory of the papal church, even though, as Clebsch puts it, "their religion was more *national* than papal."[30] Incidentally, all three attempts failed. Philip II of Spain had enormous financial resources accumulated from Spain's overseas empire, but his hope to make Madrid the center of Catholic Christendom was dashed when his armada was defeated by the British navy in 1588. Philip's great-grandson Louis XIV of France, often characterized as divine right king incarnate, who too had considerable resources gained from Africa and India, could not carry out his expansionism, which was checked effectively by William of Orange and his anti-France alliance. And finally, the attempt of Ferdinand II of Austria to establish Catholic Christendom under the Hapsburg dynasty disintegrated with the end of the Thirty Years' War in 1648. All three of them demonstrated that, notwithstanding their lip service to the reunification of the papal-church-inspired empire, they were rulers of the territorial monarchies (and masters of their colonial regimes), which depended more on the new secular civilization than on the traditional *sacerdotium*.

The apparent "success," especially enormous financial gain, of European colonialism abroad, coupled with the steady development of modern European civilization as a pseudoreligion of secularized salvation at home, brought about two great and interrelated illusions: (1) an exaggerated notion of the autonomy of human beings, especially of Europeans, who were now considered efficacious "captains of their souls," and (2) the ugly feature of racism in reference to all non-European, colored peoples in other parts of the world. Europeans' sense of autonomous humanity reached its zenith in Hegel's daring thesis, as explicated by Wilhelm Halbfass:

> The "phenomenology" or self-manifestation of the absolute merges into man's work in history, into human self-fulfillment. Man becomes "present God" (*präsenter Gott*) and continues the divine process in his own worldly presence, in taking charge of his world and discerning the dignity of the absolute in it.[31]

No wonder modern European intellectuals, especially from the period of the Enlightenment of the eighteenth century onward, began to feel that various fields of knowledge formerly circumscribed in the university by metaphysics and/or theology were now liberated and attained autonomy. In the words of Ernst Cassirer:

> They no longer look to the concept of God for their justification and legitimation; the various sciences themselves now determine the concept on the basis of their specific form. The relations between the concept of God and the concept of truth, morality, [and] law are by no means abandoned, but their directions change.[32]

Even the less intellectual masses also "inhaled" the ethos of the pervasive pseudoreligion of secularized salvation, which enthusiastically legitimated the emerging new European religious-cultural-social-political synthesis, a synthesis that vindicates Europeans' ego as creators and bearers of the most advanced, unique, and true civilization.

It was in that atmosphere that a tiny group of Pietists in both the Catholic and Protestant groups advocated the purity of "heart religion," based on the certitude of individual salvation by Christ, against the pseudoreligion of secularized salvation that had deeply penetrated churches that were dominated by the territorial monarchies in Europe. Unfortunately, space does not allow us to have any detailed discussion of Pietism and Pietists except to mention such well-known names of Pietists as Ignatius Loyola, Peter Canisius, and the Jansenists in the Catholic fold, and John Bunyan, August Hermann Francke, Philip Jacob Spener, Count Nikolaus Ludwig von Zinzendorf, and John Wesley (although obviously he was more than a Pietist) in the Protestant circle. In both Catholic and Protestant folds, Pietism on the one hand reacted against the prevailing ethos of European civilization as the pseudoreligion of secularized salvation, and on the other hand initiated and promoted the Christian world mission, that is, expanding and disseminating Christianity to the non-Western world. In this connection, probably the most representative figure among well-known Pietists was P. J. Spener (d. 1705), who in his *Pia Desideria* advocated (1) earnest Bible study conducted *"ecclesiolae in ecclesia"*; (2) the priesthood of all believers; (3) practical, and not theoretical, Christianity; and (4) a sympathetic attitude toward unbelievers "to win them, if possible, to truth," rather than denouncing their errors.[33]

As to the issue of Christian world mission, Roman Catholic and Protestant traditions faced different problems. For the Catholics, the question was how to take the initiative of the overseas missionary work away from civil authorities of the colonial powers, which carried on the church work as a part of their colonial activities in accordance with the patronage agreement. Thanks, however, to persons like Francis Xavier (a close associate of Ignatius Loyola) and his successor, Alessandro Valignano, and Matteo Ricci and others, a more religious missionary program (and less contaminated by political and other considerations) was envisaged by some of the enlightened leaders of religious orders, but eventually the Catholic overseas missionary works were consolidated in 1662 by the Congregation of the Propaganda of Faith, which brought out other complications. Besides, following the decline of Iberian colonial powers, Catholic overseas missionary activities remained at a low ebb anyway. As for the Protestant side, the national and/or territorial churches took it for granted that the spiritual welfare of peoples in overseas colonial territories was the responsibility of monarchs and civil authorities, and thus European churches had no interest or concern with Christian world mission. It was against this kind of background that Pietism took up the missionary challenge. Pietism as such did not prosper much in Germany, even though Zinzendorf's Moravian movement had started active overseas missionary work. More important was the Pietist influence on a few thinkers such as Schleiermacher and Pietism's impact on Danish and English missionary activities.

As hinted above, following the decline of Portugal and Spain, other European powers, including many Protestant nations, stepped in as masters of the new colonialism. It is interesting to note that many of the colonial authorities of Protestant nations were initially hostile to missionary work operated by groups, for example, Pietists and Evangelicals, who were not recognized or sanctioned by their home governments. For example, when the Moravian mission began its work in Dutch Guiana, "the Dutch government issued orders forbidding the Indians to join any Moravian settlement."[34] Yet colonial governments gradually recognized the value of having European missionaries who were dedicated people in carrying on educational and philanthropic activities and imparting modern European values. Those Pietistic missionaries, for their part, determined though they were in obeying the biblical missionary commandments, had no idea as to how to deal with indigenous people who had been nurtured in different cultural, linguistic, and religious modes, and they began to be more positive toward colonial regimes, which at least represented the Christian-inspired European religious-cultural-social-political synthesis. Thus there developed a strange form of coalescence, embracing this-worldly Christianity, Western culture (nurtured by autonomous science and technology), the capitalistic-paternalistic-colonial system, the coalescence of which was given blessing, sometimes grudgingly while at other times more enthusiastically, by simplistic, Pietistic Christian tradition. Meanwhile, the influence of these Pietists and Evangelicals, through the formation of private missionary societies, made the hitherto reluctant European churches conscious of their missionary obligations abroad. The private missionary societies were, in the words of Kenneth Latourette, "without exact precedent in the expansion of Christianity."[35] Eventually, these missionary societies, which had been looked down upon by both the colonial governments and the national churches, became official or semiofficial organs of European Protestant churches in conscious or unconscious cooperation with the imperialistic colonial policies of the Western powers in dealing with the non-Western world.

9

PIETY, MORALITY, AND CULTURE: EUROPEAN AND AMERICAN PERSPECTIVES

RELIGIOUS UNDERSTANDING OF RELIGION

It is rather widely known that my mentor, Joachim Wach, speculated that human beings from the dawn of history were endowed with the impulse to understand as well as the impulse to believe and worship.[1] Although many people are inclined to agree with such a conjecture, opinions vary widely about the relationships between the two impulses—whether or not, and to what extent, people have been concerned with the problem of understanding the nature of religion as such. Even in our own time, many people who hold that religion is something that is "caught" but not "taught" are prone to dismiss the relevance of the issue pertaining to the understanding of religion. On the other hand, religion as much as politics often makes people partisan, so that many people who are more modest in their opinions and competence regarding, say, art or science, are known to be pugnacious in voicing their views and judgments concerning religious matters. More often than not, their opinions are based on scant familiarity with only their own religious tradition; they most likely do not know much about other traditions or about religion in general. Also, religion shares similar reactions with language and/or money; for when one mentions language or money, many people—mentally translating almost reflexively—immediately think of "French,

185

Russian, or English" and "shilling, rupee, or dollar," without ever revert-
ing to the general issues of language or money. Similarly, when you utter
the word *religion,* many people hear Judaism, Christianity, or Buddhism.

Inasmuch as I have already depicted some of the factors that
aggravate our understanding of religion, I will mention them briefly
here.

The first factor is the infeasibility of the traditional Western
convention of dividing human experience into a series of semiautonomous "compartments" (e.g., religion, ethics, aesthetics, etc.), because human life in most places has been a seamless blending of many of
the compartments.

The second factor relates to the multiple functions of what we
call "religion." Within the seamless religious-cultural-social-political
synthesis, religion usually constitutes the spiritual or ecclesiastical tradition (often mistakenly understood as the sole feature of religion). It
serves as the invisible glue holding together the disparate elements of
life and the world. As the agent of metaphysical intuition, it defines
the kinds and levels of realities, including ultimate reality; and as such,
it provides cosmic legitimation for the respective religious-cultural-
social-political synthesis.[2]

The third factor, related to the above, is the multidimensionality
of religion itself in that it is closely related to such features as art, literature, society, culture, law, polity, and so forth, so that one can legitimately approach religion as a cultural, legal, social, political system. It
should be stressed, however, that although we benefit a great deal by
learning about various aspects of religion from cultural, psychological,
anthropological, sociological, and philosophical studies of religion, these
modes of inquiry are not adequate substitutes for our "religious" understanding of religion, more particularly, with all its multiple functions,
which so often escape people's perceptions of religion.

Obviously, religious understanding of religion is crucially important, especially in our attempt to understand a particular religious
tradition, for each tradition claims that it unfolds and actualizes, more
adequately than others, the basic core of the integrity and coherence of
invisible religious reality. The complicating factor in dealing with a particular religious tradition is the tricky art of holding in balance its inner
meaning—which is usually explored by its insiders autobiographically,
using often self-authenticating circular logic—and its outer meaning—
the more objective outsiders' view, which is not always shared by its
insiders. (Unfortunately, many people today are not even aware of the
existence of the inner and outer meanings of a religion, and it is equally

deplorable that some insiders of specific religions often neglect to square the two modes of meaning, much to the impoverishment of their understanding of their own religious tradition.) Ideally, the task of "religious understanding of religion" must envision—though it is humanly impossible to delineate concretely or to verify objectively—and try to ascertain the contour of the whole humankind's religious experiences and their expressions by empathetically and critically examining and discriminating various forms of religious data. In this sense, all particular religious traditions may rightly be regarded as parts of the whole of humankind's religious experience, and thus should be approached from the perspective of the whole.[3]

With this kind of preliminary reflection, let us now proceed to reassess our understanding of Christian tradition. We are particularly interested in collating different perspectives—more concretely, "European, "American," and "global"—which bring out somewhat different lights to illuminate the central features of Zoroastrianism, Judaism, and Hellenism (and Islam, later on) that inspired Christianity, especially its triple foci of piety, morality, and culture. Although we dealt with the European (with emphasis on Western Europe) perspective in the previous chapters, I should recapitulate at least its highlights so as to make the comparison of European and American perspectives more sharply focused. In this connection, it might also be worth remembering that from its inception, the Christian tradition, in its endeavor to reach and unfold the mystery of religious reality, emulated, followed, and appropriated the Hebrew paradigm. I refer here to the Jewish soteriological scenario based on God's promise, the Israelites' faith, the covenanted relationship that underlies the Hebrew concept of the "covenanted community," and the promised land, translated into the Christian idiom of the kingdom of God. Besides, the Hebrew tradition was instrumental in transmitting to Christianity the Persian Zoroastrian notion of *eschaton* (end of the world), together with its own version of *Heilsgeschichte* ("history of salvation," which inspired the belief in the divine initiative for the idea of progress).[4] Christianity also inherited from Hebrew tradition such cardinal views as the two natures of the divine: (1) the transcendental creator and the lord of history; and (2) the immanental indwelling in the human order (almost as a member of the covenanted community), the savior (redeemer) as a suffering servant, and that of the human being created in the image of God.

It is equally important to realize that prior to the inception of Christianity, Palestine had been incorporated into the Roman Empire (a sizable number of Jews were residing in diaspora communities in various parts of the Mediterranean world), and that the Jewish culture had been exposed to the strong impact of Hellenism, which, incidentally, produced the phenomenon of Hellenistic Jews. In this connection, the Roman Empire was both a particular nation and also an inheritor of universalistic *oikoumene*, inaugurated by Alexander the Great. Also, Hellenism was not only a cultural tradition originated in Greece; it had an aura of a cosmopolitan orientation, so that even the Hebrew Bible was eagerly translated into Greek (called the Septuagint). In such a situation, historical reality made many Hellenistic Jews realize that Judaism, as a religion as well as a culture, had both inner and outer meanings, and although they did not expect non-Jews to share Jews' autobiographical understanding of the inner meaning of the Jewish monotheistic religious outlook, they had high hopes that in the religiously pluralistic Mediterranean world, non-Jews, by means of Greek translation and approximate explication in Hellenistic thought patterns of Jewish tradition, would come to understand, however imperfectly, the general contour of monotheistic Judaism in terms of its outer meaning, namely, monolatristic particularism (the notion that different groups adhere to different supreme deities).[5]

It is hoped that the above remarks might provide us with a more realistic appreciation of the early Christians' "angle of vision," as eloquently demonstrated, for example, by (1) the Synoptic Gospels' exhortation for people to hold in balance, without rejecting either one, "things that are God's" and "things that are Caesar's"; (2) the notion that Christian community was in reality nothing but a retrieval of the historic covenanted community; (3) the thorough acknowledgment of God's transcendental and immanental characters, which gave impetus to the beliefs in incarnation and the Holy Spirit; and (4) the conviction of *imago dei* (the affirmation that human beings were created in God's image). We can also understand more readily why someone like the apostle Paul, having triple identities as a Pharisee, a Roman citizen, and a Hellenistic Jew, was so deeply concerned with three essentials: (1) piety (in Jewish or Christian senses, both presupposing the indispensability of *metanoia*, or "turning around"); (2) morality (the underpinning of citizenship as well as individual and corporate living in general); and (3) culture (called *paideia* by the Greeks, cultivation of the quality of excellence by intellectual and aesthetic nurturing). I might add that these three essentials became in medieval European history main goals of the three pivotal institutions—the *sacerdotium* (church), *imperium* (state), and *studium* (university). In the early church, these three essentials were considered as closely interrelated but separate components of equal dignity and importance, even though Paul throughout his life strongly advocated piety as the "first among equals." Furthermore, Paul was perfectly aware that Christianity had both inner (monotheistic) meaning based on the supreme piety in God through Christ, and outer (monolatristic) meaning, recognizing it as one of a plurality of religious traditions in the Mediterranean world, as he stated eloquently in 1 Corinthians 8:5–6. These two meanings were nothing but *coincidentia oppositorum* (inevitably contradictory two "faces" of the one and same reality), common to all religious traditions.[6]

It is worth noting, too, that some early Christian thinkers, following Hellenistic Jewish intellectuals in appropriating the Stoics' concept of *logos* (word, rationality, principle), affirmed that all religious and cultural traditions were endowed with scattered seeds of *logos*, which had guided them, but that they were fulfilled in the *logos*-incarnate.[7] What gave the sense of inordinate urgency to Christianity, more than anything else, was the early Christians' realistic awareness of the end of the world (*eschaton*), originally a Persian Zoroastrian notion mediated by the Jewish captives in Babylon, which quickly coalesced with the expectation of the *parousia*, or the second coming (return) of Christ. As might be expected, the anticipation of the end of the world gave unusual intensity to the Christians' fellowship, which was regarded as the spiritual community that existed in the world but not of the world. And it was only when early Christians recognized that the return of Christ was not so imminent that the Christian community began to adjust itself to the historical reality of the second century.[8]

I am persuaded that it is important to realize that the early church did not reject the idea of the end of the world coupled with the second coming of Christ or the notion that the earthly church was in effect a colony of heaven. But these ideas became accepted as doctrines and ritualized, familiar stocks-in-trade of a humanity-centered religion that preserves the contour of transcendental reference while transforming its contents to make it palatable to human conditions. Thus it becomes removed from Christians' immediate concerns. The soft-pedaling of the future-oriented *eschaton* had the effect of shifting Christians' focus to the one past event that had already taken place, that is, the Christ event, centering on the Crucifixion, as the decisive manifestation of God's mighty deed. Redemption to them became the matter of *fait accompli*, which transformed the understanding of the covenanted community from one of the "eschatological eucharistizing *koinonia*" to that of the earthly institution of exclusivistic guarantee of salvation to Christian men and women. Inevitably, the Johannine theme, that God so loved the world, was effectively transformed to that of "God so loved the church" exclusively.

In short, Christianity now had all the earmarks of a "do-it-yourself" religion, confining God's redemption to one past historical event (instead of viewing it as one, albeit an important, dot in the ever-continuing soteriological drama) of Jesus Christ, considered as a temporary earthly divine presence, who—according to pious legends—even appointed his vicar on earth. To be sure, Christianity was a tiny minority religion, one among many, in the vast Roman Empire. But it had enormous inner confidence, believing that it was unquestionably the most exclusive vehicle of salvation, thanks to the *fait accompli* nature of redemption in the drama of crucifixion, in which Christ became the sacrificial lamb for the sin of the whole world and all human beings.[9] Understandably, in that kind of spiritual climate of the early church, martyrs, who were believed to share the bloody sacrifice of the crucified Christ, were highly respected as the paragons of Christian faith.

THE EUROPEAN PERSPECTIVE REVISITED

The destiny of Christianity was decisively affected in Europe by the strange combination of the colossal vision, burning ambition, passionate religious commitment, extraordinarily cunning administrative skills, and good luck of Constantine the Great. He envisaged a new religious-cultural-social-political synthesis, which was to be given its cosmic legitimation by Christianity, the newly tolerated religion after 312 by his edict of Milan, under the supreme authority of him as the Caesaropapian emperor. Some scholars often compare Constantine, who audaciously claimed to be simultaneously secular and sacred monarch, to the "Buddhist king" Aśoka of the Maurya dynasty in third century B.C.E. in India, who was once characterized by Charles Eliot as an archbishop with an extraordinary temporal power.[10] I have no intention of blaming Constantine alone, however, for initiating a long period of "European captivity of Christianity." The Christian community, too, eager to be on the main stage in the empire, coveted the opportunity to serve Constantine, even though it had to be subservient to his will. Moreover, the church agreed to let the emperor call and preside at the Council of Nicaea. Granted, it was not easy to go against the emperor's wish; but after all, it was the crucial assembly of the church to settle some internal matters, and Constantine was not even baptized as yet. At any rate, the church leaders, reversing the biblical injunction, agreed with the new Constantinian principle "In Caesar We Trust" (in sharp contrast to a later motto of the American republic). Furthermore, the church, which in its inception was modeled after the paradigm of the Hebrew covenanted community, began to be reshaped, patterning itself after the prototype of the *imperium*. It is not surprising, therefore, that ecclesiastical leaders began to aspire to becoming the church counterparts of the emperors, monarchs, and officials, for example, "monarchical" popes and episcopates. Even Augustine of Hippo, in spite of all his spiritual insights and perceptions, condoned and furthered the authoritarian and orthodoxy-conscious trends of the church in the late fourth and early fifth century.

Admittedly, the authoritarian character of the church was rather effective in reaching the great majority of the barbarian peoples in Northern and Western Europe, bringing them into the nominally Christian fold by the end of the so-called Dark Ages. In retrospect, it becomes apparent that under the Franks, the basic framework of society centered around the inward permeation of the secular and the sacred or between the Frankish state and the Frankish territorial church.[11] In the meantime, the balance of power between the *imperium* and the *sacerdotium* shifted with the decline of the Frankish empire, and the church (which by that time had developed into the church of the empire, or *Reichskirche*) attempted to hang on to its imperial structure even after the disintegration of the empire. In this situation, many clergy, unhappy with the states' policies of clerical appointments, insisted on greater independence of the church from political rulers. And, as we discussed in the previous chapter, during the long years of the Holy Roman Empire, 962–1558, the jostling between the emperor, who aspired to be the real Caesaropapian type of kingship, and the pope, who too craved to be the "mitered" Caesaropapian monarch, continued. Inevitably, the *studium* (university), the third member of the medieval trio, which was caught between the church and the state, began to be liberated from the yoke of the church from the time of the Renaissance in the fourteenth century and through the period of territorial monarchies, 1558–1806, and the more modern era of autonomous nation-states (1806 onward). It greatly inspired and enriched autonomous modern European civilization, which in my view has all the makings of a pseudoreligion of secularized salvation. And the most amazing irony of history is that the *imperium*, which undertook colonialism, and the *sacerdotium*, which carried on Christian world mission, were destined to ally themselves once again with the *studium*, which spearheaded Western civilization, both at home and in the non-Western world, except probably in the United States.

THE AMERICAN PERSPECTIVE

Obviously, there have been a variety of views about life and the world
articulated throughout American history, but here I use such an oversimplified expression as "the American experience" primarily because I
wish to paint on the broad canvas some significant contrasts between
European and American orientations, realizing, of course, that we may
be indulging in the exercise of simplistic ideal types. Moreover, I am
aware that there seem to be different perceptions between native-born
Americans and naturalized citizens, like myself, about the selection of
significant features on the subject. My views on the American experience, therefore, are colored by my personal observations and experiences, which might or might not illuminate the discussion on this
complicated phenomenon. In this context, I would like, nevertheless, to
concentrate on three major areas: (1) the colonists' *mundus imaginalis*,
their sense of liberation from the inherited tyranny of the European
religious-cultural-social-political synthesis and their outlook toward
life in the new world; (2) Americans' historical experience, which by the
end of the eighteenth century propelled the novel (at least in Christendom) practice of religious liberty; and (3) the more recent American
scene, with the erosion of the WASP establishment that precipitated
such phenomena as the growth of cultural pluralism, the civil rights
movement, the "rainbowization" of cities, and so forth.[12] Also, the real
thrusts of the contemporary American scene must be understood in the
context of an emerging global perspective.

The American Perspective—Phase I

In discussing colonial America, we must make every effort to cut
through the rosy haze of romantic nostalgia that often unduly idealizes
the birth of the nation. Undoubtedly, there were all kinds of colonists;
and, in spite of stereotyped legends, not all colonists were Puritans.
Besides, there is no question about the fact that not every Puritan was
so pious. Nevertheless, New England Puritans were crucially important
because their angle of vision greatly influenced the general orientation
of colonial America, particularly because they had an existential sense
of history and a realistic awareness of self-identity based on their
paradigm. It is noteworthy that their religious outlook was not focused
on Pentecost but rather on the recollection of Exodus. It is well known,
according to the biblical narrative, that Yahweh had sent Moses and
Aaron to see the Pharaoh, urging him to let the Israelites go so that they

could have a feast for their God in the wilderness. Significantly, Puritans read this narrative through their own experience. They understood, therefore, that freedom, which they gained by leaving behind religious and political oppression in the old country, important though it was, was meant to be the by-product of their commitment to the worship of their deity. They also rightly discerned the tragic predicament of the human condition—that of being divided into numerous groups that are full of enmity.

Not surprisingly, the colonists applied directly the ancient biblical soteriological formula—God's promise, humankind's faith, the covenanted relationship, and the promised land—to their own situation. Concretely, they attempted to actualize the covenanted relationship in three major areas of life: (1) the domain of religion in a narrow, ecclesiastical, institutional sense (the sphere of the *sacerdotium* in medieval Europe); (2) the domain of political order with a heavy dose of religious underpinning (the traditional sphere of the *imperium*); and (3) the domain of religiously inspired culture (symbolized in Europe by the *studium*). Rejecting, however, the Europeans' acceptance of the descending model in all three domains, based on the belief that all good things come from above, the American colonists tried to keep in balance the "downward" motif (grace) in religion, the "upward" motif (morality) in political order, and the "horizontal" motif (rationality and learning) in culture. It was their sense that this tripartite covenant (which was the visible form of the emerging early American religious-cultural-social-political synthesis) was to be given cosmic legitimation by "providence," which was their favorite idiom. In a sense, the American colonists were reacting against the European pattern of the all-too-easy compromise of Christianity with this-worldly prestige, wealth, and power. The most conspicuous feature of institutional ecclesiastical development in America was the emergence of the type of institutions (later called by sociologists "denominations") characterized by the trend toward voluntary association, expansion of initiatives by laymen and laywomen, and so forth, which became common features among all religious traditions, including Protestant, Roman Catholic, and Jewish groups. The amazing vitality of religious groups throughout American history in philanthropy, overseas missionary programs, and educational activities is undoubtedly stimulated by laity activism to the extent that Daniel Boorstin even goes so far as to say that religions in America "commend themselves for the services they perform more than the truths which they affirm."[13]

As far as I can see, it was characteristic of the New England Puritans' totalistic thinking that they perceived of political order and culture also in religious terms, regarding these spheres of life as that of "civil religion," to use a contemporary term. These are fuzzy areas, because the colonists did not think of these ideas in systematic and theoretical manners. Nevertheless, in their eyes political order and culture were closely related to what came to be called the "American Way of Life," dubbed by Boorstin as "a kind of generalized American religion."[14] At any rate, in the days when Europe was governed by a series of territorial monarchies, taking for granted the notion of graded human beings (divided between those who rule and those who are ruled), American colonists struggled to hammer out the structure of government by the people (reminiscent of the Jewish notion of peoplehood), divided intricately into its three branches. Nowadays we are apt to think that the colonists must have been swimming in a vast uncharted sea; but they seemed to be certain that the Bible was their unerring compass, and that biblical narratives (e.g., those of the Exodus and of the Israelites' wandering in the desert before reaching the promised land, etc.) had anticipated—and in a sense prescribed—the scenarios of the Pilgrim Fathers' experiences in the New World. There was also an uncanny resemblance between the three branches of the government envisaged by the colonists and the three branches of the ancient Hebrew commonwealth, namely, the council of elders (the Sanhedrin), the order of elected magistrates (Judges), and the people's assembly. Evidently, they believed that it was a divine imperative for them to create a "due form of government both civil and ecclesiastical," to use their fond phrase.

Unfortunately, space does not allow a more detailed discussion as to how the task of creating a due form of government, starting with the Declaration of Independence, required the uneasy compromise and cooperation between (1) the followers of traditional, conservative Christianity, upheld by the Puritans and adherents of other wings of Protestantism, and (2) those advocates of Enlightenment-rationalist Christianity, held by some intellectual colonists who had been influenced by the thoughts of Rousseau, Bentham, and Locke, the cult of reason, and deism (rational religion). The unique features that resulted from such an unusual alliance, especially the long-range impact of the thrust of the so-called American Enlightenment, will become more evident in the next phase. Suffice it to say here that throughout the zigzag course of the Republic, the United States behaved more like "the nation with the soul of a church," with a strong sense of sacrality of the law and justice.[15] Also, I have always felt, rightly or wrongly, that the underlying ethos of the civil religion made American culture venture into the hitherto unheard-of principle of one-tier education. This was in sharp contrast to the two-tier system, practiced traditionally in Europe and elsewhere, which sharply divided the destiny of children between two classes, those who were fated to belong to the upper strata and those who were confined to the lower strata of society. The one-tier principle in education was in effect a cultural counterpart to the political affirmation of the idea of the equality of every person before the law, and it runs through the public school system and various other aspects of American cultural tradition. Significantly, Jacob Neusner observes that the same religiously inspired ethos—the "cultural Protestantism," in his phraseology—has "shaped American university perspectives until the most recent years."[16]

The American Perspective—Phase II

Among many unique thrusts that are found in the American religious universe, I would like to depict one particular principle, one that decisively shaped Phase II of the American perspective. Here I am referring to the notion of religious liberty, more commonly known by its practical consequence, namely, the separation of church and state. Coming as I did originally from Japan, which had traditionally followed the dogma of *saisei-itchi*, or unity of religion and state, at least until the end of World War II, the notion of the separation of church and state has always intrigued me tremendously. Also, although I am not an expert on this issue, I suspect that something like the concept of religious liberty will have to be explored seriously now on a global level in our religiously pluralistic world.

In retrospect, it becomes evident that this lofty principle of religious liberty had developed out of a less grandiose historical reality, characterized by the coexistence of a number of self-styled absolutistic religious groups, each convinced that it was the bearer of the final truth. It is to be remembered that most of those religious groups—Protestant, Roman Catholic, Greek Orthodox, Jewish, and so forth—had a long history in Europe, where their doctrines, liturgies, and ecclesiastical polities had been firmly fixed prior to the time when they were transplanted to the New World, with its adherents of various ethnic or national origins. Ernst Troeltsch developed various categories, such as "church" type or "sect" type, and fitted major European ecclesiastical groups into these categories. Significantly, however, all these religious groups—even those that retained church- or sect-type conviction in their theological orientation—became denominationalized in the American context. Even more significantly, these religious groups, despite their newly acquired denominational ethos, were determined to press their respective absolute claims. (Fortunately, the New World was geographically spacious, so that these competing groups could cohabit without too much obvious friction. Some of them either could not communicate among themselves because of linguistic or cultural barriers, or they took a live-and-let-live attitude on pragmatic grounds.)

At any rate, the slowly emerging notion of religious liberty—inspired especially by Enlightenment-rationalistic Christianity—in early America brought about the pattern of separation of church and state, which had both positive and negative implications. On the positive side, it ushered in an atmosphere that enabled various religious groups, each pursuing freedom to press its absolutistic claims, to coexist peacefully, if grudgingly, side by side. In the words of Wilhelm Pauck, each group was "enabled to act as if there were no other [groups] in existence, but in so doing concede to other [groups], which do actually exist as its neighbors and rivals, the right to practice the same kind of isolationism."[17] In this situation, many suspect that clerical leaders of many religious groups were presumably far less reconciled with the notion of separation of church and state or coexistence of various groups than were their lay counterparts, who were more concerned with personal, elementary, and unsophisticated piety and simple biblicism than with doctrinal differences drawn along denominational lines, as amply demonstrated in numerous revivalistic movements that were the hallmarks of American Protestantism.

It should be worth noting, too, that the American system of separation of religious and political institutions belongs to what many consider a friendly model. That is to say, they are legally separate but without enmity or antipathy. This fact becomes evident when one compares the American pattern of separation with, for example, French anticlericalism in the nineteenth century or anticlerical policies adopted in Mexico, to say nothing of many Marxist nations in our own century. J. Philip Woggaman cites the Constitution of Albania as an example of an extremely negative model: "The State recognizes no religion and supports and develops atheist propaganda for the purpose of implanting the scientific materialist world outlook in people (Art. 30). The creation of any type of organization of a fascist, anti-democratic, religious or anti-socialist character is prohibited (Art. 54)."[18]

Even then, the separation of church and state—the prominent feature of the American perspective, Phase II—was the repudiation of the Puritans' ideal of the holy commonwealth, characterized as Phase I of the American perspective earlier, in which religious principles were expected to control and direct sociopolitical and cultural orders for religious purposes. (In this sense, the American model of separation may be likened to an amicable divorce, whereby divorced and remarried persons agree to appear as fathers and mothers of grooms or brides at the wedding, but return to their separate ways after the ceremony. That is to say, divorce, however amicable, is divorce, and should be so understood.)

It is ironic that the American pattern of separation of church and state was originally motivated by the colonists' aspiration for freedom, that is, freedom from civil and religious forms of tyranny such as they had experienced across the Atlantic Ocean. As such, freedom was a powerful rallying objective for colonists of various persuasions, including conservative religionists, such as the Puritans and other Protestants, and the advocates of Enlightenment-rationalistic Christianity. Thus, Nathan Hatch cogently observes that "when Samuel Adams suggested in 1772 that 'the Religion and public liberty of a people are intrinsically connected . . . and therefore rise and fall together,' he was reflecting the common assumption that liberty always had a religious as well as a civil dimension."[19] Indeed, the cause of freedom made steady strides during the revolutionary era, as illustrated by the Virginia Declaration of Rights and the Declaration of Independence. "Most sensational of all, in that connection," says Sydney Ahlstrom, "was the enactment of complete religious liberty in Virginia, where up to 1775 restrictions had been more strictly enforced than anywhere else." Then, he continues: "With the ratification of the federal Constitution (1787) and its first ten amendments (1791), the full range of Protestantism possessed liberties enjoyed nowhere else in the world."[20]

Ahlstrom is no doubt right in saying that by the end of the eighteenth century, Americans firmly won the precious objective of liberty, both religious and civil. And the principle of religious liberty became the cornerstone of the American religious perspective (Phase II). At that time, however, people scarcely recognized and openly discussed some of the ramifications of religious liberty thus established—which became important features of the more recent American perspective (Phase III), to which we now turn.

The Recent American Perspective—Phase III

Although I have neither the competence nor inclination to go into a comprehensive analysis of modern American developments (roughly from the Civil War to World War II), I am, nevertheless, keenly interested in considering broadly recent Americans' sense of cosmic legitimation of their religious-cultural-social-political synthesis that can be contrasted to those of their forebears.[21]

I have already tried to elucidate the perception of the early colonists (who had viewed England as an "Elect Nation" but were thankful to be eluded from political and religious tyranny). They conceived of the whole of life (embracing both civic and religious facets) in religious terms. They were persuaded that such a multidimensional and yet seamless form of life hammered out in the New World (which to them was destined to develop into a new Elect Nation) would be authenticated by providence. Understandably, they put ultimate trust in God, rather than in kings, hereditary aristocrats, and/or government machineries, as the source and compass of piety, morality (both individual and corporate), and culture, all of which together would nurture democratic religion in the New World, in contradistinction to aristocratic religion in Europe. Hence came their passionate dedication to the ideal of liberty, both civil and ecclesiastical (see Phase II). Like it or not, however, recent Americans are bound to be influenced by positive as well as negative ramifications of their forebears' understanding of liberty.

It is a matter of great irony that the concept of liberty—intentionally or otherwise—effectively destroyed adhesive unity of the tripartite facets of integrated life, notably the interrelatedness among piety, morality, and culture, as envisaged by early colonists. It is not that the friendly mode of "separation of church and state" turned into a hostile relationship. However, each dimension of life was now deprived of the consolidated vision and perception that had been taken for granted in colonial days. Thus, for example, the fact that the religious notion of "religious liberty" was now translated into the legal idiom of the First Amendment inevitably shifted its arena from the unified life to the domain of constitutional reflection primarily. It is no wonder that endless debates about the plausible "original intent" behind the text of the First Amendment or the adequacy/inadequacy of the Supreme Court justices' "legal definitions of religion" have been destined to ensue throughout the modern period.[22] Concomitantly, recent Americans have been unconsciously seeking the cosmic legitimation of their religious-cultural-social-political synthesis—no longer in providence, but in the civil religion, commonly equated in the popular imagination with the "American Way of Life." This is a spiritual cousin of modern Europeans' concept of the pseudoreligion of secularized salvation (referring to the modern European civilization itself), inspired, to be sure, by the underlying notion of autonomous humanity. This fact has had a decisive impact on contemporary Americans' perception of the mutual relationships and balance among the spheres of piety, morality, and culture.

I have always been impressed by an obvious fact that American religious groups' adoption of the lofty principle of religious liberty during the eighteenth century made them stumble into—certainly not by premeditation or with theoretical sophistication—a theological formula somewhat reminiscent of the apostle Paul's two-pronged understanding of Christianity, based on monotheistic assertion of faith in one supreme God through Christ as its inner meaning, side by side with its outer meaning of monolatristic acceptance of plurality of religions. Considering the reasonableness of such a formula, I have been mystified by the seeming unpopularity of this type of two-pronged affirmation among the pious peoples. As far as I can see, the *coincidentia oppositorum* based on monotheistic assertion (inner meaning) and monolatristic affirmation (outer meaning) is an authentic formula, shared by a number of religious traditions, including early Christianity (see my earlier references to the apostle Paul).

Lamentably, such a formula had been forgotten by European Christianity, for—being the dominant, only official religion for so long—it fell into the common error of assuming that the inner meaning of Christianity, based on its self-authenticating circular logic of finality, is the uncontested self-evident universal truth. I rather imagine that even in America many denominational leaders tried to ignore, did not appreciate, and mentally resented the monolatristic implication of the principle of religious liberty. Moreover, large number of immigrants who continued to arrive at the American shore (Roman Catholics, Jews, Protestants of various persuasions) were not used to the idea of separation of church and state, to say nothing about comprehending the lofty notion of religious liberty. It is not surprising, therefore, that many pious Christians and Jews were highly critical of the 1893 World's Parliament of Religions in Chicago simply on the ground that various religious traditions were treated with equal footing and dignity.[23]

It must be candidly admitted that the friendly mode of separation of church and state, as developed in this Republic, is a murky affair, full of loopholes and contradictions. Thus, as might be expected, those purists who adopt literal interpretation of separation can find all kinds of objectionable realities and practices: military chaplaincy, chaplaincy to the Congress; invocation at a presidential inauguration, political party meetings, or a local school's commencement; some cities' display of a crèche at Yuletide, lighting of Christmas trees at the White House and/or in local cities; allocation of public funds to parochial schools and denominational hospitals; sending an ambassador to the Vatican; as well as conducting religious funeral services of the president, governor, a police officer, or fire fighter. Those who side with Jefferson's historic metaphor of "wall of separation" find Justice Rehnquist's "nonpreferentialism" (allowing government aid to religious groups without showing preference) a rejection or reversal of the historic church-state principle. I remember vividly two related questions raised in the prenomination Senate hearing of Supreme Court Justice-designate Souter. One senator asked specifically the church-state question, based on Souter's past defense, as state attorney general, of the New Hampshire governor's executive order requiring the state flag to be flown at half-mast on Good Friday in honor or Christ's crucifixion. (Souter acknowledged that today he would declare the executive order unconstitutional.) The other question had to do with the free exercise side of the First Amendment. Evidently, the state of New Hampshire refused to allow a Jehovah's Witness to strip off from his license plate the motto "Live Free or Die." The Witness had maintained that the motto was inconsistent with his religious faith. At the hearing, Souter conceded that New Hampshire, in his current opinion, had no compelling interest in requiring this motto to remain on the license plate.[24] I am fairly certain that there must be numerous other cases and examples in modern America that are to be placed on the continuum between Jefferson's and Rehnquist's interpretations of the church-state relationship.

The Role of Law

The salient feature of modern America is undoubtedly the dominant role of law that affects all aspects of individual and corporate life of the people from cradle to grave—health care, education, marriage, business, property, politics, industry, defense, government, social control, foreign affairs. Never in the history of the human race has there been any period and place like modern America in which everything depends so heavily on legal requirements, interpretation, and protection. And yet opinions vary widely as to "(1) How is law [in America] related to the maintenance of social order? (2) What is the relation between *legal obligation* and *moral obligation?* [and] (3) What are rules and to what extent is law an affair of rules?"[25] Granted that law in America, as elsewhere, has evolved out of a long historical process, influenced by legal traditions of England and the continent, Roman jurisprudence, Hellenistic thought, Jewish and Christian notions of rights, freedoms, and justice, metaphysico-social principles, and so forth. Even in the memory of American experience, we can readily see how from the time of the framing of the Constitution, various kinds of people of different persuasions have invested enormous thought and energy in hammering out the kinds of viable legal systems needed for the growing democratic nation—assuring citizens' freedom, rights, and equality before the law, and so forth. Unfortunately, those who had followed, for example, the Watergate and Iran-Contra affairs on television were compelled to realize that sophisticated and enlightened laws have made people moralistic in the sense of being aware of their obligation to legal requirements, but not necessarily moral; in fact, many people would use their legal knowledge and protection to find legal loopholes or for doing something illegal without getting caught by law.

Undoubtedly, there must be many different interpretations as to why such a highly civilized society as contemporary America, with excellent and extensive legal education, has not been able to instill in elected and appointed officials, responsible leaders of society as well as ordinary citizens, the plain fact that legality has more than some remote connection to morality.

Although I don't entirely idealize the early Americans' particular formula of tightly integrating piety, morality, and culture as such, I am equally skeptical of the other extreme of viewing each strand of the tripartite aspects of life as totally independent and self-sufficient, especially the current trend of reinterpreting morality predominantly as a sphere of legality. Inevitably, legal tradition in modern America is impoverished, partly because it has been deprived of religious, moral, philosophical, and cultural underpinning.

Having lost the transcendental sacral referent, modern America has turned to law, especially the Constitution, and the court as the sacred institutions. In fact, some people regard the Constitution as a semireligious document, much as traditional Muslims affirmed the eternality of the *Qur'an* (believed as the divine word, revealed intact to the Prophet). Some of the legal positivists assert that the framers of the Constitution had anticipated all the major problems that this Republic would encounter for many years to come.

Contrary to some peoples' impression that the Constitution and the Supreme Court are nothing but the embodiments of the fixed rule of law, these institutions and judges have been extremely sensitive to the whim of social, political, and cultural climates of the nation. Moreover, since 1803, when Chief Justice John Marshall seized the legal prerogative for the Supreme Court, the so-called doctrine of judicial review has given alleged power to the Court "to declare unconstitutional, acts of

Congress, executive orders of the President, provisions of state consti-
tutions, or state laws.[26]

I have some sympathy with people who hope that the Court will
be an independent judicial institution entirely above the political fray,
upholding the sacrality of law, especially the Constitution. William
Eaton goes so far as to say: "The danger in the Supreme Court's usurpa-
tion of legislative and amending power is that the Court will become
more and more like either agencies of the government, the legislative and
executive. It will become merely another *political,* policy-making
agency."[27] (No wonder it was Jefferson who hesitated to consider the
judges the ultimate arbiters of all constitutional questions.) Fortunately
or unfortunately, we have to recognize that judges have feet of clay, and
the only way for the Court to act as the judicial institution is for the
nation to pursue rigorously the principle of checks and balances. I might
also add that we should retrieve the insight that law and morality must be
somehow integrally related to piety and culture.

Fragmentation

The fragmentation—or at least loosening up of the seamless unity of
the tripartite facets of life—also has made culture in America vulnera-
ble and somewhat rootless, caught between its own self-understanding
and historical reality. Admittedly, the discrepancy between a culture's
own self-understanding and historical reality is not a unique American
problem, except probably its conspicuous degree and extensiveness,
due to historical reasons. From the dawn of history, as various civilizations emerged, human beings realized—as Eliade speculated—that
they "could collaborate with nature, and finally come to dominate it,
by learning how to make things more rapidly than nature."[28] Not
surprisingly, science and technology have been integral parts of human civilization everywhere. The human being, however, has not
been simply the inventor and the manipulator of tools (*homo faber*);
he or she has always had the propensity to be concerned with ideas
and ideals, language and communication, virtues and values, arts and
morality, physical and mental health, individual personal growth and
the well-being of the corporate or communal life. And specialists in
sacred things—prophets, seers, mystics, philosophers—have advanced
various theories about hidden realities, cosmic order, and so forth,
both transcendental and implicit in the world of nature. In other
words, all civilizations were instrumental in fostering their respective

religious-cultural-social-political syntheses (to use divided categories of Western mode of perceiving seamless human experience) that have provided "worlds of meaning" to various peoples and communities throughout history.[29] In this complex development, culture (*paideia*) played a crucial role in orienting people to their world of meaning, training their bodies and souls of men and women to be worthy recipients of inherited literary and philosophical traditions as well as values, virtues, and the texture of individual and corporate life in various communities.

Obviously, many of the early settlers to American colonies had been exposed, before coming to the New World, to Western European cultural traditions, characterized by territorial monarchies (following the abdication of Charles V as the last full-fledged emperor of the Holy Roman Empire), national churches (Protestant as well as Catholic, emancipated from the totalitarian domination of the European religious scene from Rome), mercantile entrepreneurship, and worldwide Western expansion in terms of cultural triumphalism and colonialism. No wonder colonists assumed that to them culture meant nothing but Western European culture, with a heavy dose of Protestant orientation! Their aspiration for emancipation from continued European political and religious authorities led them to discover the biblical theme of the Exodus. Curiously, however, their sense of joyfulness for having successfully achieved freedom for themselves did nothing to enable them to recognize and appreciate non-Western European cultural traditions of two other groups of people in the New World, namely, the Native-Americans and African-Americans, while they created fancy rhetorics of a cultural melting pot. Even today, those who have been so thoroughly and one-sidedly oriented to the "Western European, Protestant" cultural ethos wink, and try to ignore, the discrepancy between their cultural self-understanding and historical realities.

The fragmentation of life, which gives the false optimism that culture can grow all by itself without being nurtured by the inputs from piety, morality, and other aspects of civilization, often drives American culture to extreme forms of narcissism, utopianism, anomie, megalomania, and/or war-giddy patriotism. Shortly after World War I, there was a strong Americanization movement, based on the simplistic conviction that any group of immigrants from anywhere can be integrated in a relatively short time into typical American culture. Nowadays the pendulum swings to the other side, extolling the virtue of multiculturalism in America, giving the impression that there is nothing between complete absorption into a well-established, fixed American culture and cultural pluralism. Moreover, as Robert Maynard Hutchins once stated:

> The most striking paradox of American life is that this system, which must rest on individual differences, produces the most intense pressure toward uniformity. The fact that any boy can become President, instead of making every boy an individual, tends to make him a replica of everyone else. "Getting on" is the great American aspiration. And here the demoralizing part comes in; the way to get on is to be "safe," to be "sound," to be agreeable, to be inoffensive, to have no views on important matters not sanctioned by the majority, by your superiors, or by your group.[30]

The tragedy is that many people still think of culture in America primarily as a residual form of Western European cultural heritage, not recognizing that American culture, which to be sure started out with European tradition, has had its own cultural experience in the New World, enriched by the contributions of the Native-Americans, African-Americans, Hispanic-Americans, and Asian-Americans. When a gift of $20 million was given to Yale recently, I was amused that the dean of Yale College stated: "It is one of the aims of liberal education to try to provide students with a basis for understanding the world they live in and the forces that shape it. To do that the study of Western civilization is essential." Although I am, of course, in favor of the study of Western civilization, I question the simplistic assumption that American students live in the world shaped predominantly by Western civilization. It is all very well, as far as I can see, for them to study non-Western civilizations as world citizens living in the twentieth century; but, according to the dean's announcement, American colleges and universities over the last twenty years "have moved too far from the teaching of Western civilization" (implying that, after all, Western civilization is essentially the only important native tradition for American students).[31] On the other hand, I am equally alarmed by the recent trend regarding the increasing number of "would have been naturalized citizens" who are shying away from U.S. citizenship. Although I suspect that there must be various not-so-apparent reasons why the number of noncitizens, especially those of non-European backgrounds, living in the United States is increasing each year, I nevertheless lament the fact that these would-have-been-citizens, unwittingly to be sure, support some peoples' misguided notion of the Europocentric emphasis of American culture. I also regret that by not assuming responsibility as citizens, they forfeit their prerogatives of contributing to the ever-growing indigenous multiracial, multireligious, and multicultural tradition—indeed a unique blending of *paideia*, morality, and piety—in this Republic.[32]

The Consequences of Religous Liberty

As hinted several times, I am inclined to hold that one of the unintended consequences of the lofty principle of religious liberty (and its logical sequel, separation of church and state) was ironically the impoverishment of the life of ecclesiastical religion in America. By that I do not refer to the absence of government's financial subsidy to religious groups/institutions or the gradual erosion of their status in society. However, I rather suspect that the adoption of the principle of religious liberty—unintentionally and not altogether completely—terminated the pattern of uneasy coalescence between the tradition of conservative-pietistic-evangelical Christianity and that of the Enlightenment-rationalistic Christianity, which, incidentally, had made a great impact on many political and cultural leaders in the colonial period. This turn of events drove evangelical Protestants—now that they had lost the benefit of sobering restraints by their rationalistic counterpart—to indulge in what Woggaman calls the "illusion of theocracy."[33] Part of such an illusion is the trait of reading history backward, as amply illustrated by the fact that many pietistic churchmen began to have exaggerated views about the importance of their tradition in early American history. Ahlstrom quotes Philip Schaff's statement made in 1845, echoing the prevailing view among evangelical churchmen:

> Puritan Protestantism forms properly the main basis of our North American church. . . . We may never ungratefully forget that it was this generation of godly Pilgrims which once for all stamped upon our country that character of deep moral earnestness, that spirit of strong intrepid determination, that peculiar zeal for the Sabbath and the Bible, which have raised it to so high a place in the history of Christian Church.[34]

Notwithstanding such a deservedly laudatory statement about Puritan Protestantism, many people, including some notables like William Blackstone, John Clark, and Roger Williams, had difficulties with the Massachusetts theocracy, which imposed its own version of Christianity or of religious liberty, making dissension de facto civil crime.

On the other hand, especially seen from the distance of our current perspective, the effect of the illusion of theocracy, like other illusions, does not seem to be altogether that negative. We can even say with some exaggeration that theocratic ideal coupled with optimistic outlook and activistic temper—characteristics of many colonists—enabled evangelical Christians to pursue tirelessly and fearlessly with "zeal" many salutary goals such as overseas missionary programs, education—both public and religious—at home, philanthropy, and a series of activities to bring about a "Christian America," to borrow the title of Robert Handy's perceptive book on the subject.[35] It must be admitted, however, that in their eagerness for their ideals, many evangelical Protestants tended to erase the boundary line between ecclesiastical and civil religions by claiming credits for the evangelical Protestant church what had been accomplished by religiously inspired political or cultural traditions. To make the matter more complex, the illusion of theocracy was kept alive by the ambiguous statements made by well-meaning individuals (especially the advocates of the Enlightenment Christianity) who were—in spite of their misleading statements—actually upholding the cause of civil religion, as epitomized by William Penn's Preface to the Frame of Government of Pennsylvania in 1682. In his own words: "Government seems to me a part of religion itself, a thing sacred in its institution and end. For if it does not directly remove the cause, it crushes the effects of evil and is as such (though a lower part) an emanation of the same divine power that is both author and object of pure religion."[36]

In retrospect, it becomes very evident that on the one hand, ecclesiastical Protestantism has dominated the domain of religious life in American historical experience. On the other hand, partly because of its illusion of theocracy, it has been loath to confront historical realities, as illustrated by its indifference to the religious needs of the Native-Americans, Jews, Roman Catholics, Eastern Orthodox and other Christians, Unitarians, Mormons, Seventh-day Adventists, Hispanics, Asian-Americans, Muslims, Hindus, Buddhists, and so forth. Even among its own ranks, Protestantism has not been very successful in developing and maintaining a meaningful rapport among its various wings, conservatives and liberals, social gospelites and fundamentalists, rationalists and superpatriotic nationalists. By and large, the growth of ecclesiastical Protestantism owed much to revivalism, which tended to counter sectarian mentality, thus nurturing an unconsciously ecumenical spirit (even though ecumenism has often been confused with ecclesiastical consolidation movements). At home, ecclesiastical evangelical Protestants shared with the tradition of Enlightenment-rationalist Christianity the passion for education and nationalistic pride. As to education, the evangelical groups enthusiastically supported the one-tier system of education and institutions of public and private education, including the college and university. In theological education, they wanted to control their own institutions, whereas Enlightenment Christians depended heavily on private graduate universities for theological education. (It is worth noting that they have developed extensive theological curriculums, from simple Bible schools to sophisticated "theological colleges," which is a unique American phenomenon.)

One of the most baffling questions about American Christianity (especially Protestantism) is its place in the international scene. In one sense, American Christianity reflected the relative isolation of the New World, protected as it was by the Atlantic and the Pacific Oceans. However, America was very sensitive negatively and positively to the influence of religious, cultural, and economic trends of England and the Continent (e.g., scientific revolution, industrial revolution, Marxism, etc.). And, of course, immigrants came to the American shore from Europe and elsewhere. Meanwhile, the psyche of all Americans, including American Christians and Jews, was greatly affected by changing thoughts and events both domestic and international, such as the Civil War, the gold rush, the expansion of frontiers, the Spanish-American War, the Open Door policy in China, the Oriental Exclusion Act in Immigration, the peace movement, urban growth, progress (in science, technology, communication and international capitalism), Prohibition, World War I and the Great Depression, and so forth. Throughout the modern period, outsiders were mystified by such contradictory thrusts of Americans as extreme ultraism vs. nativism, quick empathy with foreigners vs. deeply rooted bigotry, outgoing open-mindedness to their cultures and religions (as exemplified in the 1893 World's Parliament of Religions) vs. exclusivistic ecclesiastical triumphalism (epitomized by the motto of the Student Volunteer Movement at the turn of the century—"the Evangelization of the World in This Generation"). Although American churches took phenomenal leadership in Christian world mission in the modern period, outsiders often suspected that American missionaries advocated the American Way of Life as much as the Christian gospel. (It reminds me of Josiah Strong's famous theme in 1893—the "Anglosaxonization of the entire world.") Much of modern Americans' religious life was affected, according to C. C. Goen, by laicism. Note his candid observation:

> Most American church members respond even to the gravest moral issues, not in terms of a conscience formed by the classical

Christian tradition, but mainly according to the social attitudes and cultural mores they have imbibed as Americans.

American Christians from the beginning have seen their country as having a special place in the purpose of God.

What we confront here is a kind of religious national- ism . . . solidly supported by most church members who are largely unaware of its idolatrous tendencies. . . .

American church members are terribly distressed over the prospect of losing America's hegemony in the world, and this is mainly because they have lost the vision of the supernational char- acter of the kingdom of God.[37]

10

PIETY, MORALITY, AND CULTURE IN GLOBAL PERSPECTIVE (1)

SOME NOTES ON GLOBAL PERSPECTIVE

I hope the title of this chapter will not be misleading. My intention is not to elucidate some concrete features and/or general characteristics of a global perspective about Christianity, and I am certainly not trying to develop anything like "a theology of religions," either. Rather, my aim is simply to reaffirm and clarify the underlying theme of this volume—already hinted at in Part I—that it is high time for Christianity to move beyond the stage of its European captivity and take its global experience and responsibility very seriously. Let me make it clear, too, that I have nothing against the long historical coalescence between Christianity and Western civilization. I have a growing premonition, however, that the Christian religion is not doomed to share its telos only with European civilization, as many insiders as well as outsiders seem to think in our time.

Implicit also is my considered opinion that Christian experience in America—in spite of the one-sided belief held by many to the effect that it has been intrinsically destined to remain as a part of, and within the framework of, Europocentric religious structure—has actually evolved many noble, indigenously American insights and perspectives unknown in European experience. Note, for example, the early

Americans' perception of the seamlessness of life (and the mutual penetration between ecclesiastical and civil religions), spiritual and political
liberty eagerly accepted by both clergy and laity with strong lay initiative, equality of all religious groups as denominational type, and separation of church and state. There have been, of course, numerous factors
that sustain the traditional view that equates American religious life to
that of Europe, for example: the natural sense of attachment on the part
of many European Americans to the traditions of their forebears; most
Americans' exposure singularly to things European in today's American education; continued influences of European theologies, ethics, and
philosophies on American soil; inferences of global confessionalism (of
Roman Catholics, Lutherans, Calvinists, Anglicans, etc.) and the ecumenical movement; the frequent exchange of visitors, scholars, and students; and the convenience of Western languages. Even so, there are
differences between European and American religious perspectives, and
it is a part of my contention that American experience will have a
salutary effect in mediating the European and global religious perspectives in the years to come.

Ironically, in America the very notion of religious liberty precipitated unintentionally the fragmentation of life (e.g., loosening of
the unity among piety, morality, and culture or between ecclesiastical
and civil religions). This fragmentation on the one hand inspired ecclesiastical churchmen and churchwomen to have the illusion of theocracy, while often equating civil religion for all intents and purposes
with the "American Way of Life," which has uncanny similarities to
the notion of modern European civilization itself as a post-Christian
pseudoreligion of secularized salvation. One of the encouraging by-
products of the erosion of WASP domination in various aspects of
American life in our own century is the gradual recognition of hitherto ignored religious-cultural traditions of Native-Americans,
African-Americans, Hispanic-Americans, and Asian-Americans, Muslims, and so forth.[1] Unfortunately, proper distinction between the
so-called rainbowization as a domestic, societal American phenomenon and religious-cultural plurality as a global reality has not as
yet been clear in the minds of many Americans, even the enthusiastic
cultural-religious pluralists.

As to the contemporary global scene, I have no intention of
spelling it out in this context. It is too vast a subject, and none of us can
claim to see the entire world from a vantage point of view.[2] Nevertheless,
we must touch upon, however superficially, such leitmotifs as (a) the end
of Western colonialism, which precipitated the rise of the peoples,

nations, and cultures of Asia, Africa, and South America; (b) the erosion of Christian world mission; the sudden popularity, especially among Western Christians, of the idea of the dialogue among religions; and the ambiguous self-identity of the so-called younger churches; (c) the growing confidence, in their own homelands, of non-Christian and non-Western religions and their appeal to many ex-Christians and ex-Jews in the West; and (d) the enormously difficult challenge for Christianity as well as other systems to reassess themselves, individually and corporately, as religious traditions in the midst of crisscrossing rival claims by nationalism, humanism, communism, capitalism, scientism, racism, consumerism, and so forth. (This last leitmotif will be discussed in Chapter 11.)

THE END OF WESTERN COLONIALISM

Some people have already made important and helpful distinctions among (a) political (plus military), (b) economic, and (c) cultural (involving religious and linguistic as well) forms of colonial expansion. As regards *political* colonialism, which had dictated the destiny of the non-Western world for the past four centuries or so, its sudden and dramatic demise during World War II and the period immediately after is well known and does not need further documentation at this point.

It seems to be a considered opinion of many people, however, that the now-defunct political colonialism is closely related to *economic* colonialism, which is still pursued vigorously both by capitalist and communist nations. Even in the recent Gulf War, it was uncanny how the oil-hungry former colonial powers, despite their notorious record of indifference to the plight of Tibetans, Laotians, people of the West Indies, Central and South Americans, Palestinians, and Ethiopians, quickly voiced in agreement their righteous anger as they fought against "little Hitler." A newspaper poignantly pointed out: "Global freedom fighters should consider what happens if the next hot spot is the land without oil."[3] I was equally depressed to speculate on the disastrous implications of what Eisenhower once called the military-industrial complex. On this topic, a columnist asked recently:

> Wouldn't it be ironic if the resounding defeat of Iraq, led by the high-tech forces of the U.S. resulted in a third world newly armed to the teeth with the smart bombs, ballistic and cruise missiles? . . . Uncle Sam himself is one of the world's biggest arms merchants— peddling $10.8 billion in conventional arms in 1989, second only to Moscow's $11.7 billion. Thus these two accounted for $22.5 billion in such sales out of a world total of $31.8 billion.

And, after citing the Bush administration's willingness to sell high-tech weapons to five Persian Gulf allies and its siding with arms contractors, the paper goes on to say:

> Administration spokesmen insist that there's no conflict with its stated aim of limiting arms sales to the third world. . . . Those spokesmen must be kidding. . . . Any way you look at it, the Bush proposal would encourage the proliferation of weapons. . . . How can that help Mr. Bush build that stable new world order to which he pays such ardent lip service?[4]

Unfortunately, this is only a very tiny segment of gigantic economic colonialism, which continues to raise its ugly head today in many parts of the non-Western world. In addition, during the long postwar period of the cold war, economic competition between the communist and capitalist nations was defended on both sides in the name of ideological conflict. Even after the decline of the aggressive communist powers, the economic colonialism continues its domination over the so-called Third World.

To make the matter more complex, as F. S. C. Northrop astutely observed shortly after World War II, the mortal fear that the non-Western world has of Western *cultural* colonialism is the one least appreciated or understood in the West. At that time, Northrop cited General MacArthur's advocacy of Christianizing Japan with a battleship full of Western missionaries, and the effort to "convert the rest of the world to the American way of life" through a "hard-hitting Voice of America." All these examples strike the people in Asia (and presumably in Africa, too) as demonstrating that the West is "withholding a political imperialism and slightly restraining an economic one merely to impose an even more dangerous cultural [colonialism]."[5] Strangely, I suspect that many people in the Western world do not even have the slightest notion that there is such a phenomenon as "dangerous" cultural colonialism. In fact, many liberal-minded Westerners, who are embarrassed by the gruesome record of Western imperialistic colonialism or incensed by the current economic exploitation of the non-Western world by the industrialized nations, seem to take it for granted that Western humanistic, scientific, and cultural expertness—including their styles, structures, symbols, logics, and taxonomies—are, or should be, universally valid and acceptable. And, from their standpoint, exporting these Westernized ideas and technologies, for example, to the non-Western world does not constitute colonialism, cultural or otherwise. It may therefore be a good idea for us to take a brief detour and place the knotty issue of cultural colonialism in the broader context of East-West relationships.

I would like to borrow William S. Haas's succinct characterizations of Western and Eastern civilizations. According to him, the hallmark of Western civilization, itself a highly developed organism, is "unity in variety"—absorbing disparate elements such as Hellenistic thought, Jewish and Christian religions, and Roman jurisprudence, and so forth. This stands in contradistinction to Eastern civilization, which has been based on the principle of "juxtaposition and identity," implying the coexistence of diverse—presumably equally valid—civilizational units, such as those of India and China.[6] Betty Heimann shrewdly observes in this connection that the notion of "system" symbolizes the dividing line between Western and Eastern civilizations, for by system the ancient Greeks asserted that there was an order in disposition and composition of ideas. Accordingly, Western civilization always understood the human mind in terms of the Greek sense of rationality and individuality.[7] As might be expected, however, the Western approach to the problem of truth-claim has always been haunted by the unresolved blending between reason, rooted in the Greek notion of rational understanding, and faith or belief, which evolves its own super-rational inner logic, as demonstrated by Hebrew and Christian "revelatory" traditions. Thus, even the notion of progress, which can be traced to the biblical affirmation of Yahweh's initiative to guide history to a righteous end, also took on new meaning in Europe as that of inching toward fulfillment of higher potentialities, in accordance with human initiative, value, and effort. In the course of time, Hellenistic understanding of humanity (as the "measure of all things," according to Protagoras) was infused with the Hebrew-Christian view of *imago dei* (human being created in the image of God), whereas the Western concept of dynamic time was compelled to develop an uneasy relationship with—and never completely coalescing with—the Persian Zoroastrian belief in the "end of the world" (*eschaton*), itself mediated by the Jewish and Christian traditions.

In retrospect, the West's attempt to absorb diverse factors into its unity-bound civilization impelled a difficult process of adjustment, often causing psychic reaction, accompanied often by overly rationalistic resolution and explanation that borders, according to some critics, on rationalization. For example, the Copernican revolution made Europeans change the way they conceived themselves in the bewildering universe. According to Samuel Miller, the uncomfortable burden of this imbalance, caused by Europeans' awareness of their smallness in this newly reconceived vast universe,

> was more influential than any other historical factor for the rise of romanticism, by which man redressed the pressure of outer space by the affirmation of an equally infinite inner world, producing the Faustian man of limitless hungers and endless possibilities. With romanticism, man [in Europe] weighted himself to stand against outer space.[8]

Similar observations have often been made about the emergence of depth psychology in the West, searching meaning and coherence in the depth of the psyche, following the discovery of the Unconscious. It is worth mentioning that although Europeans had known the existence of Muslim people from the seventh century on (and even fought against them during the long period of the Crusades), they did not come in direct contact with most other people in the non-Western world until the period of Western colonialism, which began toward the very end of the fifteenth century. My learned colleague, Mircea Eliade, often stated that the discovery of non-Western peoples, languages, religions, and cultures was as significant an experience for the West as the invention of the telescope; both provided a radically different understanding of Europeans' place in this world and in this universe. Significantly to them, the discovery of the non-Western world, much like the invention of the telescope, presented a new challenge to have this discovery absorbed into the ever-expanding process toward the unified (European) civilization. In this situation, three major forms of reaction emerged: (1) colonialism, (2) Christian world mission, and (3) self-conscious articulation of European intellectual self-identity. All three of them, be it noted, were very characteristically European responses to the new challenge, sharing in common the uniquely Western convention of dividing human experience into a serious of semiautonomous pigeonholes, such as religion, culture, society, politics, economics, aesthetics, ethics, and law. And all three of them took it for granted that such a provincial convention of perceiving the texture of human experience by dissecting it into pieces was universally the most reliable tool in understanding and dealing with all non-Christian peoples and their traditions.

1. Historically, as noted in Part I, colonialism was initiated by Portugal and Spain, the two Iberian kingdoms that unconsciously had "inhaled" the ethos of *corpus Islamicum* through the years of struggle against the Moors in the peninsula. It is worth repeating the fact that these two nations, following their agreement in the papacy-sponsored

Treaty of Trodesilhas (A.D. 1494), divided the entire world into two spheres of interest—initially, Spain following Columbus's route to the New World, while Portugal followed Vasco da Gama's route to the Indian Ocean. Following the defeat of the Spanish armada by the British forces in 1588, Iberian colonial powers declined, whereupon other European nations propelled themselves as new colonial powers (joined later by the United States). Throughout the nineteenth century and even during the twentieth century, at least until World War II, the entire world was dominated by Western (and Japanese) colonialism. Although political (and military) colonialism came to an end during World War II and its immediate aftermath, Western economic colonialism has continued to thrive in much of the non-Western world. Even so, over half of the entire world populace, whose lives had been dictated and dominated by alien colonial powers for centuries past, have now gained the measure of rights and dignity as human beings, and they have entered the main stage of world history.

2. As regards overseas Christian missionary work, it was originally conducted during the sixteenth century by the civil governments of Portugal and Spain through the *patronato* ("patronage") system. This system was terminated by the establishment in 1662 of the *Congregatio de Propaganda Fide*, which then, in principle at least, under the direction of the papacy controlled all Roman Catholic missionary activities. In the Protestant fold, it was small groups of continental Pietists and English Evangelicals, and not the national churches, that commenced overseas evangelical activities by forming hitherto unknown missionary societies, which soon became the pacesetters for Protestant world evangelism. More will be said on this subject presently.

3. Curiously, but also understandably, Europeans' growing contact with non-Western cultures greatly enhanced their self-conscious articulation of their own intellectual self-identity. (It must be candidly acknowledged that most intellectuals in the West and Western-inspired intellectuals in the non-Western world do not think of this as a matter of especially great significance today, because they live in the very Western intellectual tradition and imbibe their inspiration from it.) Of course, Europeans' sense of intellectual self-identity had undergone many phases in Europe itself, say, from the time of the Renaissance, through such experiences as the Reformation, Counter-Reformation, Enlightenment, scientific, industrial, and French revolutions, and so forth. This trend had many parallel factors that made significant contributions to the intellectual process both internally and externally. Politically, the once-powerful Holy Roman Empire gave way to a series of territorial

monarchies, which eventually turned into a series of modern autonomous nation-states. Ecclesiastically, the coherence of the medieval papal church was broken into various national churches, both Catholic and mainline as well as left-wing Protestant groups. Academically, various fields of knowledge formerly circumscribed in the medieval European universities by metaphysics and theology began to determine the concepts on the basis of their autonomous disciplines without any concern for divine legitimation.[9]

Many people use the expression "secularization" to describe the modern trend in Europeans' mental universe with some justification, because of their heavy emphasis on the critical and rational, cognitive approach, with less stress on untested belief or faith. However, I am inclined to use the designation of "pseudoreligion of secularized salvation" to refer to modern Europeans' understanding of their civilization, because it is for all intents and purposes a religion of human rationality, which now supersedes the Jewish or Christian concept of deity. On this point, no less than Hegel himself asserted that "the 'phenomenology' or self-manifestation merges into man's work in history, into human self-fulfillment. Man becomes 'present God' (präsenter Gott) and continues the divine process in his worldly presence."[10] Clearly, Hegel postulated his scheme of history, in accordance with the traditional Western understanding, as a developmental process moving toward the goal of unity. Also, he was persuaded that "the Occident supersedes the Orient, and in dealing with the Oriental traditions, it faces, in a sense, its own petrified past."[11] And it was not only Hegel but a great many other European intelligentsia who also glorified modern European civilization as having such salutary attributes as scientific objectivity, neutrality, and universality.

No wonder, during the heyday of Westernization of the non-Western world, facilitated greatly by colonialism, Christian world mission, and so forth, that many people in Asia and Africa blindly accepted the West's claim on face value that non-Western "thought is comprehensible and interpretable within European thought, but not vice versa. . . . European thought has to provide the context and categories for the exploration of thought [in the entire world]."[12] E. Husserl went so far as to say:

> Europe alone can provide other traditions with a universal frame of meaning and understanding. [Non-Westerners] will have to "Europeanize themselves, whereas we . . . will never, for example, Indianize ourselves." The "Europeanization of all foreign parts of mankind" . . . is the destiny of the earth.[13]

Undoubtedly, modern European intellectual tradition has many attractive qualities, even if those qualities are basically rooted in a semireligious faith in rationality and rationalistic speculation, such as the psychic unity of humankind as affirmed by many social scientists.[14] I refer here to qualities such as eternal truth as advocated by philosophers and theologians; potential unity and balance of power among autonomous, free, and sovereign nation-states as widely upheld by politicians; and inevitable modernization and progress as espoused by laissez-faire economists.[15] Marxists' faith and conviction regarding totality may also be regarded as a variation of the similar theme.[16]

One of the most fascinating intellectual enterprises that emerged in the West in dealing with non-Western traditions was the Western-inspired Oriental and African studies.[17] Unfortunately, space does not allow an extensive discussion of this significant problem. Briefly stated, it has undergone many stages and was related to various nonintellectual causes, too. Understandably, the initial response of Europeans to non-Western people and their traditions was to measure them against their own value systems, so that many Europeans simply assumed that all non-Western traditions possessed structures similar to those found in European/Christian heritage. If these structures proved to be different, they hoped to convert non-Westerners to the familiar ethos and ways of Europeans. In the course of time, especially after the Enlightenment, many Europeans realized that they had to interpret non-Western traditions, not through European or Christian "glasses" but on their own terms. Notwithstanding such a noble intention, they had no other intellectual recourse except to depend on their European assumptions and methodologies, and not those of non-Western peoples, to classify and interpret non-Western languages, cultures, societies, and religions. In other words, from the Enlightenment until very recent years, it was blindly and even self-righteously assumed that it is the task of non-Western peoples to present their languages, religions, and cultures, for example, as data to Westerners, who in turn would analyze and interpret them from the perspectives and through the methodologies of the Western-inspired Oriental/African studies.

As far as I am concerned, by far the most far-reaching effect, positive as well as negative, of the tradition of Western-inspired Oriental/African studies persisted in the field of religion. (Because I am quite uninformed about African, Islamic, Oceanic, and South American religious studies, I am confining my discussion at this point primarily to the studies of Asian religions.) Two concrete illustrations may be helpful on this score. The gigantic publication of the 51-volume *The Sacred Books of the*

East (1875 onward), edited by Friedrich Max Müller, and the 12-volume *Encyclopaedia of Religion and Ethics* (1908–1927), edited by James Hastings, are indeed impressive monuments of West-inspired Oriental as well as religious studies. They signify the careful selection of competent contributors, preoccupation with religious concepts and ethics, implicit assumption of a mild form of revolutionary hypothesis, and so forth. Furthermore, many European scholars of the late nineteenth and early twentieth centuries envisaged a sort of "three-storied" structure in the study of religion(s), popularly called comparative religion. The first phase (lowest level) comprised a narrow historical and cultural survey of various religions of the world, conceived as raw religious data. The second area (middle level) aimed to classify religious data, thus collecting according to what Stanley A. Cook called "certain persistent and prevalent notions of the 'evolution' of thought and . . . practices . . . in the history of culture."[18] The third area (top level) was reserved for some kind of philosophy of religion or liberal theology that was expected to adjudicate confusing and competitive religious claims. (The more conservative theologians were lured to *Missionswissenschaft* rather than to comparative religion.) Significantly, these perspectives, assumptions, and methodologies of West-inspired Oriental and religious studies are not only still influential among the current scholars in the West but also among the Westernized scholars in Asia, as well.

Evidently, we are witnessing the perpetuation of a vicious circle. Many Westerners even today see no reason to question the adequacy of West-inspired approaches and methodologies in dealing with non-Western traditions, and they justify their stances by quoting the similar views of Westernized Asian scholars, who in turn wish to keep up with up-to-date views of Western Orientalists. We can understand how such a vicious circle started, for in the heyday of Western domination of Asia, it was fairly fashionable to appropriate things Western. Besides, adopting the Western mode of scholarship was for Asian scholars the only or the easiest entree into the global academy. And of course, these Westernized Asian scholars acquired many new insights and learned many sophisticated theories from Western Oriental studies. This is how a strange phenomenon took place in modern Asia. That is to say, these Westernized Asian intellectuals started writing about the religions and cultures of Asia as though they were Westerners approaching them from the outside. Conversely, Western Orientalists can more readily understand and agree with these Westernized Asians' analysis of Asian traditions than with the views of Asian scholars who had not been influenced by Western Oriental study. Now it is almost hopeless to break this kind of self-perpetuating vicious circle!

THE EROSION OF CHRISTIAN WORLD MISSION; DIALOGUE AMONG RELIGIONS; AND THE AMBIGUOUS SITUATION OF THE YOUNGER CHURCHES

Although various authors often lump together (a) the erosion of Christian world mission, (b) the sudden popularity of the idea of dialogue among various religions, including Christianity, and (c) the current ambiguous situation of the so-called younger churches, these phenomena are independent, though related, and should be so treated.

The Erosion of Christian World Mission

I would like to lift up five points cited as early as in 1952 as factors in the "changed conditions external to the missions." They are from a pamphlet issued by the International Missionary Council and are as follows:[19]

> (1) *The demographic factor.* Partly as the result of industrialization, peoples in the non-Western world, where indigenous peoples are presumably overwhelmingly non-Christian, far outnumber the Christian population in every continent put together, so that as time goes on the Christian community is bound to become an even smaller minority on this planet.

> (2) *The rapid termination of the colonial era.* The virtual end of political colonialism in most of Asia and increasing revolts against Western colonialism in Africa instilled in the minds of Asians and Africans "a skeptical rather than a receptive attitude toward the Christian religion which in the past relied consciously or unconsciously to a considerable extent on the general prestige of the nations and cultures from which its missionaries came."

> (3) *Growing nationalism and the resurgence of indigenous religions.* It is a matter of some irony that nationalism and the concept of the modern nation-state, which non-Westerners had learned from the West, are now serving as instruments for reasserting former cultural patterns in Asia (and I presume in Africa, too). Today, in many parts of Asia, the state is taking over many of the educational and welfare functions that in the past had been important activities of Christian missions. Also, the growth of nationalism in Asia is supported by the resurgence of traditional religions and vice versa.

(4) *The growth of communist powers in Asia.* Prior to World War II, communism penetrated primarily intellectual elites in Asia, whereas after the war, communism, which is in principle against all religions, serves as the guiding ideology in such nation-states as Mainland China and North Korea. The dilemma of Christianity now is whether to regard non-Christian religions as allies for the same cause (e.g., spirituality, a religious worldview, etc.) or foes that happen to be in the same predicament as Christianity.

(5) *The changed position of America in world affairs.* (Remember that the pamphlet was written in 1952, long before the Vietnam War, which many consider reduced America's prestige in the eyes of people in the non-Western world.) After citing that the United States is now the most powerful and richest nation in the world, the report remarks: "This privileged position creates suspicion, fear, envy and hate even among beneficiaries of its use of power, as well as real gratitude among many of them. No person or nation enjoys or feels secure in a situation where livelihood and welfare are largely dependent on the goodwill of another, however well-intentioned that other may claim to be and often demonstrates itself to be."

Although the contents of this document, compiled in 1952, are inevitably dated, the report depicts many of the obvious factors that contributed to the erosion of Christian world mission. We can certainly add other factors, such as the internal division of Christendom, not only along sectarian and denominational lines but also in terms of doctrinal and theological differences (liberals vs. conservatives, evangelicals/fundamentalists vs. rationalists, traditionalists vs. pneumatics, etc.). Also, the secularizing ethos (caused, according to some critics, by the suicide of Christianity as a religious tradition) of the post-Christian culture greatly weakened Christian institutions in the West. But the same commission's report on "A Restatement of the Missionary Task in the Light of These Changes," contained in the same pamphlet, is banal and totally inadequate. It repeats the tired old notion such as the prophetic character of the Christian mission, the obvious general principle that mission must be against all injustice and must not be simply against communism. When the chips are down, the report hints that the Christian witness in the non-Christian world is probably the sole responsibility of the younger churches, known formerly as missionary churches. All in all, this pamphlet reflects fairly accurately the ethos of the Christian church, which unfortunately lost its missionary incentive.

The Dialogue Among Religions

As regards the dialogue among religions, its sudden popularity especially in the Western Christendom, which almost coincided, chronologically speaking, with the erosion of Christian world missionary activities that took place in the period immediately following World War II, caused many misunderstandings and probably needs some interpretation. Ironically, it is widely held in many circles that the nineteenth century was the age of Christian world mission, but it is no longer fashionable to talk about evangelism, because we are now living in the period of friendly dialogue with other religions. In reality, dialogue and mission, good examples of *coincidentia oppositorum*, are both legitimate and independent (even though related) activities of one and the same religion. Many religions, with the notable exceptions of some tribal, cultural, and/or national religions (which are meaningful only to specific groups) are missionary minded because they are imbued by totalistic temper. This is not because each religion wishes to dominate other peoples (though this too happened all too often in history), but more because each religion defines the levels of reality, including ultimate reality, which to the adherents of that religion is the source of cosmic, social, and human orders. Ironically, if one religion should dominate as the only (official or state) religion for any length of time in the same locality (e.g., Christianity in Europe, Hinduism in India, Islam in the Arabian peninsula, Buddhism in Southeast Asia, etc.), the adherents of that religion are prone to fall into a natural error of presuming that the truth-claim of their tradition alone must be objectively true, whereas those of adherents of other traditions, often regarded as heretics or nonconformists, are bound to be false. Fortunately or unfortunately, this kind of presumption—that one's inherited tradition alone must be correct—supplies much fuel to various religions' proselytizing passion.

After World War II, with the apparent decline of the traditional Christian evangelical approach to non-Christian religions that compelled missiologists and theologians to explore a more irenic attitude toward men and women of other faiths, the International Missionary Council and the World Council of Churches jointly sponsored the pilot project of establishing study centers for other faiths in the Middle East and several localities in Asia. These centers not only offer facilities to Christians for engaging in research concerning the other religions, but they also provide opportunities for Christians to meet and confer with the leaders and adherents of other faiths. Obviously, the motivations of those Christians involved in the study centers varied greatly. There were some who wanted to learn the mental and social habits of non-Christians in order to "soft-sell" the Christian gospel by appropriating the symbols and mores of other religions as the means for entree. On the other hand, there were others who aspired to have a fresh look, with open mind, at the mystery of non-Christian religions in the dispensation of the divine scheme. Basically, both groups of people would most likely agree with Edmund Perry's motivation for studying other religions. In his own words: "Because as Christians we are under mandate to proclaim the gospel to and make disciples of all peoples, we readily confess that our motive for studying their religions is ulterior or missionary."[20] This may account for the fact that some of the so-called interreligious dialogues devote much time for reexamining Christian soteriology.

It is interesting to note in this connection that quite apart from those whose Christian missionary motivation led them to study non-Christian religions, there are today various kinds of Western, as well as Western-influence Asian, scholars with varying degrees of sympathy with religion, who pursue study of different aspects of non-Western religions as well as Jewish and Christian religions. Many of them understandably see nothing special in Christian truth-claims; in fact, they are determined to apply the same methodological (philosophical, historical, or social scientific) principles to all religions, including Christianity, and promote interreligious dialogue under the canon of scholarly objectivity and religious neutrality. It might be helpful to depict two entirely different motivations—which might be regarded as the two ends of a line of continuum, embracing various kinds of motivations between them—for the nonmissionary-inspired interreligious dialogues.

First, the one end of the continuum is represented by secular, nonreligious or antireligious humanists and social scientists who reject the validity of all religious affirmations except as "social realities, of which deities and apparently concerns [I presume, referring to the concerns with illnesses, evils, and natural calamities, etc.] are symbolic projections," to quote one anthropologist. And, this person goes on to say, "even if people really believe what they say they do, religious thought and action are nonetheless irrational, emotional, or 'symbolic' and sharply different from secular scientific thought and action."[21] Seen from such a perspective, interreligious dialogues would be useful primarily in revealing, not various peoples' understanding of their own religious traditions or their views on religious reality itself, but the place of religions in different social, political, or cultural systems.

Second, it is extremely difficult to say much about the other end of the continuum, because it is still more or less a matter of aspiration than achievement. We can, however, at least state negatively what its perspective is not. It cannot be motivated either by any particular religion's totalistic, missionary, or apologetic aspirations or by nonreligious (antireligious) participants' objectives for articulating social, political, or cultural reality, even if it is inspired by religious factors, which, according to these participants, are *ipso facto* illusory. In other words, the interreligious dialogue cannot be operated by the rule of the game of one dominant religion or that of wishy-washy eclecticism, but its central concern has to be religious in nature, as stated poignantly by Eliade: "To try to grasp the essence of [the interreligious dialogue, although he was referring to religious phenomenon in this instance] by means of physiology, psychology, sociology, economics, linguistics, art, or any other study is false; it misses the one unique and irreducible element in it—the element of the sacred."[22] More will be said presently on this subject.

Before concluding this discussion of the interreligious dialogue, I must add briefly another complicating element. So far, participants of both the missionary-motivated as well as nonmissionary-motivated interreligious dialogues have underestimated the degree to which Western cultural colonialism had penetrated their frames of reference. And the fact that Western-inspired intelligentsia from the non-Western world had thus far willingly participated in the Western-style interreligious dialogues (giving the appearance of global conferences) keeps alive the happy illusion that provincial Western modes of perceiving human experience are the most neutral and universally valid mediums of global interreligious dialogues. As I stated elsewhere:

> If the interreligious or intercultural dialogues were primarily Western-inspired affairs, it should not be surprising that it is the Western thinkers and scholars, depending on Western concepts, methods, and rhetorics, who propose to get together with their non-Western counterparts. They are bound to have one-sided "Western" monologues with non-Western guests, who are expected to present their religious and cultural experiences and expressions primarily as "data" for the benefit of their Western hosts.[23]

Such is the almost insurmountable predicament that confronts all of us today.

The Ambiguous Situation of the Younger Churches

Inasmuch as Part I of this book dwelled heavily on many issues of the younger churches, the common designations of the churches in the non-Western lands (even though some very old churches had been known to exist in parts of Asia and Africa), we can safely dispense with general problems concerning them in this section and can concentrate only on their relationships to the increasingly less missionary-minded Western churches and to now fashionable interreligious dialogues.

It is not my intention to blame Western churches for all the troubles of the younger churches, even though my accounts may sound that way. Nevertheless, it is important to point out, as far as the younger churches are concerned, that the ethos, doctrines, and other aspects of the Christian church, including its long and varied historical experiences in Europe, were condensed in a package for them by the Western churches through their missionary enterprises. Thus to them, the Western church—the grandeur of the Constantinian type, with power, wealth, and prestige—was the only model to emulate. This type of utter dependence of groups of newly converted in the non-Western lands on the sending churches in Europe may account for missionary orthodoxy and paternalism that border on missionary imperialism. As might be expected, much of missionary rhetorics and hermeneutics was based on the self-authenticating circular logic of Western Christendom, which among other things sophistically condoned the Constantinian equation of the loyalty to God and the loyalty to the earthly king in spite of the biblical exhortation to the contrary. Similarly, the same logic found it possible to transfer the transcendental sacral authority to the earthly church, which in turn decreed that there is no salvation outside the earthly church.

One of the lamentable results of the Western missionary strategy was the establishment of the so-called mission compounds, justified on legal, economic, political, and strategic grounds to keep native converts away from further contamination by their pagan neighbors and social life. And even when the indigenous churches made considerable steps toward maturity, they retained the residual ethos of the mission compounds, characterized as they were by isolationistic, exclusive, proud, self-righteous, tight little islands, which have very little organic relationship with their surrounding societies and cultures. To be sure, members of the indigenous churches were vicariously reassured of their importance when leading missionaries were seated on public occasions next to high-ranking colonial officials (during the days of colonialism) or native government officials (when the native governments found it profitable to espouse Westernism). But following the end of Western colonialism and with the erosion of missionary incentive on the part of many Western churches, the younger churches, which had depended so singularly on the theological, cultural, and financial resources of Western Christendom, are experiencing real difficulties in growing up and developing their own resources in a hurry.[24]

As to the interreligious dialogues of various kinds, so far most of them have been initiated either by theologians/philosophers or humanists/social scientists in the West with the cooperation of Westernized scholars/religious leaders in Asia with Western languages and Western thought patterns as common frames of reference. Curiously, but also understandably, members of the younger churches (e.g., those from the Middle East, India, Southeast Asia, or East Asia), who are constantly experiencing the actual encounter between Christianity and other religions, tend to be ignored or slighted by the leading participants both from the Christian and non-Christian sides. Not surprisingly, many Western Christian participants, convinced as they are as "genuine" spokespersons of the Christian tradition, would rather directly confront leaders/spokespersons of non-Christian traditions. They feel with some justification that members of the younger churches are at best faded carbon copies of Western Christians, who do not have the benefit of unadulterated non-Christian experiences either. On the other hand, participants on the non-Christian side, those who willingly participate in the interreligious dialogues—which are more often than not sessions of simultaneous monologues[25]—do not feel they profit by the presence of younger church members, who according to their views live in a cultural no-man's land between "Christian West" and "non-Christian East." My own considered opinion is that the members of the younger churches almost physically reflect the complex religious reality on the global scene, and they should take seriously their task of sharing their unique experiences in the future interreligious dialogues.

THE GROWING INFLUENCE OF NON-CHRISTIAN RELIGIONS

There have been numerous books and articles written on the subject of the phenomenal resurgence of traditional Eastern (non-Christian) religions in Asia in the post–World War II period based on what might be called a reflex theory. It is the interpretation based on the notion that with the sudden removal of external pressures on Asia (e.g., colonialism and Christian world mission), the vacuum was quickly filled by the indigenous religions and cultures almost as a reflex action. Although there are no doubt some elements of truth in such an explanation, I am inclined to believe that we have to explore deeper issues involved, issues far deeper than what simplistic reflex theories point to. With this in mind, we might reassess briefly the Asian peoples' reaction to the Western dominance over Asia during the past four centuries or so from the beginning of the Iberian kingdoms' colonial expansion in the sixteenth century until World War II. Among many other factors that are involved, I would like to depict especially the influence of Western civilization, more particularly Western understanding, as well as the ways of dealing with Asian traditions that have directly or indirectly, unintentionally to be sure, constrained and precipitated the eventual resurgence of Eastern religious traditions.

At the expense of oversimplification, I will present three observations in this regard. First, there were roughly speaking two diametrically opposed reactions on the part of Asians throughout the modern period toward Western civilization. Although a small group of iconoclastic young intelligentsia warmly welcomed the rationalistic and critical Western tradition (based on individual's rights, liberty, equality, etc.) as a needed alternative paradigm to the deadweight (in their view) of Eastern tradition, the majority of conservative masses felt alienated from the unknown, unfamiliar alien civilization, with its strange ideas and ways of organizing society, using resources, and transmitting values and morality.

Second, strangely in this situation, both groups no longer looked directly at their own Eastern tradition. Rather, they respectively reacted primarily to the "Eastern civilization" as reflected in the Westerners' mirror. For example, the iconoclastic young intellectuals were greatly disillusioned by the crude and "uncivilized" concepts and practices of Eastern tradition as seen by Westerners' eyes. "Our present-day social practices are," stated V. Sriniva Rao, "no doubt the natural outcome of certain religious beliefs [of traditional Eastern religions]. Unless such beliefs are shaken, the present social practices [of Eastern traditions] cannot be permanently shaken."[26]

On the other hand, many conservative spokesmen lamented that the traditional Eastern ways—such as respect for aged as well as highborn peoples, unlegalistic virtue of trust in interhuman relationships, appreciation of the quality of life rather than the quantity of wealth—were before their own eyes being replaced by Western-inspired, inhuman, self-centered individualistic and legalistic ways and concepts. To be sure, even the most anti-Western Asian traditionalists were favorably disposed to some aspects of Western ideas and customs, such as equality, judiciousness, promptness, methodical and rationalistic organization; but they continued to believe that the quickly disappearing Eastern traditions, which they romantically idealized, were even better. And, they objected to Western powers for redrawing Asian maps according to their rationales and conveniences (such as artificially creating new national boundaries as in the French Indo-China or Indian peninsulas) without taking into account the sentiments of the tribes and peoples in those religions.

Third, as we look back now, it becomes evident that the first half of the twentieth century, more particularly the period between the two world wars, witnessed the increasing growth of the widespread desire among many Asians for political independence and to be freed from Western domination in general. It is noteworthy that many pro-Western Asians began to be vocal against the racism, self-idolatry, and narrow-mindedness of Western civilization itself, as well as the lack of political liberty in Asia under the Western colonial powers. Even in those parts of Asia that were not under direct colonial rule, people loudly objected to the selfishness and unfairness of Western nations in dealing with non-Western nations and peoples, as epitomized by many Asians' strong reaction against the "barred zone provision" of the anti-Asian U.S. Immigration Act of 1917, which excluded immigrants from India, Siam, Indo-China, the Malay Peninsula, Afghanistan, New Guinea, Borneo, Java, Ceylon, and Sumatra.[27] Inevitably, the sense of disillusionment with Western civilization led many Westernized Asian intellectuals, notwithstanding their continued attachment to Western concepts and values in many respects, to "discover" their own ancestral traditions and to find kinship with conservative Asian masses. Thus, for example, Jawaharlal Nehru, the epitome of English-educated Indians, dared to state: "We are citizens of no mean country and we are proud of the land of our birth, of our people, our culture and traditions."[28] Conversely, for the great cause of freedom and independence, the conservative masses in Asia were willing to cooperate with the hitherto detested Westernized intelligentsia, who represented views and mores very different from theirs.

Although many writers, both Asians and outsiders, seem to give the impression that the alliance between the Westernized intellectuals and the conservative masses prior to World War II automatically and at once released the energy to restore hitherto neglected Eastern religions, cultures, and nations, per se, I am persuaded that the situation was not that simple. I rather think that both Westernized intellectuals and traditionalists in Asia have been inspired by almost mythical images of their own religions, cultures, and lands (created in their *mundus imaginalis*, aided by their modern experience as well as by the Westerners' interpretation of Eastern traditions), which gripped what Salmon

Rushdie once called "a phenomenal collective will" of the people. Thus, for example, the modern mythical images of nations in Asia, such as India, Burma, or China, were not simply the familiar lands of their inherited traditions; concepts of their nations also had many hallmarks of autonomous, sovereign nation-states similar to those of Western nations. Their image of Hinduism, for example, was not simply religion based on the Vedas transmitted by a chain of Hindu masters; it also was a religion that has been studied and interpreted by F. Max Müller and other Western scholars as well. Similarly, the Buddhism that inspires modern Asians is more than the religion handed down by Theravada Bhikkus or Mahayana teachers. It has also been digested by Louis de la Vallée Poussin and other Western Buddhologists, and it is willing to cope with the challenges of the scientific worldview, Marxism, depth psychology, and so forth.[29]

As to what has actually happened or what is happening to individual religions (Hinduism, Buddhism, Islam, etc.) in modern Asia, I have to refer to my other writings.[30] It might be important, however, for me to cite some of the most obvious pointers—do's and don'ts—in dealing with the phenomenon of the resurgence of Eastern religions in Asia, and also to discuss briefly the impact of Eastern religions on the contemporary West. First, I hope I made it clear that contemporary Asian religions combine "old" (traditional) and "new" (Eastern as well as Western) elements. One therefore has to avoid the errors of approaching modern Asian religions primarily through the eyes of their classical forms (as we do in Western college courses) or of dealing with them as though they can be divorced substantially from their inherited traditions. Second, we have to recognize that Asians do not follow the Western convention of dividing human experience neatly into a series of compartments (e.g., religion, ethics, aesthetics, politics, law, etc.), as demonstrated again and again in their modern "collective will," which informs their *mundus imaginalis*. This fact may account for the mutual penetration between religion and nationalism, between religion and culture, and between culture and national policy/self-identity. Third, we must keep in mind the uncomfortable fact that modern Western categories, logics, and rhetorics are not the best or most reliable tools for our understanding the "religious universe" of peoples in contemporary Asia. The greatest folly is to judge Asian religions through the yardsticks of Judaism or Christianity, as so many books and articles still seem to do even today.

This may be an appropriate place for us to consider the impact of the ever-growing Eastern religions on the contemporary West, which is a relatively new phenomenon. We might recall that less than one hundred years ago—in 1893 to be exact—when the World's Parliament of Religions held in Chicago invited delegates from non-Western religions to attend "a friendly conference [based on] the golden rule of Christ; a royal feast to which the representatives of every faith were asked to bring the richest fruits and rarest flowers of their religion," Chicago newspaper reporters chased after these exotic guests primarily as curiosity items, as though they were visitors from Mars.[31] It was reported that throughout the Parliament, those foreign visitors were constantly followed by huge crowds, too, not primarily because people were eager to learn about Hinduism, Buddhism, Confucianism, and so forth, but because in their views the visitors represented the strange alien worlds characterized by Arthur Christy as "far away and long ago."[32] In this respect, most Europeans in those days shared Americans' general unfamiliarity with, and indifference to, non-Western religions.

Seven decades later, however, Hendrik Kraemer, a Dutch Protestant theologian, was alarmed by what he called a *pénétration pacifique*, the degree to which Asian cultures and religions have penetrated Europe and America: "There is evident in the fields of pictorial art, of novels, of thinking and depth-psychology, a kind of premonition. They manifest a spontaneous openness, a readiness to be invaded, to become spiritually 'colonized' by the Orient."[33] Assuming that Kraemer's observation has some validity, we might reflect on what had happened during the seven decades between the 1893 World's Parliament of Religions and 1960, the year in which Kraemer's book was published. What are some of the relevant factors that brought about such radical changes in the religious horizons in the West? We know, for example, that following the World's Parliament of Religions, small groups of Vedanta and Zen Buddhist adherents were organized both in Europe and North America, and that Buddhist and other traditional Eastern religions were transplanted to the West by Asiatic immigrants in Hawaii and on the West Coast. But the coming of these Eastern religions, important though they were in their own right, did not seem to bring about radical religious change in the West.

We are thus compelled to reexamine the internal factors in the West (religious, social, political, economic, ethical), such as growing trends toward secularization, urbanization, and industrialization—all of which tend to repudiate inherited Jewish/Christian religious beliefs and practices. Also, it does not take much imagination to conclude that internal divisions within, say, Christianity—denominational divisions among Catholic, Orthodox, Protestant traditions; doctrinal and theological factions such as rationalism, social gospel, fundamentalism, liberalism, neo-orthodoxy—did not help maintain a strong unity of religious framework in the West. Furthermore, there is undoubtedly much truth in the view that World War I (which effectively destroyed the invisible unity of Western Christian moral community), the rise of communism (based on economic determinism and religious atheism), global depression (which shook the financial foundation of the industrialized nations), the emergence of fascism and nazism (even before Europe's recovery from World War I), and World War II and the termination of Western colonialism greatly contributed to the revolutionary religious changes in the West. Although both Judaism and Christianity maintain nominal statistical stability today, many people in the West feel alienated enough from their inherited religious heritage and turn to occultism, spiritualism, and a variety of Eastern religions—not only such established familiar groups as Vedanta and Zen, but a host of new cults and religious movements from the Near East, India, Korea, and Japan, including the Hare Krishna Movement from India, the Unification church from Korea, and the Nichiren Shōshū/Sōka Gakkai from Japan. As I have stated elsewhere: "The fact that the Unification church [alone] can hire many talented young men and women for their [factories and business establishments], and at the same time bring together highly respected philosophers, theologians, and scientists—including several recipients of the Nobel Prize—to their conferences testifies to the fact that the Unification church and other Eastern religious groups are penetrating deeply into Western culture and society."[34]

Today many people, both Westerners and Easterners, keep on asking the same question that was raised recently by Wong Yong Ji of Korea: "Why [is] the West . . . so readily susceptible to these Eastern religions?"[35] In reply, I would say that modern Asian religions are different from their classical forms and cannot be so approached, as many people in the West still seem to do today. Also, many of these "religions" are not religions of an ecclesiastical type similar to Judaism or Christianity. As Wong says about the New Age Movement (NAM), for example, it is not a single religious sect or cult but is a movement that defies easy categorical understanding. Basically, the NAM is a skillful synthesis of spiritualities and practices of Hinduism, Buddhism, Taoism, Shamanism, and certain aspects of Confucianism and Christianity. As such, it poses a direct challenge to the "either-or" principle of Christianity. And, according to Wong Yong Ji:

> A "spiritual war" seems to be forthcoming in the decades to come as NAM becomes a significant threat to traditional Christianity in the 21st century. . . . The New Age [in one sense, may be regarded as] the natural outcome of spiritual hunger and moral decline in the West.[36]

Thus far, the mainline churches have been slow to respond to the challenge of the NAM, but the National Association of Evangelicals (NAE) has been already seriously warning their churches to beware of the dangers of the NAM. As one writer states:

> The New Age Movement uses religious language and a selective collection of borrowed spiritual concepts as it contends for its own utopian world vision. This makes it attractive to a largely materialistic society that is abandoning traditional Judeo-Christian beliefs, yet has failed to provide a replacement to meet the universal hunger of humanity.[37]

As well illustrated by the reaction of the National Association of Evangelicals to the rapidly growing New Age Movement, the older religious groups in North America are now resisting the encroachment of the NAM and other "Eastern" religions primarily because their self-identities do not fit into the contours of the familiar Western religious universe. However, I rather imagine in a generation or two that these new groups too will compete with Jewish, Catholic, Protestant, Mormon, Islamic, and other older religious groups without severing contacts and relationships with their counterparts in Asia.

11

PIETY, MORALITY, AND

CULTURE IN GLOBAL

PERSPECTIVE (2)

**CHRISTIANITY AND OTHER RELIGIONS
IN THE GLOBAL COMMUNITY**

We now consider the last of the four leitmotifs mentioned at the beginning of Chapter 10.

Since the Persian Gulf War, many people have been talking about a "New World Order" as though its meaning is self-evident. Actually, notwithstanding someone's facetious remark that its abbreviation (NWO) might be confused with Northwest Orient, the real problem of the New World Order is not its possibly confusing nomenclature but its mammoth multidimensionality. Because the expression itself grew out of the recent international scene, which witnessed the decline of the USSR as a superpower and the victory of the American-initiated Allied coalition against Iraq, some politicians and columnists have frequently cited the current de facto unipolar world as the permanent feature of the New World Order, in which war-giddy Americans will continue to dictate the rules of the game in international affairs. And because such a political overtone will remain paramount in the popular understanding of a new world order, let me now quote a newspaper editorial entitled "Caveat for Pax Americana: Military Victory shouldn't make the U.S. trigger happy; such success is a heady but fleeting phenomenon" and divulge my own sense of anxiety concerning the role of my adopted homeland in the future of the global community. The editorial reads:

> Winning has already gone to America's head. Now the U.S. has to avoid the temptation of becoming addicted to military solutions. . . . The war got in our blood. The adrenalin rush banished the ghosts of Vietnam and the Iranian hostage-taking, restored national pride and purpose, and promised to jump start our misfiring economic engine. . . . Another reason for caution is the nature of our Persian Gulf victory. We beat up on the second-rate military of a Third World nation run by a fourth-rate hooligan. . . .
>
>   During the war, Bush warned us repeatedly to avoid euphoria. He was right, and we should carry this realism with us as we face the challenges ahead. Ultimately, the Roman legions couldn't protect Rome. A Pax Americana supported chiefly by military power can't survive either.[1]

Although my own international political sense may not be very accurate, I have a hard time convincing myself that the political future of the New World Order, if it is to become actualized, will be based on the unipolar principle. I may be wrong, of course, but I expect to see some sort of the multipolar world with intricate crisscrossing of ethnic, national, regional, cultural, economic, and other factors making it infinitely complex. By now, all of us have learned how inseparable all these factors actually are. For example, in order to achieve and maintain stability of the world in a political sense, one has to have a minimum of military forces to defend society; and in order to have a functional military strength, one has to have up-to-date technologies and sufficient capital; so it goes. On the other hand, artificial political power or military strength alone cannot win the hearts and minds of the people, as was learned by the Japanese militarists during World War II in Asia, France in Algeria, the USSR in Afghanistan, Eastern Europe, and the Baltic nations, the white minority government in South Africa, Israel in occupied territories, and the United States in the Persian Gulf. I remember after the Suez Canal conflict in 1956, John Wilson, an Egyptologist in Chicago, wrote a perceptive article entitled "Nasser Wins by Defeat," in which he pointed out the fleeting nature of a military solution when many other factors are so inseparably interpenetrated.[2]

   On economic matters, I suspect that the current preoccupation everywhere with the economic orders that are influential at the moment, either capitalism or Marxism, with such built-in assumptions as progress, development, laissez faire principle, and automatic harmony of interests, may solve the problems only for a limited number of peoples in the global community. To be sure, I have learned a great deal about the intricacies of international economics and some of the possible advantages of current economic systems from many articles in the *Wall Street Journal*, the *Economist*, and numerous other magazines and books, including J. H. Makin and D. C. Hellmann's *Sharing World Leadership? A New Era for America and Japan.*[3] But I am still not altogether persuaded that the so-called postwar economic miracles of Germany and Japan are solidly stable and permanent, and I also can readily see the possibility that even America's economic and technical superiority in our time might be threatened by an unexpected turn of events in the next century. Such threat will probably not come from Marxist quarters, which are now busily trying to change directions from their Moscow-oriented economic systems. But capitalism itself, too, has come under serious criticisms from such diverse quarters as from Octavio Paz,[4] Robert S. Ozaki,[5] and John Paul II.[6] Somehow, it seems to me that the economics of the New World Order will have to enhance human values, fairness, and distributive justice if individuals and groups of diverse backgrounds are to share the common life of the global community.

GENERAL CONCERNS

Among all the dimensions of the New World Order, which I believe will be bound to propel itself somehow into the twenty-first century, my own particular concern is with its cultural, religious, and spiritual components. It is my considered opinion that Christianity will have to carry very heavy burdens—for itself, for the sake of all religions, and for the global community. One of the predicaments for Christianity and all other religions alike in our time is the ambiguity of the definition of religion that is based on the provincial Western convention of dividing human experience into a series of semiautonomous pigeonholes (e.g., religion, aesthetics, ethics, law, culture, society, politics, economics). I personally see no reason to reject the validity of such taxonomy where it is applicable, but in the long run, I share Eliade's lament that "it is unfortunate that we do not have at our disposal a more precise word than 'religion.'"[7] We learn from European history that it was a perennial temptation for *imperium* to resort to a literal interpretation of religion so demarcated (e.g., the belief in, and worship of, a deity, etc.) and try to confine the activity and influence of *sacerdotium* to a narrow "religious" sphere in order to avoid possible conflict or threat from religious quarters. Conversely, the *sacerdotium*, using the broad interpretation of the vague definition of religion, such as the view that everything is ultimately related to the salvation of humankind, attempted to claim authority over *imperium*. In all fairness, given the Western notion of the ambiguous meaning of religion, both *imperium* and *sacerdotium* were probably more than a little right and more than a little wrong.

As one turns to a larger canvas of the human situation, however, one discovers that many civilizations regard all phases of life as a unified, seamless whole, what amounts to a religious-cultural-social-political synthesis (to use Western categories) or an intricate blending of what the West tends to think of as semiautonomous compartments. And the most challenging concern before us today is not what religion is or does, but how we can gain adequate understanding of the relationships between what the Western tradition usually identifies as religion and the religious-cultural-social-political synthesis, which is the seamless whole of life itself. On this score, I have repeatedly urged reflection on what religion does *within* this synthesis, and also on what religion does *to* the synthesis itself. Briefly stated, religion (1) evolves a spiritual, moral, and ecclesiastical tradition, (2) serves as a glue to disparate elements, such as art, economics, cultural life, and sociopolitical order, and (3) serves as the metaphysical agent to determine the kinds and levels of reality. Moreover, religion provides cosmic legitimation—based on its self-authenticating, circular logic, which is affirmed by "insiders"—to the particular religious-cultural-social-political synthesis.[8]

Unfortunately, many people ignore the fact that religion has both inner and outer meanings, or they simply assume that insiders' autobiographical understanding of the inner meaning of religion is the only authentic statement about religion, forgetting the existence of the legitimate biographical approach to outer meaning, such as the sociological, phenomenological, and cultural aspects of religion. It is to be noted that it is not only religion but also culture, language, national community, and scientific discipline that have both inner and outer meanings, and they can be approached by both autobiographical and biographical modes of perception. Nevertheless, this kind of very obvious general phenomenon is often overlooked by many religious people in favor of their misguided conviction that their autobiographical understanding of the inner meaning of their own religion alone has ultimacy, finality, and universality. Thus everything else, including other peoples' religious traditions, has to be approached and adjudicated only from this one perspective, as was commonly done previously by many Western Christian missionaries in Asia and Africa. (This kind of mental habit was not confined to Western Christian missionaries, however. It is widely asserted by people of many different religions, especially by those of absolutistic or fundamentalistic orientations. More ironically, many allegedly fair and objective—but actually exclusivistic—individuals among philosophers, rationalistic scientists, and even theologians in the West as well as in the East also suffer from this malady today.)

A PRELIMINARY GLIMPSE INTO THE FUTURE

The above discussion on inner/outer meanings of religion as well as autobiographical/biographical modes of perception, simple and elementary though it is, may provide useful prolegomena to our reflections on the métier of religion in general and Christianity in particular in the forthcoming New World Order of the global community. In all fairness, I should at this point note some of my premises about future religious problems in general.

First, I do not foresee the emergence of one universal world religion, nor do I believe that any one of the existing religions, be it Buddhism, Islam, or Christianity, or any other newer syncretistic religion—despite wishful thinking—will develop into such a decisively overwhelming dominant world faith, swallowing up all others into its own tradition.[9] Furthermore, I am not persuaded that underneath or behind various contradictory empirical religions there is in fact an invisible unified gnostic religion of one kind or another existing already, even though that kind of speculation is intellectually alluring.[10] These are my premises, and of course I may be wrong, but basically I accept the fact of plurality of religions as a part of the human pilgrimage on this planet. Of course, I should not preclude the possibility that I might be happily surprised to see the emergence of one super world religion. On the other hand, we have learned from experience that "modernity"—rather than burying religions—seems to nurture an infinite variety of religious forms.

Second, I have a hard time convincing myself that either "faith" or "reason" in a generic sense will triumph, burying the other in the years to come. I have a strong suspicion that faith and reason will continue to carry on their muddled relationship, and the sooner we recognize that we need both, and thus need to nurture genuine rapport between them, the better. Having been exposed to the post-Enlightenment mental universe, I have profound respect for the courageous revolt that reason took against the unwarranted postmedieval religious, moral, and intellectual authority claimed by the *sacerdotium.* And I take seriously Darwinian, Marxian, and Freudian negative judgments of religion as needed; they offer a constructive critique of empirical religion (*religionskritik*). It might be added here that the eighth-century Hebrew prophets were just as stringent, if not more, in their criticisms of the self-righteous and self-centered piety of empirical religion. In the history of Asia, too, there have been many sages and wise men who sharply criticized blind piety, moral laxity, and the degradation of sober rationality.

Appreciative though I am of the profound and legitimate critique of religion inspired by human reason, I do not share the view of some rationalists that reason now makes human beings completely self-sufficient and thus antireligious, by implication. According to Hegel, "The 'phenomenology' or self-manifestation merges into man's work in history, into human self-fulfillment. Man becomes 'present God' (*präsenter Gott*) and continues the divine process in his own worldly presence."[11] Such exaggerated glorification of reason makes men and women trust only what their eyeballs can observe or what their senses can verify, and thus condemns human beings to a life of insipid banality, totally cut off from faith, which is "the assurance of things hoped for, the conviction of things not seen" (Heb. 11:1). There is no question that rational, critical thinking, rooted in the life of reason, will be badly needed by the global community in the years ahead. But the New World Order would be a sorry state if it is dictated only by reason, without art and culture (*mundus imaginalis*) and faith to enrich the quality of what Fichte once called *Die Bestimmung des Menschen.*

Third, on a more empirical level, I am reconciled to the future prospect of seeing many different types of religious traditions (e.g., theistic and nontheistic, exclusivistic and relativistic, elitist and folkish, conservative and liberal) crisscrossing the face of the earth. Some of these contradictory traits will always be found within one and the same tradition, too. Even the most elaborate series of articles of faith and rules of behavior, imposed by arbitrary monolithic ecclesiastical authority, cannot enforce unified religious conformity on the part of adherents as long as they remain human.[12] I realize that in some parts of the world, conversion from one's ancestral faith to another is forbidden by law, whereas the religious maps of other areas are changing constantly. Nevertheless, my own assumption, which of course may not be correct, is that the arbitrary law of religious conformity will eventually decline, and the world will gradually witness the arrival of the "free market of religion," at least theoretically, despite strong inertia on the part of people for various inherited traditions. (In so stating, I also realize that there will be a strong push for various kinds of antireligious movements, too.)

Fourth, related to the above premise of a religious free market in the future is my assumption that all religious traditions will have to learn in the years to come the uncomfortable art of holding in balance the two contradictory objectives, namely, mission and dialogue (which were earlier depicted as *coincidentia oppositorum*). There is much truth in someone's observation made long ago that religion is a response by the totality of the human being to the totality of existence. Understandably, insiders of a given religion, whose life experience has been nurtured by their autobiographical understanding of the inner meaning of their religion, tend to have a totalitarian outlook toward the meaning of life. They and their co-religionists live and breathe in that particular kind of "world of meaning," supported and reinforced by their common language, mores, art and culture, and communal life. Curiously, such a particularistic approach to the totality of existence often provides energy for a universalistic vision of salvation for universal humanity. And when such a universalistic soteriological vision becomes an imperative, mandate, or vocation, the adherents of that religious tradition or ideologies, for that matter, pursue the task of mission, as we have seen in the cases of Buddhism, Christianity, Islam, communism, Bahā'i, Sikhism, pseudoreligion of secularized salvation (modern European civilization), American civil religion, Mormonism, and a host of modern new religions, Eastern and Western.

It is a great mystery of religion that each religious tradition, notwithstanding its conviction about its finality, is surrounded by other religious traditions with similar truth-claims, and thus has to develop some kind of rapport with them. Frequently in our time, various traditions are engaged in interreligious dialogue. Of course, plurality of religions is nothing new in human history, but the vogue of dialogue among them is rather new. On this issue, which involves many precarious questions, Stanley Samartha wryly observes:

> If all religions are "true," dialogue is hardly necessary. If only one religion is "true," dialogue is impossible. No, the question is rather how, in a world of many living faiths and ideologies, men and women can best work together on the basic issues of human life. We need not often talk about dialogue itself, but the climate which genuine dialogue produces provides the indispensable climate of trust and freedom in which the real issues can be appropriately raised and discussed.[13]

And if the global community should ever evolve anything like a New World Order, it is hoped that genuine interreligious dialogues will hammer out a common thrust of *humanum* (a humane ethical code) without which human unity will be unthinkable.

MATTERS OF SOME URGENCY

My reflection on some of the main burdens for Christianity for the future of the global community, especially about its relationship to other religions, reflects my own autobiographical understanding of the inner meaning of Christian tradition, which I hope transcends the confines of the European Christians' historical experience. In so stating, I am not rejecting Europeans' understanding of Christianity as false. I do reject the view, however, that only Europeans—obviously the transmitters of Christian culture for many centuries—can attain authentic perception of that tradition. Having been originally a product of a younger church in Asia and having been exposed to *religionswissenschaftliche* and theological studies on both sides of the Pacific, I hope I have proper appreciation and respect for the Western Christian tradition without being enslaved to it. Also, I have come to learn over the years the inevitable differences that developed between European and American perspectives on the piety-morality-culture stratifications.

My main concern for the future directions of Christianity is that it has to face several far-reaching and demanding tasks simultaneously and soon. Briefly stated, resorting to the dialogue language for the sake of simplification, Christianity can ill afford to neglect (1) internal dialogues between its inner and outer meanings, (2) dialogues between it and *religionskritiks*/antagonists, and (3) dialogues between it and other religions, which too came into being as responses to the totality of existence. In addition, like it or not, Christianity in America has to carry on within American borders serious dialogues with new and/or Eastern religions and traditionally non-Western cultures, all of which will inform and affect the religious universe of many citizens in the years to come. There must be some way for these religious and cultural traditions, including, of course, Christianity, to join forces in order to provide cosmic legitimation to the ever-changing religious-cultural-social-political synthesis instead of leaving this crucial task primarily to civil religion, as has been the case up to this point.

It should be stated clearly, however, that the various types of dialogues mentioned above will not solve all the knotty religious problems of the world—or for Christianity, for that matter. As I stated elsewhere:

> A dialogue is not meant to be a religious counterpart of the Rotary Club, [either]. In fact, as Professor Takeuchi remarks, "where there is an enchanted possibility of mutual appreciation there is also the increased risk of misunderstanding." Admittedly, those who participate in the coming dialogue will learn something from one another, and the chances are that *their understanding of their own faiths will undergo changes. Those who feel that they have nothing to learn from others have very little to contribute to such a dialogue.*[14]

Bearing these factors in mind, I want to mention one example of the historic burden that has been inflicted on Christianity, especially in the West, the nature of which can be clarified, thanks to various dialogues. (Whether or not such a clarification has been welcomed by the Western Christian tradition is another matter. From the global perspective, with the necessity of interreligious dialogues for the future in mind, I am personally in favor of such clarification of the nature and identity of Christianity itself, which understandably has serious implications for its relationship to other religions of the world.)

The example I have in mind has to do with the false (partially, at least) claim of absoluteness or finality of Christian faith—identified with the whole Christian religious tradition by many—which has been discussed variously in connection with the problems of relationships between general and special revelations, natural and revealed theologies, *missio dei* vs. human initiative for mission, faith vs. knowledge, Jesus' *kerygma* of God's kingdom vs. the messenger (Jesus Christ) as *kerygma* itself, the kingdom of God vs. the Christian church, salvation vs. enlightenment, transcendence vs. immanence, religion vs. philosophy/science, grace vs. human striving, true vs. false religions, and so forth.[15] Although we cannot discuss in detail all the genetic, historical, theological/philosophical, and cultural/sociological/political factors involved in this one huge bundle of issues, we should at least briefly touch upon its main thrusts.

It is worth recalling in this connection my earlier quotation of the simple "genetic" observation made by Hamilton Gibb to the effect that to outsiders Islam is a religion of Muslims but to the Muslims it is the religion of truth. I am certain that the same principle is applicable to other religions, too, inasmuch as they all try to cope with the totality of human existence. And usually the insiders' autobiographical perception of the inner meaning of their religion is rooted in the circular self-authenticating logic. (E.g., I believe that my religion is true because it was revealed by the god whom I believe, and so the circular logic goes round and round. In this respect, I can understand the Christians' in-house rhetoric of the finality and absoluteness of their religion, just as adherents of other faiths assert their supreme loyalty to their faiths.) Historically, this kind of very conventional religious perception takes on a dogmatic, sinister, authoritarian character when one religion (e.g., Christianity in Europe, Buddhism in Southeast Asia, etc.) remains as a dominant or the only official tradition in the same locality for any length of time.

Thus Christianity, which had emerged as a persecuted, minority religion surrounded by many other powerful systems, underwent a radical change in its outlook, following the Constantinian twist. (1) Loyalty to God became prerequisite to the loyalty to Caesar, rejecting the biblical exhortation to separate the sphere of God from the things of Caesar. (2) Inevitably, not unlike Israelite kingship after the time of Samuel that often overshadowed divine kingship, Roman emperors after Constantine and Theodosius expected their subjects in the realm to pay allegiance to them as divinely-ordained sacred kings. (3) Although prior to the time of Constantine, the Roman Empire, following the example of Alexander the Great, depended on the plurality of religions to provide cosmic legitimation to its religious-cultural-social-political synthesis, the post-Constantine Roman Empire depended on the religious unity, or singleness, of religion (Christianity) to authenticate its *raison d'être*. (4) Inevitably, the imperialistic political character was rubbed into the Christian religious community, which developed a monarchical episcopate, doctrinal orthodoxy, authorized rituals, clerical hierarchy, canon laws, and rules of behavior.

The Europeanization of Christianity involved both internal and external transitions. Internally, this religious tradition, having emerged originally as an offshoot of Hebrew religious heritage, took seriously the notion of the *dynamis* (power) of God who "acts" (based on the Hebrew notion of *hāyāh*, meaning "to act," "to become," "to happen"). Accordingly, Paul spoke for many Christians when he declared: "Jews demand signs and Greeks seek wisdom, but we preach Christ crucified, a stumbling block to Jews and folly to Gentiles, but to those who are called, both Jews and Greeks, Christ the power (*dynamis*) of God and the wisdom of God" (1 Cor. 1:22–24). Moreover, Paul was persuaded that "the kingdom of God does not consist in talk (*logos*) but in power (*dynameis*)" (1 Cor. 4:20).[16] It was natural, therefore, for early Christians to look forward to the *parousia* (the second coming of "Christ the power") and the arrival of *eschaton* (end of the world), which were to be initiated by the dynamic God. Following Pentecost, however, Christians realized that the anticipated *parousia* was not impending, and they had to come to terms with the historical reality of life in the second and third centuries. Also, under the strong impact of the intellectual climate of the day of the church, the hayathological and prophetic modes of thinking (from the Hebrew heritage) began to recede in favor of the more rational Hellenistic mental habit as well as the Roman tradition-inspired legal reasoning that were more useful for the infant religious communities, which had to structure their doctrines, liturgies, and ethics.

It was during that volcanic period of transition of the Christian church from the divine *dynamis*-inspired group of humble Christians to a more settled church in Roman society that we might see the figure of the lonely seer John and his Book of Revelation. Although he was getting old in his exile at Patmos, he solidly stood in the tradition of the prophets of Israel, who had lived in the days of the imperial powers of Egypt, Assyria, and Babylon. John's world was dominated by the mighty empire of Rome, and he knew that Christians were caught between their fidelity to the God of Jesus Christ and the loyalty to Caesar (who assumed divine prerogatives). John was painfully aware of the precarious destiny of those who pledged their loyalty to the transcendental deity but had to live under the sway of a mighty earthly empire, which demanded compromise and allegiance in the name of security and safety. In fact, John anticipated very astutely the many troubles and predicaments that were to descend on the Christian communities that were compelled to sell their souls to gain security, wealth, and power from the earthly empires from the second to the twentieth centuries. On his part, John—by using the grotesque symbolism of the old Hebrew apocalyptic tradition, presumably to disguise his in-house anti-Roman messages in order to keep them from the eyes of Roman officials—encouraged the persecuted Christians not to lose faith in God. Throughout his apocalypse runs a theme that has a uniquely contemporary ring to it, namely, that a nation or a civilization that pretends to have absolute authority and power is bound to be doomed, and that in the long run (although it may take a long time), God's dominion will prevail by bringing renewal of world order and of humanity.

Externally, notwithstanding John's counsel, however, the Christian church during the third and the fourth centuries quickly and successfully transformed itself to be a this-worldly religion and, following the reigns of Constantine and Theodosius, grew into the official state religion. As such, it willingly provided cosmic legitimation to the emerging European form of the religious-cultural-social-political synthesis, which integrated, among other things, Christian religion, Hellenistic thought, and Roman jurisprudence. In this process, as has been frequently mentioned already, the church became one of the three pivotal institutions in medieval Europe, namely, the *sacerdotium, imperium,* and *studium.* Significantly, both the church (*sacerdotium*) and the university (*studium*) came under the spell of Hellenistic thought, which was reintroduced to Europe through the mediation of Muslim and Jewish intellectuals in the Iberian peninsula. Hellenistic thought, especially the Greek form of rationalistic ontology (which was diametrically opposed to the ancient activistic Hebrew hayathology) greatly aided scholastic theological systematization and enabled theology to claim to be the queen of science in the medieval university. According to Greek-inspired theology, God is now portrayed no longer as the dynamic deity and the lord of history and the universe, as indicated by the Hebrew notion of *hāyāh,* but rather as a static unmoved mover, sitting on a solitary throne of transcendent immobility, whereby the earthly church, amply armed with dogmas, rituals, canon laws, clerical hierarchies, and monastic disciplines acts and speaks on behalf of the heavenly deity. The church even invaded the divine territory of salvation by declaring the dogma of "no salvation outside the Christian church" and condemned those to anathema who refused to come under the church's authority. By that time, an important motif of the Johannine Gospel that "God so loved the *world*" was forgotten in favor of the new belief that "God loved primarily the *church*." And the church, which now shares the political fortune with *imperium,* is willing to be engaged in armed crusade against Muslims (who were labeled as infidels instead of children created by God) in the name of the Prince of Peace!

The influence of Hellenistic thought, a part of which was warmly welcomed by the church, brought about some adverse effects, too. Europeans now learned not only Aristotelianism (which aided the theology and the church immensely), but also Greek antiquity and art that inspired the new cultural movement called the Renaissance. The impact of Greek rationalistic tradition, rooted in the prominence of reason, also aided the growth of scientific revolution, much to the chagrin of the *sacerdotium.* Worst of all, European universities, which at one time acknowledged the preeminence of theology and metaphysics, began to recognize the autonomy of various disciplines. Moreover, Protestant reformers, many of whom had been educated in the universities, defied the papal monopoly of the *magisterium* (teaching authority on religious truths and morals) on the ground that what they learned in the universities also had truth-claims, though they were different, to be sure, from what the *sacerdotium* unfolded. Meanwhile, the Holy Roman Empire—which had managed to survive, thanks to the mixture of friendly and antagonistic cooperation with the church— eroded and gave way to a series of territorial monarchies, which eventually were taken over by a number of modern autonomous sovereign nation-states. Side by side with such a trend of political liberation from the yoke of the church and the empire was an intellectual current that exalted human autonomy and rationality, which now ushered in a strong impulse for secularization.

WHAT ARE THE PROSPECTS?

And now, being at the tail end of a turbulent century, or rather coming close to the threshold of an unknown new age, what kind of future prospect of religion in general and Christianity in particular do we or can we anticipate? On this subject, a few preliminary remarks may be in order.

First, there is a "curious contradiction" of modern life, as George D. Kennan recently pointed out:

> As medicine prolongs man's span of life, the headlong pace of technological change tends to deprive him, at an earlier age than was ever before the case, of the only world he understands and the only one to which he can be fully oriented. . . . We older people are the guests of this age . . . like the guests in a summer hotel. . . . [I]t is not our hotel. . . . [W]e shall be leaving it; the personnel, while sometimes cheerful, sometimes competent, sometimes strong, are nevertheless terrifying to us for the things that are not written on them.[17]

Even so, notwithstanding our incompetence to conjecture the things to come, we must do our very best to speculate about the future for three reasons: (1) what will take place in the years to come cannot be divorced altogether from the factors and currents we have known in the past and present, (2) what we mortals now call "future" itself will always have to be seen by future mortals as a pale shadow of the real "world (*oikoumene*) to come" (Heb. 2:5), and (3) I believe, rightly or wrongly, that one's long years of experience enable one to attain some sort of integration and perspective.

Second, if religion in the future will be anything like religion we have known thus far, it will hardly be separable from the whole of a seamless life as such (characterized earlier as the religious-cultural-social-political synthesis), with a number of different functions in it.

Nevertheless, we have to lift up, as much as we can possibly do, specific religious issues for the future.

Third, we are familiar with uniquely conservative, elitist, defensive and yet assertive exclusivistic qualities shared by various religious traditions of the world, and it will not be easy for them to foresee that the current equalitarian thrusts will increasingly foster a climate that approximates something like a "religious free market" in the next century. A part of their backwardness is due to the strong inertia derived from many religious traditions' questionable conviction that the only reliable salvation or enlightenment had been already completed in the past (*fait accompli*). This kind of conviction nurtures a mental habit to read history backward rather than looking ahead, which encourages religious leaders to resort to the past soteriological formula as the only trustworthy tool for the future. Thus they tend to feel that there is something incongruous to think of the *future* as *future;* it is almost as difficult as it is for the male celibate ecclesiastical hierarchy (who in the end will have the authority to decide) to consider the question of women's ordination or clerical marriage. Like it or not, however, the destiny of religion in the future will not be completely in the hands of ecclesiastical leaders alone. For example, the recent Polish voting shows that Poles, who no doubt had appreciated the Vatican's support of their solidarity movement, had overwhelmingly rejected the antiabortion bill, dubbed as "the papal gift."[18]

Evidently, Christianity more than many other traditions has been burdened with more of these potential and actual problems, for it remained as the only and official religion in Europe for so long, that its ecclesiastical leaders have become used to thinking that insiders' (i.e., European Christians') autobiographical perception of the inner meaning of Christianity alone was unquestionably true and universally valid. Of course, other religions in other places under similar circumstances could fall into the same error, as indeed they have. At any rate, the lack of rival traditions deprived European Christianity of a spiritual mirror that would show Christians some images of the outer meaning of Christianity, as seen by outsiders. (Prior to the fall of the Muslim regime in Grenada, Spain, in 1492, there was at least a slight opportunity for a mutual image existing between the *corpus Christianum* and the *corpus Islamicum*. A mutual image to be sure did not guarantee a correct mutual image, however, as illustrated by the Europeans' frequent characterization of the caliph as the Islamic pope, and the Muslims' referring to the pope as the Christian caliph. Even such a distorted outer meaning of Christianity was no longer accessible to Christians later on.) I sincerely hope that my recommendation of the three measures mentioned in the section "Matters of Some Urgency" might at least initially help the Christian tradition to be emancipated from its long years of European captivity and start moving forward as a universal religion, which it is in the new age. Let me now briefly touch upon each one of them.

The Dialogue Between Christianity's Inner and Outer Meanings

I hope the Christian tradition will realize that the European captivity has made Christianity hermeneutically illiterate, and that one of the first necessary remedies from this symptom is to develop an "internal dialogue" between its inner and outer meanings. For too long European Christianity has depended solely on its own autobiographical perception of the inner meaning of Christianity, and has behaved as though its outer meaning either did not exist or, if it did, it did not illuminate anything. This may account for the happy illusion of many European missionaries who have gone abroad believing and declaring that Christianity has nothing to do with European colonialism. (At least David Livingstone's slogan of "commerce [colonialism] and Christianity" was more honest and realistic, even though it greatly distorted the Christian *kerygma* in Africa.) It would be helpful if European Christians' image of Christianity can be contrasted at least to the secular historians' image of European Christianity, too. (The usual German distinction between *Kirchengeschichte* and *Dogmengeschichte* is useful in this respect.) The worst part of hermeneutical illiteracy is the lamentable confusion between authentic doctrine and "pious opinion," whereby a variety of superstitions and folk beliefs had invaded Christianity in the name of biblical inerrancy and sacrality of church tradition.

The other side of the hermeneutical illiteracy was the false conviction that European Christians' self-authenticating understanding of Christianity provides the most unerring instrument to approach and interpret any and all non-Christian and non-Western religions and cultures. (More will be said on this problem presently in connection with the interreligious dialogue.) In so stating, I want to state that, important though hermeneutical literacy is, it is not the final answer to all our religious problems of the world. To be sure, Christianity will benefit immensely from hermeneutical insights that would enable us to "recognize" that which had been "cognized" by others, past and present, as well as point to the importance of our "re-experiencing" that which had been "experienced." For example, note the certitude of salvation that was experienced by the disciples narrated in the New Testament or the discovery of God's hand in raising an alien King Cyrus as God's anointed in the experience of the Hebrew prophet (Isa. 45:1). The hermeneutical insight also would enable us to observe and appraise our own belief and experience as though they were something apart from ourselves.[19] But hermeneutics will help articulate primarily our ability for deduction and understanding, but will do little regarding the domain of the certitude of salvation, which is central to Christianity and various other religions of the world.

The Dialogue Between Christianity and *Religionskritiks* / Antagonists

I hope that, side by side with the internal dialogue between its inner and outer meanings of Christianity itself, Christianity will take a positive stance in considering *religionskritiks* /antagonists more as our dialogue-partners rather than simply as foes and infidels. Historically, all religious traditions have had their share of the rebellion or criticism of insiders, and the disputes or open combat of outsiders. Understandably, many religious traditions have developed mostly confrontational attitudes toward those whom they considered as heretics, schismatics, critics, and mortal enemies. On the other hand, it must be honestly admitted that all religious traditions have learned much from those who have disagreed with their convictions. And it might be possible from time to time for all religious traditions to adopt a more positive attitude toward those who differ with them. Such a posture will not only bring more benefit to religions but might become inevitable and necessary in the years to come.

I fully realize that this is far easier said than done. After all, as far as religious traditions are concerned, deviation from what they regard as truth is a serious matter because of their "concern, not for any truth, but for truth regarding the sources of life and death. In other words, in religions truth is not a matter of satisfying the intelligence but of fulfilling existence."[20] This is more particularly true with European Christian tradition, which for so long had justified its truth-claims singularly by means of self-authenticating circular logic. This was proclaimed as self-evidently the most complete verity by the teaching authority of the self-styled ecclesiastical agent on earth of the heavenly sacred deity, who allegedly had commissioned the church to act and speak on the deity's behalf according to its autobiographical understanding of biblical revelation and the tradition of the church. Unfortunately, the church had a difficult time adjusting to the changing intellectual climate, because it wanted to concoct and preserve almost artificially a comprehensive and coherent worldview for all time, based primarily on the resources of the past, such as scriptures, the writings of the Church Fathers, and a series of theological resolutions inspired by Greek and Latin rhetorics. Even then, the church served fairly well as a civilizing agency in elevating the cultural standard of barbarians within the imperial border. In retrospect, it becomes evident that the influence of Aristotelianism brought mixed blessings to the medieval church. On the one hand, it helped the creation of the architectonic scholastic theology and boosted the prestige of theology and metaphysics in the universities. On the other hand, its impact hardened the rigidity of the papal church's dogmatic assertions, especially after the Lutheran Reformation and the Counter-Reformation, as demonstrated by the all-too-arrogant Inquisition's condemnation and imprisonment of Galileo Galilei (1564–1642). In this respect, Protestant churches were not much better in adjusting to the changing cultural climate.

As a matter of fact, it was the antiecclesiastical rationalists/positivists who broke the spell of the rigid, narrow, and myopic European churches' truth-claims. I am never sure whether it was European Christianity that pushed the Renaissance/Enlightenment out from its fold, or whether rationalistic humanists happened to live in the emerging alternative mental universe, which transcended the inflexible and tenacious churchly truth-claims. At any rate, by encountering the reality of the non-Western world and the new cosmic map by telescope, among other things, many European intellectuals after the time of Galilei bypassed the allegedly all-comprehensive and normative truths asserted by European Christianity. And, under the impact of Copernicus, Newton, Descartes, Darwin, Vico, Marx, and Freud, the reluctant European Christianity was compelled to face—however belatedly—the reality of critical and rationalistic modern thought patterns.

We should also remember, however, notwithstanding the current positivists' idealization of the eighteenth century as "the Age of Reason," that it was, in the words of the Polish poet-Nobel Laureate Czesltaw Milosz, actually "the Age of *Pious* Reason." Some of the scientists (e.g., Isaac Newton and Carolus Linnaeus, in particular) were committed believers, and it was also the age of mystical writers (e.g., Claude de Saint-Martin, Emanuel Swedenborg, and William Blake). Milosz points out that many of those scientists affirmed God in spite of their basically materialistic philosophy:

> The notion underlying all its artifacts is that of order. God established the immutable laws for the movements of the planets, for the growth of vegetation, for the working of the animal organism, and

the life of man on the earth is providentially arranged in accordance with the universal rhythm. Some ideas, like the idea of the inalienable rights of every human being seem to imply a stability underneath the changing forms of social existence. The *episteme* of the 18th century, centered upon order, is best expressed in its music.

Then, he continues:

The next century, the 19th, would exacerbate some tendencies of its predecessor and elaborate what can be called a scientific *Weltanschauung*. In fact [it would seem] quite distant from those harmonious visions of the earlier scientists. Destructive of values, it would prompt Friedrich Nietzsche to announce the advent of "European nihilism."[21]

Fortunately or unfortunately, we in the twentieth century have been haunted by the mixed blessings of the last century's legacy of the scientific objectivity advocated by empirical thinking based on a presumably coherent scientific vision of the world, which, however, shows very little regard for meanings, values, and orders. Nevertheless, we have to acknowledge at least the cleansing, purifying, and illuminating effect that rationalistic humanism has brought to Christianity.

Lamentably, Christianity and rational/scientific/humanistic thinking have often reacted to the wrong image of one another, images that each side assumes that the other side has of its counterpart. Accordingly, the mutual criticisms that would have brought about much benefit to both have not come about easily. But make no mistake; on this point we are destined to move on these two (religious and rationalistic) parallel tracks in the coming century. Furthermore, people in the non-Western world too will be destined to follow similar parallel tracks.

The Interreligious Dialogue

As though the internal dialogue between its inner and outer meanings and the dialogue between it and *religionskritiks*/antagonists were not enough, Christianity in the years to come will have to participate seriously in the interreligious dialogue with other religions of the world. It is worth mentioning that the idea of the interreligious dialogue is fairly fashionable in our time, and various such dialogues have already been held with a variety of motivations (social, cultural, political, etc.), all of which have their own significance but have very little to do with *religious* interreligious dialogues. Even the religiously motivated interreligious dialogues can be, and actually have been, inspired by different visions and models. For example, according to one kind of vision, different religions are basically the same; this vision believes that people sing songs with the same theme but according to different tunes. However, a second vision holds that each religious tradition has its unique, non-transferable meaning-structure. To the former, the uniqueness of each religion is its disgrace, whereas to the latter, universality implies the surrender of truth. Even linguistic labels are often misleading, for as Hendrik Kraemer reminds us, some of the more aggressive spokespersons of inclusiveness are really "exclusivists in a concealed way" in the name of inclusiveness, by claiming that interreligious dialogues are possible only when all religions drop at the outset their uniqueness and accept solely the tenet of the one, universal religion.[22]

In this connection, it might be pertinent for me to mention the two well-known historic, religiously motivated, interreligious dialogues. The first was sponsored by the Mughal (Muslim) emperor Akbar (reign 1556–1606) of India. A religious reformer of a sort, Akbar was persuaded that the unity of humankind was attainable only through the unity of religions and common worship, and he built the Hall of Worship at Fathpur Sikri for the purposes of common worship and of interreligious discussions over which he himself presided. We are told that these discussions were attended by "Sunni ulamā , Sufi shaikhs, Hindu pundits, Parsees, Zoroastrians, Jains, and Catholic priests from Portuguese Goa."[23] As might be expected, Akbar's religious policy was not supported by everybody; it was received negatively by many, especially by the orthodox Muslims in his own court. Akbar had many piercing insights about religious matters, but he did not make constructive contributions to the cause of interreligious dialogue. And eventually, his own religious search took him to enunciate in 1582 his own eclectic faith called "Divine Faith (Dīn-i-Ilāhī)," which disintegrated when he died.

The second was the 1893 World's Parliament of Religions, held in Chicago as a part of the Columbian exposition. Originally proposed by a Swedenborgian layman, C. C. Bonney, the Parliament was strongly supported by many civic and business leaders, as well as by liberal Jewish, Roman Catholic, and Protestant leaders. The fact that it was the first occasion for spokesmen of Hinduism, Buddhism, and Chinese and Japanese religions to occupy Western platforms was no doubt a very significant event, but the Parliament had a strong Christian overtone. Besides, notwithstanding the Parliament's official statement that its guiding spirit was the then-emerging general science of religion (Religionswissenschaft) and not Christian theology, many Westerners who had warmly welcomed guests from Eastern religions assumed rightly or wrongly that the religious yearning of Easterners would eventually be "fulfilled" by the Jewish-Christian telos. Furthermore, the Western hosts at that time completely missed two significant factors (and I rather suspect that these two blind spots have been inherited even by many current Westerners who are presumably interested in interreligious dialogues): (1) Many of these Eastern delegates did not represent the classical Eastern religious traditions (whereas Western students of Eastern religions have continued to study the classical Hinduism, Buddhism, etc., thinking that these classical forms have remained normative). Rather, they were what I once described, for lack of a better designation, as "modern religious reformers."[24] Although they did not question the essential viability of their respective inherited religious traditions, they had also been exposed to the Western-inspired rationalistic mood, which had salutary effect in cleansing much of the meaningless deadweight of bygone features of traditional religions. Thus there were some discrepancies between what Western hosts expected of these Eastern religions and what these Eastern delegates actually presented at the Parliament. (2) Probably of more importance, these modern religious reformers quickly learned that the Western formula of "fulfillment" could be legitimately appropriated by Eastern religions, so that a genuine interreligious dialogue should not follow just "one way traffic" (meaning the fulfillment of Eastern religions in the Jewish-Christian religious universe) but ought to be the sharing of religious insights by dialogue partners of equal standing.

I hope the foregoing will at least make it clear that what we need in interreligious dialogue is not a new method or new gimmick, but our willingness and determination to "re-vision" afresh our own religious tasks for the new age. I understand that for Christianity, which has been boxed in for so long in European captivity, the initial impulse is not to "re-vision" but "revise"—and make more up-to-date—the answers and formulas that had been "completed" in the past and have been handed down by the official churches. But I share the conviction of Edward Schillebeeckx that what we need most of all is to re-vision "a mutually critical correlation" between "the whole tradition of the experience of the great Jewish-Christian movement" and "the contemporary, new human experiences of both Christians and non-Christians."[25] Then, perhaps it will become more apparent to us that the task of our own self-understanding of Christianity depends on mutual understanding (between our inner and outer meanings of Christianity, between it and the image of Christianity held by the *religionskritiks*/antagonists, and between Christianity and other religions). In other words, our self-understanding must be based on understanding of mutual understanding. This is particularly true in the framework of the interreligious dialogue.

Having attended a fair number of such meetings labeled as interfaith or interreligious dialogues over the years, I have spotted some common fallacies that have often been tolerated in the name of politeness. In some extreme cases of Western Christian-sponsored conferences, interreligious dialogue is considered de facto primarily as a new softer strategy, replacing the now-defunct aggressive missionary approaches to adherents of other religions. Even those who have no proselytizing motivation are often under the happy illusion that one can have a genuinely meaningful interreligious dialogue by depending on mostly Western languages, Western philosophical/theological categories, logics, and rhetorics, and by inviting non-Western representatives who are familiar with the Western intellectual climate for the purpose of discussion of various religious traditions, their doctrines, ethics, and rituals. Sometimes participants of such dialogues take undue interest in linguistics or symbolic "accidental" similarities between various religions, and at other times they are mesmerized by some prominent Westerners' pet theories of Eastern religions, such as Albert Schweitzer's characterization of Indian religious tradition as world-and-life negation, or some of the French philosophs' notion of Chinese religion as the highest form of natural religion. I remember once in an interreligious conference in Europe, it took more than one full day for some of us to convince Western participants that it is a dangerous oversimplification to view all Asians through the category of "Völker von ewigen Stillstandes." Similarly, oversimplified categorizations and characterizations, such as the nonspiritual materialism of Western traditions, have haunted many conferences in Asia. I am bewildered as to why members of the so-called younger churches, that is, those Asian and African Christians who have been raised in the non-Western world, have not been more active in the interreligious dialogues. Although I recognize the eagerness on the part of Eastern dialogue-partners to exchange views with leading Christian thinkers in the West, and vice versa, I regret that thus far the dialogues have not seen fit to take more advantage of younger church members, who in a sense daily go through interreligious conversations in their own personal lives and who, if asked, can potentially relate themselves meaningfully both to the representatives of Eastern religions and the Western Christian dialogue-partners.

CLOSING REMARKS

Considering the importance of the interreligious dialogue for the future of the world, I offer some closing remarks, thereby sharing my reflections on some do's and don't on the subject.

First, we must avert the spectacle of "simultaneous monologue" in the name of interreligious dialogue by avoiding the temptation of making statements about our own as well as other religions based solely on insiders' autobiographical understanding of inner meanings of their own religion. For example, some insiders of the Christian fold sincerely believe (and they are certainly entitled to hold these views as their pious opinions) that there is one continuous religion called the Judeo-Christian tradition, or that Islam came into being because of a misunderstanding of the *wesen* of Christianity. Also, it is fairly common for some Hindu insiders to assert that Buddhism began as an offshoot, or one of the heterodox schools, of the great Hindu tradition. Notwithstanding the sincerity of those Christians or Hindus who are thus persuaded, such premises will bring only disaster to interreligious dialogues, because self-respecting Jews, Muslims, and Buddhists most likely will not accept such one-sided interpretations. Also, one must explain carefully to others unique accents or nuances of certain categories that have come to be accepted as common vocabulary inside respective religious traditions—such as "revelation" (in Jewish or Christian senses), "*maya*" (in Hinduism), "*tao*" (in Chinese traditions)—instead of presuming that these notions are self-explanatory and should be understood by other dialogue-participants. In the context of the interreligious dialogue, which must be based on the principle of the equality of various religions' starting points, it is also important for all participants to view that each religion is—following Hamilton Gibb's insight—"an autonomous expression of religious thought and experience, which must be viewed in and through itself and its own principles and standards."[26]

Second, acceptance of the equality of various religions' starting points naturally leads to the realization that each religion has its own history and involvement in the respective religious-cultural-social-political synthesis, and that each tradition is undergoing simultaneously (a) internal dialogue between its outer and inner meanings, (b) its dialogue with *religionskritiks*/antagonists, as well as (c) interreligious dialogues. Recognition of these factors makes it possible for us to carry on religiously motivated dialogue, which is based on a simple premise that we have to approach, understand, and interpret religion as something religious. In the words of Mircea Eliade: "To try to grasp the essence of such a phenomenon by means of physiology, psychology, sociology, economics, linguistics, art, or any other study is false; it misses the one unique and irreducible element in it—the element of the sacred."[27] The implications of this type of thinking are clear: the dialogue-participants on the one hand should be sufficiently religious themselves; and on the other hand, they must "have a readiness to take a candidly self-critical view of the empirical reality of their own religions," following Kraemer's insight.[28] This does not mean that the interreligious dialogues should be preoccupied, as so many of the dialogues have been thus far, with doctrines and dogmas. After all, a religion is not primarily a system of doctrines, coherently constructed for the convenience of an interfaith debating society. Also, our understanding of religion based solely on observable factors (as some social scientists insist on doing) is quite misleading: "It would be like the description of a man founded only upon his public behavior and leaving out of account his secret passions, his nostalgia, his existential contradictions and the whole universe of his imagination, which are more essential to him than the ready-made opinions he utters."[29]

Third, something should be said regarding the feasible agendas of such interreligious dialogues. On this question, we must start with the contention that religions are responses of the totality of human beings to the meaning of the totality of human existence and experience. It is conceivable that some traditions assume on this point that the meaning of the original totality of human existence is embodied completely in the sphere of visible nature, based on the principle that the natural is the original. Other traditions affirm the transcendental (absolute) realm side by side with, or above, the empirical (relative) realm. The latter traditions are again divided between those who view the transcendental sphere in nonpersonal terms (like Buddhism) and those who view it in a personal manner (like Judaism, Christianity, and Islam). Nevertheless, all these traditions—although realizing that they cannot perfectly actualize their ideals—attempt to come to terms with the totality of reality, the totality of the meaning of human experience and existence. And the first order of the interreligious dialogues in the emerging global community is not to compare the stereotyped doctrines and ethical systems of various traditions, but to share each tradition's endeavor to substantialize, objectify, and materialize that mystery and religious insight into the puzzling reality, into temporal religious forms, constituted by doctrines, ethics, rituals, and ecclesiastical-sociological structures. In such a process of sharing, each tradition will no doubt learn something from others, and each tradition might also undergo a series of internal and external changes.

The second great agenda of the genuine interreligious dialogue in the years to come is for various traditions jointly to hammer out viable planetary ethical systems of mutual responsibility that can be mutually acceptable to men and women of various as well as no religious traditions. It is to be noted, of course, that every religious tradition is concerned with germinating and articulating meaningful human ethics, known in the Christian tradition as the *humanum*, in contradistinction from the *divinum*. One of the better-known projects in this area is the *Humanum Studies* of the World Council of Churches in Geneva. Understandably, a natural temptation for many Christian leaders is to advocate the Christian understanding of the *humanum* as a de facto substitute for the interreligious vision of the *humanum*. But what concerns us is an attempt to articulate a global scheme of the *humanum*, which has to be based on religious inspirations of various religious traditions, and not one tradition like Christianity, however advanced the Christian understanding of the *humanum* is. Obviously, all men and women in every continent and every tradition are deeply concerned with such common problems as the ecology, human rights, equality of men and women, sexual preferences, discrepancy between the rich and the poor, and so forth. And all religious traditions are duty-bound to confront the issue of the *humanum* as the most urgent task for the present and future.

It must be kept in mind (and here Christians should readily understand it) that the *humanum* cannot be separated from the *divinum*. I personally believe that the agreement among hidden resources of various traditions that authenticate a respective religion's understanding of the *humanum* will not be forthcoming for years to come. In that sense, the interreligious dialogues are never-ending affairs so long as different religious traditions crisscross various continents on this planet. Nevertheless, today all of us realize that what human beings have produced can actually destroy, not just Christians, Muslims, or Buddhists, but all human beings. The realization of this plain fact alone instills in everybody's consciousness a new universal meaning to the originally provincially inspired notion of the *eschaton*, and thus all religious traditions have urgent imperatives to develop a mutually acceptable scheme of global human ethics.

It is my sincere hope that the above suggestions will be taken seriously by those who are concerned with the global perspectives for Christian tradition. In so stating, it is not my intention to reject

Western Christianity. All of us are greatly indebted to the religious insights and illumination derived from European and American experiences. Moreover, I have come to believe that the members of the so-called younger churches have much to reflect on from their rich spiritual heritage, and must cooperate with Christians in the West and adherents of other religions in the East for the sake of the religious task ahead for all of us.

The question that has run through this volume is whether or not there is a future for the Christian tradition beyond its European captivity, and I trust readers will gather that my considered opinion on this is affirmative. But I am also a firm believer that we will have to "re-vision" the entire *mundus imaginalis* of all human beings, going forward beyond Christianity's long years of European captivity. Thus, if we use the term "revelation" from a global perspective, I accept the view of Nathan Söderblom, the late archbishop of Uppsala: "All genuine religion in the concrete religion is revelation. . . . [E]ither there is real revelation outside the Biblical sphere, or there is no revelation at all, not even in the Bible."[30] I also affirm, as did William Temple:

> Only if God is revealed in the rising of the sun in the sky, can He be revealed in the rising of a son of man from the dead; only if He is revealed in the history of Syrians and Philistines, can He be revealed in the history of Israel; only if he chooses all men for His own, can He choose any at all; only if nothing is profane can anything be sacred.[31]

All religions, including the Christian tradition, must struggle with the *coincidentia oppositorum* involved in our *mundus imaginalis*. I hope I have learned in my eventful life the depth of spiritual wisdom advocated by the fourteenth-century Zen master, Daitō Kokushi, who said:

> From eternity to eternity [the Absolute] and I are separated from each other, yet, at the same time he and I do not fall even for a single moment. All day long he and I live facing each other, yet he and I have never a chance to meet each other.[32]

Such is the mystery of the religious universe.

APPENDIX

SOME PERSONAL REFLECTIONS ON AUTOBIOGRAPHICAL AND BIOGRAPHICAL MODES OF PERCEPTION

Many people at a certain point in life feel an urge to write memoirs or autobiographies. I, too, have reached an age when recollection of the past seems to be more rewarding, at least for me, than anticipation of a seemingly limited future. Fortunately for the world at large, many of us lack the necessary incentive, literary talent, intellectual honesty, and courage to follow through with what is essentially a misguided impulse in unfolding our own lives and thought in print. Besides, general readers are not interested in the personal accounts of most of us unless we can claim unusual professional achievements, important public services, or notoriety of one kind or another. Be that as it may, I realize that the lure of the autobiographical genre lies in its characteristic way of viewing life, events, and the world from one's own personal perspective or from the perspective of one's family, nation, culture, or religious group— singularly "from within," as it were.

On the other hand, even though it might sound contradictory in one sense, we are nevertheless attracted by some features of the bio-graphical genre as well. It is not easy to explain adequately why some other persons' lives, historical or contemporary, captivate us. After all, people everywhere, regardless of cultural, ethnic, or religious back-ground, go through similar experiences, such as biological cycles, proc-esses of socialization, or stages of human growth. But it may be that the fascination of the biographical perspective, unlike its autobiographical counterpart, is derived from the fact that through biography we can view other persons' lives, their inherited traditions, and the world as well as the time in which they live "from without." We can view them partly as a mirror to our lives and partly as aspects of our general knowledge about life and the world, with no direct responsibilities on our part, exercising what we consider critical faculties without being involved in the nitty-gritty of actual life situations. Today some people think that they can collapse autobiographical and biographical perspectives, following the glaring examples of politicians and movie stars who write "autobiographies" with the help of ghostwriters' biographical perceptions. For the most part, the result is neither good autobiography nor insightful biography, however. Basically, even the most optimistic collapsing of the two must evidence qualitative differences between autobiographical and biographical modes of apprehending the meaning of life and the world, even though both modes can rightly claim to be equally legitimate, though different, ways of perceiving reality.

ON TWO SETS OF PERCEPTIONS OF THE IMMIGRANT

All of us, in the process of growing up, learn how to appropriate simultaneously and almost intuitively a series of autobiographical and biographical perceptions, because each one of us is both an insider and an outsider of numerous coteries (e.g., family, professional guilds, cultural, linguistic, or religious groups, etc.) that constitute intricately overlapping concentric circles of our life. Like it or not, our all-too-fragile balance of autobiographical and biographical perceptions is severely threatened when we leave our familiar setting and move into a new situation, especially if we cross cultural lines. Such is the familiar tale of immigrants, who have to take up new sets of autobiographical and biographical senses in their newly adopted society, while their old modes of discerning the map of reality still cling to them. Indeed, probably the most demanding and disturbing—and yet little recognized—psychic burden to a vast majority of immigrants (except very young ones) is that of sorting out the old and new sets of autobiographical and biographical modes of perception. This problem is certainly far more disconcerting than the much-talked-about and well-known difficulties in adjusting to and adopting the new language and mores, as well as the legal, economic, educational, and other norms and practices of their newly adopted countries.

For years I have been mystified by many Americans' hyperbolic expectations of new immigrants. I use the expression "new immigrants" advisedly, because most Americans are proud of being descendants of "old immigrants" and as such are supposed to understand and appreciate some aspects of the tragic realities of more recent immigrants. But nowadays, in many cases, people here show little understanding or sympathy when they deal with new immigrants. Often, indeed too often, new immigrants are expected to "pay their dues" by demonstrating that they have made a complete break with their past and the lands and cultures of their ancestors. They are expected to behave and function as though they were average native-born Americans. On the other hand, on some special occasions, such as certain festivals involving non-American cultures or when prominent guests from other nations visit American cities, these new immigrants—who otherwise are expected to have been recycled into pristine 200 percent Americans—are called upon as resourceful experts of foreign cultures or instant emissaries of international goodwill. It is my sincere hope, however, based partly on my own personal experience, that new immigrants be more fully understood by descendants of old immigrants for what they are—products of two cultures, having a normal sense of attachment, coupled with appreciative as well as critical awareness, to both. Indeed, they are thus destined to have two sets of autobiographical and biographical modes of perceptions, which are simultaneously a curse and a blessing to their psyche.

ON THE INVISIBLE ESTABLISHMENT AND HYPHENATED AMERICANS

Obviously, the problem of autobiographical and biographical apprehension is a serious one for the American populace, which embraces a wide variety of ethnic, cultural, and religious groups within it. To be sure, according to some peoples' autobiographical sense, there has been—and an amazing number of individuals and groups still try to hang on to such an image—one dominant, full-fledged "American ethos," derived primarily from former Western European white, predominantly Protestant residual traditions. These traditions dominate other ethnic, cultural, and religious traditions and groups, which have their own respective sets of autobiographical and biographical perceptions. The latter are considered less than fully and genuinely American elements and are often called ghettos or marginal groups. In a sense, Americans learned nothing new from Alexis de Tocqueville (1805–59), famous French historian, who in the 1830s observed that there are three "racial groups"—Native-Americans, Euro-Americans, and African-Americans—cohabitating in the territory of the United

States. However, according to the autobiographical sense of the majority of the Euro-American dominant group, what Tocqueville called "racial groups" were interpreted mentally and immediately in effect as "social classes." The notion of "class" penetrated deeply into the American social fabric, whereby the hierarchical model of "color caste" in interracial relationships found its counterpart in the oppressive pattern of religious bigotry, discriminating against certain hyphenated Americans as well as Jews, Roman Catholics, and other religious groups. In other words, what the prevailing group (or class) affirmed as an egalitarian, democratic polity ("all men are created equal"), offering a haven to anybody seeking freedom and opportunity, on one level, unwittingly spawned a series of marginal groups of peoples who cannot be easily assimilated into an idealized American social and cultural pattern on the dominant group's terms. Inevitably, one finds profound tension in American history between two major types of autobiographical-biographical perceptions—one representing the prevalent group and the other representing the marginal groups, especially the hyphenated Americans.

As to the so-called marginal groups in general, it is my personal observation and experience that their coherence is greatly exaggerated by outsiders (based on their biographical perspective, one might say). Let me cite a concrete example of an ethnic minority group. I happen to know something about the Japanese-American community, which has developed out of the social/cultural/linguistic/legal/economic community of Japanese immigrants in the United States. Largely ignored by the Japanese government, and barely tolerated by American officials, those Japanese immigrants, ineligible for naturalization by American law until recently (like other Asiatic immigrants), resorted to communal organizations of their own for survival as much as for mutual encouragement and fellowship. Understandably, all kinds of professional, religious, recreational, and other groups were represented in those communities. There were also at least three types of peoples within such communities: (1) those who intended to return to Japan after making some money, (2) those who were determined to settle in this country, immigrants usually referred to as *Isseis* ("first generation"), and (3) their children, called *Niseis* ("second generation"), who were American citizens.

As far as their orientation and outlook are concerned, the first group of people (who intended to return to Japan) did not face any complicated problem, whereas the second group of people, like other immigrant groups, were saddled with two (Japanese and American, in their case) sets of autobiographical and biographical modes of perception, and they often felt caught between two cultures and value systems. The third group, Americans of Japanese descent, had by far the knottiest orientation, which was not what it appeared to outsiders, even to their *Issei* parents. Some of these Japanese-Americans, not sure of their own senses, suffered from severe cases of identity crisis. At the root of their mental and psychic uncertainty and agony was the tension between two cultural traditions, but be it noted that what they knew of Japanese tradition was once removed from the living entity in Japan and was mediated primarily by their own immigrant parents and embodied in the Japanese community in America. For the most part, their perceptions of autobiographical and biographical modes, which were very American, molded by public education, their exposure to playmates, newspapers, radio, television, and so forth, could not be divorced from the impact of their parents and the Japanese community.

In all fairness, it should be pointed out that many of the mental burdens of Japanese-Americans were not of their own making. (Here I am referring to the particular problems of the *Niseis*, but I rather imagine that children of other immigrant groups have their own unique sets of problems.) United States law did not permit Japanese immigrants to be naturalized, so their young children, being citizens, became legal owners of their parents' shops and farms; therefore, their parents (de facto owners) officially worked for their children. However, these children did not view Japanese cultures and value systems autobiographically as their parents did, but rather as outsiders (i.e., as Americans), much to the bewilderment of their immigrant parents. It is not surprising, therefore, that the usual tension between parents and growing children grew out of issues rooted in differences between two cultures. Thus, caught between a dominant society, which did not accept them as full-fledged Americans, and the world of their parents, which could not fully understand them, average Japanese-Americans, who were too young to assert themselves before World War II, made the best of their unhappy lot in life. Most tragically, when war broke out, they were forcibly removed from their homes on the West Coast, losing most of their financial assets, without any due process of law, and were incarcerated with their noncitizen parents in various internment camps euphemistically called "Relocation Centers." In short, in a crucial moment, their American "citizenship" did not count—so the government policies vividly demonstrated to Japanese-Americans, and by implication, to members of other minority groups—in the eyes of the dominant society in their own country.

ON THE EROSION OF THE INVISIBLE ESTABLISHMENT AND RAINBOWIZATION OF THE UNITED STATES

Thus far, I have attempted to analyze the Japanese-American community—as much as possible "from inside"—hoping that it could serve, if anything, as one concrete example of the so-called marginal groups and minority groups, each one of which, to be sure, has its own particularities. It must also be acknowledged, however, that the character of American society, notably the relationship between the prevailing group (class) and marginal groups, has undergone considerable changes over the years. Although we cannot possibly cite all the pertinent factors that brought about or accelerated such changes, the following features should not be overlooked.

Polity

Rejecting traditional European notions that important good things descend from above, early Americans attempted to balance (a) the upward movement of political life—government by the people, (b) the downward movement of religion—divine grace, and (c) the horizontal thrust of culture/education. This balance was to enhance the three necessities of life—morality in political life, piety in religion, and knowledge/rationality in cultural life. Each of the three dimensions was to uphold and restrain the other two. In retrospect, it becomes evident that various liberalizing measures in American history (e.g., from Lincoln's Emancipation Proclamation to the 1964 Civil Rights Act, or ever-expanding suffrage, and/or simplifying immigration and refugee laws), despite some counteracting factors and practical difficulties in their implementation, are deeply rooted in the way the tripartite polity of this Republic was originally envisaged: To guarantee freedom and equality of all persons and just protection of all individuals under the law, at least in principle.

Education

In contradistinction from the two-tier system common in Europe and elsewhere, whereby only select youngsters are encouraged to choose schools that would prepare them for institutions of higher learning while the rest are given practical training for trades and professions, the American public school system has introduced and consistently followed the one-tier system whereby children of diverse financial, cultural, linguistic, and religious backgrounds, if they so choose, are given the same educational opportunities. And, notwithstanding numerous troubles and difficulties that have menaced education all these years, it has been one of the most equalizing factors in American society.

Immigration and In-Migration

The vitality of American society has been constantly refreshed and re-furbished by the coming of immigrants from other shores, even though U.S. immigration laws have been known for many of their negative measures, such as discriminating against certain groups on real or imagined grounds. Nevertheless, thanks to a great extent to immigration, the United States has been maintaining its position as one of the more populous nations of the world, together with India, China, and the Soviet Union. Inevitably, the infusion of various ethnic, cultural, linguistic, and religious groups (e.g., the Jewish, Roman Catholic, East Asian, Southeast Asian, Latin, and other groups) changes however slowly the face of America, enlarging the lower strata of society. Also significant is the in-migration of individuals and various groups within the United States, which is both cause and result of the high mobility of people in our time.

Religion: Separation of Church and State and Religious Liberty

This is not the occasion to rehearse the existence of the variety of religious patterns in American colonies before the Revolution. Briefly, the First Amendment separation of church and state clause in the U.S. Constitution precipitated and provided legal justification for the phenomenon of religious liberty in eighteenth-century America. To be sure, earlier in various colonies there might have been some informal practice of religious freedom among some groups that took the familiar "live and let live" attitude. But the axiom of religious liberty assumed that each of the Jewish and Christian groups (or any other religious group, for that matter, at least in principle) officially recognize de facto the principle of "monolatry" (implying the allegiance to one supreme deity, recognizing, however, other groups' prerogatives to adhere to their respective one supreme deity) as an outer meaning of their religions, while holding to "monotheism" (at least for Jewish and Christian groups) as an inner meaning of their faiths.

On the one hand, these factors, together with other far-reaching trends such as urbanization, industrialization, and secularization, played important roles in the erosion of the invisible establishment of the once-dominant WASP culture. On the other hand, they precipitated the "rainbowization" of American society by loosening up certain rigidities that traditionally enveloped the communal structures of ghettos, and minority and marginal groups. It should be noted that the more recent immigrant groups, such as those from Latin America or Southeast Asia, still tend to hang on to a self-protected shell of rigidity. However, other groups that have existed here for a longer period have become for all intents and purposes fraternal, philanthropic, recreational, and/or mutual aid societies with more flexible "revolving-door" policies than the tightly organized ethnic/cultural/linguistic/legal communities of decades ago. Also, today many individuals simultaneously belong to a variety of other organizations as well, judging from the membership lists of, for example, the Chicago Japanese-American Council, the Japan America Society (with a large number of members who are not of Japanese descent), the Japanese Chamber of Commerce and Industry of Chicago (geared to the representatives of commercial firms from Japan), and the Asian-American professional, civic, political, and recreational groups (with members who are descendants of other Asian immigrants). I am told of census figures showing that in 1980 alone 20 percent of all Asian-Americans in California were married to a partner of a different ethnic or racial group, reflecting the national trend that Asian-American communities are not as isolated today as they once were, even just ten years ago. It should be noted, however, that there is still a long way to go before gaps between the prevailing group (class) and the marginal groups in this country are lessened to a significant degree. To be sure, certain individuals of minority backgrounds have by now broken into more visible academic, technical, and professional arenas in society, and not a few have accumulated considerable wealth. Some members of nonwhite ethnic backgrounds have become elected officials. But mentally, psychologically, and psychically, those who live in the orbit of the now-disintegrating world of the WASP and those who belong to marginal groups are still very much apart, each side not having altered to a significant degree its inherited set of autobiographic and biographic modes of perception.

ON ECCLESIASTICAL AND NONECCLESIASTICAL FACETS OF CHRISTIAN HERITAGE

It may sound strange for me to discuss at this juncture the métier of the "Christian tradition" of the marginal group. Of course, churches have played significant roles, religiously and in other ways, in the African-American community as well as in some other groups. My particular concern at this moment, however, is not to reassess the Christian tradition in all marginal groups, but to reflect on it in the Asian-American community, more particularly, the Japanese-American community. It must be admitted that the Christian fellowship (not to be only or even primarily equated with Christian ecclesiastical institutions) in the Asian-American context thus far has been a tiny sub-subgroup within a numerically small ethnic and cultural group. Even then, this insignificant minority within a minority group, if motivated spiritually and intellectually, can turn out to be an effective instrument in retrieving creative, reflexive, and prophetic Christian insights regarding love and justice; can be a small but alert harbinger within Christendom in American culture and society; and can even play a modest but important role in discerning and articulating religious reality in global human experience.

As far as can be ascertained, Christian groups in Asian immigrant communities on the West Coast have had unusually checkered and multidimensional activities from the latter end of the nineteenth century. As is well known, unlike various European immigrant groups, their counterparts from Asia were not easily absorbed into American society, especially because historically they arrived on this side of the ocean after the Civil War, an event that had made America acutely race conscious. The United States adopted a series of measures against Asiatic immigrants, so they not only were barred from naturalization but were discouraged from participation in the broader social, cultural, and economic life. In this situation, many Christian groups played a variety of roles, offering worship services in vernacular languages and serving as centers of social, recreational, and philanthropic programs, which were provided partly as expressions of Christian love for fellow human beings and partly as a means of proselytizing. With the coming of their children, the Christian groups among Japanese immigrants, as among other Asiatic newcomers, entered another phase, adding a new dimension. Inevitably, the ethos of the first generation church groups, often characterized by a simplistic evangelical piety, the temperance movement, and rigid moralism, had to be modified by the educational, social, and recreational needs of children. English-speaking volunteers had to be recruited to conduct church school classes and other activities for young people, such as scouting programs. How to meet simultaneously the needs of the older and younger generations presented serious problems, and most Christian leaders felt they were not adequately prepared for meeting the ever-growing demands in such a rapidly changing situation.

It must be candidly acknowledged, however, that it is quite common for any religious group to be oriented simultaneously to diverse objectives, thereby often being pulled in opposing directions. It is taken for granted that there are at least three related but different levels of meanings attached to all religions, including Christianity: (1) religion per se, usually consisting of an ecclesiastical component (dealing with faiths and spiritual matters, cults, doctrines, sacred books, etc.) and a nonecclesiastical facet (e.g., morality in practical living, service to others, etc.); (2) religion as a cultural system; and (3) a religiously inspired (or rooted or oriented) sociopolitical order. All religions assert that human beings, in order to be really human, must see all existence in relation to Ultimate Reality, however differently it is understood, and such an affirmation is the very cornerstone of the first level of meaning, both its ecclesiastical and nonecclesiastical dimensions. On the second level, religion shapes and nurtures culture, which is the domain of values, arts, and imagination. On the third level, religion is integrally related, implicitly or otherwise, to the actual sociopolitical structures and organizations. Like it or not, the greatest temptation for any religion is to resort to "ecclesiasticism," which would view all aspects of religious tradition, including the nonecclesiastical facet of the first level, culture (second level), and sociopolitical order (third level) as the legitimate and proper sphere of only the ecclesiastical component of the first level of religious meaning. To be sure, ecclesiastical and nonecclesiastical dimensions of religion often point in opposite directions, but it is the paradoxical task of religion to preserve, without artificially compromising on either side, the integrity of both dimensions.

It is worth repeating here that the perennial temptation for ecclesiasticism is to develop an unwarranted presumption of unified meaning-structure, insinuating that all aspects of nonecclesiastical dimensions of religion, as much as life itself, must be completely subservient to the behest of the ecclesiastical institution and/or its clerical leadership. On this score, Christianity in the West has made double or triple somersaults historically. For example, at one time, the faithful were advised to hold two realms separately but in balance—to render "unto Caesar the things that are Caesar's" and "unto God the things that are God's." After the fourth century, when Christianity was made the religion of the empire, however, the faithful were expected to express their allegiance to God and Caesar concurrently, by means of resolute submission to Caesar, who now reigns over the ecclesiastical leadership as well. Strangely enough, this basic formula was not abandoned when monarchy as such was toppled by other forms of political power. It continued to be assumed that all citizens should owe supreme, and almost semireligious, allegiance to the state. Significantly, as mentioned earlier, only in early America was it understood that (1) ecclesiastical Protestantism (which was the dominant religion among the colonists) was not to dominate but to coexist with (2) the semireligious political entity of the Republic (characterized by someone as a "religion wearing a secular mask") and (3) cultural Protestantism, each supporting but also checking the other two dimensions. And, as is well known, the second and third dimensions of American life were usually combined and called "civil religion" by sociologists. Clearly, the eighteenth-century American principle of religious liberty (as much as the theory of the separation of church and state) had been nurtured both by the ecclesiastical and nonecclesiastical (civil) religious traditions, and certainly had not been spawned primarily by ecclesiastical Protestantism alone.

In a way, the erosion of the invisible establishment of the dominant WASP ethos precipitated the breaking down of the vision that had held together the intricate balance of the (1) ecclesiastical, (2) sociopolitical, and (3) cultural dimensions of American religion. Understandably in this situation, Jewish, Catholic, and Protestant ecclesiastical groups became imbued with sectarian ecclesiasticism, according to whose rhetorics the ecclesiastical religion singlehandedly had nurtured the spiritual life of colonial America. They were determined again to reshape the Republic according to their designs.

Ironically, this kind of presumptuous, self-authenticating but hollow rhetoric characteristic of various denominational churches was "inhaled" by many Christian traditions in marginal groups, especially in the immigrant communities, as epitomized by the churches in Asian-American communities on the West Coast. Thus, notwithstanding their noble intentions, coupled with exaggerated spiritual and philanthropic goals, various Christian institutions in Asian-American communities have remained ineffective religious fellowships barely staying alive institutionally by offering a variety of practical programs catering to men and women, old and young, of their particular segregated communities. To be sure, those Christian groups maintain nominal relationships with their respective denominations in North America, but so far their religious, social, cultural, or political impacts on those denominations and/ or American society have been practically nil. Even within the confines of their own ethnic-based communities, they tend to shy away from controversial issues and stress narrowly defined religious functions (e.g., worship, church school, etc.), offering conventional wisdom and

nonpolemical activities for their members. It is not surprising, therefore, that their members very rarely (except socially) meet members of
non-Christian religious groups within the same communities. In short,
for the most part, the autobiographical sense of Asian-American Christians has been conditioned primarily by two factors—denomination
and ethnic affiliation.

ON THE DEBATE BETWEEN ONE SINGLE AMERICAN TRADITION VS. PLURALISM

The discussion of ethnic, racial, cultural, and other minority groups
often gives a misleading impression that members of these groups are
doomed to live and die within the boundaries of the "givenness" of their
communities alone. Of course, I hope I have more than casual sympathy
with, and understanding of, those who feel that their lives are boxed
into their segregated communities or who reduce all the major troubles
of our society to the evil of racism. Also, I think I am painfully aware
myself that the suffering, humiliation, and frustration caused by racial
discrimination will not go away tomorrow; in fact, they probably will
not disappear entirely for generations, in spite of all the efforts made by
many individuals and groups along the objectives of civil rights. But I
do firmly believe at the same time that members of ethnic or racial
minority groups (the so-called hyphenated Americans) are genuine full-
fledged Americans and, like it or not, are destined to shoulder as much
as all other citizens both the shortcomings and strengths of America as
citizens of this Republic. In other words, their autobiographical senses
must simultaneously and existentially be directed to and rooted in both
American society and their ethnic minority communities.

Such a double-edged autobiographical mode of perception must
be securely grasped by Christians of, say, Asian-American ancestry. This
is partly because an increasing number of Asian-Americans intentionally
have now only tenuous connections with Asian-American communities
as such; and even in the traditional ethnic communities on the West
Coast, churches are no longer monopolized by just one ethnic group
alone but are expected to serve individuals and groups of various backgrounds who happen to live in the immediate neighborhood. And I am
aware that more persons of Asian-American background are taking active part in all sorts of enterprises of various denominations. I trust,
however, that they will not equate "Christian vocations" only with
"denominational vocations." It should be noted that this principle is to be
adhered to not only by Christians of Asian-American or other minority

group backgrounds, but by all Christians. However, in view of their and their parents' unhappy experiences in this country—derived to a great extent by America's loss of balance among ecclesiastical, sociopolitical, and cultural dimensions of religion (in a large sense of the term)—it is my fervent hope that Christians of Asian-American and all other ethnic and racial minority groups will more readily comprehend and capture the wisdom and necessity of retrieving the invisible but realistic equilibrium of a tripartite scheme—namely, piety in religion, morality in political life, and knowledge-rationality in culture—without, however, any prevailing group or class posing as the guardian, thereby monopolizing such a scheme (as was the case of the WASP in the past).

Not so long ago in a television interview, a reporter asked Richard Nixon for his comments on the rising nations in Eastern Europe and East Asia. The former president commented that none of the other nations, however wealthy or strong today, are real superpowers like the United States, because they do not have nuclear power. Similarly, I know many people who argue about America's superiority and greatness in terms of economic might and excellence in technology and industry. Although I can readily see what all these people are driving at, I do hope that we will not be overly impressed by only the visible accomplishments of America. And from my perspective as a naturalized citizen, concerned as I am with the religious health of the country, I will strongly advocate the crucial significance of the invisible balance among religious, sociopolitical, and cultural dimensions of our national life, which was believed by early Americans to be the *raison d'être* of this Republic.

Apparently, all Americans, regardless of their religious commitment or lack of it, are caught by two diametrically opposed views—a utopian notion of America as a melting pot and a view of extreme pluralism. The former was represented by the so-called Americanization movement that developed after the outbreak of World War I. Earlier it was believed that assimilation of different peoples (at least those from Europe) was an automatic process. As early as 1782, J. Hector St. John de Crèvecoeur asserted that, upon arriving at the American shore, a person of any ethnic or cultural background becomes simply an American. In his colorful language, the immigrant, he says, "leaving behind him all his ancient prejudices and manners, receives new ones from the new mode of life he has embraced, the new government he obeys, and the new rank he holds."[1] World War I, however, revealed that some new Americans still maintained cultural and emotional affiliations with their old countries (or two sets of autobiographical and biographical perceptions, in my language). The sudden realization of this fact prompted the government and civic leaders to organize programs to teach the essentials of American citizenship, such as the English language, American history, and the structures of American polity, to those who were considered not fully assimilated into American life. In their eagerness, however, some advocates of Americanization paid little attention to the complexity of the social, psychological, and cultural factors that are involved in the personal adjustment of many immigrants.

In the meantime, the decline of the Americanization movement, especially after the Great Depression, inevitably gave added impetus to the opposite view that the uniqueness of American democracy lay in its ethnic, cultural, and religious pluralism. Ironically, often many of the ecclesiastical denominational spokesmen, unwittingly or otherwise, gave endorsement to the pluralist principle, too. Although there are no doubt many shades of pluralism, some of the advocates of this view even insinuate that there is no such person as a typical American, for every American is a member of a certain separate group or community, and they strongly argue in favor of preserving different ethnic, religious, and cultural groupings within the boundary of American society. Evidently, to some people, such a debate between all-out, almost monolithic integration and extreme pluralism is important primarily as a theoretical issue; to members of ethnic, racial, and cultural minority groups, however, such a debate presents not only theoretical, but very pragmatic and existential questions that have immediate as well as far-reaching implications and consequences.

ON DIFFERENT PERCEPTIONS (SINGULARITY VS. PLURALISM) OF AMERICAN TRADITION

The above-mentioned controversy also presents a whole series of theoretical and practical disputes to American education, with legal, civic, social, economic, and political implications. It provokes debates between those who take for granted the existence of a single distinct American culture (most likely a carryover, with some modifications, from Western European tradition) and those who lean toward the view that American culture is essentially an uneasy composite of various disparate traditions that were inherited and brought to this country by different ethnic, racial, linguistic, and cultural groups. Although we cannot even superficially consider the seriousness of this issue on education in general, we should not overlook the relevance of this debate to "religious studies" programs (now mushrooming in private and state colleges and universities in North America) and "theological studies" in freestanding denominational seminaries and in some other institutions of higher learning.

For the most part, at least from my perspective, both religious studies and theological studies in North America tend falsely to equate domestic and global issues without making adequate distinctions between the task of dealing with cultural-religious backgrounds of Americans of, for example, Asian ancestry, which is clearly a domestic problem, and that of dealing with other religious and cultural traditions, which is essentially a global issue. Of course, it is impossible to generalize about religious studies programs, because no two of them are exactly alike. Some religious studies programs embrace within them Jewish studies, African-American studies, and/or womens' studies, while in other situations those specialized studies exist outside the programs of religious studies. In many instances, it is not always clear whether Jewish studies and African-American studies are directed to historical Judaism and African religious-cultural traditions or whether they are focused more on the religious issues of American Jewish communities and African-American communities. Also, unfortunately not many institutions are prepared at the moment to sort out as to how to proceed with both Islamic studies on a global basis and the study of Black Muslims in North America.

The case of theological studies is more complicated (I confine my discussion only to "Christian" theological studies, because my knowledge of Jewish and other theological studies is practically nil), because most theological studies have not squarely confronted theological problems in connection with ethnic or cultural communities in North America; many of them tend to stick to their stock in trade, notably promoting funding for African-American or Hispanic ministerial candidates. (There have been some attempts made to deal with theological problems pertaining to some ethnic or cultural backgrounds, e.g., Asian and Pacific Americans, Korean immigrants, etc., but those programs often confuse the domestic and global issues.) For the most part, theological studies are more sensitive to hyphenated Americans' or marginal communities' sociological, economic, and political problems than to their theological problems. More often than not, theological studies, influenced as they are by the strong impact of denominationalism and ecclesiasticism, equate—even in the context of ethnic or cultural minority groups—Christian tradition only with the activities of institutional churches.

Although it is far from my intention to discuss various aspects of the study of non-Christian religions at this time, I must at least applaud the good intention of religious studies programs in various North American colleges and universities to expose students to different religious traditions of the global community. I am concerned, however, with two issues that religious studies programs can ill afford to ignore. First is the tendency of many of those who are in religious studies to overlook the relevance of the study of one religion (e.g., Judaism, Buddhism, Islam, or Christianity) on the ground that it is too narrow and subjective. Granted, each religion, especially when it is studied by its adherents, tends to stress its self-authenticating logic, giving the impression that its teaching is the most unbiased truth (which incidentally is all too often a common trait of Christian theological studies). Nevertheless, there are legitimate reasons—often not fully explored by theologians, however—why one religion can unfold more adequately than many religions the wholeness of religious reality, especially demonstrating piercing insights into the inner meaning of religion, which is not altogether accessible to the more objective (and thus inevitably external) approach of religious studies. Second is the questionable and widely held assumption that Western approaches (philosophical, religious, historical, social-scientific, etc.) to religion consist of the most adequate, universal logics, symbols, and methods, so that all that non-Western peoples have to do is to present their religions as "data" for Western scholars to analyze and interpret for them as well as for us. There is hardly ever the realization that non-Western and non-Christian religions and cultures are based on very different (at least from Western) conventions of dividing and perceiving human experience and the nature of reality.

ON INTERRELIGIOUS DIALOGUE VS. SIMULTANEOUS MONOLOGUE

This may be an appropriate occasion to reflect upon various enterprises now called interfaith and intercultural dialogues, which have come to be a favorite intellectual activity among many scholars of theological and religious studies in our time, especially in the West. It was probably fortuitous that three noteworthy phenomena—namely, the end of Western colonialism in Asia, the loss of missionary incentive of Christian churches in the West, and the sudden popularity of dialogues—took place almost simultaneously following World War II. It is not surprising, therefore, that some adherents of Asian religions across the ocean try to find causal connections among these three phenomena. In the West, too, an amazing number of people seem to feel that the dialogue procedure came into being in order to rectify the past mistakes made in the missionary approach to adherents of non-Christian religions. It should be stressed, however, that although these three phenomena are connected, they are not necessarily *causally* connected. Certainly, evangelism (or missionary witness) and dialogue are two separate, autonomous, and equally legitimate enterprises, and they must be independently, though in many cases simultaneously, pursued. Of the two, my greater concern at this point is to reflect on the significance of dialogue, which is not adequately understood, rather than on evangelism, with which most people are better acquainted (even though their reactions, positive or negative, to this endeavor may be very biased, too).

The term *dialogue* could mean different things to different persons. In the main, it refers mostly to a conversation or an exchange of views and opinions in the hope of ultimately reaching agreement. Such a notion of dialogue, hopefully expecting to reach agreement ultimately, presents an almost insurmountable problem to an interreligious (similarly to an intercultural) exchange of views, because each tradition has both inner and outer meanings, as mentioned earlier, and because an insider's autobiographical understanding of the inner meaning of his or her tradition is usually based on a self-authenticating logic, which probably would not make any sense to outsiders. Thus, in a conversation between two persons—for example, a convinced Christian and a convinced Buddhist—if they both make statements based solely on inner meanings of their faith, which they approach autobiographically, their exchange of views will not likely have any hope of ultimately reaching agreement. And yet, this is precisely what I term "simultaneous monologue," which is advertised widely but erroneously as dialogue nowadays. I am not belittling the value of such simultaneous monologues altogether, because in such situations, conversation partners on both sides become familiar with the other side's religious dialectics, and sometimes it is known that outsiders might stumble into hidden meanings that insiders unwittingly neglect.

But I am very much afraid that even a stimulating simultaneous monologue-dialogue harbors happy but unrealistic illusions. Let me cite two concrete examples.

1. I happen to know, and greatly admire, the erudition and seriousness of the so-called Kyoto school of philosophers. Most of them are convinced Buddhists, but they are well versed with Christian (Roman Catholic, Russian Orthodox, Protestant) theologies as well as with Greek, German, French, and Anglo-American philosophies. In the words of Y. Takeuchi, a leading contemporary scholar of this school:

"Adopting Western methods, utilizing Western categories, and at the same time criticizing both, [these Kyoto philosophers] endeavour to find a new way to express their original philosophical insights and often, in view of the results so far achieved, their own life and world views, nurtured in the tradition of Oriental thought."[2] Recently, many of the Kyoto philosophers' books have been translated into English, German, and French, much to the joy of many Western Christian theologians, who learn from these writings a great deal not only about Asian, especially Buddhist, traditions but also about Christian theology and Western philosophy. My own uneasiness, however, lies in the fact that Kyoto philosophers and Christian theologians find more agreement in terms of underlying Greek ontology and Western metaphysics, both of which they appropriate, than about the religious meanings of Christian and Buddhist religions. Equally questionable is the exaggerated wishful thinking of some Western scholars who try to find hastily the "point of contact" (Anknuepfungspunkt) between Judeo-Christian and Eastern religions, with unwarranted assumptions that Western language, logics, and rhetorics are the only and the best media of interreligious dialogues. No wonder they are eager to find Buddhists or Hindus, for example, who are sufficiently Westernized enough to carry on interreligious dialogues in Western theoretical frameworks. Curiously, they have no intention of reversing the procedure by carrying on dialogues using non-Western symbols, syntaxes, theories of knowledge, and hermeneutics that have not already been Westernized.

2. The second example represents familiar quests by different religionists who get excited by discovering some similarities in theoretical or practical traits crossing religious and cultural lines. I am not here referring to the many features of doctrinal, scriptural, or liturgical commonalities and/or affinities among the three monotheistic traditions of Judaism, Christianity, and Islam, because that is a very special and too large a subject for me to discuss in this context. Rather, I am thinking of more unlikely resemblances and parallels, say, between the Christian and Indian traditions of grace, as pointed out by Rudolf Otto, or between Luther's approach and the Japanese Pure Land Buddhists' utter dependence on Amida's mercy, as observed by Hans Haas and many recent Western and Japanese scholars. When we are confronted by these actual apparent similarities of certain features across historic religious lines, prudence should caution us to differentiate sharply those cases in which we can plausibly trace connections based on known encounters of different religious traditions (e.g., Northwest India prior to the beginning of the common era, where A. L. Basham

and many other scholars affirm that Persian Zoroastrian notions of the savior motif penetrated Hindu and Buddhist religiosities) and other cases where similarities of different religious features can be attributed to the simultaneous emergence of similar phenomena. And, although we discover that we have many cases of accidental or casual similarities, we have to be extremely judicious not to pursue what we like to think of as dialogues on the basis of these scattered similarities, however tempting they may be.

ON THE STEPS TOWARD "DIALOGUE"

How then can we proceed with interreligious dialogue? Unfortunately, there are no widely accepted road maps to guide us in this uncharted sea. And, although I have no grandiose proposal that may be termed as something like the "canon of dialogue," it may be worthwhile for me to share my own personal reflections on the matter, because this quest has been close to me both academically and existentially. Incidentally, my reflection must begin with a strange confession. That is, after studying the history of religions (*Religionswissenschaft*) professionally for many years, I now agree wholeheartedly with Mircea Eliade's considered opinion that "it is unfortunate that we do not have at our disposal a more precise word than 'religion' to denote the experience of the sacred."[3] But because we have not found a better term, I will persist in using the term *religion* to refer to the totality of human experience vis-à-vis existence in this mysterious cosmos. Indeed, religion, according to Hocking,

> has promised to give the human individual the most complete view of his [or her] destiny and of himself [or herself]. It projected that destiny beyond the range of human history. It speaks for "the whole"—a totality discernible only by thought—and a presumed ultimate source of right guidance. It provides standards of self-judgment not alone in terms of behavior, as does the law, but also in terms of motive and principle—of the inner man which the state cannot reach.[4]

We must remind ourselves in this connection that the religious community—be it Jewish, Christian, Buddhist, Islamic—is an empirical institution one step removed from religion as such. This obvious distinction has been often ignored by religious people, especially by Christians who tend to equate Christianity so thoroughly with the church. It is worth noting that, although existing within a particular time and space, the religious community or tradition must nevertheless attempt to articulate and transmit its understanding of the truth-claims of religion to the present generation in order to interpret—without falling into the pitfall of overtly sectarian rhetoric—the meaning of contemporary events in light of transhistorical, transnational, and transcendental references. Ironically, however, empirical religious communities or traditions have not been particularly willing or successful in exploring and explicating how each of them has been trying, with varying degrees of success, to unfold and embody the wholeness (without distorting or misrepresenting) of the invisible religious reality.

Given this situation, it would be foolhardy for a Christian insider of empirical Christian tradition and community, for example, to make a statement based on his autobiographical understanding of the inner meaning of Christianity, such as *extra ecclesiam nulla salus* ("no salvation outside the church")—which was based on the self-authenticating logic, common to one's family—in the context of interreligious dialogues. This misguided assumption, incidentally, was one of the greatest weaknesses of the past Christian missionary approach to non-Christians, especially because most simplistic missionaries knew only the "inner Christian lingo," which they expected to have direct universal meaning to outsiders. Actually, the reaction of non-Christians to this kind of one-sided approach of many Christian missionaries was, as Tillich astutely observed, "not so much that they reject the Christian answer *as answer*, as that their human nature is formed [by their own autobiographical and biographical understandings of inner and outer meanings of their own traditions] in such a way that they do not ask the questions to which [Christianity] gives the answer. To them the Christian answer is not an answer, because they have not asked the questions to which [empirical] Christianity is supposed to give the answer."[5] I quote Tillich's assessment of the obvious fallacy of misguided past Christian missionary approaches because similarly one-sided complacent logics on both sides of dialogue partners have often destroyed the very meaning of interreligious dialogue.

Unfortunately, the vogue of dialogue has often been based on the erroneous and self-deceiving notion that we have a ready-made common cultural background, what German friends call *gemeinsamen Bewusstseinsbestand*, crossing empirical religious and cultural lines. Rather, our common task now is to work from scratch to establish and solidify the ground floor of a genuine interreligious dialogue. With this in mind, I take very seriously the following two steps, which will not in themselves automatically bring about actual dialogue, but will probably help us to inch along toward our lofty goal. The first has been traditionally resisted by many Christians, whereas the second has been spurned by many adherents of religions in Asia.

1. I have already mentioned the reluctance of many empirical religious communities, each one of whom has been persuaded by its own self-authenticating logic as the most unrivaled, truest tradition, to explore how genuinely each religious system has incorporated the full substance of underlying, invisible religious reality. Ironically, many Christians have taken the attitude historically that this way of assessing their religion is incongruous with the ethos of the Christian church, which—to be sure, according to the inner meaning of its heritage—was founded by divine mandate and not created by human initiative. Some of them are confident that the truth-claim of the inner meaning of Christianity, which they understand autobiographically, is so self-evident even to all outsiders that inasmuch as Christianity exists in its unique plane, it has nothing in common with all non-Christian traditions. Fortunately, not every Christian depends solely on such an autobiographical, self-authenticating sense of the inner meaning of empirical Christian tradition. Nathan Söderblom (1866–1931) of Uppsala is one of the most articulate spokesmen of *Religionswissenschaft*-inspired theology, which rejected the simplistic dogmatic assertion—based solely on the inner meaning of Christian tradition—that insists upon a preeminent place for Christianity in the religiously pluralistic world history. Thus he was persuaded that "'the general history of religion' (*Allgemeine Religionsgeschichte*) had achieved one result above all: to show that *religion, though multiform, actually is one interlocking entity, 'an interconnected series of phenomena, of which Christianity is also a part.'*"[6] For that reason, Söderblom made every effort to perceive the nature of religious reality with its diversity, as epitomized by his writings on animism, power, tabu, mana, revelation, prophetology, holiness, and so forth, and at the same time attempted to explore how specific empirical religions, being parts of the whole, unfolded the wholeness of religious reality as such. I share his conviction that sharing, cooperating—with the willingness to engage in mutual criticism and edification among different empirical religious traditions, each trying to analyze and assess its own theoretical and practical superstructure—rather than engaging in simultaneous monologue, based upon each tradition's autobiographical understanding of the inner meaning of itself, seems to be a more constructive first step toward the far-reaching objective of pursuing dialogue. It is a matter of regret that this way of laying the groundwork for genuine dialogue has been neglected by many dialogicians, especially by those in the Christian tradition.

2. The second step, which also in my opinion is a constructive first step to dialogue, pertains to stringent self-criticism of each empirical religious tradition vis-à-vis the three layers of meaning of religion mentioned earlier: (1) the level of the narrow sense of religion, embracing both ecclesiastical and nonecclesiastical facets, (2) religion as unfolded in culture, and (3) the religiously inspired sociopolitical order. Historically, however, many religious traditions in Asia have on the one hand insisted on the amorphous, seamlessness of all aspects (sociopolitical, cultural, spiritual, etc.) of life, and yet on the other hand have leaned toward a restricted meaning of religion in terms of spiritual and ecclesiastical activity and/or institutional form. Thus medieval Europeans' perceptions of the three pivotal, divinely ordained institutions (i.e., *sacerdotium* [church], *imperium* [state], and *studium* [university] or early Americans' sense of three kinds of religious life (i.e., ecclesiastical, political, and cultural) are quite foreign to many traditional non-Christian religions. Thus they recognize, of course, the religious import of spiritual liberation, compassion, and/or holy wisdom, for instance, but freedom, justice, equality, fraternity, and so forth, are conceived of largely as religiously once-removed human-civic virtues.

It should be noted that one of the precious legacies the modern West left in Asia is the keen sense of freedom as a necessary ingredient of being fully human.[7] And I have high hopes that various religious traditions—including those of Asia that traditionally were indifferent to dividing disparate dimensions of life or were reluctant to hold spirituality and morality, compassion and justice, or spiritual/cultural/social/political dimensions of life too closely—will now pursue rigorous examinations as to how they correlate the religious métier of each dimension of life. And here again, sharing, cooperating, with the willingness to engage in mutual criticism and edification in this enterprise among various empirical religious traditions, will be a constructive step toward the goal of dialogue. In this context, Christian dialogicians should be aware, however, that the provincial Western convention of dividing human experience into a series of semiautonomous pigeonholes is not the most reliable tool in interreligious dialogue.

NOTES

Preface
1. Arnold Toynbee, *Christianity Among the Religions of the World* (New York: Charles Scribner's Sons, 1957), 11.
2. Adolph Keller, *Christian Europe Today* (New York: Harper & Brothers, 1942), 4.

Chapter 1: The Asian Christian Perspective of Christianity
1. The four chapters in Part I were published earlier under the general title "The Asian Christian Tradition—with Special Reference to Japan," *Anglican Theological Review* (1989–1990) 71, no. 3: 241–250; 71, no. 4: 406–424; 72, no. 1: 62–84; 72, no. 2: 175–198. I would like to thank the editor of *ATR* for permission to reprint these articles here. Furthermore, each of the four chapters was based on an earlier article. For example, Chapter 1 is an adaptation of my "Divided We Stand," in J. M. Kitagawa, *Religion in Life* 27/3 (Nashville: Graded Press, 1958), 335–351. The publisher graciously permitted me to revise my earlier article.
2. See J. M. Kitagawa, *The Quest for Human Unity: A Religious History* (Minneapolis: Fortress Press, 1990), 2–3.
3. Ibid., 3–4. This theme is also expounded in my Introduction to J. M. Kitagawa, ed., "Religious Studies, Theological Studies, and the University-Divinity School," forthcoming.
4. Bernard Lewis, *The Political Language of Islam* (Chicago: University of Chicago Press, 1988), 2.
5. J. M. Kitagawa, "Religious Visions of the Unity of Mankind," *Crossroads* (SWTS) (June 1988): 10.
6. Ibid., 12.
7. R. C. Zaehner, "Zoroastrianism," in *The Encyclopedia of Living Faiths*, ed. R. C. Zaehner (New York: Hawthorne Books, 1959), 209.
8. Cf. Ernst Benz, "The Theological Meaning of the History of Religions," *Journal of Religion* 41, no. 1 (January 1961): 5.
9. Robert M. Grant, *Religion and Politics at the Council of Nicaea* (Chicago: University of Chicago Press, 1973), 9.

10. Quoted in ibid., 12.
11. Reuben W. Smith, ed., *Islamic Civilization in the Middle East: Course Syllabus* (Chicago: University of Chicago—Committee on Near Eastern Studies, 1965), 40.
12. For more on this subject, see Gustave E. von Grunebaum, *Medieval Islam: A Study in Cultural Orientation* (Chicago: University of Chicago Press, 1946), 334–335.
13. Albert J. Nevin, "Patronato Real," in *Concise Dictionary of the Christian World Mission*, ed. S. Neill, G. H. Anderson, and J. Goodwin (Nashville: Abingdon Press, 1971), 474.
14. K. M. Panikkar, *Asia and Western Dominance* (London: George Allen & Unwin, 1959), 27.
15. For more on this fascinating subject, see René Grousset, *The Rise and Splendor of the Chinese Empire* (Berkeley: University of California Press, 1952), 247.
16. See Nigel Cameron, *Barbarians and Mandarins: Thirteen Centuries of Western Travelers in China* (New York and Tokyo: Walker-Weatherhill, 1970), esp. 90–106.
17. William W. Sweet, "Christianity in the Americas," in *A Short History of Christianity*, ed. A. G. Baker (Chicago: University of Chicago Press, 1940), 227.
18. H. Cnattingius, *Bishops and Societies* (London: SPCK, 1952), 4.
19. See Robert T. Handy, *A Christian America: Protestant Hopes and Historical Realities* (New York: Oxford University Press, 1971).
20. Cf. H. Richard Niebuhr, *Christ and Culture* (New York: Harper & Brothers, 1951), esp. chap. 2, "Christ Against Culture."
21. Much of this information is taken from Sir Reginald Coupland, *India: A Restatement* (New York: Oxford University Press, 1945), 42–70.
22. Stephen Neill, *The Christian Society* (New York: Harper & Brothers, 1952), 250.
23. Eugene A. Nida, *Customs and Cultures* (New York: Harper & Brothers, 1952), 253.
24. Robert K. Merton, *Social Theory and Social Structure* (New York: Free Press of Glencoe, 1949), 152, 153, 155, 157, 158.
25. Hendrik Kraemer, *The Christian Message in a Non-Christian World* (London: The Edinburgh House, 1938), 36.
26. See my discussion on "The Case of the Younger Churches," *Pastoral Psychology* 5, no. 45 (June 1954): 27–32.
27. Cf. J. M. Kitagawa, "Evanston—West Meets West?" *Occasional Bulletin*, Missionary Research Library, vol. 5, no. 8 (July 12, 1954).
28. Irving Kristol, "The 20th Century Began in 1945," *New York Times Magazine*, May 2, 1965, 25.

Chapter 2:   The Asian Christian Perspective in Global Revolution

1. Part of this section was originally published as "Imperialism, Racialism and the Christian World Mission: A Commentary on K. M. Panikkar's *Asia and Western Dominance*," *Overseas Mission Review* 6, no. 2 (Epiphany, 1961): 30–55.
2. This theme was more fully elaborated in J. M. Kitagawa, *Spiritual Liberation and Human Freedom in Contemporary Asia* (New York: Peter Lang, 1990).
3. Edward W. Said, *Orientalism* (New York: Random House, 1979), 1.
4. Ibid., 37.
5. William S. Haas, *The Destiny of the Mind: East and West* (London: Faber & Faber, 1956), 55.
6. Mircea Eliade, *The Two and the One*, tr. J. M. Cohen (London: Harville Press, 1965), 9.
7. Cf. Said, Orientalism, 42–43.
8. William Ernest Hocking was well known as chairman of the Commission of Appraisal of the so-called Laymen's Inquiry After One Hundred Years, which published *Re-Thinking Missions* (New York: Harper & Brothers, 1932). For his own views, see *Living Religions and a World Faith* (New York: Macmillan, 1940), and *The Coming World Civilization* (New York: Harper & Brothers, 1956).
9. F. S. C. Northrop, *The Taming of the Nations* (New York: Macmillan, 1952).
10. Most pertinent for our purpose are Paul Tillich's two books: *Christianity and the Encounter of the World Religions* (New York: Columbia University Press, 1963), and *The Future of Religions*, ed. J. C. Brauer (New York: Harper & Row, 1966).
11. Although Arnold Toynbee's numerous other writings are also important, we should at least mention his *Civilization on Trial* (New York: Oxford University Press,

1948), *The World and the West* (New York: Oxford University Press, 1953), and *Surviving the Future* (New York: Oxford University Press, 1971).

12. K. M. Panikkar, *In Two Chinas* (London: George Allen & Unwin, 1955), 179.

13. Panikkar, *Asia and Western Dominance.* The following paragraphs contain several quotations from this book. The page numbers cited are in parentheses and follow each quotation.

14. In this section, I am trying to revise and update parts of my earlier article "Glimpses of the Christian Church in Asia," *Overseas Mission Review* 5, no. 2 (Epiphany 1960): 5–52.

15. (Author unknown), *The Revolt in the Temple* (Colombo, Sri Lanka: Sinha Publications, 1953), 499.

16. J. M. Kitagawa, ed., *The History of Religions: Understanding Human Experience* (Atlanta: Scholars Press, 1987), 163.

17. U Khyaw Than made many other thoughtful comments to the author in the winter of 1959 in Rangoon, Burma.

18. International Missionary Council, *The Growing Church, Madras Series*, vol. 2 (New York: International Missionary Council, 1939), 276.

19. From the report of the Indian Ecumenical Study Conference, which was published in the Indian Journal of Theology 1, no. 2 (November 1952): 41–65. This report is the source of the following seven observations. Page numbers are noted in parentheses where applicable.

20. These quotations are taken from *Documents of the Three-Self Movement* (New York: National Council of the Churches of Christ in the U.S.A., 1963), 14–16.

21. David Tracy, "Some Reflections on Christianity in China," *Criterion* 21, no. 2 (Spring 1982): 20.

22. Quoted in *China Update: A Quarterly Newsletter* (Autumn 1988): 72.

23. Cf. Douglas J. Elwood, ed., *Asian Christian Theology: Emerging Themes* (Philadelphia: The Westminster Press, 1976).

24. Jose M. de Mesa, "Re-Thinking the Faith with Indigenous Categories," *Inter-Religio*, no. 13 (Summer 1988): 18.

25. Quoted in Elwood, *Asian Christian Theology*, 15.

Chapter 3: The Emergence of Christian Dilemma, with Special Reference to Japan

1. J. M. Kitagawa, "Some Reflections on Theology in Japan," *Anglican Theological Review* (October 1961): 1–19.

2. Although it is dated, the bibliography of Charles H. Germany, *Protestant Theologies in Modern Japan: A History of Dominant Theological Currents from 1920–1960* (Tokyo: IISR Press, 1965), 225–234, establishes the fact that many books and articles in Western languages were already appearing between 1961 (when my article appeared) and 1965.

3. Harold Isaacs, *Scratches on the Mind* (New York: John Day, 1958), 39.

4. For a fuller discussion of these issues, see my "Prehistoric Background of Japanese Religion," in J. M. Kitagawa, *On Understanding Japanese Religion* (Princeton: Princeton University Press, 1987), 3–40.

5. Muraoka Tsunetsugu, *Studies in Shinto Thought*, tr. D. M. Brown and J. T. Araki (Tokyo: Japanese National Commission for Unesco, 1964), 58.

6. Donald L. Philippi, tr., *Kojiki* (Tokyo: University of Tokyo Press, 1968), 28.

7. This system was called the *Manyō-gana*; it was a form of syllabry used in compiling a collection of poetry called the *Manyō* or *Manyō-shū* ("Collection of Myriad Leaves") and was the forerunner of the *hiragana* and *katakana*, the two syllabries that have been used until the present time.

8. Hans-Georg Gadamer, *Philosophical Hermeneutics* (Berkeley: University of California, 1976), 26.

9. Donald Keene, comp. and ed., *Anthology of Japanese Literature: From the Earliest Era to the Mid-Nineteenth Century* (New York: Grove Press, 1955), 19.

10. Quoted in *Chicago Maroon* 69, no. 60 (February 24, 1961): 2.

11. For a discussion of all these Buddhist schools, see Takakusu Junjirō, *The Essentials of Buddhist Philosophy* (Honolulu: University of Hawaii, 1947).

12. See Kitagawa, *On Understanding Japanese Religion*, xii.

13. For a fuller discussion of the Buddhist development during the Kamakura era, see J. M. Kitagawa, *Religion in Japanese History* (New York: Columbia University Press, 1966), chap. 3, "The Pure Land, Nichiren, and Zen," 86–130.

14. Those who are interested in this subject are referred to George Elison, *Deus Destroyed: The Image of Christianity in Early Modern Japan* (Cambridge: Harvard University Press, 1973, 1988).

15. Kitagawa, *Religion in Japanese History*, 139.

16. See Kitagawa, *On Understanding Japanese Religion*, xiii–xiv.

17. On this fascinating phenomenon—not dissimilar to the cases of the Muslims and Jews, who were forcibly converted to Catholicism in Spain during the fifteenth century, but who preserved their ancestral faiths sub rosa—see Kataoka Kenkichi, *Kakure Kirishitan: rekishi to minzoku* (*Hidden Christians: History and Customs*) (Tokyo: Nihon-hōsō-shuppan-kyōkai, 1967).

18. Ichikawa Sanki, "Foreign Influences in the Japanese Language," in Nitobe Inazō et al., *Western Influences in Modern Japan* (Chicago: University of Chicago Press, 1931), 141.

19. On other schools established by Western missionaries during the early Meiji period, see Winburn T. Thomas, *Protestant Beginnings in Japan: The First Three Decades, 1859–1889* (Tokyo and Rutland, Vt.: C. E. Tuttle, 1959), chap. 5, "Education," 96–116.

20. Quoted in ibid., 115.

21. Quoted in Marius B. Jansen, *Japan and Its World: Two Centuries of Change* (Princeton: Princeton University Press, 1980), 69.

22. Kishimoto Hideo, comp. and ed., *Japanese Religion in the Meiji Era*, trans. and adapted by John F. Howes (Tokyo: Obunsha, 1956), 241–242.

23. Ibid., 143.

24. Ibid., 202–204.

25. Thomas, *Protestant Beginnings in Japan*, 79.

26. Kishimoto, *Japanese Religion*, 242.

27. Thomas, *Protestant Beginnings in Japan*, 13–14.

28. There are now an abundance of studies of this movement. One might profitably consult R. Tsunoda et al., comp., *Sources of Japanese Tradition* (New York: Columbia University Press, 1958), the section on Uchimura Kanzō, pp. 847–856. Incidentally, Emil Brunner wrote a rhapsodic (not very critical) account of this movement in his article "A Unique Christian Mission: The Mukyokai ("Non-Church") Movement in Japan," in *Religion and Culture: Essays in Honor of Paul Tillich*, ed. W. Leibrecht (New York: Harper & Brothers, 1959), 287–290.

29. Raymond Hammer, *Japan's Religious Ferment* (New York: Oxford University Press, 1962), 118.

30. Quoted in Kishimoto, *Japanese Religion*, 207.

31. Ibid., 204.

32. Niebuhr, *Christ and Culture*.

33. Kishimoto, *Japanese Religion*, 302.

34. See Handy, *A Christian America*.

35. Hocking, *Living Religions and a World Faith*, 207; italics mine.

36. Quoted in Kishimoto, *Japanese Religion*, 197.

37. See Notto R. Thele "From Conflict to Dialogue: Buddhism and Christianity in Japan, 1854–1899" (Ph.D. diss., University of Oslo, 1982).

38. See Kitagawa, ed., *The History of Religions*, app., "The 1893 World's Parliament of Religions and Its Legacy," 353–368.

39. Quoted in Kishimoto, *Japanese Religion*, 265.

40. See Vera Micheles Dean, *The Nature of the Non-Western World* (New York: The New American Library, 1957).

Chapter 4: Christianity in Japan: Some Reflections

1. Gerardus van der Leeuw, *Religion in Essence and Manifestation: A Study in Phenomenology*, tr. J. E. Turner (London: George Allen & Unwin, 1938), 273.

2. M. A. C. Warren, "General Introduction" in Hammer, *Japan's Religious Ferment*, 10; italics mine.

3. Ibid., 5–6.

4. Haas, *The Destiny of the Mind*, 134.
5. See J. M. Kitagawa, s.v. "Japanese Philosophy (historical)," *Encyclopaedia Britannica*, 1966 ed., vol. 12, pp. 958G–959.
6. Takeuchi Yoshinori, s.v. "Japanese Philosophy (modern)," *Encyclopaedia Britannica*, 1966 ed., vol. 12, pp. 958J–959.
7. One of the best ways to understand Hatano's thought is to read *Hatano Seiichi Zenshū*, vol. 5, *Toki to Eien* (*Time and Eternity*) (Tokyo: Iwanami Shoten, 1949).
8. See Akimoto Mitarō, *Yamamuro Gumpei no Shōgai* ("Life of Yamamuro Gumpei—Commanding General of the Salvation Army in Japan," d. 1940).
9. Iinuma Jirō, "The History of Rural Gospel-Preaching in Modern Japan," *Kirisuto-kyō Shakai-mondai Kenkyū* (*The Study of Christianity and Social Problems*) 36 (March 1988): 149.
10. Tetsu Katayama, "Hachijūnen no Shōgai to Shinkō (My Life of Eighty Years and My Faith)," *Seikōkai Shimbun* (November 20, 1967).
11. Carl Michalson, *Japanese Contributions to Christian Theology* (Philadelphia: The Westminster Press, 1960).
12. Germany, *Protestant Theologies in Modern Japan*.
13. Ibid., 87.
14. Kumanó Yoshitaka, *Shumatsu-ron to Rekishi-tetsugaku* (*Eschatology and Philosophy of History*) (Tokyo: Shinkyō Shuppansha, 1949).
15. Michalson, *Japanese Contributions*, 52.
16. Germany, *Protestant Theologies in Modern Japan*, 127.
17. Quoted in Hammer, *Japan's Religious Ferment*, 176–177.
18. Cited in ibid., 175. Hammer also quotes the statement of William P. Woodard, who had worked in the SCAP: "Apparently the drafters [of the Constitution and the emperor's Rescript quoted above] were even willing to secularize the State [of Japan] completely rather than run any risk of a revival of Shinto as a national cult" (ibid., 177). Incidentally, the most reliable Western work on the SCAP's religious policy is William P. Woodard's volume *The Allied Occupation of Japan 1945–1952 and Japanese Religions* (Leiden, Neth.: E. J. Brill, 1972).
19. See Kitagawa, *On Understanding Japanese Religion*, 282.
20. "Nanzan Studies in Religion and Culture," including such volumes as Nishitani Keiji, *Religion and Nothingness*, tr. Jan Van Bragt (Berkeley: University of California Press, 1983), and Tanabe Hajime, *Philosophy as Metanoetics*, tr. Takeuchi Yoshinori (Berkeley: University of California Press, 1986).
21. See *Inter-Religio* (a newsletter published twice annually by the Nanzan Institute).
22. A statement quoted in Germany, *Protestant Theologies in Modern Japan*, 171.
23. Ibid., 172.
24. See my introduction "*Verstehen* and *Erlösung*" to Joachim Wach, *Introduction to the History of Religions*, ed. J. M. Kitagawa and G. Alles (New York: Macmillan, 1988), xi–xxxiv.
25. I elaborated this threefold scheme vis-à-vis Buddhism in J. M. Kitagawa, "Buddhism and Social Change," in *Buddhist Studies in Honor of Walpola Rahula*, ed. S. Balasooriya et al., (London: Gordon Fraser, 1980), 84–102.
26. Quoted in Germany, *Protestant Theologies in Modern Japan*, 191; italics mine.
27. Elwood, *Asian Christian Theology*, 60–61.
28. Available now in an English translation; see Kitamori Kazoh, *Theology of the Pain of God* (Richmond: John Knox Press, 1965).
29. Michalson, *Japanese Contributions*, 95.
30. Takeuchi Yoshinori, "Buddhism and Existentialism: The Dialogue Between Oriental and Occidental Thought," in *Religion and Culture*, 301.
31. Michalson, *Japanese Contributions*, 74.
32. Ibid., 95–96.
33. Germany, *Protestant Theologies in Japan*, 183. In a personal conversation with Katayama in Chicago after his cabinet was defeated by a more conservative Liberal Democratic Party (neither so liberal nor so democratic), which was supported by big-scale financiers, vote-hungry local politicians, and many in Washington who never made the proper distinctions between socialism and communism (but were concerned primarily with making Japan a strong anticommunist power in Asia), he

said that he was very disappointed with the political sense of the average Japanese Christians and church leaders.

34. I personally was flabbergasted when a certain high-ranking church leader commented on the volume *American Refugee Policy: Ethical and Religious Reflections*, ed. J. M. Kitagawa (New York: The Episcopal Church; Minneapolis: Winston Press, 1984), saying that Japan, being an ethnically more homogeneous country, is fortunate not to have such serious problems regarding the refugees as we have in America.

35. Germany, *Protestant Theologies in Japan*, 215.

36. Nitobe Inazō is well known as the author of *Bushidō*. A famous Quaker, a holder of doctorates both in jurisprudence and agricultural science, he was the principal of the First Higher School (*Daiichi Kōtō-gakko*) in Tokyo (which has produced a large number of scholars and leaders in modern Japan). Nitobe's (also Uchimura's) lectures on *Ningen-kyōiku* ("education for humanity") were not confined to academic circles. Nitobe was also a member of the House of Peers and Chairman of the Japanese Council of the Institute of Pacific Relations, and he served at one time as Under-Secretary General of the League of Nations in Geneva.

37. For nearly twenty years I have been talking about the importance of understanding the real significance of these new religions. See, for example, J. M. Kitagawa, "New Religions in Japan: A Historical Perspective," in *Religion and Change in Contemporary Asia*, ed. Robert F. Spencer (Minneapolis: University of Minnesota Press, 1971), 27–43.

38. Takenaka Masao, "Christian Art in Asia: Signs of a Renewal," in *Asian Christian Theology*, 161-173.

39. F. Sierksma, *The Gods As We Shape Them* (London: Routledge & Kegan Paul, 1960), 49; italics mine.

40. Jean Higgins, "East-West Encounter in Endō Shūsaku," *Dialogue and Alliance* 1, no. 3 (Fall 1987): 12–21.

41. In Japanese, Endō Shūsaku, *Chimmoku* (Tokyo: Shinch-o-sha, 1966); in English, Endō Shūsaku, *Silence*, tr. William Johnston (New York: Taplinger, 1969).

42. Higgins, "East-West Encounter," 16–17.

43. Elison, *Deus Destroyed*, 190.

44. Higgins, "East-West Encounter," 16–17.

45. I am paraphrasing these statements from the Japanese edition; Endō, *Chimmoku*, 221-223.

46. Endō, *Silence*, 259. I have substituted "you" and "your" as a more faithful translation than Johnston's "men" and "by men"; italics mine.

47. Endō, *Chimmoku*, 225. I am presenting a very literal translation in order to convey the nuance of Endō's literary language.

48. Ibid., 223.

49. Higgins, "East-West Encounter," 17.

50. Charles W. Iglehart, *A Century of Protestantism in Japan* (Tokyo and Rutland, Vt.: C. E. Tuttle, 1959), 346.

51. Ibid., 347.

Chapter 5:   The Saga of Asian-Americans

1. Franz Werfel, *The Song of Bernadette* (New York: Pocket Books, 1947).

2. Quoted in Milton R. Konvitz, *The Alien and the Asiatic in American Law* (Ithaca, N.Y.: Cornell University Press, 1946), 5–6. The following paragraphs contain several quotations from this book. The page numbers cited are in parentheses and follow each quotation.

3. See Morton Grodzins, *Americans Betrayed: Politics and the Japanese Evacuation* (Chicago: University of Chicago Press: 1949), 133, 284, 402.

4. Quoted in J. tenBroek et al., *Prejudice, War, and Constitution* (Berkeley: University of California Press, 1954), 263.

5. Quoted in Bradford Smith, *Americans from Japan* (New York: J. B. Lippincott, 1948), 180.

6. Konvitz, *The Alien and the Asiatic in American Law*, 248–249.

7. Grodzins, *Americans Betrayed*, vii.

8. *The New Encyclopaedia Britannica: Micropedia* 12:363.

9. D. J. Boorstin, *America and the Image of Europe* (New York: Meridian Books, 1960), 12–13.
10. Robert Maynard Hutchins, *No Friendly Voice* (Chicago: University of Chicago Press, 1936), 1.
11. Edward Shils, "The Culture of the Indian Intellectual," *The Sewanee Review* (April and June 1959): 45–46.
12. Ibid., 46.
13. From *A Little Anthology of Poems in Modern Japan*, tr. Hisakazu Kaneko (Tokyo: Hisakazu, 1973), 1–2.

Chapter 6: The Mass Evacuation: Recollections and Reflections

1. This section is based on my address on the assigned topic at Hillel Foundation, Chicago, in Spring 1980.
2. Claire Huchet Bishop, *France Alive* (New York: The Declan X. McMullen Co., 1947), 1–2.
3. Grodzins, *Americans Betrayed*, 2.
4. This section is based on an address, "The Legacy of the *Isseis*," given at St. Peter's Church, Seattle, on September 5, 1978.
5. This section is based on an article written in the Minidoka War Relocation Center in Hunt, Idaho, in October 1945, a few weeks before the camp closed. The text was published in *The Living Church* 111, no. 19 (November 4, 1945). I dedicate this section to the over 10,000 fellow evacuees who were "there" with me, 1942–45.
6. Daisuke Kitagawa, *The Race Relations and Christian Mission* (New York: Friendship Press, 1964), 67.
7. Ibid., 72–73.
8. *New York Times*, 28 August, 1990. According to "California Firm on View of War Internment," *New York Times*, 31 August, 1990, Ferguson's bill was soundly—60 to 4—defeated in the California Assembly. Similar attempts will no doubt be repeated in the future, however.
9. Konvitz, *The Alien and the Asiatic in American Law*, 123.
10. Ibid., 248.
11. Ibid., 244, 255.
12. *The Christian Century* 105, no. 1 (January 6–13, 1988): 32.
13. Quoted in *The Chicago Shimpo* 42, no. 8 (August 31, 1988).

Chapter 7: Religion(s), Community, Communication, and Faith: The Hebrew Paradigm of Christianity

1. See Part I, Chapter 1 of this volume.
2. Mircea Eliade, *Patterns in Comparative Religion*, trans. Rosemary Sheed (London: Sheed & Ward, 1958), xi.
3. Recall Bernard Lewis's statement quoted in Part I, Chapter 1, no. 5.
4. On this question, Hendrik Kraemer made some astute observations in his article "The Problem of Communication" in *Motive* 17, no. 6 (March 1957): 2–3.
5. Louis de la Vallée Poussin, *The Way to Nirvana* (Cambridge: Cambridge University Press, 1917), 138.
6. For more on Wilhelm von Humboldt, see Joachim Wach, *Essays in the History of Religions* (New York: Macmillan, 1988), 65–80.
7. Quoted in Harry E. Barnes et al., eds., *Contemporary Social Theory* (New York: D. Appleton-Century, 1940), 55.
8. Louis Wirth, *Community Life and Social Policy*, eds. E. W. Marvick and A. J. Reiss, Jr. (Chicago: University of Chicago Press, 1956), 10.
9. Van der Leeuw, *Religion in Essence and Manifestation*, 243.
10. Kraemer, "The Problem of Communication," 3.
11. Robert Redfield, *The Primitive World and Its Transformations* (Ithaca, N.Y.: Cornell University Press, 1953), 12–13.
12. Josephus, *Against Apion* 2, 82. I owe this quotation to Daniel J. Boorstin.
13. Van der Leeuw, *Religion in Essence and Manifestation*, 252.
14. James Muilenburg, "The Ethics of the Prophet," in *Moral Principles in Action*, ed. R. N. Anshen (New York: Harper & Brothers, 1952), 536.

15. Joachim Wach, *Sociology of Religion* (Chicago: University of Chicago Press, 1944), 348.
16. This notion of spiritual covenant was taken very seriously by the early Christians.
17. See J. A. MacCulloch, s.v. "Eschatology," in James Hastings, ed., *Encyclopaedia of Religion and Ethics*, 1951 ed., vol. 5, 281.
18. This passage was immediately followed by the most universalistic claim of Yahweh: "Before me no god was formed, / nor shall there be any after me. / I, I am the LORD, / and besides me there is no savior" (Isa. 43:10–11).
19. The tension between the primacy of the codified Torah and the primacy of existential religious experience has remained one of the most profound issues throughout the history of Judaism ever since.
20. J. M. Kitagawa, "A Historian of Religions Reflects Upon His Perspectives," *Criterion* 28, no. 2 (Spring 1989): 8.
21. Joseph R. Levenson, "'History' and 'Value': The Tensions of Intellectual Choice in Modern China," in *Studies in Chinese Thought*, ed. Arthur F. Wright (Chicago: University of Chicago Press, 1975), 146.

Chapter 8:   The Christian Church and Western Civilization
1. Edward J. Thomas, *The History of Buddhist Thought* (New York: Barnes & Noble, 1933, 1951), 14.
2. Among numerous works on the subject, the following two are noteworthy: Tor Andrae, *Muhammad, The Man and His Faith* (London: George Allen & Unwin, 1956); and Annemarie Schimmel, *And Muhammad Is His Messenger* (Chapel Hill: University of North Carolina Press, 1985).
3. Cited by Judah Goldin, "Early and Classical Judaism," in C. A. Adams, *A Reader's Guide to the Great Religions* (New York: Macmillan–Free Press, 1965), 310.
4. Morton Scott Enslin, *Christian Beginnings* (New York: Harper & Brothers, 1938), 154. It should be noted, however, that the compilers of the New Testament must have rearranged some materials in order to present a more convincing argument about the greatness of Jesus' personality. No doubt, transferring a postresurrection narrative of the transfiguration story to a pre-Easter context was not farfetched for the mentality of the compilers of the Gospels. See John Dominic Crossan's view on this particular point in *Four Other Gospels* (Minneapolis: Winston/Seabury Press, 1985).
5. L. S. Thornton, *The Common Life in the Body of Christ*, 3d ed. (London: Dacre Press, 1950), 9.
6. Muilenburg, "The Ethics of the Prophet," 536.
7. On this subject, see William Temple, *The Church Looks Forward* (London: Macmillan, 1944), 183ff.
8. See E. G. Hinson, s.v. "Irenaeus," in M. Eliade, ed., *The Encyclopedia of Religion*, vol. 7 (New York: Macmillan, 1986) 280–283.
9. Ernst Troeltsch, *The Social Teaching of the Christian Churches*, vol. 1, trans. Olive Wyon (New York: Free Press of Glencoe, 1949), 70.
10. Thornton, *The Common Life*, 5.
11. Van der Leeuw, *Religion in Essence and Manifestation*, 267; italics mine.
12. Troeltsch, *The Social Teachings*, 72.
13. Ibid., 75.
14. See Stephen Neill, *The Christian Society* (New York: Harper & Brothers, 1952), 29.
15. Clebsch informs us that only Emperor Diocletian, "and he very briefly, tried to force all Christians to declare their loyalty to the holy empire and the sacred emperor." William A. Clebsch, *Christianity in European History* (New York: Oxford University Press, 1979), 36.
16. Christopher Dawson, *Enquiries into Religion and Culture* (London: Sheed & Ward, 1933), 211.
17. Ibid., 257.
18. Peter Brown, *Augustine of Hippo* (Berkeley: University of California Press, 1967), 214; italics mine.
19. See Massey H. Shepherd, Jr., "Christianity and the Fall of Rome," in *A Short History of Christianity*, ed. A. G. Baker (Chicago: University of Chicago Press, 1940), 69.
20. Troeltsch, *The Social Teachings*, 235.

21. Ibid., 229–230.
22. Ibid., 234.
23. On this dogma, see John Hick, "Whatever Path Men Choose Is Mine," in *Christianity and Other Religions*, ed. J. Hick and B. Hebblethwaite (Glasgow: Collins, 1980), 171–190.
24. See "Empire," in *Encyclopaedia Britannica*, 1971 ed., s.v. "Roman Empire," vol. 8, pp. 344–345.
25. Kitagawa, *The Quest for Human Unity*, 150–158.
26. See Clebsch, *Christianity in European History*, 193–210.
27. Ibid., 188–189.
28. See Kitagawa, *The Quest for Human Unity*, 2.
29. Haas, *The Destiny of the Mind*, 303.
30. Clebsch, *Christianity in European History*, 183.
31. Wilhelm Halbfass, *India and Europe* (Albany, N.Y.: SUNY Press, 1988), 93.
32. Ernst Cassirer, *The Philosophy of the Enlightenment* (Princeton: Princeton University Press, 1950), 159.
33. See article on "Pietism" in James Hastings, ed., *Encyclopaedia of Religion and Ethics* 1951 ed., vol. 10, p. 7.
34. Charles H. Robinson, *History of Christian Missions* (New York: Charles Scribner's Sons, 1915), 53.
35. Kenneth S. Latourette, *A History of the Expansion of Christianity*, vol. 3 (New York: Harper & Brothers, 1939), 50.

Chapter 9: Piety, Morality, and Culture: European and American Perspectives

1. See my Introduction, "*Verstehen* and *Erlösung*," in Wach, *Introduction to the History of Religions*, ed. Kitagawa and Alles.
2. Kitagawa, *The Quest for Human Unity*, 2.
3. For more on this mode of inquiry, see Kitagawa, ed., *The History of Religions*, 152ff.
4. See Tillich, *The Future of Religions*, 64ff.
5. Kitagawa, *The Quest for Human Unity*, 3–4.
6. Ibid., 4.
7. This theme of the *logos* ("word") is assumed in the Prologue to the Gospel of John.
8. For more on this subject, see Kitagawa, *Spiritual Liberation and Human Freedom in Contemporary Asia*, app. 2, "Religious Visions of the End of the World," 179–191.
9. It is to be noted that these idioms and symbols of the early church had been borrowed from the Hebrew temple tradition.
10. See Kitagawa, *Spiritual Liberation and Human Freedom in Contemporary Asia*, app. 1, "Some Remarks on Buddhism," 165–178.
11. Troeltsch, *The Social Teachings*, 215.
12. For more on these analyses, see my Introduction to Kitagawa, ed., "Religious Studies, Theological Studies, and University-Divinity Schools," forthcoming.
13. Daniel J. Boorstin, *The Genius of American Politics* (Chicago: University of Chicago Press, 1953), 136.
14. Ibid., 157.
15. See Sidney E. Mead, *The Nation with the Soul of a Church* (New York: Harper & Row, 1975). This may be an appropriate occasion for me to express my indebtedness to Mead's exposition of Enlightenment-rationalistic Christianity in early America.
16. Jacob Neusner, "Judaism in the History of Religion," in *History and Theory*, suppl. 8, *On Methods in the History of Religions*, ed. J. B. Helfer (Middlebury, Vt.: Middlebury College, 1968), 37.
17. Wilhelm Pauck, "Theology in the Life of Contemporary American Protestantism," *Shane Quarterly* 13 (April 1952): 49.
18. Quoted by J. Philip Woggaman in his "The Illusions of Theocracy as Model of Relationship," *Report from the Capital* 45, no. 10 (November–December 1990): 4.
19. Nathan O. Hatch, *The Sacred Cause of Liberty: Republican Thought and the Millennium in Revolutionary New England* (New Haven: Yale University Press, 1977), 72.
20. Sydney E. Ahlstrom, *A Religious History of the American People* (New Haven: Yale University Press, 1972), 380.
21. Although I cannot possibly cite all the people who have enlightened me on the subject of the modern American religious scene, I should acknowledge my special

indebtedness to Martin E. Marty's recent volume *Modern American Religion*, vol. 2, *The Noise of Conflict* (Chicago: University of Chicago Press, 1991).

22. Among numerous works on these subjects, see particularly James E. Wood, Jr., ed., *The First Freedom: Religion and the Bill of Rights* (Waco, Tex.: J. M. Dawson Institute of Church-State Studies, Baylor University, 1980), and a brief but informative article by Eric Michael Mazur entitled "Definitions of Religion in Supreme Court Decisions," *Report from the Capital* (Washington, D.C.: Baptist Joint Committee on Public Affairs, September 1990), 4–11.

23. Many perceptive books and articles have been written on the subject in recent years, e.g., Eric J. Ziólkowski, "Heavenly Visions and Worldly Intentions: Chicago's Columbian Exposition and World's Parliament of Religions (1893)," *Journal of American Culture* 13, no. 4 (1990): 9–15.

24. All questions and answers of this Senate hearing were carefully documented in the *New York Times*. See also J. Bruce Walker, "Views on the Wall," *Report from the Capital* 45, no. 10 (November–December 1990): 6.

25. On these questions, see *International Encyclopedia of the Social Sciences*, 1968 ed., vol. 9, pp. 73ff.; italics mine.

26. See Rollin Bennett Posey, *American Government* (Ames, Iowa: Littlefield, Adams, & Co., 1954), 33.

27. William Eaton, *Who Killed the Constitution? The Judges v. The Law* (Washington D.C.: Regnery Gateway, 1988), 7.

28. Mircea Eliade, "*Homo Faber* and *Homo Religiosus*," in *The History of Religions*, 5.

29. See J. M. Kitagawa, "The Asian's 'World of Meaning,'" in *Glaube, Geist, Geschichte*, ed. G. Müller and W. Zeller (Leiden, Neth.: E. J. Brill, 1967), 469–476.

30. Hutchins, *No Friendly Voice*, 1–2.

31. See "Yale Gets $20 Million Gift for Western Studies Course," the *New York Times*, 18 April, 1991.

32. "Fewer Aliens Want to Be Citizens," *San Francisco Chronicle*, 12 March, 1991.

33. See the previously quoted article by J. Philip Woggaman on "The Illusions of Theocracy."

34. Quoted in Ahlstrom, *A Religious History of the American People*, 512.

35. See Handy, *A Christian America*.

36. Quoted in Ahlstrom, *A Religious History of the American People*, 122.

37. Taken from the tribute "C. C. Goen: Superb Scholar, Gentle Encourager," *Report from the Capital* (February 1991): 11, 14.

Chapter 10: Piety, Morality, and Culture in Global Perspective (1)

1. The 1991 opinion poll on religious affiliation, commissioned by the Graduate School of the City University of New York, unfolds an illuminating reality of contemporary American religious life. See the article "Portraits of Religion in the U.S. . . .," *New York Times*, 10 April, 1991.

2. I have stated parts of my limited views on this gigantic problem in my other writings, especially in *The Quest for Human Unity* and *Spiritual Liberation and Human Freedom in Contemporary Asia*.

3. "Caveat for Pax Americana," *San Francisco Examiner*, 10 March, 1991.

4. See Tom Wicker, "Arming the New Order," *New York Times*, 27 March, 1991.

5. Northrop, *The Taming of the Nations*, 67.

6. Haas, *The Destiny of the Mind*, chaps. 1 and 2.

7. Betty Heimann, *Indian and Western Philosophy: A Study in Contrast* (London: George Allen & Unwin, 1937), chap. 1, "Introduction."

8. Samuel H. Miller, "Commencement Address," *The* (Virginia) *Seminary Journal* 11, no. 4 (July 1960): 6.

9. On this point, see Cassirer, *The Philosophy of the Enlightenment*, 159ff.

10. Quoted in Halbfass, *India and Europe*, 93.

11. Ibid., 88.

12. Ibid., 96; italics mine.

13. Quoted in ibid., 437; italics mine.

14. See Klaus-Peter Koepping, *Adolf Bastian and the Psychic Unity of Mankind* (St. Lucia: University of Queensland Press, 1983).

15. See E. Bradford Burns, *The Poverty of Progress* (Berkeley: University of California Press, 1980).
16. See Martin Jay, *Marxism and Totality* (Berkeley: University of California Press, 1984).
17. Readers would find many illuminating discussions on this subject in Edward S. Said's somewhat controversial book *Orientalism*.
18. Quoted in Hastings, ed., *Encyclopaedia of Religion and Ethics*, vol. 10, p. 664.
19. The pamphlet, "The Missionary Task in the Present Day," constitutes the Report of Commission IV of the IMC. It was compiled by Wynn C. Fairfield (New York: International Missionary Council, 1952); all quotations in this section are found in the pamphlet, pp. 2–5.
20. Edmund Perry, *The Gospel in Dispute* (New York: Doubleday & Co., 1958), 84.
21. Stewart Guthrie, *A Japanese New Religion: Risshō-Kōsei-Kai in a Mountain Hamlet* (Ann Arbor: Center for Japanese Studies, University of Michigan, 1988), 193.
22. Eliade, *Patterns in Comparative Religion*, xi.
23. Kitagawa, *The Quest for Human Unity*, 232.
24. On this problem, I have learned much from many sources, especially from *Nihon-jin no mita Kirisuto-kyo (Christianity Seen Through Japanese Eyes)*, ed. Suzuki Norihisa and Joseph J. Spae (Tokyo: Oriens Shukyo-kenkyujo, 1968).
25. On the problem of simultaneous monologue, see J. M. Kitagawa, "Tillich, Kraemer, and the Encounter of Religions," in *The Thought of Paul Tillich*, ed. J. L. Adams et al. (San Francisco: Harper & Row, 1985), 197–217.
26. Quoted in J. N. Farquhar, *The Crown of Hinduism* (Oxford: Oxford University Press, 1913), 110.
27. Konvitz, *The Alien and the Asiatic in American Law*, 26.
28. Jawaharlal Nehru, *The Discovery of India* (New York: John Day, 1956), 579. Before he came under the spell of Mahatma Gandhi, the Harrow- and Cambridge-educated Nehru felt no congeniality with India and Indian civilization. It is interesting to note that his own father, Pandit Motilal Nehru, before he became a nationalist under the influence of his son and Gandhi, was a very Westernized Indian himself, who was reputed to have shipped his shirts regularly to the laundry in London.
29. I have briefly discussed how modern Hinduism and Buddhism have appropriated the traditional Christian formula of "fulfillment" in their effort to establish their respective apologetics. See Kitagawa, ed., *The History of Religions*, app., "The 1893 World's Parliament of Religions and Its Legacy," 353–368.
30. See J. M. Kitagawa, ed., *Modern Trends in World Religions* (LaSalle, Ill.,: The Open Court, 1959); J. M. Kitagawa, *Religions of the East* (Philadelphia: The Westminster Press, 1960; rev. ed., 1968); idem, *Spiritual Liberation and Human Freedom in Contemporary Asia*. See also my contribution to Robert F. Spencer, ed., *Religion and Change in Contemporary Asia* (Minneapolis: University of Minnesota Press, 1971). I also wrote on Asian religions annually for many years in *Britannica Yearbook*.
31. Statement by C. C. Bonney, quoted in George S. Goodspeed, ed., *The World's First Parliament of Religions: Its Christian Spirit, Historic Greatness and Manifold Results* (Chicago: Hill & Schuman, 1985), 56.
32. Arthur E. Christy, ed., *The Asian Legacy and American Life* (New York: John Day, 1942), 37.
33. Hendrik Kraemer, *World Cultures and World Religions* (Philadelphia: The Westminster Press, 1960), 18.
34. Kitagawa, *The Quest for Human Unity*, 222.
35. Wong Yong Ji, "The Challenge of Eastern Spiritualities to Western Society," *Theology and Faith* 4 (1990): 228.
36. Ibid., 226.
37. "The New Age Movement," *Leaves of Healing* 125, nos. 7–8 (July–August 1990): 7. *Leaves of Healing* is a publication of the Christian Catholic Church.

Chapter 11: Piety, Morality, and Culture in Global Perspective (2)

1. "Caveat for Pax Americana," *San Francisco Examiner*, 10 March, 1991.
2. See also Paul Kennedy, *The Rise and Fall of the Great Powers* (New York: Random House, 1987). Kennedy relates how from A.D. 1500 to 2000 the political fortunes of great powers were influenced by economic change, military conflict, and other factors.

I do not endorse his interpretations altogether, however. On the Egyptian situation itself, see Derek Hopwood, *Egypt: Politics and Society, 1945-1984,* 2d ed. (Boston: Unwin Hyman, 1982, 1985).

3. J. H. Makin and D. C. Hellmann, eds., *Sharing World Leadership? A New Era for America and Japan* (Washington, D.C.: American Enterprise Institute for Public Policy Research, 1989).

4. I have already quoted Paz's critical remark about "progress"—which has given people things but not being—in Kitagawa, *The Quest for Human Unity,* 238.

5. See Robert Ozaki's article on "The Humanistic Enterprise System in Japan," *Asian Survey* 28, no. 8 (August 1988): 830–848.

6. See the text of John Paul II's encyclical *Centismus Annus* in the *New York Times,* 3 May, 1991.

7. Mircea Eliade, *The Quest: History and Meaning in Religion* (Chicago: University of Chicago Press, 1969), Preface. I have discussed this concern of mine in numerous other occasions, especially in my article "A Historian of Religions' Reflections Upon His Perspective," *Criterion* 28, no. 2 (Spring 1989): 5–9.

8. For more on this subject, see my *The Quest for Human Unity,* "Introduction."

9. Although there are far too many dilettantish works on the subject of "world faith," I will cite at least one sober discussion of this difficult problem by mentioning Hocking, *Living Religions and a World Faith.* Concerning respective religious traditions' claims to be the world faith, see missiological works of various religions, old and new. One of the best-known Christian works on the subject, even though somewhat dated, is Kraemer, *The Christian Message in a Non-Christian World.*

10. I cannot possibly cite all the major works of this tradition, variously called *philosophia perennis, sophia perennis,* or *religio perennis.* I learned a great deal about this tradition from S. H. Nasr, *Knowledge and the Sacred* (New York: Crossroad, 1981).

11. Halbfass, *India and Europe,* 93.

12. Mircea Eliade, *The Sacred and the Profane* (New York: Harcourt, Brace & Co., 1959), 203.

13. Stanley J. Samartha, ed., *Living Faiths and Ultimate Goals* (Geneva: World Council of Churches, 1974), x.

14. Kitagawa, *The History of Religions,* 264; italics mine.

15. See Joachim Wach, *Understanding and Believing,* ed. J. M. Kitagawa (New York: Harper & Row, 1968), chap. 4, "General Revelation and the Religions of the World," 69–86.

16. More about *dynamis* and *dynameis,* see F. E. Peters, *Greek Philosophical Terms* (New York: New York University Press, 1967), 42–45.

17. See George D. Kennan, "Age and Grace," *The Anglican Digest* (Pentecost A.D. 1991): 8.

18. See *Chicago Tribune,* 18 May, 1991.

19. See my Introduction, "*Verstehen* and *Erlösung*" in Wach, *Introduction to the History of Religions,* ix–xxxiv.

20. Arthur C. McGill, "The Ambiguous Position of Christian Theology," in *The Study of Religion in Colleges and Universities,* ed. P. Ramsay and J. F. Wilson (Princeton: Princeton University Press, 1970), 107.

21. Czeslaw Milosz, "The Fate of the Religious Imagination," *New Perspective Quarterly* 8, no. 2 (Spring 1991): 6-a, 6-b.

22. Kraemer, *World Cultures and World Religions,* 364 n. 1.

23. William Theodore de Bary et al., comps., *Sources of Indian Tradition* (New York: Columbia University Press, 1958), 438.

24. Kitagawa, *The History of Religions,* 358.

25. Edward Schillebeeckx, "Salvation and Experience" (Mimeographed, n.d.), 1.

26. A. R. Hamilton Gibb, *Mohammedanism: An Historical Survey* (New York: Oxford University Press, 1953), vii.

27. Eliade, *Patterns in Comparative Religion,* xi.

28. Kraemer, *World Cultures and World Religions,* 356.

29. Mircea Eliade, *Myths, Dreams and Mysteries* (New York: Harper & Brothers, 1960), 107.

30. See Kraemer, *Religion and the Christian Faith* (Philadelphia: Westminster Press, 1956), 210.

31. William Temple, *Nature, Man and God* (New York: Macmillan, 1949), 306.
32. Quoted in Y. Takeuchi, "Japanese Philosophy," *Encyclopaedia Britannica*, 1968 ed., vol. 12, p. 961.

Appendix: Some Personal Reflections on Autobiographical and Biographical Modes of Perception

1. J. Hector St. John de Crèvecoeur, *Letters from an American Farmer*, ed. E. Rhys (New York: E. P. Dutton, 1912), 43.
2. Takeuchi Yoshinori, s.v. "Japanese Philosophy," *Encyclopaedia Britannica*, 1968 ed., vol. 12, pp. 958J–959.
3. Eliade, *The Quest*, Preface.
4. Hocking, *The World Civilization*, 47.
5. Paul Tillich, *Theology of Culture*, ed. R. C. Kimball (New York: Oxford University Press, 1959), 204–205.
6. Quoted in E. J. Sharpe, *Nathan Söderblom and the Study of Religion* (Chapel Hill: University of North Carolina Press, 1960), 143; italics mine.
7. For more on this subject, see Kitagawa, *Spiritual Liberation and Human Freedom in Contemporary Asia*.

INDEX

INDEX

Afghanistan, 108
African-Americans, 40, 203, 204, 210,
    263, 269
  communities, 262–272
  studies, 275
Agape, 69, 70
Alameda County Jail, 123
Alaska, 121
  evacuation of Japanese, 120
Alexander the Great, 7, 9, 154, 188, 242
Alexander VI, 12
American Baptist Free Mission Society, 53
American experience, 192–202
  Declaration of Independence, 194, 197
  government, 111
  and the law, 202
  and pluralism, 272
American Methodist church, 53
American Revolution, 267
Amherst College, 53
Anderson, Marian, 149
Andover Theological Seminary, 53
Ankor, xi
Apostles' Creed, 67
Aquinas, Thomas, 10
Aquino, Corazon, 38, 40
Arab-Americans, 137

Aramaic, 151
Aristotle, 10
Aristotelianism, 244, 249. *See also*
    Metaphysics
Army Internment Camp. *See* Detention
    Camps
Asia, 25, 29–30, 219, 230
Asian Americans, 204, 206, 210, 262, 268
  and American culture, 110–111, 113
  community, 268–272
  cultural heritage, 114
  Democratic and Republican parties,
    103
  dilemma of, 102, 103
  during and after W.W. II, 106, 107–14
  identities, 111–12
  and immigrant parents, 93, 100, 117
  Oriental Exclusion Act (1924), 134,
    207
  racism, 91, 92, 93, 113
  religious groups, 104
  repeal of Chinese exclusion laws, 105
  role of education, 112
  stages of the marginalized person,
    100–101
Asian Christian tradition, x, 4, 22, 30–31,
    33, 34, 40, 65, 66, 68, 83, 88, 221, 227

297

Asiatic immigrants, 93
    Americanization after W.W. I, 203,
        273
    and Babylonian captivity, 41
    Chinatowns, 97
    Chinese immigrants, 95
    Christian work among, 98, 99
    cultural and religious syncretism,
        114–15, 116
    guiding principle of, 116
    in Hawaii, 94
    as manual laborers, 97
    as a marginal group, 100
    and naturalization, 97
    refugees and asylum seekers, 107–109
    and segregated community life, 101
Assembly Center. See Detention Camps
Augustine (of Hippo), 172, 173, 174,
    191
Autobiographical genre. See Perceptions:
    autobiographical

Babylon, 8, 167, 189, 243
Babylonian exile, 153, 154, 156
Barman Declaration, 77
Barth, Karl, 76, 78, 79
Baptism, 62
Benedict XIV, 14
Bennett, John C., 78
Bentham, Jeremy, 194
Bill of Rights, 135. See also American
    experience
Bishop, Claire Huchet, 119
Biographical genre. See Perceptions:
    biographical
Blackstone, William, 205
Boat people, 82
Boniface, 174, 175
Boorstin, Daniel J., 111, 193, 194
Boxer Rebellion, 57
Britain, 58, 66
Brown, Peter, 172
Brown, S. R., 52
Brunner, Emil, 78
Buddha, 44, 146
Buddhism, 32, 46, 48, 58, 62, 63, 79, 145,
    148, 150, 228, 229, 237, 239
    Dharma and samgha, 47, 147
    founding myth, 159–60
    and hidden Christians
        (kakure-kirishitan), 51, 52
    into Japan, 44–45, 47
    and suffering, 80

Buddhist, 52, 83, 128, 143, 206
    Japanese Pure Land, 46, 47, 48–49, 278
    thought, 49, 51, 69
    traditions on death, 115
Buddhist-Christian Conference, 62, 63
Bultmann, Rudolf, 78
Bunyan, John, 182
Burlingame Treaty (1868), 95
Burma, 66
Bush, George, 212, 234
Byzantine Empire, 10, 170

Caesaropapism, 9, 170. See also
    Constantine
California Joint Immigration Committee,
    106
Carey, William, 20, 29
Carolingian rulers, 172, 173
Cassirer, Ernst, 182
Catholicism, Roman, 39, 48–49, 52, 55.
    See also Iberian peninsula
Ceylon (Sri Lanka), 32, 33
Charles V, 177, 203
Chinese Catholic Patriotic Association
    (CCPA), 38, 40
Church. See Sacradotium
Chiang Kai-shek, 108
Chimmoku. See Silence
China, 92, 207, 213
    Han empire, 44
    Shin-Butsu Shūgō, 47
Chinese characters, 45
Christian theology, 70
Christian theologians, 80
Christianity, American, 208, 237, 239
    dialogue with antagonists, 240, 248–50,
        254
    internal dialogue, 240, 247, 254
    interreligious dialogues, 239, 240, 241,
        250–53, 254
    rationalistic humanism, 250
    separation of church and state, 195–97
    See also Religion: American
Christianity, Western, 145, 150, 151, 230
    apologists, 8, 170
    biblical interpretation, 171
    bureaucracy, 18, 19
    canon law, 178
    clerical marriage, 246
    community, 4, 7, 157, 168, 169, 172
    cult of saints, 171
    in the dark ages, 191
    and denominations, 196, 229–30, 278

ecclesiastical structure, 146, 147
in Europe, 242
founding myths, 160
Good Friday, 200
Hebrew views of divine, 187
heresies of Wycliff and Huss, 177
horizontal versus vertical dimensions,
7–8
medieval, 175
Meiji's harsh treatment of, 52
Petrine doctrine, 176
and the pope, 40, 173, 174
and purgatory, 174
revelatory tradition, 215, 254
and salvation, 34
Church. *See* Sacradotium
Civil Liberties Act, 136, 137
Civil War, 94, 197, 207, 269
Clark, John, 205
Clebach, William, 179
Clement XI, 14
Clement VIII, 177
Coincidentia oppositorum, 145, 167, 189,
199, 221, 239, 257
Colonialism, 35
administration, 17
and Christianity, 16
decline of, 29
economic and cultural, 212
and missionary societies, 18
political and economic, 211
western, 20, 210, 211–20
See also Iberian peninsula
Columbia University, 92–93
Columbus, Christopher, 12, 215
Communism, 25, 35, 37, 230, 239
Community Enterprises, 128. *See also*
Detention camps
Comparative religions, 142–43
interreligious dialogue, 221–23, 225
Oriental studies, 24, 218–19
Concentration camps, German, 119,
135
Conference of Religionists. *See*
Buddhist-Christian Conference
Confessionalism, global, 4, 6, 210
Confucius, 44
Confucianism, 46, 47, 69, 229
Congregation of the Propagation of the
Faith, 183
Constantine, 8, 67, 168, 170, 171, 175,
176, 178, 190, 224, 242, 243
Constitution of Albania, 196

Copernicus, Nicolaus, 179, 213, 249
Cook, Stanley A., 218
Corpus Christianum, 11, 173, 174, 246
Corpus Islamicus, 173, 176, 177, 214,
246
Council of Florence, 67, 174–75
Council of Nicea, 9, 170, 190
Council of Trent, 177
Counter-Reformation, 11, 12, 14, 48, 85,
177, 215, 249
Coupland, Sir Reginald, 17
Covenantal motif. *See* Hebrew Bible:
paradigm
Crèvecoeur, J. Hector St. John de, 273
Criticism, postructuralist, 142
Cromer, Earl Evelyn Baring, 23–24
Crucifixion, 189, 190, 200. *See also*
Christianity, Western
Crusades, 10, 11, 13, 28, 173, 174, 176,
214. *See also* Iberian peninsula
Cyrus (of Persia), 154, 156, 248

Daimyos (feudal lords), 49, 50
Daitō Kokushi, 257
Darwin, 249
Deng Xiaoping, 35
de Nobili, Roberto, 14–15
Descartes, 249
Deism, 194
Department of Interior, 107
Department of Justice, 106
Depression, 102, 125, 207, 274
Detention camps
and adult education, 128
Amy Suzuki's account, 131
army internment camp, 121
Ashio Copper Mine Incident, 61
assembly centers, 121, 135
author's account, 120, 121, 122,
123–29
four types, 121
Kimura's account, 131–132
Minidoka War Relocation Center
(Idaho), 121, 126, 127
in New Mexico, 120
Sato Family, 129–131
War Relocation Authority (WRA), 121,
127, 128, 129, 130, 131
See also Japanese Americans
DeWitt, John L., 106, 135
Dialogue
definition of, 277
interreligious, 41, 276–82

Diaspora communities, 154, 187
Dibelius, Martin, 161
Diet, 80, 81
Diet of Augsburg, 177
Diocletian, 176
Divine Faith, 251
Doshisha College, 53
Dutch learning (Rangaku-sha), 51
Dutch Reformed Church, 53
Dynamics, 242

Eaton, William, 202
Easter tradition, 226, 227. *See also*
    Christianity, Western
East India Company, 27
Economist, The, 235
Ecumenical movements, 3, 4, 6
Egypt, 23
Eisenhower, Dwight David, 211
Ekklesia, 67, 163, 168, 174, 178
Eliade, Mircea, 24, 25, 143, 145, 202, 214,
    223, 235, 254, 279
Emperor cult, 57, 58, 66, 76
Endō Shūsako, 84
Enlightenment, 175, 178, 179, 181–82,
    194, 205, 206, 215, 217, 249
Episcopal church, 52
Epithumia, 70
Eros, 70
Eschatology, 7, 72, 76–77, 156
Eschaton, 153, 165, 166, 167, 187, 189,
    213, 242, 256. *See also*
    Zoroastrianism
Essenes, 151
Ethics, 256. *See also* Perceptions
Europocentric, 24, 54, 204, 209
Evangelicals, 15, 74, 75, 184, 205, 206,
    215, 269
Evangelism, 52, 277
    and Goa, 14, 251
Extra ecclesiam nulla salus (no salvation
    outside the church), 59, 64, 67, 72, 175

Federated Christian Church, 128
Feudalism, 173
Fichte, Johann Gottlieb, 54, 238
Formosa (Taiwan), 57, 80
France, 57, 58, 66, 196
    and revolution, 215
Francke, August Hermann, 182
Freedom of Information Act, 136
French Revolution, 180
Freud, Sigmund, 249

Gadamer, Hans-Georg, 45
Galileo, 249
Gama, Vasco da, 13
Gandhi, Mahatma, 149
Gashin-Shōtan, 57
Gibb, Hamilton, 241
Goen, C. C., 207–208
Grant, Robert, 9
Gregory I, 9. *See also* Corpus
    Christianum
Gregory VII, 177
Germany, 57
    postwar miracle, 235
Goa, 27, 28, 251
Goble, Jonathan, 53
Grodzins, Morton, 120
Gulick, Sidney, 99

Haas, William, 24, 26, 62, 69, 180, 213,
    278
Haiku, 79
Haole (wealthy whites), 94
Hammer, Raymond, 56
Hapsburg dynasty, 181
Harrison, Earl G., 105
Hatano Seiichi, 70, 82
Hawaii, 93, 94, 97, 99, 102
    Asian Americans in, 106, 109, 110
    See also Asian Americans
Hayathology, 152, 243, 244
Hearst Press, 106
Hebrew Bible, 154, 188
    Abraham, 155, 161, 162
    Amos, 152
    Daniel, 123
    Davidic kingdom, 151
    Deutero-Isaiah, 153–54, 156
    Exodus, 152, 155, 164, 165, 192, 194,
        203
    Ezekiel, 153
    Genesis myth, 147
    heritage, 242, 243
    Isaiah, 248
    Moses, 155, 172
    new covenant, 153
    Noah, 155
    paradigm, 147, 149, 151–57, 161,
        187
    Prophets, 153, 238
    Psalms, 124
    Samuel, 152
    Tower of Babel, 155, 165
Hegel, Georg W. F., 181, 216, 238

Heilsgeschichte (history of salvation), 153, 155, 156, 157, 161, 187
Hellenism, 7, 147, 151, 154, 166, 169, 187, 188, 189, 200, 213, 243, 244
Hellmann, D. C., 235
Henry the Navigator, 12. *See also* Iberian peninsula
Henry IV, 177
Hepburn, J. C., 52
Herford, R. T., 163
Hermeneutical literacy, 247, 248
Herodians, 151
Hideki Yukawa, 92–93
Higgins, Jean, 84, 85, 87
Hinduism, 62, 143, 145, 200, 228, 229
Hispanic-Americans, 204, 210
Hocking, William Ernest, 62, 279
Holland, 69
Holton, Daniel C., 62
Homo faber, 202
Homoousios, 9
Hotoke (God), 48
Holy Spirit, 6, 160, 165, 167
Human experience, 20, 21. *See also* Perceptions
Humbolt, Wilhelm von, 148
Hutchins, Robert Maynard, 112, 204

Iberian peninsula, 12, 15, 172, 244
    and anti-Islamic, 14
    colonial powers, 215
    conquistadors, 14
    1494 treaty, 36
    Inquisition, 12, 28
    patronage system, 12, 14, 15, 180–81
    Portugal, 11, 12, 13, 178, 214, 226
    Spain, 11, 12, 13, 178, 214, 226
    Spanish Armada, 15, 215
    synthesis of religions, 13
    See also Perceptions
Ichikawa Sanki, 52
Iglehart, Charles, 87
Imago dei, 166, 188, 213
Immanental theocracy, 74
Immigration and Naturalization Act (1952), 108
Imperial Rescript, 57, 73
Imperium (state), 10, 147, 166, 173, 174, 175, 176, 177, 178, 188, 191, 193, 235, 236, 244, 282. *See also* Christianity, Western
India, 37–38, 44, 47, 48, 49, 51, 61, 66, 82, 108, 213

Indian Civil Service (ICS), 17
Indian Ecumenical Study Conference (1952), 37
Indian Police Service (IP), 17
Indonesia, 27, 66
Industrial Revolution, 180
Innocent III, 174
Inquisition. *See* Iberian peninsula
International Missionary Council (IMC), 33, 66, 219–20, 221
Iraq, 233
Iran-Contra Affairs, 201
Irenaeus of Lyons, 167
Isaacs, Harold, 43
Ishiwara Ken, 82
Islam, 5, 143, 145, 172, 237, 239
    and Christianity, 10–11
    falsafah, 10, 179
    founding myth, 160
    and Granada, 12
    in India, 48
    Muslims, 201
    See also corpur Islamicus
Isseis. *See* Japanese immigrants
Isoo, Abe, 61, 71, 82

Janes, L. J., 60
Jansenists, 182
Japan, 14
    aestnetics-oriented culture, 83, 87–88
    as an anticommunist citadel, 74
    Buddhist institutions attacked, 48
    Christian situation, 50, 57, 60, 64–65, 68, 75, 78, 84, 85, 264
    Christian social action, 70–71
    chronicle of, 46
    Communist Party, 61
    denominational divisions, 56, 60
    economic prosperity, 109
    geography, 44, 65
    honji-suijaku belief, 47
    ideological weapons, 58
    interracial marriage, 55
    Jesuit-inspired groups, 48–49
    Jesuits and Franciscans, 50
    Kamadura era, 47
    linguistic thought forms, 46, 52
    Marxist group, 58
    and mores, 61
    national learning (koku-gaku), 51
    national Shinto, 59, 76
    and philosophy, 69
    postwar Christianity, 78

Japan *(Continued)*
  postwar communism, 79
  postwar recovery and development
    of, 235
  Religious Bodies Law, 59
  saisei-itchi, 195
  state Shinto, 47, 51, 58, 62, 63, 66, 72, 76
  status of women, 81
  theology in, 82
  Tokugawa shogunate, 66
  westernization, 54–55
  and writing, 45
  See also Perceptions
Japanese Americans
  and evacuations, 107, 122, 134
  first generation immigrants (Issei), 121,
    123, 124, 125, 264, 265, 269
  patriotism of, 107, 136
  Quota Act (1924), 124
  racism and war hysteria, 120, 125
  redress movement, 136
  second generation (Niseis), 121, 125,
    126, 130, 132, 134, 264, 265
  Student Relocation Council, 122
  third generation (Sanseis), 126
  and women, 63
  See also United States Supreme Court;
    Detention camps; Women
Jehovah's Witness, 200
Jesus of Nazareth (the Christ), 8, 80, 86,
    147, 151, 160, 162, 173, 190, 241
  agent of new covenant, 164
  disagreement with the Pharisees, 163
  and the Kingdom of God, 164, 165
  logos incarnate, 169
  and Mary, 171
  See also Hebrew Bible; Christianity,
    Western
John (of Patmos), 243. *See also* New
    Testament
John Paul, II, 235
Josephus, 150
Judaism, 145, 146, 150, 187, 230
  ancient Hebrews, 180
  apocalyptic tradition, 243
  and Hellenistic Jews, 154
  revelatory tradition, 215
  and synagogue, 168
  as a tribal community, 156
  understanding of God, 164

Kagawan Toyohiko, 71, 82
Kaifuso, 45

Kami (emperor's nature), 73. *See also*
    Japan
Katayama Sen, 61
Katayama Tetsu, 71
Keene, Donald, 46
Kennan, George D., 245
Kierkegaardian dichotomy, 80
King, Martin Luther, Jr., 137
Kitagawa, Daisuke, 133
Kitamori Kazoh, 79, 80
Kitetsugaku, 69
Kiyoko Takeda Cho, 79
Knox, George W., 62
Koinonia, 163, 165, 189. *See also*
    Christianity, Western
Kojiki (Records of Ancient Matters), 45, 46
Kokumin-no-Tomo (Friends of the
    People), 63
Konvitz, Milton R., 96
Korea, 49, 57, 58, 75, 92, 109
Korean War, 74, 93, 104, 107, 108
Kotoku Shusui, 60
Kozaki Hiromichi (Kōdō), 59, 60
Kraemer, Hendrik, 20, 150, 229, 251,
    255
Kristol, Irving, 22
Kumamoto School, 60
Kumano Yoshitaka, 71
Kyoto School, 53, 69, 70, 76, 277, 278
Kyushu rebellion, 50. *See also*
    Catholicism; Iberian peninsula

Laicism, 207–208
Latourette, Kenneth, 184
Leo III, 172
Lewis, Bernard, 5, 144
Liggins, L., 52
Little Tokyos. *See* Asiatic immigrants:
    Chinatowns
Lippmann, Walter, 121
Livingstone, David, 16, 247
Lloyd, Arthur, 62
Locke, John, 194
Logos, 8, 53, 54, 115, 168, 169, 189, 242
Louis XIV, 181
Loyola, Ignatius, 182, 183
Luther, Martin, 11, 177
Lutheran, 76

MacArthur, Douglas, 73, 74, 212
Magisterium, 11, 244
Magnus, Albertus, 10
Makin, J. H., 235

Manchuria, 57, 58, 59
Manchurian Incident, 58–59
Manyō-shū, 45, 46, 285
Mao Tse-Tung, 26, 108
Martel, Charles, 10
Martyrdom, 170, 171, 176, 190. *See also*
    Christianity, Western
Marx, 249
Marxism, 196, 207, 228, 234
Maya (Hinduism), 254
Medieval Europe, 173, 175
Meiji
    constitution, 57
    emperor, 51, 69
    regime, 54, 55, 56, 58, 59, 61, 73, 80
    See also Japan; Perceptions
Merton, Robert K., 19
Mesa, Jose M. de, 40–41
Messianic cults, 51
Metanoia, 188
Metaphysics, 176, 278. *See also*
    Aristotelianism
Michalson, Carl, 71, 79
Middle Ages, 67, 168–169
Miller, Samuel, 213
Milosz, Czesltaw, 249–250
Missionaries, 68, 207
    American, 61
    in Asia and Africa, 231
    and education, 53
    Pannikkar's view, 26
    philanthropy and education, 32
    political aggression, 29
    and Protestants, 56
    See also Iberian peninsula
Missionary Conference, 35
Missionary programs, 193, 206
Missionary societies, 16–17, 18, 19, 53,
    68, 184
Mission churches. *See* Younger churches
Missions, 11, 12
    American, 15
    and Baptists, 15
    boards, 18, 19
    Christian world, 178, 214, 216, 219,
        221, 222, 280
    compound, 18, 31
    erosion of, 211
    Franciscans, 13
    and indigenous churches, 18
    to the New World, 12
    Portuguese and Spanish, 14
    Protestant, 15, 16

Roman Catholic expansion, 13, 14, 28,
    180, 182–83, 215
    women's education, 61
    See also Iberian peninsula
Monastic system, 172, 176, 178
    disciplines, 244
Monolatry, 5, 7, 67, 154, 167, 188, 199,
    267
Monotheism, 5, 67, 167, 188, 199, 267,
    278
Mormons, 206, 239
Muhammad, 10, 11, 160, 172, 173
Muilenburg, James, 152
Müller, F. Max, 36, 228
Mundus imaginalis, 192, 228, 238, 257
Muslims, 210, 214, 251
Mystery cults, 145, 168
Mystical writers, 249
Mystics, 202

Nagasaki, 51
Nakajima Nobuyuki, 61
Nambara Shigery, 82
Nanzan Institute, 76, 80
Naoye, Kinoshita, 61
Napoleon, 177
National Association of Evangelicals
    (NAE), 231
National Council of Churches (NCC),
    76
Nationalism, 57, 63. *See also* Asia; Japan
Native Americans, 91, 133, 203, 204,
    206, 210, 263
Native Sons of the Golden West, 106
Naturalization, 96, 105. *See also* U.S.
    Supreme Court
Nazi Germany, 105
Near Eastern religions, 145
Neesima, Joseph Hardy, 53
Nehru, Jawaharlal, 227
Neo-Confucian (philosophy), 50, 53, 54,
    69, 72
Nestorian church, 13
Netherlands, 66
New Age Movement (NAM), 230, 231
Newman, John, 149
New Testament
    Acts, 160, 164, 165
    canonical form, 169
    Hebrew paradigm, 163
    Johannine gospel, 164, 189, 244
    Mark's gospel, 162, 163
    and salvation, 247

New Testament *(Continued)*
  synoptic gospels, 162, 188
  See also Hebrew Bible; Jesus of
    Nazareth
Newton, Isaac, 249
New World, 107, 195, 196, 198. *See
  also* Missions
New World Order (NWO), 233, 234,
  235, 237, 238, 239
New York Times, The, 134
Nichiren Shoshu (Sika Gakkai), 48,
  230
Niebuhr, H. Richard, 16, 60
Niebuhr, Reinhold, 78, 83
Nietzsche, Friedrich, 250
Nihon-gi. *See* Japan: chronicle of
Niijima. *See* Neesima, Joseph Hardy
Niseis. *See* Japanese Americans: second
  generation
Nishi Amane, 69
Nishida Kitaro, 69, 71
Nitobe Inanzo, 53, 82
Nixon, Richard M., 273
Nobel Prize, 230
Northrup, F. S. C., 25, 212

Ō-bō (emperor's law). *See* Perceptions:
  Ritsuryo synthesis
Oda Nobunaga, 48, 49
Oikoumene, 245
Onishi Hamime, 63
Ontology, 152, 244, 278
Osius (Hosius) of Cordoba, 9
Otsu, Prince, 45
Otto I, 173
Ozaki, Robert S., 235

Paideia (culture), 203, 205. *See also*
  Perceptions
Pan-Anglican group, 66
Panikkar, K. M., 26, 27, 28, 29
Parochial schools, 199
Patripassionism, 79
Patronage system, 215. *See also* Iberian
  peninsula
Pauck, William, 196
Paul (the Apostle), 7, 67, 166–68, 169,
  188, 189
Pax Romana, 167
Paz, Octavio, 235
Pearl Harbor, 106, 123, 127, 130. *See also*
  Japanese Americans
Penn, William, 206

Pentecost, 7, 8, 160, 161, 163, 164, 165,
  167, 168, 192, 243. *See also* New
  Testament
Perceptions, 261–282
  American Synthesis, 193, 198
  of Asian Christians, 65
  autobiographical, 4, 6, 34, 36, 59, 67,
    72, 142, 143, 146, 160, 167, 171,
    172, 186, 188, 236, 237, 239, 240,
    241, 246, 247, 248, 254, 261–65,
    272, 273, 277, 281
  biographical, 4, 8, 67, 142, 143, 236,
    237, 261–65, 273, 280
  Constantinian synthesis, 8–9, 180
  of education, 266–267
  Hegelian synthesis, 80
  of immigrants, 262–63
  Meiji synthesis, 51, 52, 72, 74
  and polity, 266
  of religion, 5
  Ritsuryo synthesis, 45–46, 47, 48, 49,
    51, 72
  sacred and profane, 145, 146
  space and time, 144
  Tokugawa synthesis, 49, 50, 51, 69, 72
  western convention, 3, 5–6, 20, 34,
    144, 179–180, 182, 186, 192,
    202–203, 214, 235, 236, 240, 242,
    243, 245, 254, 276
Perry, Edmund, 222
Perry, Matthew, 65–66, 73
Persian Gulf War, 211, 212, 233, 234
Pescadores Islands, 57
Pharisees, 151, 163
Philippines, 14, 50, 66, 92
  Filipinos excluded from naturalization,
    96
  independence of, 40, 108
  See also Aquino, Corazon
Philo of Alexandria, 8
Philo-ousia, 69
Philosophy, 69
  of religion, 70
Pietists, 15, 31, 178, 182, 183, 184
Pilgrims, 205
Pontifex maximus, 170
Portugal. *See* Iberian peninsula
Poussin, Louis de la Vallee, 228
Presbyterian Church, 52
Protestant Christianity, 11, 52, 55, 70, 197
  reformers, 244
  See also Christianity, Western;
    Reformation

Protestantism, 196, 206, 207
Purgatory, 174. *See also* Christianity, Western
Puritans, 192, 193–194, 197, 205

Qahal, 163
Qur'an, 160, 201

Racism, 181, 272. *See also* Japanese Americans
Reagan, Ronald, 136
Reason, cult of, 194
Redfield, Robert, 150
Reformation, 11, 67, 175, 177, 215, 249
Refugee Relief Act (1953), 108
Reischauer, August Karl, 62
Religion
  American experience, 209–210
  in ancient world, 159
  and communication, 148, 149, 150
  Darwinian, Marxian and Freudian judgments of, 237–38
  definition of, 145, 279
  field of, 217–18
  function of, 180, 185
  future of, 245–47
  history of, 281
  levels of, 270–72, 282
  and liberty, 205–208, 267, 271–72
  meaning of, 5
  pluralism, 9
  study of, 274–76
  topography of, 35–37
  and traditions, 279
Religionskritiks, 238, 240, 248, 252. *See also* Dialogue
Religionswissenschaft (science of Religion), 4, 251
Relocation Centers, 265. *See also* Detention camps
Renaissance, 11, 15, 24, 175, 176, 178, 179, 244, 249. *See also* Christianity, Western
Revelation, Jewish & Christian, 254. *See also* Hebrew Bible; New Testament
Ricci, Matteo, 14, 183
Rikkyo (St. Paul's) College, 53
Rites Controversy, 14
Ritsuryo synthesis. *See* Perceptions: Ritsuryo synthesis
Roman jurisprudence, 24, 147, 171, 200, 213, 244
Roman Catholic Church, 128

Roman Empire, 7, 167, 169, 170–72, 173, 177, 178, 180, 187, 188, 215, 245. *See also* Christianity, Western
Roosevelt, Franklin D., 105
Roosevelt, Theodore, 57
Rousseau, Jean Jacques, 194
Rushdie, Salmon, 227–28
Russia, 26, 29, 57, 58
Russian Orthodox, 52, 55
Russo-Japanese War, 57, 58, 61

Sacerdotium (church), 10, 11, 15, 147, 166, 173, 174, 175, 176–77, 178, 181, 188, 191, 193, 282, 235–36, 244, 245. *See also* Christianity, Western
Sadducees, 151
Saito MiBuo, 61
Salvation Army, 71
Samartha, Stanley, 239
Sanhedrin, 194. *See also* New Testament
Sanseis. *See* Japanese Americans: third generation
Satori, 87
Schaff, Philip, 205
Schillebeeckx, Edward, 252
Schleiermacher, Friedrich, 183
Schweitzer, Albert, 253
Seleucid dynasty, 154
Septuagint, 188
Seventh Day Adventists, 206
Shakai-Minsho-to (Socialist Democratic Party), 71
Shaku Soyen, 62
Shamida Saburō, 61
Shils, Edward, 113, 114
Shingon school, 46
Shinko Shukyo, 83
Sixtus IV, 12
Shogun, 50
Shogun, 14
Sierksma, F., 84
Silence, 84, 85, 87
Sino-Japanese War, 63
Socialization, 21, 100. *See also* Japanese Americans
Söderblom, Nathan, 257, 281
Song of Bernadette, The, 92
Soteriology, 144, 145, 146, 161, 174, 187, 190, 193, 222, 239, 246. *See also* Hebrew Bible
Spain. *See* Iberian peninsula: Portugal and Spain

Spanish-American War, 207
Spener, Philip Jacob, 182
Strong, Josiah, 207
Student Volunteer Movement, 20
Studium (university), 10, 11, 147, 166,
    173, 174, 175, 176, 178, 188, 191,
    193, 244, 282. *See also* Christianity,
    Western
Study of religion. *See* Comparative
    religions
Suez Canal, 236
Suffering servant, 156, 162, 163, 187. *See
    also* Hebrew Bible: Deutero-Isaiah
Supreme Commander of the Allied Powers
    (SCAP), 73, 74, 81
Sweet, William, 14

Tai sho Democracy, 58
Taiwan, 108, 109
Takakura Tokutaro, 71
Tanabe Hajime, 80
Tao, 47, 145, 254
Taoism, 46, 47
Taxonomy. *See* Perceptions: western
    convention
Telescope, 24, 214
Temple, William, 59, 257
Tendai school, 46
Theocracy, 47, 49, 205, 206, 210
Theodosius, 67, 170, 242, 243. *See also*
    Christianity, Western
Theological education, 206–207, 216
Thirty Years' War, 181
Thomas, Edward J., 159
Three-self movement, 38–39
Tiananmen tragedy, 108
Tillich, Paul, 25, 46, 78, 280
Tocqueville, Alex de, 263–264
Tokugawa feudal regime, 52, 59, 60, 65, 85
Tokyo Imperial University, 53
Tokyo University, 82
Tokugawa Iyeyasu, 48, 49
Tokugawa synthesis. *See* Perceptions
Toyotomi Hideyoshi, 48, 49
Tracy, David, 39–40
Transfiguration, 162. *See also* Jesus of
    Nazareth
Treaty of Nanking, 27
Treaty of Trodesilhas, 12–13, 215
Troeltsch, Ernst, 169, 173, 195
True Pure Land Sect. *See* Buddhism;
    Japanese Buddhist groups
Tsuda Masamichi, 69

Uchimura Kanzo, 53, 54, 56, 60–61
Ultimate Reality, 36, 144, 270
Unification Church from Korea, 230
Unitarians, 61, 62, 206
United Church (Kyodan), 79, 81
USSR, 233, 234
United States, 58, 66
United States Constitution, 136, 197, 198,
    201. *See also* American experience;
    United States Supreme Court
United States Immigration Act, 227, 267
United States Supreme Court, 124, 198
    definition of Caucasian race, 96
    Justice Field, 95
    Hirabayashi vs. U.S., 135
    Korematsu vs. U.S., 135
    Justice Marshall, 201
    Justice Murphy, 135
    Justice Rehnquist, 200
    sacrality of law, 202
    Justice Souter, 200
    Justice Sutherland, 96
University. *See* Studium
University of Chicago, 141

Value history motif, 156
Valignano, Alessandro, 14, 183
Vandals, 172
van de Leeuw, Gerardus, 67, 150, 151,
    168
Vedanta, 230
Verbeck, G. F., 53
Vesalius, Andreas, 179
Vietnam War, 35, 74, 93, 104, 107, 108,
    220, 234
Virgin cults, 176
Virginia Declaration of Rights, 197
Visigoths, 172

Wach, Joachim, 77, 144, 185
Wa-Kan style, 46. *See also* Japan:
    linguistic thought
War Relocation Authority, 107
War Relocation Centers. *See* Detention
    Camps: War Relocation Centers
Warren, Earl, 106
Warren, Max A. C., 68
Watergate, 201
Werfel, Franz, 92
Wesley, John, 182
West Coast, 93, 97, 99, 121, 122, 134,
    265, 269, 271
Asian American communities, 109–110

California gold rush, 95
discrimination of Asian immigrants, 94,
    95–96, 102, 103
evacuation of Japanese, 105, 106, 120,
    128
returning evacuees, 132, 133
See also Japanese Americans
Western-Byzantine, 6. *See also*
    Christianity, Western
Western Civilization, 204, 213
Whitehead, Alfred North, 179
William of Orange, 181
Williams, Channing Moore, 52, 53
Williams, Roger, 205
Wilson, John, 234
Wirth, Lois, 150
Women
    arrival of Asiatic women immigrants, 97
    Issei women, 124
    and ordination, 246
    See also Asian immigrants
World Council of Churches, 81, 187, 221,
    256
World Lutheran group, 66
World's Parliament of Religions, 62, 63,
    199, 207, 229, 251–252
World War I, 207, 230
World War II, 276
    awareness of Asia, 43

experience of incarceration, 119
postwar Christian development, 77
Japanese postwar constitution and
    religious liberty, 73, 74, 75
and postwar interreligious dialogue,
    276–79
See also Supreme Commander of the
    Allied Powers; Japanese Americans

Xavier, Francis, 14, 28, 48, 85, 182–83

Yale University, 204
Yin-Yang school, 46
Yokio Tokio, 63
Yonejiro Noguchi, 116
Yanaibara Tadao, 82
Yüan rulers, 13, 251
Younger churches, 3, 6, 7, 18, 19, 20–21,
    22, 33, 35, 36–41, 220, 223–25, 240,
    253, 257

Zealots, 151
Zen Buddhists, 46, 50, 115, 230
Zinzendorf, Nikolaus Ludwig von, 182,
    183
Zoroastrianism, 7–8, 145, 153, 187, 213,
    251